The Strangest of Theatres

Poets Writing Across Borders

EDITED BY

Jared Hawkley, Susan Rich, and Brian Turner

CONSULTING EDITOR

Catherine Barnett

HARRIET MONROE POETRY INSTITUTE

"POETS IN THE WORLD" SERIES EDITOR

Ilya Kaminsky

POETRY

FOUNDATION

MᶜSWEENEY'S BOOKS

SAN FRANCISCO

The Strangest of Theatres: Poets Writing Across Borders is a copublication of The Poetry Foundation and McSweeney's Publishing.

For more information about McSweeney's, see www.mcsweeneys.net
For more information about The Poetry Foundation, see www.poetryfoundation.org

McSweeney's and colophon are registered trademarks of McSweeney's Publishing. "The Poetry Foundation" and the Pegasus logo are registered trademarks of The Poetry Foundation.

Hardcover ISBN: 978-1-938073-26-7
Paperback ISBN: 978-1-938073-27-4

First printing, 2013

Should we have stayed at home and thought of here?
Where should we be today?
Is it right to be watching strangers in a play
in this strangest of theatres?

—Elizabeth Bishop, "Questions of Travel"

Contents

Editors' Note

The information in this book is provided as a resource and source of inspiration for poets considering travel abroad. Ideas and knowledge about international travel are ever changing, so we present this book in the spirit of an evolving conversation. The content derives from a broad spectrum of contributors who have an extensive range of viewpoints and experiences. Their discussions often describe the general issues at hand and include ideas about resources or poems; however, this information is not meant to be exhaustive or to address any reader's specific situation, and inclusion is not an endorsement of specific content or of a particular course of action. Readers are invited to consider the materials and topics raised in the book, as well as other available resources, while they make thoughtful decisions based on their values, priorities, and circumstances. Readers should seek answers, resources, and legal counsel, as well as relevant laws, that address their specific circumstances, wishes, and needs.

The authors of the essays made great efforts to provide accurate, relevant information on a wide range of topics. However, many details are liable to change and, in many instances, are subject to interpretation. The publishers cannot accept responsibility for any consequences arising from the use of this book.

Acknowledgments

The Harriet Monroe Poetry Institute recognizes with deep gratitude the kindness, collaboration, and generosity of spirit of all of the contributors, editors, and many others who worked so hard to bring this book into existence. In particular, this project owes great thanks to the following: John Lusk Babbott, Susan Briante, Patricia Chao, Fred Courtright, Charlotte Crowe, Zachary Cupkovic, George Foy, Kathleen Graber, Garth Greenwell, Susan Hogan, Jill Jarvis, Chelsea Hogue, Gabriel Kalmuss-Katz, Jessica Kovler, Lauren Ricke, Jess Row, Jennifer Scappettone, Michelle Coghlan, Roy Scranton, Sarah Marie Shepherd, Tiffany Tuttle Collins, Ryann S. Wahl, G.C. Waldrep, McSweeney's Publishing, the Trinity College Office of International Programs in Hartford, Connecticut, and most especially Ethan Nosowsky, Beth Allen, Daniel Moysaenko, and Kathleen White.

Introduction: Beyond the Visible Horizon

No matter where we are, the horizon—retreating, drawing near—adds its quiet definition to the moment we live in. This happens whether we are crossing the Ambassador Bridge into the streets of Detroit or taking the Red Line to Braintree somewhere down in the subterranean world of the Boston suburbs; it happens even at an altitude of thirty-nine thousand feet in a twin-engine turboprop over Coeur d'Alene, Memphis, Kailua-Kona, Sioux City, or Nome, the world below erased in cloud. Once the bus pulls over or the subway line ends or we climb down the rolling stairs to stand on the tarmac, we become fixed within the stations of our lives—circling the sun at about sixty-seven thousand miles per hour with our hair perfectly still, yesterday falling like ash within each of us, the day ahead as yet unknown.

The maps we scroll open across our desks or buffer into resolution on our iPads and laptop screens offer a conceptual framework that makes employing the cartographer's trade and navigating the world easier. To say that these maps partially define us may sound like a simple bromide or platitude, but it is difficult to sidestep the fact that we live in the (politically) very real abstractions of city, county, state, and federal jurisdictions. For those who cross the wrong invisible line without the proper documentation, these concepts become very real, very quickly. Rarely can we physically "see" the map delineated on the landscape itself, though.

Recognizing the surveyor's marks expressed in us and within the language we bring to the page is often even more difficult. In a very literal sense, there are exceptions to the mapmaker's abstractions. In parts of present-day Berlin, for example, bricks in the roadbed denote the wall that once separated East and West Berlin; one can stand with one foot in the former Soviet bloc and the other in what was previously called the Federal Republic of Germany. In Uganda, roughly forty miles southwest of the capital on the Masaka-Kampala Road, it is possible to stand with one foot in the Southern Hemisphere while placing the other foot in the Northern Hemisphere. Those who travel to Struga for the annual poetry festival on the northern shores of Lake Ohrid might come face-to-face with the reality that the people living there consider themselves citizens of the Republic of Macedonia; in the halls of the United Nations, at the urging of Greece, those same people are known as citizens of the Former Yugoslav Republic of Macedonia, or FYROM. Satellite technology, over-the-counter GPS units, and smartphones track and plot people's movements on Earth's surface with incredible precision and accuracy, in some cases down to a ten-digit grid (or roughly the equivalent of an area ten meters square). The invisible divisions and demarcations of the world crisscross the landscapes of human lives with profound effects, both subtle and overt.

It is the editors' hope that this book might serve as a guide or trail marker, a series of possible azimuths travelers might set their courses by, a collection of lyric revelations and sober assessments that travel beyond national borders might reveal or encourage. "One of the obligations of the writer," Denise Levertov once wrote, "and perhaps especially of the poet, is to say or sing *all* that he or she can, to deal with as much of the world as becomes possible to him or her in language."

Sometimes, as William Logan writes, "poets behave like conquistadors wherever they roam, picking up a new verse form, a lover, some inventive cursing, a disease." Still, he goes on to point out, "Would Byron have been Byron without Italy and Greece? What would Eliot and Pound have become without the hostility of London? Can we imagine Hart Crane without the Caribbean or Elizabeth Bishop without Rio?" The politics of travel is one of the through lines of this book and one of its consistent challenges: How do we embark upon these journeys in meaningful, responsible ways? How do we avoid the tropes of colonialism—and, for that matter, how might we recognize them at work within ourselves? Do we venture out as literary voyeurs, cousins to tourists, continually smashing champagne bottles across the bow of experience? Do we travel to escape the noise of our lives, driven by a need to create livable spaces for ourselves, places in which to breathe? Do we sense a necessity in the art of witness, sharpening our pencils in the journalist's trade?

Whatever the initial reasons and internal pressures we may have as we set out into the larger world, "the insight must be earned as much as the poem." These words, from Jack Gilbert's essay "The Landscape of American Poetry in 1964," ring with great clarity several decades on. They might serve as a guidepost, though we may not immediately be able—as writers and as human beings—to recognize the depths of the insights we've garnered through experience and crafted to the page. Sometimes the language we bring to the page teaches us what we didn't previously realize or comprehend. As Mark Doty says, "Poetry is an investigation, not an expression, of what you know."

In this sense, *The Strangest of Theatres: Poets Writing Across Borders* is also a call to action. It is our hope that poets might serve, in some ways, as envoys to the greater world, offering American poetry newfound sources of engagement with language and a renewed engagement with what being a global citizen means. With gratitude, we recognize the journeys of those who have gone before us; we recognize the immensity of what those journeys have added to literature as well as to our ways of perceiving the world in which we live and the ways in which we live in the world. This book is a celebration of poets who have ventured beyond the visible horizon and brought back verse; it may also offer insights into how others might emulate these travelers by forging paths into the world beyond the United States. The editors hope these essays will inspire, encourage, be talismanic, serve as harbingers or mercurial whispers, perhaps, or as epistles from the far shore imploring us and warning us along our own ways. The work of these writers enlarges the world available within us; this work augments us.

The Paths Before Us

Where would American poetry be today without the journeys our poets undertook into the wider world? The ebb and flow of entire schools and counter schools of poetic thought owe their existence, in part, to the conversations that took place across the far seas. Where would American poetry be, for example, without a poet such as Langston Hughes, who traveled extensively and served in the early 1960s as a cultural emissary for the US Department of State (though decades earlier, he found himself wanting to return to the United States after being robbed and stranded while en route to Italy—"stranded" when a homeward-bound ship wouldn't hire him because he wasn't white, so Hughes wrote "I, too, sing America"). Where would American poetry be without the Vietnam-era visits to Hanoi by Grace Paley and Muriel Rukeyser (whose last book, *The Gates*, sprang from her attempts to visit the South Korean poet Kim Chi-Ha, who was serving a life sentence in prison)?

In all shapes and forms, American poets have wandered the globe and encountered other writers engaged in similarly picaresque journeys. After World War II, W.S. Merwin, a former US poet laureate, lived in Europe, ending up in Majorca, where he tutored the son of the poet Robert Graves. Although not all poets may have the good fortune to find employers who are also literary patrons, the options are myriad—there are farms to work, bars to tend, bookshops to run, schools and wells to build, ships to crew as they ply the whale roads of old.

Travel may even encourage writers to diverge from their usual genres and allow them to share their work internationally. Galway Kinnell was moved to write his first and (so far) only novel, *Black Light*, which was influenced by time spent living and working in Tehran (1957–1960). Coleman Barks and Robert Bly have journeyed to Iran and Afghanistan, speaking to audiences large and small of their engagement with ancient poetics and how that interaction has affected their work. Barks—whose versions of Rumi are well known for their unconventional approach to the art of translation—received an honorary doctorate from the University of Tehran.

Other poets choose to gather the poetic traditions they encounter abroad to foster an international dialogue and to widen the poetic compass of poets and thinkers back home. This functions, perhaps, as a form of literary hybridity or cross-pollination. In 1971, for example, John Balaban returned to Vietnam during the war, a heavy tape recorder slung over his shoulder so that listeners might hear the voices of Vietnamese poetry sung in the rice paddies and monasteries and villages decades later. I was fortunate enough to hear these voices when he played the recordings at a poetry reading at the Marfa Book Company in the tiny West Texas town of Marfa in 2008. In addition to writing verse and sharing the recordings he has preserved from years ago, Balaban has also brought to readers of English the eighteenth-century Vietnamese poetry of Hô Xuân Hương (*Spring Essence*, 2000), whose work was originally created in Chữ Nôm, an ideographic script now nearly extinct.

Work along these lines often leads to the development of lifelong friendships with writers and thinkers we meet during our travels. "That poets today can form a *confraternitas* transcending distances and language differences," the Polish poet Czesław Miłosz wrote, "may be one of the few encouraging signs in the current chaotic world order."

Curiosity often leads poets to the far corners and beyond. As is often the case, curiosity searches out the genius available through the centuries of thought we inherit as well as the genius we discover in our contemporaries. I think, for instance, of the poet, scholar, and multilingual translator Willis Barnstone. Through his many travels, Barnstone has returned to the United States with translations of Machado, Lorca, Sappho, Wang Wei, Rilke, Heraclitus, a play by Neruda, and much more. Many poets have wandered out into the larger world in search of its poetic treasures so that they might apply the translator's art and carry the verses back home to the rest of us. Kenneth Koch may have been right when he said "reading poems in translation is like kissing someone through a shower curtain," but I prefer Charles Simic's vision of translation as he articulated it in the *New York Review of Books*—"To translate is not only to experience what makes each language distinct, but to draw close to the mystery of the relationship between word and thing, letter and spirit, self and world."

We can serve as champions for the language we encounter abroad. For example, Sandy Taylor (1931–2007), poet and founder of Curbstone Press, traveled widely and brought back the work of poets from many nations around the globe, often publishing poetry collections and novels that would likely have been overlooked or refused print by some of the larger, more prominent presses of the day. In 1999, Curbstone published Carolyn Forché's translation of *Saudade* (or *Sorrow*), penned by the Nicaraguan poet Claribel Alegría, whom Taylor had met by chance on a bus in Managua. "I was down there in support of the Sandinista regime," he once said, "... reading poetry to the police, army, and coffee workers." Poets such as Taylor remind us that, just as poets and poetry can be discovered on a bus in Managua, they can be discovered wherever our feet take us in the world. And, perhaps more important, the poetry we experience abroad has the capacity to create profound change and influence on the poetic landscape back home.

The textbook image of the American poet abroad is sometimes envisioned as the famously irascible Robert Frost meeting with the diplomatic and gracious Anna Akhmatova in Moscow in 1962, near the end of both of their lives. As the story goes, Frost's translator (the poet F.D. Reeve, the late Christopher Reeve's father) had to "smooth over" Frost's gruff manner in his presentation to Akhmatova. Roughly fifteen hundred miles away and nearly five decades earlier, Frost had often walked with the English poet Edward Thomas through the Dymock countryside near Ledbury, England. Those walks have attained a near-mythic quality in the years since and led to the work some consider among the foundation stones of American poetry in the past century, "The Road Not Taken." According to the postulate, travel affected the poet and inspired the poem, but the poem remained uniquely American, lacking the visible and subtextual traces of the journey that spawned it.

Other poets, such as Allen Ginsberg, threaded their travels into the poems themselves so that the work became an electric conversation with the journey itself or an amalgamation of the world's overflowing riches tumbling line by line into verse. For example, in Paris during the "winter-spring" of 1958, Ginsberg wrote,

> Here in Paris I am your guest O friendly shade
> the absent hand of Max Jacob
> Picasso in youth bearing me a tube of Mediterranean
> myself attending Rousseau's old red banquet I ate his violin
> great party at the Bateau Lavoir not mentioned in the
>   textbooks of Algeria
> Tzara in the Bois de Boulogne explaining the alchemy of
>   the machineguns of the cuckoos
> he weeps translating me into Swedish ...

In a very different mode, C.K. Williams's visit to the Ugandan chimpanzee sanctuary on Ngamba Island doubtless added to the depth of insight he brought to his poem "Apes":

> The chimps Catherine and I saw on their island sanctuary
>   in Uganda we loathed.
> Unlike the pacific gorillas in the forest of Bwindi, they
>   fought, dementedly shrieked,
> the dominant male lorded it over the rest; they were, in
>   all, too much like us.

As it happens, I visited the same island at the northern end of Lake Victoria in 2007, saw—most likely—the same chimpanzees and many of the same caretakers on the island, visited the same veterinarian's facilities, and hurled jackfruit over the fence line at feeding time from the same wooden viewing platform where Williams and his wife must have stood before. I imagine I would write a poem very different from Williams's own. Though the doorway into a poem may derive from the same place (and often from very similar experiences), the poem—if fully realized—will journey through language and the wide landscape of self to discover a new place.

The world works its way through writers just as much as we work our way through the world. So, too, with language. As poets, part of our service to the art is being aware of the language we carry as well as the new language we acquire along the way. We must attend to the nuances and subtleties involved when we graft newly acquired language onto the words we carry within us, the words we might refer to as our "mother tongue."

Quayside

The poet Amy Lowell left in her will a mandate to send American-born poets abroad (stipulating that they leave North America) for a year at a time; poets have undertaken this particular journey since E.L. Mayo set out in 1953, Stanley Kunitz to follow the year after. Lowell had a mind of great prescience. She recognized the deep need for American poets and, by extension, American poetry to experience the larger community of nations, as she had done. In recent years, low-residency writing programs and writers' conferences abroad have formalized the overseas writing dynamic.

Even with some structures set in place to help them travel, few American poets venture abroad. In contrast, leading news agencies and magazines routinely send journalists out on assignment to the far corners of the Earth. These reporters serve as witness to world events so that we might expand our field of vision. As reporters and photojournalists lift off the tarmac on outbound flights, business executives and company employees also travel to all points on the map. Low-echelon members of the US Department of State serve in remote consular offices and in labyrinthine constructions of the mightiest embassies in major capitals worldwide. At the same time, the American military (from straight-leg infantry soldiers to covert operations teams) has forces and hardware deployed to countries far and wide. Unlike Rukeyser's and Paley's and a few others', the passports of most American poets are rarely stamped. As one Vietnamese poet and former NVA soldier once remarked to the poet Bruce Weigl (paraphrased here), "You Americans are strange: first you send your soldiers and tanks—then you send your poets." Telling as that statement might be, how much more so might it be if the poets never "deployed" at all?

At the time of Amy Lowell's death in 1925, writers traveling to Europe or South America mostly went by ocean liner, their trunks packed for journeys that often lasted months. But in many ways, the world moves exponentially faster now. In the present day, it's possible for poets to attend international poetry festivals in Medellín, Dubai, or Durban during a week's vacation from work. Over a series of trips such as these, it is possible for writers to develop lifelong friendships and colleagues in the art. When the Jasmine Revolution reaches Tahrir Square in Cairo or Bangladesh relaxes its bans on travel or the prime minister of Romania threatens to resign and a country of twenty million people finds itself in historical flux, poets can hop on planes and witness such moments through the lens of their own humanity. The information age—the age of Twitter, YouTube, and Facebook—makes it possible for poets to recognize where momentous challenges and changes are taking place in the world. Poets who choose to witness the events of our time now have the ability to experience them firsthand. The editors hope that the work assembled in *The Strangest of Theatres: Poets Writing Across Borders* might inspire a new generation of writers to take part in the global conversation that is already underway, regardless of a trip's duration.

Sails in the Wind

During the creation of this book, several of the poets whose work appears were engaged in journeys beyond American shores. Yusef Komunyakaa (author of *Dien Cai Dau* and *Neon Vernacular*, among other books) visited Nairobi, where grenade attacks took place after he left. Gregory Dunne (author of *Home Test* and *Fistful of Lotus*) continued his teaching in Japan, though the country was reeling in the aftermath of the Tōhoku earthquake of 2011. Between news assignments, Eliza Griswold (author of *Wideawake Field: Poems* and *The Tenth Parallel: Dispatches from the Fault Line Between Christianity and Islam*) went surfing in El Salvador.

Sandra Meek (poet and editor of the anthology *Deep Travel*) had her car tires slashed while visiting the Silvermine Nature Reserve atop the Table Mountain plateau overlooking Cape Town, South Africa. All her belongings (passport, cash, credit cards, and even her food and water) were stolen from her car as she was out trekking. High up in the mist overlooking an ocean she couldn't see, she received a text message from her sister telling her that their father had been hospitalized. Meek had to work with South African Home Affairs and the US consulate in Cape Town, among other agencies, before she was able to make it home—just in time to be with her father before he passed away.

We can't plan all that will take place along our journeys, and in equal measure we can't plan all that might occur in our communities back home. That said, the immutable laws of travel offer an encouraging note within their somber tone: not every journey involves pain, disaster, and heartbreak. As Pound reminds us, "Each age has its own abounding gifts." Still, what can we do if that gift is the eruption of a caldera beneath Iceland's Eyjafjallajökull and if the airspace over most of Europe is closed because of volcanic ash and debris, leaving us stranded in foreign airports? What if our passports are stolen? Whose voice do we turn to when inner-city Bangkok shifts to a place of riot and conflict, a place where the renegade Thai military general Khattiya Sawasdipol can be shot in the head as he responds to a reporter's questions on a city street? The contributors to this book can't propose a solution to every problem, but the intent is to offer roads into the wider world as well as possible sources of help and guidance. The editors hope that the work compiled here may be of use to both the long- and the short-term traveler.

In the grand tradition of the expatriate, you may choose for the remainder of your life to pull up stakes and move to another country or to a series of countries, as one might traverse the garden via many stepping-stones along the way. A.E. Stallings lives with her family in Greece while continuing to have an active presence in contemporary American poetry. Similarly, Tamar Yoseloff and Eva Salzman have forged lives in London. In Wales, Florida-born Amy Wack (who graduated from the Columbia University MFA program) serves as the poetry editor at Seren Books. A beacon across the water, Gertrude Stein and her influence resound to the present day; she is proof that American writers not only travel but also forge and sustain literary lives far beyond their native shores.

In contrast, many writers choose to become temporary denizens of other countries. Jorie Graham has spent a good deal of time in Normandy, and it's difficult to imagine how she might have written *Overlord* without such meditative proximity to the actual landscape where the invasion forces stormed ashore and fought their way inland. Not too far afield from those Normandy beaches, Cyrus Cassells has taken research trips to Germany in order to access the world of poems he fashioned for his latest book, *The Crossed-Out Swastika*. I think of Jack Gilbert's "self-imposed isolation" and the poetry written after his first collection (*Views of Jeopardy*) won the Yale Series of Younger Poets, when Gilbert lived in Greece and also traveled to a variety of countries as a lecturer for the US Department of State. I'm also thinking of Sam Hamill in Mexico as I write this. I'm thinking of Martín Espada visiting Neruda's Casa de Isla Negra in Chile. I'm thinking of Bruce Weigl and Kevin Bowen returning to Vietnam to visit friends and writers they once fought against when their counterparts were part of the North Vietnamese Army. I'm thinking of

Ken Taylor, winner of the recent FISH poetry prize (for the poem "string theory") and how he used the money to help fund a trip to the West Cork Literary Festival set amid the raw green beauty of County Cork, in Ireland.

Poetry can be a doorway into a new circle of friends and colleagues. For some poets, the layered places of history call in ways we may not fully understand until we can interact with the land itself or the people who live there. We may need to breathe in the air—to inspire it, from the Latin *inspirare*, from which the word *inspiration* is derived—as we witness the conversation between dusk and dawn; our poems may need to wander through the streets and fields of the world, searching out the shady groves and the brilliant vistas, the junkie alleyways and the industrial wastelands.

Once the journey is done and we return home and our poems have found their way to the page, we often learn about the world in which we live. In this way, poetry unfolds and unravels the journey we may have thought long over. Our bags may be unpacked, our clothes washed and folded away, our passports tucked into safe-deposit boxes or cubbyholes in back rooms, but the poems—the poems are extensions of the journey. Poems offer pathways into the countries within, paths that might otherwise grow wild and unnoticed by the eyes of daydreamers leafing through sheaves of photos from their time abroad.

Passports and Entry Visas

As with all anthologies, imperfections abound here. As editors, we have done our best to be inclusive and wide-ranging in gathering the work you now hold in your hands. Early on, we grappled with how the book might consider the terms *American* and *United States* in the first place. What parameters would we apply to the work we sought? How might the voices and traditions and experiences of Hopi and Navajo and Iroquois poets, for example, of Cherokee and Choctaw and Cheyenne writers, instruct us in what it's like to be a poet traveling out from a sovereign nation, traveling through the counties and states and jurisdictions of what others call the United States of America? When we spread a map of the world before us, we had many long conversations about where we might travel with poets vis-à-vis the essays they had written, whether in newly commissioned essays or in reprints culled from a variety of sources. The necessary questions of identity politics, that which makes a nation and that which makes a citizen, the inherent possibility of marginalization and erasure that argue against the creation of anthologies as a form, as well as the tricky territory of who we are as editors and who we are drawn to for new work and old—these issues and concerns form a good portion of the interior architecture of this book, its underlying aesthetic awareness. You might ask—where are the words of John Ashbery in France? Where are the travels of Adrienne Rich? Muriel Rukeyser? Gerald Stern and C.D. Wright and Rita Dove and Brenda Hillman? Where are poets and travelers from centuries gone by? There are also poets who came to the United States and offered Americans new ways to see themselves and the wider world—here I'm thinking of Auden and Lorca and Miłosz, for example. Contemporary poets in this vein might include Li-Young Lee, Eavan Boland, Valzhyna Mort, Khaled Mattawa, Dunya Mikhail, Tomaž Šalamun, and Oliver de la Paz. Their poetry rises into this world from multiple geographies and expands the poetic landscape in the United States. For these reasons and many, many more, of course, *The Strangest of Theatres: Poets Writing Across Borders* is an incomplete book. In a variety of ways, it waits for the pages readers will add.

In terms of structure, the editors worked to create a book both useful and insightful about the logistical aspects of travel as well as the more sublime and intellectual elements that travel engenders. For example, if a writer encourages carrying an Olympus Digital Linear PCM recorder while traveling, we hope that the practicality of the instrument will prove useful and also help travelers connect more deeply to their possible roles as witnesses, archivists, human beings who cherish the words that others offer and wish to preserve and care for them. Likewise, when a traveler describes in detail the sublime experience of separation from the world she or he comes from (as well as, likely, the world entered into), we hope readers will recognize the value of this for their interior lives. Perhaps they will also ponder the deep and cherished relationships they may have at "home" and how, for example, they might want to make certain that their bill payments are set up before they go, living wills set in place should they never return, powers of attorney set up (should they plan on being overseas for an extended time), and more. In essence, people's choices revolve around their best attempts to be responsible citizens of the world as they travel. The essays that follow cover a wide range of possibilities, and all of them highlight, in one way or another, these basic attributes.

The Poet in the World: You

The aim of this book isn't to encourage writers to choose an escapist route and turn away from that which most needs work. Far from it. The editors recognize the necessity of the interior soliloquy. We realize that our country needs what one might colloquially term "homegrown" poetry. Now, just as in years past, poems will rise from the squad car in Portland, the frying pan at Oklahoma Joe's in Kansas City, the out-of-gas motorcycle on a county road on the outskirts of Tehachapi, the vegan bakery in Jackson, and Rudy's Car Wash in Allentown. There are necessary poems to be written about Alabama and Wisconsin and Puerto Rico. And we will need the poems from our maternity wards, our school yards, our prisons, our gardens and our slums, the beds that we make love in as well as the beds where we lie down to die.

As much as these necessary poems deserve attention, it is the editors' belief that this is a time in which a deep, sustained, and global interaction is necessary to reinvigorate the poetic landscape at home. Stated baldly, the country needs more polymath poets—hybrid creatures who have listened to the voices outside of their field of view, poets who return to American poetry a renewed sense of connection with the language we share. They just might be able to do this if they journey beyond the known. As Lucille Clifton once said, "Poems come out of wonder, not out of knowing." That's why Gertrude Stein's wisdom rings as true today as when she said it long ago: in Paris, "Americans can discover what it means to be American." Substitute the name of any number of foreign cities, towns, villages, hamlets, homes for the name *Paris*. At the same time, the poems created from experiences abroad can serve as dispatches, as entry points, as vehicles of mystery and profound insight. As Eamon Grennan said in the *Irish Times*, "Good poets are the explorers of the world. Out on the frontiers, they send back bulletins."

In compiling this book, the editors gathered an array of voices and experiences and travel possibilities. I worry that this might lull us into a false sense of security. Some may think, given the many travels of poets described in these pages, "Ah, with so many American poets going abroad, what's the point of this book?" For the most part, sadly, these poets stand in sharp contrast to the norm (in terms of international travel). A large number of poets go from one educational institution to another, to one MFA or another, without investigating the wider world. It is precisely because of the dearth of sustained and meaningful interaction with the world beyond our borders that the editors assembled this book.

The far horizon for one person may be the opposite horizon for another. And the idea of "the far horizon" itself deserves study—it is someone else's center of the world, someone else's firm footing, someone else's native ground. The map as construct serves mostly as a frame in which to recognize where we writers are in the world and where we are in our lives. Why not expand the available topography? To expand the knowledge available within the landscape we might dub our "internal borderlands," we would be wise to follow US poet laureate Philip Levine's advice: "If you're going somewhere new and undiscovered you have to trust the imagination, you have to truly believe the poem knows better than you and thus follow where it leads."

Here it is at last—the time to set sail with the writers assembled in the pages that follow. Our own journeys are hinted at and encouraged and guided by those who have gone before—Bishop, Walcott, Levine, and many more. The possibilities stretch far beyond the pages of this book. The fado singers lift their voices over the rooftops in the Bairro Alto of Lisbon. Giant stone turtles announce the mandarins in the Temple of Literature in Hanoi, just as they have done for centuries. Monastery bells toll over the hillsides at dawn. The muezzin rises in the minaret to sound the call to *adhan*. Bathers stand waist-deep in the headwaters of the Ganges, fringed in the gold light of sunset. The brogue of language calls its landscape into being, whether on the steps to Machu Picchu, beside the intricate locks of the Panama Canal, or under the awning of a street kitchen in Surabaya along the Madura Strait. The world awaits our curiosity and our deep attention. The great travelers and journeyers—they all set out into the unknown to make a record of what they experienced. And they each recognized one fundamental truth: each age requires its own journeys.

Let us not make of the world, as Spalding Gray phrased it, "one big piece of calendar art." Let us engage our curiosity and our humanity in that which exists beyond our own horizon line with our sails fully opened—to riff off a phrase of Bertolt Brecht's—so that our verses might travel further in this life than they might otherwise have done.

—*Brian Turner, for the editors*
  Göteborg, Berlin, Dubai, Orlando, 2012

New Cartographies

The Poet in the World

Poets Crossing Borders

Kazim Ali

He is looking into my book, turning each page slowly, looking at, reading the faded blue marks there. Every once in a while he touches his fingertip to the page, leaves it there before slowly turning to the next.

"What is it?" I ask, knowing what he sees there. He does not answer. "My name is Mohammad Kazim Ali. I am a professor at Shippensburg University. You can call up the school's web page and see my profile there." He does not answer. "I am a *poet*," I say.

It is the spring of 2006. It is still a year before a student, dressed in army fatigues, will see me in the parking lot outside my office in the English Department carrying a box of recycling to the curb. He will call the police to report suspicious activity. The campus will be temporarily shut down. In the rush to fulfill all the emergency procedures, the officers will forget to notify the department secretary still inside the building at her desk. At some point in the afternoon, she will look out the window and see the bomb squad and panic. I am not aware of this. I am in my little love bug, driving north to Carlisle, humming along with the radio. Maybe poetry *is* dangerous?

"Okay," says the passport control officer, shutting my book and knocking its edge against the counter between us. "You need to go with this man," he says and hands the passport to a waiting officer.

Because he is also Asian, a Filipino, I get bold. "Do we really need to do this?" I ask him. "You realize I have to go through this *every* time."

He does not answer.

I heft my shoulder bag. He does a quick double take when he catches a glimpse of my fingernails, painted in what I think is a fetching slate blue gray. He keeps walking. Which is more disturbing: That he doesn't immediately understand that I would pose no al-Qaeda-supported security threat? Or that somehow I take this sign of my westernization and postmodernity to be a marker of queerness that thus excuses me from scrutiny, an evasion that perhaps any other Muslim man with more heteronormative behavior would not be able to escape? That somehow I am trying, from a position of odd privilege, to be clear that I am not "that kind of Muslim," that I am not *like them.*

Any Muslim body is strange now, other, worthy of scrutiny.

And to cross any border means to submit one's own body to the law.

The law marks the body, documents it, scrutinizes it, registers it, permits it, manipulates it, suppresses it, denies it, forbids it, kills it.

Linguistically, the word *national* often refers to where you were born. Within that conception is an intrinsic connection (of political loyalty, yes, but also physically in the tissues and organs themselves) of a human body to the geographic location or space in which it entered the world or currently resides.

To be *international* means to be "between" nations, between loyalties, between the human body and the very idea of a law that seeks to control it. It must be a good place for a poet to be, a person who speaks with a forked tongue, who understands that the difference between *sky* and *caelo* may be just a little drifting but that between *sky* and *ciel* is immeasurable distance, not mere vowel and consonant, *ciel* holding not only the root syllable for the English *ceiling* but also a synonymous word in French for *heaven*. Only to the bilingual speaker will the word quiver so in between the languages.

At Babel we were given fractured tongues, and the notions of multiplicity and infinity opened themselves in our mouths. Say something. Say something more.

It is not when I cross a border but when I cross *back*—back to my own home, my "nation," as it were—that my body is subjected to various technological interventions. I am separated from the group. X-rays pass through me. An image of me, a naked ghost, appears somewhere and then disappears. I disappear. Led by a man—usually younger, usually a man of color, usually joking to hide his discomfort—to the cordoned-off room. Here we are: me, shoeless and trembling, trying to ignore his uniform and gun, his hands moving up and down my body. He is giving me—it must be part of the training—a running narration of his activity.

I am touching your chest. I am touching your stomach now. I am going to touch your groin. I will use only the back of my hand. I am touching the inside of your thigh. Your hip.

My body is the dark one. My name is a Muslim one. Your name is in our system. We know it isn't you. You should change your name. What is your father's name. What is your grandfather's name. Who are you. Where do you come from.

Body, you do me well and dangerous, slip between nations, between tongues, slip yourself naked between night and day, between genders and genres.

Or will you write yourself in code, download your short-term memory into machines, slide credit cards under the skin of your palm, be tagged by an electronic surveillance device. Will your physical location be monitored like the airplane on the little screen embedded in the seatback in front of you, slowly crawling across the Midwest to New York, crawling from New York to Iceland, from Iceland across Europe and Turkey to Tel Aviv.

What is your father's name. What is your grandfather's name. Wrote Mahmoud Darwish, "My homeland is not a suitcase." My suitcase is opened, all my things taken out, rubbed with special cloth. The cloth is taken away to be tested. For what, I don't know.

This is how a poet crosses borders.

I was driven from the sea through the mountains to Jerusalem, where every street has three names that do not always translate from one to another. Street of the Mujahideen, meaning "martyrs" in Arabic, translated into English and Hebrew as "Lions Gate." The mujahideen in this case refers not to the twentieth-century martyrs but instead to the men who fought with Saladin nearly one thousand years earlier.

History has long arms in a country crossed and recrossed by lines. Buildings, neighborhoods, and whole cities are built one on top of another. Sound familiar?

The first thing I wanted to see in Jerusalem was al-Aqsa, the open plaza called by Muslims the Far Mosque, called by Jewish people the Temple Mount because it was the location of the Temple destroyed in 70 CE. As we climbed the creaky wooden causeway for non-Muslim worshipers, we could see through the slatted walls Jewish worshipers who had come to the small fragment of the Western Wall. It was an emotional sight: a people still wandering in the only land they call home, still hovering at a remnant and in very temporary settings—sitting in plastic lawn chairs or dragging over makeshift podiums on which to place their prayer books. Perhaps the temporariness of the furnishings is meant to acknowledge the fleeting nature of the ruin, or perhaps it is a form of resistance—that to have more permanent accoutrements would be to accept that the Temple was lost and would never be reclaimed. And there, just ahead of us on the causeway, the other side of the whole equation—twenty or thirty body-length riot shields, stacked within easy reach for quick use. Then I remember how some places are used as symbols of the "nation," how Ground Zero is used, how this place is used for swearing-in ceremonies for different units of the Israeli army.

In this open area—besides the gardens and paved areas for worship—is the enormous Dome of the Rock and an indoor mosque, itself built and destroyed many times. Around the mosque in the great tree-lined park, many small groups of men recite the Qur'an. As with many Muslim mosques, it is not the building but the space itself that is the actual mosque, the place people pray. When you go inside the structure called the Dome and see the actual Rock (it is massive), you only want to get closer. A little stairwell under the Rock leads into the so-called Well of Souls. Where one can and can't pray here is fraught with all kinds of meaning. When a group of Jewish men came up onto the plaza, the Muslim men began reciting loudly at the top of their lungs, a sonic resistance but a resistance nonetheless. One of the Arab men called the Jewish people "settlers," which I didn't at first understand.

Though I had always thought of settlers as people out in the territories building their kibbutzim, it wasn't so. There were settlers inside Palestinian cities like Hebron, and there were even settlers buying up or confiscating Palestinian buildings and apartments inside the Muslim Quarter of the Old City and in East Jerusalem. I knew them by the enormous Israeli flags hanging from the roof and by the barbed wire, surveillance cameras, and other security measures.

I cross the border—the fake border, the invisible one, the Green Line, so called because it was drawn on a map with a green crayon—between Jerusalem and Qalandia by cab. Though others must dismount and walk through the checkpoint in four stages by advancing through metal cages, I pay my cab driver 250 shekels to drive me straight through. It is the same coming back.

As far as borders go, this one has high drama—border patrols, metal detectors, full searches, plus a thirty-foot-tall concrete wall wrapped in barbed wire and mounted with observation posts. The soldiers aren't much more than children, but I think children grow up quickly in this country. On the Israeli side the bare concrete was licked here and there by the odd piece of liberation graffiti—OCCUPIERS OUT! FREE PALESTINE!—and on the Palestinian side it was covered with a rich tapestry of art: twenty-foot-tall portraits of Yasser Arafat and Marwan Barghouti, drawings of birds, flowers, animals, a young girl holding balloons being borne up and over the wall.

It is not a wall in every place. For long stretches of countryside it is "nothing more" than a high chain-link fence with layers of barbed wire. An electrified fence.

If you want to think about how the machinery of "nations" works against the individual human body, there is no better body to start with than the Palestinian body, specifically the body of Mahmoud Darwish, on August 6, 1982, on his hands and knees, crawling down the hallway of his third-floor apartment while bombs hit the upper floors of the same building, crawling down the hallway to the kitchen so he can make a pot of coffee.

Coffee during bombs: "I want nothing more from the passing days than the aroma of coffee," he says. "The aroma of coffee so I can hold myself together, stand on my feet, and be transformed from something that crawls, into a human being." It is in the midst of war or occupation that people reach for the smallest thing—like Darwish's coffee, "the virgin of the silent morning," "the sister of time"—that gives the body's experience back to itself.

Occupied by the time of war and invasions, the natural places in the world—not only mountains and forests but also cities and towns and human settlements—give up their identities to steel and fire. Darwish writes of the sparkling Mediterranean: "The sea has been entirely packed into stray shells. It is changing its marine nature and turning into metal. Does death have all these names?"

In myths of creation it is given to humans to name things in the world, that is, to give all the particularities of the world their significances. When we tried to climb back into formlessness, namelessness—God?— the tower fell, and we were punished—rewarded?—by the splintering of tongues, the *Babel*.

When I went to France, I went without language. I lived nearly mute as the soft, sanded-off edges of French disappeared into my ears without cognizance. It took *reading* for me to learn the words and be able to speak. It took *writing* for me to be able to make sentences. I lived alone on Corsica, having an easier time understanding Corsican French, French with an Italian accent if you will.

Even so, I could write in English only what I knew in French, and the translation wasn't by meaning but by sound. "I am sending you the sands of Corsica," I wrote on a postcard. And under it, led by the assonance between verb and object, I left the sand as itself—*sable*—but found a new verb to sound off it, "*j'oublie les sables de la Corse*," translated literally, though not in sound, as "I forget the sands of Corsica."

So I slipped between tongues. Urdu and Arabic, since I was young, had always been in my ear, and Arabic had been in my mouth too, but French was the first other tongue that traveled between them. My muscles—my tongue, the shape of my mouth and lips, the constriction of my throat—all had to change to accommodate it. But they—my throat in particular—had had good practice from Arabic. And sound does give meaning. "*La mer sans cesse*," I whispered to myself one blustery November morning while walking along the Oregon coast. I could not translate it.

So untranslated, my genre: essays called poems, poems called novels, and some things that call themselves nothing, call themselves wind. A novel, a notebook, a score. Score, not that you won something but that you marked something down on the stone or the wall.

So what is a body for? Questions of language, nation, and individual human body—its fears, its lusts, its sweetness and kindness—are not unrelated.

Darwish knows he is in trouble when the birds stop singing: "Perhaps one of the worst Arabic words is *Ta:'irah*—airplane—which is the feminine form of *Ta:'ir*—bird.... Two wings of steel and silver versus two made of feathers. A nose of wiring and steel against a beak made of song.

A cargo of rockets against a grain of wheat and a straw. Their skies no longer safe, the birds stop singing and pay heed to the war."

When cyborg studies theorist Donna Haraway asks, "Why should our bodies end at the skin, or include at best other beings encapsulated by skin?" she means to explain the idea that our environment—the natural and the made objects within it—is an expression both inward and outward of our individual, communal, bodily, and national desires. So these extensions—the things that make us "cyborgs" or compromise our biological distinctiveness—can in reverse tell us who we really are, what we value, what we fear, how we define the functional existence of ourselves as bodies.

In the case of Mahmoud Darwish, the technologies that intervene in the Palestinian body—airplanes, bombs hitting the apartment building, guns in the hands of soldiers of various factions, the sea covered in metal, the sky a helmet of steel, surveillance equipment, cameras that photograph the body, scanners that read code on ID cards and passports, systems that take measure of the body's shape, bullets that enter it— have defined the conditions under which those bodies have existed and continue to do so.

And the poet himself by page thirty of his book? Still in the kitchen, painstakingly describing the making of Arabic coffee, a difficult prospect under the best of circumstances, and then: "Turn off the heat, and pay no heed to the rockets. Take the coffee to the narrow corridor and pour it lovingly and with a sure hand into a little white cup: dark-colored cups spoil the freedom of the coffee...."

What if a "nation" is just another way to organize political power, which means another way to organize wealth? I want to define the "international" as anyone who moves against this grain, who crosses and recrosses borders, not with allegiance or loyalty to the original idea that physical proximity or natal origin creates intrinsic physical, spiritual, or emotional connection that must then be defended with steel or cash but with a refutation of that concept, with an embrace of community through shared values and an adherence to sustainable and peaceable coexistence with other communities of differing—or similar—values.

I don't think any such nation—whether one is in a place far across the waters from one's home, with a different language and culture defining it, or in one's own birthplace or familiar home surroundings—can be seen except through fractured sight, spoken of with a fractured tongue. Because we cannot remove ourselves, we must live and find it in the actual world. So we are already dependent on the ability of poets to write the future of the society. In her book *In the Heart of the Heart of Another Country*, poet and novelist Etel Adnan writes of Beirut: "It was a refuge for all sorts of political opponents to the various governments in the region, and the matrix for all the tensions that were tearing the world apart.... In that whirlwind, any living body, human or animal, looked fragile...."

When Adnan posits Beirut as a city of refugees, she means it is a city that has stopped being a "capital"—a representative of national ideals and aspirations—but is rather an *international* city, a site of resistance of the individual and human to the systemic structures of institutional power, whether political, military, or national. She herself is a multinational writer, born of a Syrian father and a Greek mother, who has lived her life between California, France, Lebanon, and Greece.

The book I use to cross borders, to move from one nation to another, is as good an essay as any about the American experience with place. On each page of my little passport is a quote relating to the "destiny" of the American project. This "destiny" seems to be endless expansion, expansion without clear purpose. On one page, Lyndon Johnson says, "For this is what America is all about. It is the uncrossed desert and the unclimbed ridge. It is the star that is not reached and the harvest sleeping in the unplowed ground.... Is a new world coming? We welcome it—and we will bend it to the hopes of man."

On another page, George Washington suggests, "Let us raise a standard to which the wise and honest can repair." This second quote I cannot see in my own passport because pasted over it is my multiyear visa to India. India is the home of my parents and grandparents and my family for at least two hundred years back. Do I belong there any more than the place I happen to live now? At any rate, I have the option of becoming an "Overseas Citizen of India," which affords me the same rights as Indian citizens living abroad and many rights while traveling in India as well.

What is the origin of a body of multiplicity? For example, one like mine that was born in England, spent early childhood in India, and then was taken to the cold places—first Winnipeg, Manitoba, on the prairies of Canada, then north to Jenpeg, where it snowed in early October and I never saw a deciduous tree. The only Indians I knew were from the Cross Lake Indian Reservation; we bought our fur-lined suede gloves and boots from them. The hydroelectric project my father was working on brought cheap and plentiful power to the city of Winnipeg far to the south but devastated the local environment. Where are you from, a person is often asked. Where indeed? I have no answer.

When Etel Adnan returned home to Beirut after seventeen years away, she had no way of approaching the task of writing about the return. She instead opted for the form of the short paragraph, borrowed from the book she was reading at the time, *In the Heart of the Heart of the Country*, by William H. Gass. In the title story, Gass writes brief entries under various headings, including "Place," "Weather," "My House," "A Person," "Wires," "The Church," "Politics," "People." Sometimes the categories combine, as in "My House, This Place and Body." In this form of divided intention, Adnan is able to approach—like a cubist painter, like Gertrude Stein in *Tender Buttons*—the same place, the same people and subjects, from multiple perspectives. In the following decades of her life Adnan would rewrite this same essay three separate times, using the same headings: once about her return to California, once about a time in Libya, and the last time about moving between these places and her home in California.

Adnan wants to know if the body's experience really is tied in any meaningful, actualizing way to "locality" (which might or might not mean "nationality").

"The world is somewhere else, in Mexico, in India," she suggests. "Why should it always be in a named place? Why should it, altogether, *be*?"

So "home"—or "homeland" if you insist—may not be a place in the world, a geography. It may be within—the experience of the single body inside one's skin. "It's not about history, not about suffering," Adnan insists. "It's not about people, it's about a child gone crazy with power." It is interesting that she positions the idea of "nation" as infantile, suggesting that maybe we could try to develop a model of nationality based on motherhood, a social or political entity whose purpose is nurturing in a certain way the interests and productivity of those people who live within it. Such a nation would have the resources under its own earth available, would belong to the people who live inside it.

Adnan's folded, refracting, repeating way of exploring "nation" or "country" is typical of many multinational writers. One cannot choose a single frame or single narrative or single experience. They all happen at once, one after the other, sometimes overlapping, sometimes playing backward:

> I understand how the muezzin's last call to prayer spreads within the sky and sinks in the direction of the mounting darkness. I'm losing my hold on the sliding day, and sitting on a chair seemingly firm, I feel that I am engulfed by an invisible wave that is carrying me into this geometry we call "the world," and also into something else for which we do not have a name.

In the meantime, on the wrong sides of various borders we wait. My sister and her family, having purchased plane tickets, do not receive their visas for travel to India in time for a cousin's wedding. We all theorize it has to do with our father's Pakistani citizenship. He wasn't born there but moved there just before Partition and became a citizen upon the creation of the Pakistani state.

When nations—Pakistan, Israel, India—come into existence, a whole history, a whole nationality, sometimes a whole language has got to be written, and quickly, to account for them. The large-pearl couscous prepared by Arabs in the region and referred to there as "Palestinian couscous" is labeled "Israeli couscous" in the West.

These nations—most of the new ones of the twentieth and twenty-first centuries anyhow—received their political legitimacy from mandates of European powers. England in particular—as Robert Moses of New York State highway-planning infamy did—indulged in the strategy of "partition," brutally effective at separating communities, creating political and social unrest, and killing any chance of popular resistance against the mechanism and the machines of empire. In this way "postcolonialism" became continuing economic and political colonialism, "post" only the trappings of political empire.

And when a nation is split, people are split from one another and sometimes split inside themselves. Adnan's fractured narrative is one artistic solution to the problem, but in *Schizophrene*, Bhanu Kapil explores the connection between migration and schizophrenia. Is a body removed from its nation, its familiar soil, really subject to partition not just of the political sort but also inside the brain itself?

The dramatic heart of this poetic dream-essay of a book is the narrative of an incident of domestic violence in the British-Punjabi community. It is between a butcher and his wife and the chorus of neighbors who peek in through the windows of the house. (Even the neighbors' criticism of the violence stems from their racism: *"You fucking Paki, what do you think you're doing? This is England, you bleeding animal."*) The neighbors are not quite sure whether they are witnessing a murder or whether the blood splattered across the dining room table is from the blood-smeared clothes of the family that works at a butcher's shop.

And me, how am I seen, when someone looks at me? When I read lines of poetry by Gillian Conoley, I felt at last defined: "I approached / as an alias, trachea / without sound, my signature, bright felon."

This confusion of what is seen reflects less on the witnesses and more on the immigrants themselves, whose very existence is governed by the inability to perceive or to be perceived properly in the new environment.

In Kapil's book, the trauma is not limited to the subjects of the book but the subject of the author herself. Threaded through *Schizophrene* is the story of its writing—or rather the failure of its writing:

On the *night* I knew my book *had failed*, I threw it—in the form of a *notebook*, a hand-written final *draft*—into the garden of my *house* in Colorado.

Christmas Eve, *2007*. It snowed that *winter* and into the *spring*; before the weather turned truly *warm*, I retrieved my *notes*, and began to write again, from the *fragments, the phrases and lines* still legible on the warped, *decayed* but curiously rigid pages.

It's a good thing Kapil really threw her book into the garden and wasn't just trying to make a further metaphor for the alienation of a subject from perception; I know because I held the book-as-compost object in my hands. She didn't—as she later claims in *Schizophrene*—throw the composted object into the bin when she was finished transcribing what she could from it—or if she did, then she fished it out again and handed it off to Boulder mapmaker and artist Jarvis Fosdick, who created an artist-book/sculpture of the decaying, shredded pages.

Fosdick's object manifests another version of *Schizophrene*, different from the recently published book in standard format. In Fosdick's object, the pages are lashed together with twine and bound between boards covered with sequences of repeating numbers, like geographic coordinates: they seem to be maps to places that can't be found. The body of the schizophrenic is dizzy between localities, unable to place herself. This composted book *can* be read, but not completely. One must peel away shredded layers to read sentences and phrases written below. In a "Notes" section at the end of the book, Kapil theorizes the benefit of a book in shreds, one she tried to re-create textually:

> From cross-cultural psychiatry, I learned that light touch, regularly and impersonally repeated, in the exchange of devotional objects, was as healing, for non-white subjects (schizophrenics) as anti-psychotic medication. In making a book that barely said anything, I hoped to offer: this quality of touch.

Even this "Notes" section becomes a part of the body of the main text. In six short paragraphs, it situates *Schizophrene*, outlines its creation in a learning community of writers and thinkers at Naropa University, describes how its editing process engendered Kapil's next project (an anticolonial novel, *BAN*), and gives a listing of the journals and collaborations (including with Kapil's sister, the visual artist Rohini Kapil, whose work graces the cover of the book) in which the work previously appeared. These integrative acts seem to serve as the artist/writer's own effort at reversing the damage of mental distress caused by the immigrant condition of migration from familiarity to the new nation, a journey more often than not marked or caused by other stresses—social, political, economic, familial.

The "Notes" section ends with a brief and telling sentence:

> Finally, I would like to extend my gratitude to Olga Visio's *Unseen Mendieta*, a document of Ana Mendieta's silueta

works that inspired *Schizophrene*, and which I tried to make myself, as close to the border of India and Pakistan as I could get, which was my own mother's garden in Punjab.

So at last we have a statement of influence, in this case a statement of absence, the imprint of Mendieta's body, the outline of it, the trace of it. Absence is what makes the condition of a body without nation after all, absence from language, absence from landscape, and—no joke!—absence from the food of one's mother and one's mother's people, which is the easiest and the surest sign of the loneliness of the immigrant—just as that rich smell of curry in the air is the surest sign you have entered an Indian neighborhood or household.

And here also, in the final lines of the book, after the formal "border" of text and "apparatus" has already been crossed, one finds another border, the national border, the one between India and Pakistan. And when Kapil says she made silhouette works in her mother's garden—itself an archetypal place of creation—"as close to the border" as she could get (like my sister and her family, Kapil could not get the stamp of national legitimacy into the book of her passport)—I believe she made them: pressed the skin and flesh of her bare body into the damp earth.

Body and soil meet at the close of the book at the "national border," which is a false one—that border in particular, the one that runs through Punjab, the one that separated Amritsar from Lahore, that ripped open the dream of a different nation, Khalistan, one like Palestine that occupied (for the moment) no map, that false border, soaked with the blood of countless bodies—and try through physical contact to stitch what was torn apart whole again with the body of the writer-artist, a body-worker herself, pressed into the earth.

In *Schizophrene* and in her books *Incubation* and *Humanimal*, Bhanu Kapil takes as one of her many departure points the interrogation of the immigrant body as either a monster—an entity unexplainable by and unable to function properly within the social and legal structures of a given society—or a cyborg, a body that by subvention and subversion surrenders parts of its own sovereignty to the external processes of the environment around it. In either case it is a body in crisis, one whose very existence and function and processes call into question the efficacy of nationality or nationhood in describing it.

In the bitter midwinter cold of Brampton, my cousin and I watch the old Indian ladies in their saris and parkas and snow boots striding purposefully from their housing developments to the supermarket. In the fall it is cardigans and sneakers. In the summer it is a light jacket and *chappals*. It is never quite warm enough to wear the sari unaccompanied and besides, the sari wearer is usually an older woman, in her fifties or sixties at least, and the skin of her bare stomach and back, revealed by the sari "blouse," really little more than a halter bra, seems unseemly in the repressed West, just one more reason for her to be seen as monstrous.

"It is psychotic to draw a line between two places," says Kapil, and then, "It is psychotic to submit to violence in a time of great violence and yet it is psychotic to leave that home or country, the place where you submitted again and again, forever." If the mind itself comes under pressure and duress from the various patterns of forced migrations, what are the coping mechanisms of the immigrant, nearly a monster in the new country, with monstrous customs, deviant sexuality, strange language, strange smells and tastes and clothing?

How does a body, a small one, a South Asian queer body, the body of a poet with a little blue book in his hand, cross borders then? Accompanied by verses extolling American expansion, he receives little marks of his legitimacy. A stamp from Uruguay, a stamp from India, and though he doesn't need them, shouldn't need them, stamps from the Canadian government too, and from Spain and France, both countries with open-border agreements with the United States that render visa stamps extraneous. He is annoyed when they stamp—no one else needs this stamp—but grateful for it when he comes home, is separated from his traveling companions, taken to the room in the back, stands there while a stranger runs his hands all over his body. Once he is asked to remove his shirt. Another time he is asked to remove his pants. The weird intersection between sexuality and the apparatus of nationhood and alienation—*his* alienation—is not lost on him.

I am touching your chest. Your throat. Your stomach. Please unbuckle your pants. Please lower your pants. I am going to touch your thigh. Your groin. I will use the back of my hand.

It *does* remind him that here in this place, in every American place, he is less than human. He is reminded that even though he is a citizen, he is—will always *be*—suspect and *a* suspect.

And the last page of his passport frightens him. There is a graphic of Earth seen from space—the moon is in the foreground, a satellite floats above—as if to confirm Lyndon Johnson's earlier discourse on the United States: that its mission is continual expansion, continuing homogenization, that once the western limit of the continent is reached, the nation will (did) spread out into the Pacific, that once the reaching arms of nationality encircle the planet and meet (they have), they will reach out into space for the star yet unvisited.

Opposite this graphic, in large letters, is the following statement: "This document contains sensitive electronics. For best performance, do not bend, perforate, or expose to extreme temperatures."

Electronics? But where, he wonders, turning the book over in his hands in alarm. True, the covers are thick and stiff. *Inside* the covers, he wonders. On the front cover below "the United States of America" there is a small gold rectangle with a circle inside it. Is this chip in the cover underneath that rectangle, he wants to know. And what information is on that chip? About me? Where I have been, which borders I've crossed? Or does it track my movement, track it like the plane on the little screen in front of my seat when I am flying?

As Kapil says, "It is psychotic not to know where you are in a national space."

The favorite security questions of the TSA echo back to me at the passport control office of Ben Gurion airport but in my interrogator's broken English: What is you father-name. What is you grandfather-name.

My "father-name" is not even real: our family name is Sayeed. My father's actual name wouldn't tell anything about us, migrants for generations—from Egypt to India, from India to Britain, from Britain to Canada. And in the one place of ultimate rootlessness, we are the most fixed into otherness. Every male relative of my father's shares the same first name, and my father chose to drop the family name. *Kazim* and *Ali* are my two middle names, not my first and my last. So who am I? You can't even begin.

And no one has yet asked me: what is your mother's name.

A poet, a maker of things, using the very language that was designed to control, obfuscate, curse, becomes his own mother. In the myth, the goddess Athena, born of no mother, wants the scariest mother of them all—Medusa—to adorn her shield. Medusa has all the symbols of the best of poets: she has snakes, that ancient symbol of wisdom, for hair, and when she looks into your soul, she can transfix you to the spot. True to form, once slain, from her open throat—source of her voice—flew the winged horse Pegasus, icon of poetry.

In practical terms, asking one in the brutal forum of interrogation what one's mother's name is must necessarily conjure for the interrogator his or her own mother. How would one be able to continue?

How does a body cross a border? How do borders cross bodies? The poet Meena Alexander writes of returning from a trip to her home and reading a passage from Darwish's *Memory for Forgetfulness*:

> She realizes that these words, composed in another place,
>   in another language, words written in a time of war,
>   translate well.
> Where she is, migrant memory pitches its tent.

This is her home ground, this borderland of desire and
meaning making. No elsewhere.

Is that it then? A book as a home, a book to wander with. A book as a
passport, not the passport as a book.

The book must give us tools, then, for seeing the individual body
against the landscape it inhabits. The book can help us see the landscape
not as political territory or economic potential but *as a place* itself, with
topographical, spiritual, and biological values utterly intrinsic and at the
same time knitted thoroughly together with the lives and the lifestyles of
the biosystems, plant life, people, and animals that inhabit it.

When I was writing *Bright Felon: Autobiography and Cities*, I had no
intention of writing "poems" or a "book of poems." Perhaps you could
say the entire text is a single poem—or reads that way. But I knew that in
order to write about my life, or more accurately *write my life*, I would have
to use not literary but geographic form, architectural form: the form of
the cities that I had traversed and lived in, even for short periods of time.

The map on the cover of *Bright Felon* is by the cartographer, artist,
and DC statehood activist Nikolas Schiller. It is an aerial photo of Lower
Manhattan and Brooklyn refracted and formed into a geometric pattern.
It is no mistake that it appears as a classical Islamic motif. Some maps
are conceptual.

Just as cities are concatenations of time acting in space (I pointed
out once while giving a walking tour of Walt Whitman's SoHo the build-
ings that were original to Whitman's time, including the theater that
was once a firehouse, a guesthouse now a shop, and a parking lot once
a hospital), my book passes through space and time, moving both back-
ward and forward, once discursive, then lyrical, first essayistic, then
poetic, sometimes all things at once. Sentences without consequence,

one leading into the other, shine into the unexplored and unexamined life: *why* had I been silent for so long? The book stutters itself open finally. What begins in clotted and endless sentences opens out into monosyllables and long vowels. Function follows form sometimes. Someone once said that pentameter is the length of a breath and iambic is the rhythm of pulse. It might be medically true, but only if you are tuning your fork to two of the many systems in your body, two of the many that exist in the planetary entity, of the many that resound through the cosmos.

The book is part sculpture perhaps, part geometry, part calligraphy. On the cover, in the form of orange calligraphy surrounding the subtitle, is a second subtitle, a secret, a line of American poetry translated into Urdu and copied there. I've never told anyone what the line reads. I want a reader like me—someone who can read the Urdu text but who also knows enough American poetry that he or she would recognize it. It's happened twice so far.

A map is a dangerous and useless thing, warns Hakim Bey in his groundbreaking text of popular and artistic resistance, *Temporary Autonomous Zone*. "The 'map' is a political abstract grid," he says, "a gigantic *con* enforced by the carrot/stick conditioning of the 'Expert' State, until for most of us the map *becomes* the territory." But in the actual moment of mapmaking itself, one can find intentions more directly connected to the body: where is the highest point from which to see the terrain around you, where is the closest source of fresh water, where is there shelter from sun or rain. In a world, as Bey points out, in which every square inch of territory, whether land, water, or air, is claimed by some political entity or another, there are critical questions: "How can we separate the concept of *space* from the mechanisms of *control*? The territorial gangsters, the Nation/States, have hogged the entire map. Who can invent for us a cartography of autonomy, who can draw a map that includes our desires?"

In *A Lily Lilies*, poet Josey Foo and choreographer Leah Stein make an effort to map the terrain of the desert landscape of the Navajo Nation. They write that their effort "maps space through language, language through movement, and both space and movement through pictures." The book of poems, choreography, and photographs presents an interesting new way the abstract of "nation" can be personalized and brought into the individual body.

In one photograph, you could be looking at the water, at the sky, at the inside of a mouth—it isn't clear, though you know it is a landscape you are seeing. The parts of the body and the parts of the landscape are not so distinguishable, at least not in the dance. Stein writes, "Contrast between architecture of the body—bones suggesting buildings, kite and ridge—and movement of arms, wrists, elbows, head.... Arms, wrists, elbows and head seek wilderness." The sensuous forms of the poems on the page imitate biomorphic shapes of eroded tree branches, wind-shaped hills, and the sinuous line of the horizon itself. Dancers become birds, poems become choreography, bodies turn into one another.

This moment—bodies turning into one another—is the moment of "chaos," the moment that precedes most creation myths. It's the moment that Bey believes needs to be preserved against the interests of "Nation/States," which always require regulation and submission to law in order to increase maximum productivity for the benefit of as few people as possible (in order to maximize the amount of benefit). "Don't just survive while waiting for someone's revolution to clear your head," Bey exhorts. "Act as if you were already free ... carry your Moorish passport with pride, don't get caught in the crossfire, keep your back covered—but take the risk, dance before you calcify."

In *A Lily Lilies*, words change into themselves: "The sun *shines* but the sun *is* the shine." Dancers change into animals before finally one can be two things at once: "*She is both daughter and river.*" If you can be a citizen of two nations at once—really owe ultimate loyalty to both countries—it can mean only one thing: that war, the most unimaginative and boring method of resolving conflict, must really be over.

"Imprint," the final sequence of the book, explores the contact between physical bodies and the soil of the land; this contact *is* and *can be* a productive part of oneself, not as territory to be owned but as place, nourishment, locality. "I carry a candle to the river / and acquire my life," writes Foo. In a final note, Stein explains the choreography: "Each dancer's movement 'imprints,' becomes part of the other's movement, all movements become one imprint."

Perhaps Foo and Stein—who has choreographed site-specific works in train garages, open fields, corner parking lots, vacant city lots, historical sites, gardens, and burial grounds—should team up with Bhanu Kapil and create some pieces for all the invisible borders that run under the ground of the American continent, its current political borders so new, so recent not only in the eyes of the Earth but in any conception of human inhabitation here.

Kapil threw her book into the garden to undergo transformative processes, and Foo and Stein talk in their introduction about their book as a "transportable site," hoping it "will travel to very many places." That leaking of the main text in both of these books into what is traditionally thought of as "apparatus"—the index, the notes, the introduction, the biographical data—is exciting because it prefigures an idea about the book as a body or the book as a nation. A nation could have multiplicity as a founding concept, but such an idea necessarily contravenes the possibility of "empire"—doing away with borders would mean awarding ownership of what's in the ground to whoever rightly inhabits that space. Deep in the ground of a book, one thrown into the garden or one constructed in somatic movements in open air, for example, one discovers new ways of reading it.

Who is the human here, then, and what can it all mean? On the macro level, in a conflict between nation and individual human body, nation would always seem to win. Bodies can be pierced, killed, sullied, lied about, suppressed, erased. Nations have many tools, mechanical and otherwise, at their disposal. But I am tempted to say that in a conflict between nation and individual on a micro level, the individual always wins. A nation is a fiction, a story everyone has decided to agree is real because it seems either convenient or necessary at the moment; a person is a collection of infinite kindnesses, loves, and, indeed, joys.

It is always the human who acts, who transcends the national myth that has been created. Darwish, in his book *Absent Presence*, writes, "Do not look upon yourself in the way they write about you. Do not investigate the Canaanite in you in order to establish that you exist. Rather, seize this reality, this name of yours, and learn how to write your proof. For you are you, not your ghost, the one who was driven away in that night."

The individual must find those zones of liberation—as Bey would advise, that "tactile tasty physical space (ranging in size from, say, a double bed to a large city)"—in order to actualize an individual spiritual awakening, one to generosity and kindness, pleasure and the abandonment of "world-hatred & shame."

Well, I myself am a Temporary Autonomous Zone then, with my Moorish passport, refusing to write the laws of the nation on my body but instead learning through the language of poetry what it really is that binds one human to another in community.

WORKS CITED:

Adnan, Etel. *In the Heart of the Heart of Another Country*. San Francisco: City Lights Publishers, 2005.

Alexander, Meena. *Poetics of Dislocation*. Ann Arbor: The University of Michigan Press, 2009.

Bey, Hakim. *T.A.Z. The Temporary Autonomous Zone, Ontological Anarchy, Poetic Terrorism*. Brooklyn, NY: Autonomedia, 2003.

Darwish, Mahmoud. *Absent Presence*. London: Hesperus Press, 2010.

Darwish, Mahmoud. *Memory for Forgetfulness: August, Beirut, 1982*. Berkeley: University of California Press, 1995.

Foo, Josey, and Leah Stein. *A Lily Lilies*. Callicoon, NY: Nightboat Books, 2011.

Haraway, Donna. *Simians, Cyborgs, and Women: The Reinvention of Nature*. New York: Routledge, 1990.

Kapil, Bhanu. *Schizophrene*. Callicoon, NY: Nightboat Books, 2011.

Astral Summer

Katharine Coles

The only time my parents took me out of the United States as a child, I was nine. That Christmas break, they loaded my two brothers and me into the old International Travelall and drove us south into Mexico. We stayed in run-down motels until we left the cold weather behind and reached our beachfront hotel—also probably run-down but glamorous in my memory, maybe because I'd slept in far more tents than hotels or maybe because the restaurant served turtle soup—outside San Blas. San Blas has since been developed as a surfing destination, but back then the road leading to the hotel was a rutted track my father nosed the shock-sprung truck carefully down, its headlights at night lunging wildly against dense jungle foliage strange to a child born and raised in the desert.

Most of our time in Mexico we spent either on the beach, digging for shells and bodysurfing the enormous waves, or out in the jungle, hiking and canoeing and stalking iguanas. Only once or twice did we go into town. The place was still remote enough that women on the street would stop us so they could run our white-blond hair—my brothers' in 1968 grown almost as long as mine—through their fingers. Since I didn't understand Spanish, our communication occurred through those touches. There, I had my first sense of the foreignness not only of others or the world but also of myself. I understood myself to be a stranger, worthy of examination.

This was my first awareness of a sense I've spent much of my life as a poet seeking and cultivating. I humped a backpack loaded with Homer and Sappho around the Greek islands during graduate school. Shortly after September 11, when Americans were taking travel advisories seriously, I spent three weeks alone in Indonesia, where my mother had been born and spent her early childhood; for days, I didn't see another Western face, and again I understood how little privacy anyone has who is visibly marked as other. I traveled on a small boat up the Amazon; I went to Cuba, where the highways are so poorly marked you have to hire someone to ride with you out of Havana, just to make sure you're on the right road. Sometimes, traveling, I thought I knew in advance what I sought. But even though it can be useful to have a destination in mind, the most important things I found would be those I didn't know to look for. The shaman in the Amazonian village who pressed his thumb next to my blue eye, then gave me a spear he'd made. A lion carved in a stone lintel. The house my mother was born into in what was then Batavia, the house my grandmother had sketched in the margin of one of her letters home, which I found seventy-odd years later by luck and accident.

For most of my young adult life, I thought my parents parochial and unadventurous in their travel, which mostly involved camping or car trips to visit extended family in the Midwest. They'd been limited in where they could go by children and money. My mother's father was a geologist and an explorer (eventually the chief geologist for Standard Oil, then head of exploration for Petrobras in Brazil), and, after a childhood spent moving from Indonesia to Central America to Cuba in the wake of his career—a path I've erratically followed on some of my own journeys as I've tried to write about my grandparents—my mother for years was content to explore the spectacular desert landscape they'd made home. And, finally, it hadn't occurred to them to travel in pursuit of the human. I was the one who wanted to spend weeks outside her language, who, having grown up in a western town settled a bare one hundred years earlier, wanted to walk great cities redolent with history and see their museums and churches. I preferred an ancient botanical garden, planted and cultivated over centuries by human hands, to an untouched natural vista. What I wanted was to feel my otherness. In nature, especially in the Utah desert that had been so exotic to my parents, I felt at home, having spent much of my childhood playing under its spectacular sandstone formations and vast sky. Hanging from a cliff face by a rope or rafting the wild waters of a western river was, thanks to my parents, part of my ordinary life.

In December 2010 I spent a month in Antarctica, sent to Palmer Station by the National Science Foundation to write poems. The desire and the comfort to go to such an extreme must have been rooted in my childhood. Indeed, my sense of estrangement in Antarctica arose out of just what my parents had been seeking when they moved to the American West: a landscape vaster and less welcoming than any I had known. Made entirely of water, sky, ice, and the light they all reflect, Antarctica was a place I literally had to teach myself to see. I am not alone in this. Ernest Shackleton, in *South*, describes watching, on May 8, 1915, the sun, "which had made 'positively his last appearance' seven days earlier," rise and set again not once but three times over two and a half hours. With sinking hearts, he and his crew had watched the final sunset in the north—and it had really occurred. The subsequent risings and settings were reflections and refractions cast by water onto clouds. And those repeated sunsets— were they any less disheartening for being unreal?

When I was there (summer, the light never altogether failing), the mountains on the horizon might appear one place in the morning then shift leftward that afternoon; they might turn upside down or temporarily vanish into a cloud bank or a clear day. Everything came to the eye via reflection and refraction; everything observed was an image cast, partly or wholly mirage. And so I found my way to see it. It was like nothing so much as the desert, where landscape is also made largely of light and light's deceptions. I learned to remember what my parents had taught me: that my senses are wholly untrustworthy, even at home. Next to this estrangement, the somewhat odd culture of science that dominates station life was, well, a negligible obstacle to overcome. Still, the locals never would let a poet forget that she was the foreigner among them, the stranger worthy of observation.

I should say that over time, my parents began sometimes to join me on my travels—both of them for part of my trip to Greece and to Cuba, my mother following me, again in my grandfather's footsteps, up the Amazon. It is now December 2011. A week from today, my parents, who are seventy-nine and eighty-two, will step onto an airplane. A few days later, they will be on a ship off the Antarctic Peninsula, not far from where I lived during that month. After spending so many years stalking history—of human culture, of my own family—I will be thinking of them there, following in my footsteps to a place I never would have gone without them. I will be beside myself with envy.

It seems to me that the poet's job is just this: to stand beside herself, outside herself, in order to understand something about how an individual human subjectively encounters the world, in which and against which she is a stranger, even to herself. In doing so, she may become able to illuminate something important about the human condition, the fact that in this world we are all in some sense foreigners, estranged by consciousness from our essential, immediate relationship with reality. Without this awareness, we believe in what we see—the mountains just there; the sun setting; the wavering on the desert horizon that seems to promise cool water where there is only dry rock and sand.

Some poets, I know, can remember this estrangement, can feel it again and again, without leaving home. Emily Dickinson, for example. But for me, to be out of my element—my language, my culture, my known landscape—reconnects me in a powerful way to my sense of the world, which I will never fully know, and through it to the part of myself that is equally unknowable.

Field Poet

Nick Flynn

Strange, that we sometimes have to put ourselves in another place—unfamiliar, foreign—in order to wake up. Strange in that we wake up every day, just where we are. We wake up, but before we open our eyes, we say, this is my bed or this is my room or this is my apartment. This is my corner, this is my box, this is my cell. My castle, my dungeon, my iron lung. My armchair, my wheelchair, my coffin … yet we barely remember the moment our eyes closed last night. Neuroscientists, I've read, understand sleep, but why we wake up is still a mystery. Try this: lie in bed (box, dungeon, iron lung) with your eyes closed—can you list everything you would see on the mantel (sidewalk, floor) if you were to open your eyes?

Ten years ago now, I made my way to a lake in the center of Africa, a lake almost the size of Ireland. Because I flew there from Ireland, I thought I would understand. I went, ostensibly, to help someone I'd just met make a documentary film, which he described as a parable about fish and guns and globalization. His name was Hubert, the lake was Victoria, the fish was Nile perch. Nile perch is flaky and white, and it feeds soldiers and lots of folks in Europe and the United States and is perfect for Filet-O-Fish sandwiches. The guns—well, arms merchants supply the guns, and the arms merchants come from the same countries that import the fish. This is the way the world works.

The first night Hubert and I met, in Rome, he showed me some early footage of what he was working on. I was so moved that I offered to meet him in Africa the next time he went. To help, whatever that meant. But I was a poet, not a filmmaker—what could I do? I went to Paris—which is where Hubert was based—a few times in the months before the trip. To buy equipment, to look at footage, to be filled in on that part of the world. Hubert had spent the past ten years in and out of Africa—to listen to him was like having a veil pulled back, like waking up. Africa had seemed, from my reading of headlines, like a nightmare of chaos—endless war, endless famine, all of it somewhat incomprehensible. Hubert, with his parable of guns and fish, was attempting to put things into context.

As a child, I hadn't had much opportunity to see the world; my family didn't have that kind of money. I had to learn what I could from books ("when I walked into the jungle, I was seventeen. When I walked out I was twenty-one. And, by God, I was rich!"), from Tarzan movies, from Mutual of Omaha's *Wild Kingdom*. My mother didn't have the money to fly us anywhere, except once to Montana—Helena—to stay with cousins for a month. I was eight, and that trip to Montana is a vivid nail driven into those days. I learned to ride a bicycle in Montana! We made Lego fortresses for locusts! On a road trip to Glacier National Park, we stopped at a roadside stand and bought turquoise and rabbit pelts and rubber tomahawks from real Indians. In the back was a sad zoo with a sad bald eagle bent over in a too-small cage—that eagle is all I remember. The mountains were always in the distance, so unlike anything in our hometown, and we were driving toward them. Locusts splattered on the windshield; we had to pull over at every gas station to scrape their bodies off. By nightfall, we would touch a glacier.

Our hometown was Scituate, on the Atlantic Ocean. We lived on Third Cliff, which was slowly—sometimes suddenly—eroding into the sea. Each year, a house or two was pulled over the cliff as the ocean forced its way inland. I would lie on my belly on the edge of the cliff, stare into the ocean, try to imagine eternity. That was when I was awake. Or I'd wander the salt marshes, strewn with detritus from all over the world—parts of ships, brightly colored lobster buoys, the corpse of a white dog.

Annie Dillard, in her essay "Total Eclipse," muses:

> We teach our children one thing only, as we were taught: to wake up. We teach our children to look alive there, to join by words and activities the life of human culture on the planet's crust. As adults, we are almost all adept at waking up.... Yet it is a transition we make a hundred times a day, as, like so many will-less dolphins, we plunge and surface, lapse and emerge. We live half our waking lives and all of our sleeping lives in some private, useless, and insensible waters we never mention or recall. Useless, I say. Valueless, I might add—until someone hauls their wealth up to the surface and into the wide-awake city, in a form that people can use.

This is what Hubert was doing on Lake Victoria all those years. This is why I wanted to meet him there, to help. It meant getting a raft of vaccinations—yellow fever, typhoid, et cetera. It meant taking a pill daily (mefloquine hydrochloride)—psychosis was one possible side effect. It meant not drinking any water unless it was bottled or had been boiled— it doesn't help anyone if you get sick. It meant learning how to work a camera and a boom mic, to carry the money, to guard the equipment. It meant, mostly, opening my eyes.

Now Hubert is one of my best friends, and the footage I saw that first day in Rome has become the film *Darwin's Nightmare*, which won awards at about a dozen international film festivals and was nominated for an Academy Award for Best Documentary Feature in 2006. In the credits, I am listed as artistic collaborator and field poet, a term I borrowed from the Vietnamese, who for thousands of years included a poet in each military unit (a field poet), whose job was to write poems in order to give meaning to each day. In Africa, it simply meant I tried to be fully awake to each moment we were there, and part of that was to transcribe what I saw. It was the best I could offer.

Thirteen Ways of Working in a War Zone

Eliza Griswold

1. **Stock a first-aid kit:** Carry a broad-based gut antibiotic, such as Cipro or Proquin. (It's hard to be sure of quality in many places.) The opposite is true for antimalarials. If you need one, stop in the first big city and buy Coartem or Riamet at the best pharmacy. Take on first sign of infection. Also purchase oral rehydration salts. They are less than a dollar in some places (less than ten dollars on average) and can cure diarrhea, a preventable disease that kills more than three million people a year, mostly kids.

2. **Locate yourself:** On arrival, check in with the US embassy or the legation of whatever country claims you as a citizen. If the situation is uncertain, the embassy might urge you to leave for precisely the reasons you've come. Still, it's worthwhile to let someone know your whereabouts.

3. **Carry the right papers:** If working as a journalist, you may need a government-issued press pass, which can take months to procure. Check the country's visa requirements online before you apply. It

might be easiest to use a visa service, which will act as an intermediary with the arcane embassies of many troubled or closed countries.

4. **Organize your communications:** A working phone is a priority. Satellite phones aren't a requirement in most places. Usually it is simple and much cheaper to pick up a SIM card in the airport. Don't buy one until asking locals which service is best. To that end, be prepared to buy a secondhand phone from a man standing on the street, probably your driver's cousin. A local line is invaluable.

5. **Organize your work:** Bring three sturdy notebooks and keep a daily journal; the more quotidian detail it records, the better—rickshaws, roasting meat, the sweet smoke of a garbage heap, the muezzin's call competing with evangelical hymns over loudspeakers. These will be useful later, especially for the half lines of poems scrawled in the margins.

6. **Hone your method:** Slow down. You may be tempted to accelerate through interviews and places to *get the story*. This frustration—a fear of failure—is part of the reporting process, especially under tough conditions with limited time. Gathering the scenes and facts that long stories require comes with various pressures, including deadlines and the necessity to think through the character detail required on the page later. There's a certain parallel between serving as a soldier and being a foreign correspondent. Both require the capacity to outwait boredom.

7. **Be prepared for more than the work:** There are cases in which interviews, if guided by a gentle intuition, can provide a form of healing. On occasion, a survivor of physical trauma, including rape or abduction, builds a home for her spirit in the air just above her head. She builds a safe castle in the sky where, by not occupying her body, she

is certain to protect herself from harm and the memory of harm. In these cases, posttraumatic stress can manifest as a kind of sleepiness, a daze. You might gently speak to her, repeat the phrases she uses in order to affirm her story. She may return to her physical self for a few minutes.

8. **Travel safely under fire:** In a car, keep your windows rolled down if there is gunfire. Bullets shatter glass, which becomes a secondary weapon. Always park so that you don't have to turn around to get out of a bad situation. Ask about land mines. Listen to your driver. If he says a road is a no-go, then it is a no-go. In some situations, it is a good idea to send a security car ahead to investigate the route.

9. **Find fixers:** Often local journalists, teachers, or aid workers are available for a day or a week. They are invaluable, not only for the perspectives they bring but also for making contacts, which might take months to track down otherwise. Find a fixer before arrival, if possible. Begin your search by contacting the country's leading news-paper, the local BBC or Reuters bureau, and/or local human rights organizations.

10. **Shoot video, whether you like it or not:** Carry a lightweight video camera. I recommend one called the Flip, with some versions being as inexpensive as $100. It will catch and hold details the human eye might not, for instance the accurate number of bee boxes the minis-ter of bees tends in Afghanistan.

11. **File frequently:** If you are working in a place where your notes or camera might be seized before you leave the country, then take the time to upload materials, notes, and photos and e-mail them home every night so they are safe.

12. **Know the rules and responsibilities:** If anything goes wrong—and it will—remember that the people who will pay most for your mistakes are the local driver, translator, and/or friends who will not be leaving when the story is finished. To that end, follow every protection for which they ask, including leaving names out of your work.

13. **Take time to reacclimate:** Be gentle with yourself and those at home. Avoid large supermarkets. Experiencing such a surfeit of food can be nightmarish. Remember, you chose to go. Choose to let painful moments render you tender rather than tough. The act of writing poetry will encourage this process; poems encourage us to return to what baffles us, to return to the site of a disaster and sift through what floats after a crash.

What Is the Wind: The Changing, Unchanging Gertrude Stein

Jared Hawkley

Among the books in her library, *Robinson Crusoe* was a favorite of Gertrude Stein's for the way it examines the behavior of a man separated from his familiar world, stranded on an island he doesn't know. There is a scene in the novel in which the yoke of reality comes crushing down on the hero's shoulders. It happens as he is walking along the beach on the island that he'd presumed deserted.

> It happened one day about noon, going towards my boat, I was exceedingly surprised with the print of a man's naked foot on the shore, which was very plain to be seen in the sand. I stood like one thunderstruck, or as if I had seen an apparition. I listened, I looked around me; I could hear nothing, nor see anything.[1]

Stein sometimes referred to this scene in the novel because of what

---

1. Daniel Defoe, *Robinson Crusoe* (New York: Barnes & Noble Classics Series, 2003), 150.

she thought to be Crusoe's state of mind at the moment he sees the foot-print, calling it "one of the most perfect examples of the non-existence of time and identity": he's so startled that he doesn't immediately understand what he's looking at.[2]

Before she turned six, Stein had already lived in a handful of places—first Pennsylvania, then Austria, France, Maryland, and finally California. After losing both parents by the age of seventeen, she invested several years toward a degree in psychology at the prestigious Radcliffe College, then enrolled at Johns Hopkins to study medicine, but dropped out of school after realizing the work didn't suit her. Around that time she had also drafted—and then shelved—her first novel, *Q.E.D.*, a veiled autobiographical account of a hot-and-cold, ultimately unsuccessful love affair involving her and two other women during her college years.[3] After this early series of false starts and failures, Stein left her home in Baltimore in 1903 and sailed to Paris, intending to join her beloved brother Leo, leave behind her confused American life and the world at large, and become a writer.

Stein later reflected that living in Paris was necessary for her; it allowed her to write and to be a writer, not so much because it was Paris but because it wasn't the United States. "This separation is important in making literature," she explained, "because there are so many ways for one to feel oneself and every new way helps, and a separating way may

2. Gertrude Stein, *What Are Master-Pieces* (New York: Pitman Publishing Corporation, 1970), 93.
3. Gertrude Stein, *Fernhurst, Q.E.D., and Other Early Writings* (New York: Liveright Publishing Corporation, 1996), xi.

help a great deal, indeed it may, it may help very much. And this did."[4] She asserted that "writers have to have two countries, the one where they belong and the one in which they live really. The second one is romantic, it is separate from themselves, it is not real but it is really there."[5]

⚬

Stein channeled her sense of separation into what became her best-selling work, *The Autobiography of Alice B. Toklas*, written entirely in the persona of her muse and wife, Alice. Paraphrasing herself in the voice of Alice, Stein explained that her social isolation, exemplified partly by her steadfast allegiance to the English language, was to a large degree intentional:

> No, she replied, you see I feel with my eyes and it does not make any difference to me what language I hear, I don't hear a language, I hear tones of voice and rhythms, but with my eyes I see words and sentences and there is for me only one language and that is english. One of the things I have liked all these years is to be surrounded by people who know no english. It has left me more intensely alone with my eyes and my english. I do not know if it would have been possible to have english be so all in all to me otherwise. And they none of them could read a word I wrote, most of them did not even know that I did write.[6]

Stein confessed that she wanted to be "intensely alone." She used expatriation as a tool, a precisely planned and executed exercise in

---

4. Catharine R. Stimpson and Harriet Chessman, eds., *Gertrude Stein: Writings 1932–1946* (New York: The Library of America, 1998), 202.
5. Gertrude Stein, *Paris France* (New York: W.W. Norton & Company, Inc., 1996), 2.
6. Gertrude Stein, *The Autobiography of Alice B. Toklas* (New York: Vintage Books, 1990), 70.

moving away. She was essentially placeless: no longer part of her home-land and not part of her adopted home either.

With the turn of the century came a new generation of writers, philoso-phers, and scientists who began to dismantle the foundation stones of basic knowledge. Darwin had claimed that the Bible may not be literally true, and Nietzsche and Marx were suggesting that ethics and social class may be socially constructed; Freud was advocating his theories of sexual impulses, and the world was in the throes of industrialization. Much of the great reconstructive effort began with the artists converging in Paris. From her vantage point there, Stein was perfectly poised to sift through the debris of the nineteenth century, salvaging what remained to com-pose the scaffolding of the new twentieth century.

In time, the accumulated change of that era came to be known as modernism—a movement in literature and the arts characterized by a precipitous plunge into uncertainty and the ensuing trek back out. Among the first to detect this plunge was Henry James; Stein noticed in his writing "the disembodied way of disconnecting something from anything."[7] This was, she felt, a sign of the times—this way of things sep-arating, becoming disembodied.

I don't mean to imply that Stein was reclusive—quite the opposite. She welcomed many artists of the new generation into her home and learned from them; her house at 27 Rue de Fleurus was famously a gathering spot for a pantheon of writers and painters, including F. Scott Fitzgerald, Ernest Hemingway, and Henri Matisse. In particular she was profoundly

---

7. Stimpson and Chessman, 222.

influenced by Pablo Picasso and his peers, most of whom were not French either, having convened in Paris for their own reasons.

Compelled by the artist's approach to representation and receptive to the undertones of coming unrest, Stein began to be changed. She saw her close friend Picasso working toward a new mode of perception, a new composition "of which one corner was as important as another corner."[8]

Reflecting on Picasso, Stein recalled that he "once remarked I do not care who it is that has or does influence me as long as it is not myself."[9] Soon after they first met, Stein agreed to let Picasso paint her portrait. It was the winter of 1905, and Picasso had yet to take up his cubist modes. Over the course of more than eighty sittings, Picasso finished all but his subject's face. After three times scraping down to the underpainting and revising the view from profile to three-quarters, he finally wiped out the face in aggravation, declared, "I can't see you any longer when I look,"[10] and left for Spain.

Returning to Paris in 1906, inspired by the new African masks and sculpture prevalent in France due to an increasing number of French colonial campaigns, Picasso sat down with the portrait of Stein and finished her face without a reference, without looking at her.

Reportedly, the finished portrait was criticized on the basis that Stein did not resemble it.[11] But Picasso, realizing the impossibility of painting a definitive static image to encompass all of Stein, had instead painted the likeness of a transformation. He saw that she herself was in flux,

8. Gertrude Stein, *Picasso* (London: B.T. Batsford Ltd, 1939), 11.
9. Stein, *What Are Master-Pieces*, 85.
10. Stein, *The Autobiography of Alice B. Toklas*, 53.
11. Picasso's reply: "She will."

and one might say that, at least in part, he extracted the idea of cubism from within his subject: a view of real objects as fleeting, shifting, and unknowable.

In 1909, Stein returned the gesture in the first of what would ultimately become a triptych of word portraits of her friend. Word portraits were exercises in freeing their subjects from containment—a practice Stein had developed between 1906 and 1908 while composing *The Making of Americans*, essentially an extended portrait of three generations of a fictional American family. In the writing of this novel she exploited the power of repetition and rhythm, with subtle changes, to render characters, contemporaries, and life itself. She refined this method in "Picasso," a more restrained work limited to seven verbs in the progressive tense: *following, needing, working, bringing, coming, having,* and *being.*

> This one was one having always something being coming out of him, something having completely a real meaning. This one was one whom some were following. This one was one who was working. This one was one who was working and he was one needing this thing needing to be working so as to be one having some way of being one having some way of working. This one was one who was working.[12]

Curiously, Stein's portrait begins by describing Picasso as "one who was working" and ends by claiming that "he was not ever completely working." By the last line, Stein has asserted several contradictory observations, all ostensibly under the banner of one and the same man. The result is a case study in the process of becoming. Stein essentially

12. Gertrude Stein, *Picasso: The Complete Writings* (Boston: Beacon Press, 1970), 97.

describes a man who, like every man or woman, isn't ever only one thing—who can't truly be known.

❧

In 1912, progressing from portraiture to still lifes, Stein wrote the bulk of the work that would be collected in *Tender Buttons*, a series of household poems that seem to obscure the subjects unveiled by their titles. But Stein had the opposite intention. She hoped to discover true essences through a concentrated study of the fleeting and changeable.

In an interview,[13] Stein explained her process during the composition of these poems:

> You must remember each time I took something, I said, I have got to satisfy each realistic thing I feel about it. Looking at your shoe, for instance, I would try to make a complete realistic picture of your shoe. It is devilish difficult and needs perfect concentration, you have to refuse so much and so much intrudes itself upon you that you do not want it, it is exhausting work.[14]

Through her perfect concentration, Stein managed to create "complete realistic pictures" of mundane domestic objects without naming them. She saw her subjects as they really were—many elements at once, all of them true, all of them contributing in some small way to the actual nature of the subject.

---

13. The interview was arranged by Robert Bartlett Haas and conducted by William Sutton in France in 1946.
14. Robert Bartlett Haas, *A Primer for the Gradual Understanding of Gertrude Stein* (Los Angeles: Black Sparrow Press, 1971), 29.

A LONG DRESS.

What is the current that makes machinery, that makes
it crackle, what is the current that presents a long line
and a necessary waist. What is this current.

What is the wind, what is it.

Where is the serene length, it is there and a dark place
is not a dark place, only a white and red are black,
only a yellow and green are blue, a pink is scarlet, a
bow is every color. A line distinguishes it. A line just
distinguishes it.[15]

In "A Long Dress," Stein also works at what it is that causes change:
that mysterious current, a force as sure and as baffling as the wind. By
focusing on what things are changeable and therefore inessential, she
begins to uncover what is not affected by this wind, in this case guessing
that its line is what distinguishes the dress from other things.

Stein's aversion to naming household objects paralleled her strug-
gle with naming herself. Part American, part Parisian, part writer, part
theorist, part matriarch: to Stein, the problem with assigning names was
that "the name was not new but the thing being alive was always new."[16]
Names, she thought, impose a false certainty, robbing a thing of its mys-
tery and mutability.

---

15. Gertrude Stein, *Tender Buttons* (New York: Claire Marie, 1914), 17.
16. Stimpson and Chessman, 330.

At one point, she phrased her struggle with identity as a question: "What is the use of being a boy if you are going to grow up to be a man."[17] To her, a person was divided into discrete parts; the boy and the man were two unconnected beings. She seemed to be grappling with the growing difference between the person she once was and the person she was continuously, inexorably becoming. In his book *Sum*, neuroscientist David Eagleman describes what I think tormented Gertrude Stein, this division of selves as a "group of individuals touchingly searching for a common theme"[18] but finding none.

At its heart, travel is composed of two inverse functions: travel toward and travel away. Both occur simultaneously, though a traveler usually characterizes a journey as one or the other. The question is, toward what? Away from what?

By her own admission, Stein moved to Paris to be alone and separate from where she had come. A sort of method acting for the writer, this distance from the familiar certainties of home opened Stein up to all the change radiating from Paris and freed her from the confines of identity. But distance from home didn't make the inner conflict disappear; it didn't mean never coming back. It may have paradoxically guided her closer to understanding her own abandoned past.

Despite her best efforts to be placeless and nameless, Stein surmised that "it is not what France gave you but what it did not take away from you that was important."[19] After thirty-three years spent forsaking her previous identities, she perceived that something remained inside her—something true, irreducible, and foundational.

---

17. Stein, *What Are Master-Pieces*, 90
18. David Eagleman, *Sum: Forty Tales from the Afterlives* (New York: Vintage Books, 2009), 74.
19. Gertrude Stein, "An American and France," Oxford University Lecture (New Haven, CT: Yale University Archives, 1936).

Ultimately, her work in understanding a new century may have led her to experience a brief and blinding moment of Crusonian clarity, a revelation Wallace Stegner describes in his story "The Traveler": "For from the most chronic and incurable of ills, identity, [she] had looked outward and for one unmistakable instant recognized [her]self."[20] Seeing that she was, in fact, a part of a world of parts, Stein could have finally stooped to collect the shuffled, themeless pieces of her identity, even as the winds stirred up from the darkest corners of her heart.

20. Wallace Stegner, *The City of the Living* (Boston: Houghton Mifflin, 1956), 206.

The Door of Return

Yusef Komunyakaa

I began to reread Pablo Neruda's *Memoirs*. A poet who'd left footprints on numerous cities, countries, and continents, whose work had guided me, Neruda had spoken to my heart through his imagination and feeling for the larger human world.

Distant places. I had seen a photograph of a Portuguese cannon aimed out of Elmina Castle toward the Atlantic. I could already see Ghana—a wooded savanna in my mind's eye—a zone of forests swollen with daily rainfall. I knew something about African lore, the kings of Songhai, Mali, and Ghana who drained swamps and cut canals for farms, who bartered gold for the lifeblood of salt. I knew sleeping sickness was spread by the tsetse fly. Hundreds of images populated my head.

I had gone to Africa many times in daydreams and poems long before I set foot in the land. So in early 2004, when Arthur Whitman, my former poetry student at Princeton University and one of the founding members of the Ghana Education Project, invited me, I said yes without hesitation. As a member of the board, I was already familiar with the organization's mission: to establish small libraries, to promote literacy, and to combat HIV/AIDS through education. I understood I wasn't embarking on a tourist safari but rather leading a group of writers to confront a very real pandemic. And in this moment, I realized that poetry was a tool, or an instrument, for preparing my psyche for the journey.

I always say poetry is confrontation and celebration. I suppose I had to attempt to confront some unspoken part within me that did not exactly want to encounter the severity of that world. My acute imagination had already jump-started, and I knew I had to align my mind with my heart. A deep dreaming had begun to claim my body.

One reason for the trip was to attempt to establish a dialogue confronting the devastating reality of AIDS. I knew we would meet with schoolchildren and with the fishermen of the village of Komenda. It was in anticipation of meeting the fishermen that I began writing the poem "Dead Reckoning," and in the lines "Now, lost in the old clothes of unreason, / & wanderlust, their nets sag with the last / of its kind, with bountiful fish stories..." I was perhaps attempting to bring the abstract into focus, to live in that world for a moment, where a story becomes a bridge between people, countries, and cultures. In this way, poetry can be a first step toward initiation. It is a place where one can transform borders and reconstruct time.

Traveling can also force one to become extremely practical. Aside from preparing mentally, I, of course, had to plan quite literally for the trip, asking, "Is this the right shirt and trousers? Do I need to take a jacket? Wouldn't sandals be more comfortable? Where's my shot record?" The University Health Center provided a consultation, inoculations for tetanus and yellow fever, and malaria pills, which I started a few days before leaving; I was lucky not to experience any side effects. I carried dysentery pills with me, as well as mosquito repellent. The trip required a visa, which was expedited because of the organization's positive reputation.

As I was preparing myself for the trip, we were still trying to raise additional funds for the program. Arthur and Ram Devineni, a filmmaker and the publisher of Rattapallax Press, managed the financial plans for the trip as well as the itinerary. We all agreed to give two readings: one on a Sunday afternoon at the White Dog Café in Philly, the other at The New School with Sonia Sanchez and Danny Glover.

It was mid-March, and I arrived at JFK International Airport, where I met Ram, Thomas Glave, and Willie Perdomo, among others. I was glad to be traveling with writers I knew, friends. The flight had a long layover in Amsterdam, so our group ventured out to the city in the early morning before our flight to Ghana later in the afternoon. I hardly remember the flight. I can't recall what I was reading, whom I was seated next to, or how I passed the time. Growing up in Bogalusa, Louisiana, I never thought I'd fly anywhere. On that flight, I felt I was living a life for more than just myself.

That evening, when we landed at Kotoka Airport, diplomatic workers processed us swiftly, so we didn't have to go through customs. In less than thirty minutes, we were zooming along the highway. The images, fragments of memory, continue to bleed together for me. I wanted merely to experience the place, to let the landscape wash over me. I must admit, I was surprised by how the lights swarmed over the skyline. I don't know why I expected darkness. Great anticipation grounded me, and I wanted to see everything in full daylight. We dined that evening in Accra, but in no time jet lag overtook us.

Traffic. Ghanaians in a floating throng of colors. Stone colonial houses. Forts. Apartments. Palm, bougainvillea, cassia, and mango. The lighthouse. And then the desolation of Jamestown beside the sea. Now we were speeding out of the city in a brownish sedan, the young driver with pleasant determination on his black face. The Atlantic waves seemed dark and sluggish. The people seemed to change with the country landscape. Women and children along the roadside sold vegetables and handicrafts. Someone pointed and asked, "What's that?" From the car window, we saw a boy holding a big, flattened, roasted rat in a wirelike grill, as if it had been cooked in a trap. I believe it was Arthur who said, "No, that's a nutria."

It was sunny when we arrived at the sewing club in Komenda. The girls—mainly teenagers—were dressed in green-and-black-checkered skirts and tan blouses, and some hid laughter behind their hands when they saw our faces. We had come across the Atlantic to talk about AIDS. We were straightforward, but we weren't there to cast stones. A few of the girls were also direct, raising the question about how AIDS had come to their small fishing village. Perhaps they were momentarily freer because we were strangers, and this allowed them to discuss things they would never have discussed openly in their homes, schools, and churches. We were listeners, and at that moment, this was what they needed: strangers as confidants.

We needed to talk with the fishermen, but we had heard that they wouldn't meet with us. This was heartbreaking; they were the main reason we were there in Komenda. Maybe they'd feel like walking targets when our eyes met theirs.

Finally, the day before we were to depart Komenda, the fishermen agreed to meet us at sunset. An array of colorful boats had been pulled onto the sandy shore, and men sat in the shifting light, waiting for us. Young and old, they all seemed seasoned by the salty winds of the sea. We stood there, facing them, but no one said anything. What was the protocol? We were visitors. We had requested the meeting. I felt as though everyone was looking at me. Who spoke first? Was it Arthur, Ram, Willie,

Bob, Thomas? Or maybe I said, "Hello. This is my first time here, but it seems that I've come home." (If I said that, it was because nearly everyone I had met over the past few days had said to me, "You're Ghanaian." Before my trip there, I'd always thought I was Ibo.) Or maybe I said to the fishermen, "Look, we're here to talk about the dangers of venturing over to the Ivory Coast and then returning to Komenda." I was the eldest of our group, and I must have been the one to speak first. At least, that's the way it is in my dreams. But the fishermen were silent. They were stone still until one young man said, "I know what you are talking about." It was as if someone had struck a brass bell. For a moment, everyone seemed to talk at once. Then an older fisherman spoke in a harking voice about how the fishermen from Komenda had to venture farther and farther out because the waters close to shore were depleted of fish, and they had to go a greater distance—all the way to the Ivory Coast—and some of the fishermen slept with the women there, and they returned to Komenda, but didn't know they had contracted HIV.

Something terrifying shifted underneath the image. It was still a beautiful picture. The men were talking and gesturing with their hands, caught in some ancient dance. The sun was sinking into the sea.

Our caravan of two or three sedans headed back to Accra. The drivers were young men who didn't waste any time; the rented sedans slid into blind curves, and sometimes the foot traffic scattered. I wanted to warn them.

We spent hours at Elmina Castle, a slave compound that housed a small library the Ghana Education Project had built. The monolithic structure was erected in the late fifteenth century by the Portuguese, who were following the rumors of gold. The building's architecture defined domination; I could see the brute force of the slave trade, which in the seventeenth century infiltrated the structure, in its thick walls, in its height, in its presence, in the scale of the project, and I knew indeed why it bore the infamous name the Door of No Return.

It wasn't the skull and bones crafted into the concrete or the chains mounted on the walls but the small chapel at the heart of the fortress that evoked unspoken fear. Perhaps more than anyone else, the poet recognizes the power of symbols because symbols continue to speak across the abyss of time. The dead keep on speaking. One can imagine—especially a poet—that in this space, these men who exacted brutality also bowed to a god.

I stood beside the Cave Canem sign that read BEWARE OF DOGS. A high fence surrounded the house of W.E.B. Du Bois, the man who had once edited *Crisis* magazine, who wrote *The Negro, The Souls of Black Folk, Dark Princess, Dusk of Dawn*, among others, and who in 1963 became a citizen of Ghana, having moved there in 1961.

Standing there, trying to remember a poem of his, "The Song of Smoke," I could recall only the refrain: "I am the Smoke King, / I am black!" At that moment, so were most of the faces around me. The heavy iron gate opened, and we stepped into the big yard. There were no dogs. No one to greet us Americans. Soon a caretaker, or someone posing as a caretaker, appeared and unlocked the door of the house to show us the final pages of this great man's life. We wandered through, asking hardly any questions, among the dust-covered books and papers that hadn't been catalogued or protected. I wondered how many items had disappeared through the years and were now on eBay. There, entombed in a mausoleum of stone and garniture, I was reminded that true elegance usually resides in simplicity. While standing in the house among the last shadows the man cast, I stood awestruck by this citizen of the world. Isn't that what a poet is, a citizen of the world? Du Bois was an internationalist before he was a Marxist. I stood there thinking of what Vijay Prashad writes in *The Karma of Brown Folk,* how he picked up a copy of *The Souls of Black Folk* in Kolkata and his whole life changed. I wondered if anyone at the W.E.B. Du Bois Institute for African and African American Research at Harvard University was aware of the man's notes and books covered with dust in this distant land, how hard nature works to bring everything down to the ground equally.

I attempted to prepare myself mentally for our visit to the hospital to see the smallest patients—babies who were one, two, and three years old. I tried to call up a moment of my religious tutelage back in Bogalusa, to glimpse my forays into Buddhist meditations through the decades, to go back to those few years I had worked as a peer counselor at the University of Colorado, but soon I realized that little or nothing could have prepared me for what we witnessed.

The children were frail and tiny; their vulnerability was so transparent that there was no way for anyone not to perceive the depth of their pain and suffering. It's hard to say how many children were there in the hospital. Maybe fifty. Maybe one hundred. It was more terrifying than the dislocated images on television. The few nurses there seemed completely overwhelmed. But the courage and heroic presence of the grandmothers who rocked their grandchildren in their arms was astonishing; some were silent and others whispered almost breathless words that seemed to have come from a great distance. The strength in their faces contrasted so starkly with the children, and perhaps this is what magnified the pain and desperation in that place.

At first, feeling that we were intruding on some sacred rite of passage, that our eyes would wound them more deeply, I wanted to retreat. Of course, wasn't this also the fundamental question for the poet: isn't it the duty of artists to witness, to hold ourselves accountable? Indeed, this bore the familiar distress of a battle zone, where the most vulnerable are singled out and attacked with brutal certainty. But I stood there completely overwhelmed, uncertain about what we could do, almost defeated by what I saw that day in Ghana. I also knew that we were seeing only a fraction of the suffering on the African continent.

We were going to meet a king. Would he embrace our effort to establish a dialogue about AIDS, or would he simply shrug his shoulders and begin a litany about esoteric rituals locked in the recent past? Weren't our clothes too typical, too ordinary? A king, huh? I visualized him in his kingly garb, sitting on a golden throne and holding a golden staff. Should we bow? The protocol was beyond me.

There were three "kings." The two older kings seemed so alike, especially in their austerity. They seemed so upright in posture and demeanor. The third king was younger; he seemed not fully initiated. Yet there was something about him that also seemed more cosmopolitan, more modern. They all seemed to possess at least symbolic power—absolutely ceremonial. Their fat gold rings caught the eye. Their colorful robes and cowrie adornments spoke silently of authority, and the carved canes the two older kings clutched were pragmatic. It seemed more like poets meeting poets, and in this sense one understands Shelley's statement:

> Poets are the hierophants of an unapprehended inspiration; the mirrors of the gigantic shadows which futurity casts upon the present; the words which express what they understand not; the trumpets which sing to battle, and feel not what they inspire; the influence which is moved not, but moves. Poets are the unacknowledged legislators of the world.

We weren't there to pose questions through metaphors. The kings were probably experts with metaphors, but we hoped that they also understood the gut-level reality of AIDS in Ghana. Our ritual was discussion. Maybe kings never show alarm or their deep, heartfelt thoughts, especially when facing strangers. Their emotions seemed stately. Contained. Goaded by the younger king, the two elders slowly agreed to assist in the efforts of the Ghana Education Project. Sitting there, facing these three men of traditional and symbolic power, it was difficult for me not to think of Kwame Nkrumah, the first president and first prime minister of Ghana, a Pan-Africanist who had studied at the University of Pennsylvania and was, in many ways, an everyday man. The ghost of him possessed more power than the folkloric platitudes of these three kings. I sat there trying not to think of Dudley Randall's poem "Ancestors":

Was the Old Country a democracy
where every man was a king?
Or did the slave-catchers
steal only the aristocrats
and leave the fieldhands

...

My own ancestor
(research reveals)
was a swineherd
who tended the pigs
in the Royal Pigstye
and slept in the mud
among the hogs.

We strolled into the room of the hospice to see Kiki Djan. He was a sack of bones, but there was still something in him that said, Look, I'm a damn genius. And we were dumbfounded by what drugs and AIDS can do to a man. He sat on the bed hugging a portable recorder, rocking back and forth while he played his last recording over and over, a pop song full of energy and crafted passion. He was still good, still burning with genius and belief in himself, and one felt that perhaps this could keep him alive. Or maybe he believed this so deeply, we also believed it through a mental osmosis. He would beat the monkey on his back; he would even outsmart the specter of AIDS. Kiki had played keyboard with the legendary band Osibisa, which he had joined in 1971, and I remember how that band's sound was different from anything I'd ever heard. The music had a positive authority that left its listeners thunderstruck. It's said that after splitting from the group, he did a twenty-four-hour gig in London. He was friends with Mick Jagger and Elton John and hung out with jet-setters cruising off to the Caribbean. He bragged about making £8,000 in a single weekend, saying that he was the most gifted keyboardist on the London scene. But here he was back home—Kiki Djan from Takoradi in western Ghana—hugging a battered recorder, pleading with the ghosts of ancestors. He seemed surprised that a group of writers and poets from America was standing at the foot of his bed. He'd stare out the window, and I sensed this was his last torture on Earth—glimpses of passing figures in bright clothes caught by the March sun.

Close to our departure, we moved from the small quarters where we had been sleeping to a beach hotel. The hotel was huge and sprawling and stood in complete contrast to the world we had just witnessed. There was a high fence built around the perimeter as if to keep out the common locals, the everyday Ghanaians. Beside the sea, shops sold paintings, handicrafts, gold and diamonds, clothing, and tchotchkes made for tourists. From their garb and overall demeanor, I gathered the African clientele was made up of upper-middle-class professionals. It was impossible for me to feel comfortable in my American jeans and sandals alongside their colorful robes.

That night, Arthur took us to a Portuguese-owned seaside pub. I recall the music playing and the voice of a fado singer whose longing suspended me between Africa and the West. I felt more comfortable in my American clothes, which seemed to blend in with the European feel of the pub. And for a moment, I was glad to recognize the Portuguese language spoken by the staff and a few of the patrons. Then I thought of Elmina Castle, and it occurred to me that even the hotel might have been European owned. And then I understood the complexity of the diasporic spirit; we may feel more at home in the culture we've inherited but at a loss for the rituals and customs of our ancestors.

After returning to the United States, I tried for years to write poems that capture the images of those babies, of the slave castle, of Jamestown, and of Kiki. In fact, I've traveled to many places, including Vietnam, Australia, Eastern Europe, New Guinea, Mexico, Chile, India, and Brazil, but I've written poems about only a few of those places. Neruda once wrote, "*I have come out of that landscape, that mud, that silence, to roam, to go singing through the world.*" Now I'm realizing that encountering the world leads one both farther from home and closer to it because that world is always in dialogue with the deepest self.

Perhaps for me, it takes a long time for these acquired images and experiences to distill into poetry. Though travel is an action, and poetry at times can be defined as an action, the two together need a space that resides in silence, meditation. The truth is, an act of poetry, the moment a poem comes forth, is often unpredictable because it springs from some place not fully conscious but informed by everything that has made us who we are.

Poetry Peddler

Naomi Shihab Nye

My endless wandering / becomes my language

—Amina Saïd, "Freedom's Faces"

I was raised in a savory, slightly strange household. The walking homesickness household. I guess it makes sense that a wandering poet would be born from a father in exile and a renegade mother who defied the codes of her own strict upbringing even to marry him.

Because he had a voice, my father, Aziz Shihab—a dapper man who loved bow ties and cologne, who engaged in vigorous shoe polishing, who still liked a folded white hankie tucked into his breast pocket—embodied the hugeness of a people's suffering. He found a way to wrap his melodious, perfectly pitched voice around a room, send it out in a letter, weave it into Christmas talks about the Holy Land at local churches, without becoming shrill or arrogant. He was human size.

But his voice was bigger. He did not understand why dialogue seemed so difficult for so many people in power, but he believed humiliation would never last and arrogance could never win and someday, justice might take a deep breath again. He exercised his own voice every way he could toward that goal.

When my father died, he was still aching for Palestine, its quirky rhythms and ancient traditions, which people tried to say weren't ancient after all. "You lived here a hundred years?" they might have said. "Sorry, you're invisible."

Wherever he wandered, whichever border he crossed, he was Palestine: his soft, olive-tinted skin carried almond blossoms, green fields, goat cries at sunset. He had a rich wit, a gentle sense of irony, a passion for education, pride.

Why was it so easy to downgrade, or overlook entirely, the Palestinian legacy, as if it didn't exist, as if its people would just—*pouf!*—vanish in a pollen cloud? Surely one never thinks, in the hopeful flush of growing up, "By the time I'm twenty-one, my people will be invisible."

Though I lived in Palestine in 1966–1967, only a short time myself, I felt obliged, whenever wandering, and also at home, to try to speak up about it, wherever appropriate. I wanted to make it real for people who had never considered its existence. It was not my only topic, of course, but the conditions and issues of rootedness and exile rested at the center of all my topics—respect for dailiness, mutual exchange, and simplicity.

When introduced as a "peacemaker," I'd think, well, I'm a total failure then. Because there is no peace, not for the people of Palestine. Not yet.

It was easy to feel like a failure. But I kept talking. When you feel rotten, talking and writing always help. And sometimes, such as yesterday, when I met two seventeen-year-old girls representing Hand in Hand: Center for Jewish-Arab Education in Israel and their respectful, mutual descriptions of shared life, I know with conviction that talking and writing are the only and very best things we can do.

My father believed in a better day, in human potential, in the poetry of possibility, in the dignity of details. To honor him, I had to keep telling his story. Though he died frustrated, he told the hospital chaplain right before his last day he was sure things would eventually work out.

I hear an unexpected echo in this wide world from Hawaiian students familiar with legacies of occupation nodding gravely, from far-flung village Alaskans and Native Americans in Wyoming: sorrowful repetitions of injustice.

And I tried not to think too often of the chant one of my dearest writer friends used to filter his own penetrating writing—"So what?"

Those words didn't help me.

So—everything.

If a girl in Alberta, Canada, who has never been out of her own province, reads a poem or story about a Palestinian girl and then asks her mother to make her baba ghanoush, saying, "I will never think of the Middle East in the same way again," does that mean a poem or story has done its humble job? How many girls like this, and the two I met yesterday, might be needed to make peace in the world?

No, I don't wish I'd gotten a regular job somewhere along the way.

Not even for benefits.

I've had my benefits. A thousand towns, beds, hotels, friends. A hundred thousand young poets with notebooks, pencils, clicking pens, far gazes.

***

I think of my friend M., who said when we were twenty in a condescending voice, "So what are you going to do in your life? Be a poetry peddler?"

I stood up straighter, hurt, saying, "Yes, that's what I'll be, I'd be honored to be that."

The word *peddler* made me think of wheelbarrows and ragbags, two things I really like.

***

So, the gift of being a poet out in the wide world, on the avenues, in the airports, carrying scenes and voices, is immense.

I remember the worried Iranian mom who appeared in a school library one day, wanting to read from her journals to me—is it okay to be a writer if one has not been officially trained? To allow one's soulful longing for connection to be the flag of one's true country? I think of the Saudi girls with covered faces who will remove their hijabs only if we meet in a completely enclosed space—what is it they want to talk about? Photography! All the images they are recording on their fancy little digital cameras! Plants, doorways, tile work, light falling down onto palms! Even two sessions with them will change entirely the sense I have of their deep eyes, peering out, when in public, from between folds of dark cloth.

Why is it so hard for politicians to believe that people who don't match us exactly might nevertheless harmonize with us in deeply agreeable ways? Girls with covered heads might be visionary artists. Why are people always picking out differences, painful contrasts, instead of making kinder links?

Poetry gives these realities a place to abide: in the Asian grocery store in Abu Dhabi, in a steaming hammam in Rabat, in the wildly dancing, finger-cymbal-clicking streets of Fez, on Berlin's Ringbahn at twilight. I am certain that human beings think in layers and that everything new to any one of us is simultaneously old, new, precious, passing. Talking about poetry all over the stricken Earth, with children as well as adults, gives us a shared, more humanized side.

The seventh grader with neatly combed black hair is crying. He's trying to pretend he's not crying, but every time he removes his fists from his eyes, big tears roll down.

"Speak to us," I say. "What's happening?"

We're sitting in a circle in the school library. Graceful students from all over the planet, notebooks open on their laps, stare so quietly at him, at their hands. They look humbled by his pain.

"I am worried about my country," he gulps. We're in Saudi Arabia, at King Abdullah's magical liberal graduate university. Yes, it exists. Women can drive on this campus. My head is not covered. Boys and girls are going to school together here, at King Abdullah University of Science and Technology, aka KAUST.

I'm with the children of the university professors, students, and staff at the edge of the glistening Red Sea, whose other side touches the shores of this boy's home country, Egypt.

For days now, brave demonstrators have been gathering in Tahrir Square, raising their arms and voices, shouting for freedom, setting up tents, carrying one another on their shoulders. They must be exhausted. I've left CNN International on mute in my room for hours, watching what happens next, even at two in the morning, thinking about the past, just a few years ago, when I felt oddly secure hopping off the underground metro and dashing across that very square by myself, even late at night.

"What will happen to Egypt? I don't want my grandparents or neighbors or neighborhood to be hurt," the boy says, growing more confident when no one titters. "If I were the head of the chess club and everyone said they did not want me to be the head, if everyone stood in the hallway shouting, 'Go, go, go, we want a new head! You had your turn!' I would go. I would go very fast. So why won't President Mubarak go?"

Acknowledging our own essential questions helps us think about them.

This is the point my journals return to: in Bangladeshi classrooms, in Pakistani girls' schools, in the poetry salons behind a school cafeteria in India, we share our questions and dilemmas in the company of others. We may not be able to solve all our problems, but the making of analogies and metaphors, the making of poetry, feels like a possible solution, diffuses the scariness.

Here, slant of light. Now, think about this again.

From such abundance and raw material, from the glitter of open questioning among friends or strangers equally, poems have always gathered for me, and for so many students, bouquets of voices and scenes. Sometimes we need confirmation from one another; even if we can't solve these problems, it's helpful to speak about them across borders, cultures, religions, ages. Guiding others to try simple writing tactics and strategies is always a good reminder for ourselves too. It's all contagious—if one student witnesses another writing from a place of personal uncertainty, odds instantly grow that more will try a deeper, questioning style.

In coming months, far from one another, we'll be wondering the same things, but more urgently, about Libya and Syria. Hey, you guys in power! Haven't you had your turns? The chess club demotes you!

Tyranny will feel like a modern word again—not something from history books.

Before school every day, a studious Lebanese boy composes book reviews on an international children's website. Indian twins carefully letter a giant page with the poem they wrote together yesterday. A giggling Tunisian girl brings me wrapped gifts every morning—a shiny necklace, a tiny stitched pouch.

After I return home, a Korean girl living in Rabat who loves poetry more than the whole wide world, more than skyscrapers, even, more than the ocean and the beach and the sand that stretches to the mountains, keeps writing me e-mails with yellow blinking smiley faces attached. One day her message says, "My page is empty. What if I can't write anything? Does this ever happen to you? What do you do?"

All the way across the ocean, in south Texas, where the rain has not fallen for months and the old lakes named Medina and Canyon are going dry, I stare at gray doves scrapping on a nearly empty green bird feeder hanging outside my window. When I refill it with sunflower seeds, the hungry birds gobble them within hours.

To my pen pal, pecked out carefully: "I take a walk, look at all the windows around me, and wonder who lives inside them."

When she writes back days later, her message says simply, "I tried it. It's working."

❧

At the American School in Rabat, which has no prominent sign, on the day the fourth graders write odes, Omar is the first volunteer to read his poem. His classmates and teachers look surprised when he raises his hand. I, of course, don't know anyone's history. Not knowing who generally succeeds or fails in any classroom anywhere has always been a benefit—a visitor carries no preconceptions, welcomes all participation equally.

Tourists and travelers might wish for as much open anonymity in the markets and streets. Too often we're identified by what previous travelers have desired or spent.

Most in Omar's class wear bright-red T-shirts, the school color, but he wears what can be described only as a golden satin tunic. Omar clears his throat. He addresses his home country of Egypt, describing a "yellow flower calling to me." Across the countries between, across Libya, Tunisia, Algeria, he can hear its plaintive cry. Now he is "stuck in sad Morocco"—forced to make a new home, far from his yellow flowers. But he vows to go back someday. He has written an ode to belonging, to a better life where he felt grounded and secure.

I look around. Tears are rolling down his teacher's face.

The students seem mesmerized. They crowd around Omar after the lunch buzzer trills, begging him to sit with them at the picnic tables outside, mentioning that Morocco has lovely white flowers popping their petals open before dawn even in the schoolyard, on the soccer field, that they are happy he is here. He looks—thunderstruck.

"What's up?" I ask the teacher.

"He has been here since September," she says. "This is the first time we have heard his voice."

It is a moment that underscores what poets and poetry do.

To say something true to you and have it acknowledged, accepted, recognized as real by people around you—what better treasure? Belonging to everyone. And if that stranger in our classroom said we could talk about these things, express our love and longing—we might just keep doing it, no? Even after she leaves, even more than usual, even with the new ones, the awkward ones, even on days when it hurts to do it.

A poet walks on to the next class, the next city, the next country, fortified, knowing that all the occasions in classrooms when things didn't seem to "click" as well have just been transformed by a perfect, essential moment.

It's the same when we're writing by ourselves alone at a desk.

All those scribbles, diversions, little lost impulses and lines absorbed, uplifted by the moment one line or group of lines sings.

I heard my mother say, "Be your best self, use your voice" when I stepped out onto the gravel driveway and headed up Harvey Hill to elementary school, in old St. Louis, humid city of melancholy and great architecture. It would take years of living to appreciate the challenge of that simple code.

I heard our beloved second-grade teacher, Harriett Barron Lane, age ancient, age eternal, say, "A poem can save you." Her husband had died a long time before. She had no children. We were all her children. She wore 1950s pink and green plastic bangle bracelets stacked up both arms. Anyone inattentive or reluctant received a bop on the head with those bangles. A poem can save you.

So can a window, I remember thinking, staring out the tall classroom windows in the hundred-year-old building.

Mrs. Lane felt Emily Dickinson to be real in all our lives, more real than the school principal or the mayor of St. Louis. If we stumbled, acted ridiculous, got the giggles in the middle of a lesson—what would Emily think of that? The fact that Mrs. Lane imagined we could know was deeply compelling.

I recall reading, and feeling befriended by, the Bengali poet Rabindranath Tagore on the day my best friend told me her family was moving away. Tagore, who had won the Nobel Prize in Literature, used to send his words out in small boats on a running stream, hoping some stranger would find and unfold them and "know who he was." Tagore knew loneliness.

Tagore would understand.

Carrying poems in one's brain is a remedy stretching far beyond the sweet meadows, ditches, and fragrant hideouts under looming pine trees where we had all wandered together, making a larger family of friends. I still hear familiar echoes guiding my steps—I'm nobody, who are you? Hope is the thing with feathers.

My first day in Berlin, the day before the Internationales Literaturfestival Berlin began, I got lost among birds at the zoo. Why hadn't I learned German? I had studied it for two years. I had attended recitation contests, speaking poems from memory in German. I had had German grandparents.

The great, complicated, multilayered city of Berlin, a city that had known true sorrow, a city that had been bombed and wrecked and rebuilt and reinvented, a city with vast empty spaces, a city still recovering, was a city whose story was inextricably linked with my father's Palestinian refugee status.

My wandering journalist father would have stood, as I did, staring at haunting memorial markers in front of Berlin homes whose Jewish inhabitants had been evicted, evacuated, massacred. He would have understood that pain.

Was this partly why he always struggled for perfect grammar and simple, strong sentences? To find a fluent home in a paragraph or a few well-weighted lines must have felt very comforting to one whose refugee family had lost its physical home and grounding.

For how many of us has poetry always felt like the genuine home? As a traveler, deficient in other vocabularies, I seem to remain on the edge, the outside, but poetry in any form—original or translated—calls me inside. *Who would I have been*, I mused, wandering among the depressed zoo bears and surly elephants of Berlin, *had I never studied Spanish or Arabic, had I not crowded my pitiful acquired-language domain with three languages? What if I had focused better?* But a poet's main concern is focus and connection—did I use my energies otherwise? Have my endless attempts to encourage students to focus and connect been meaningful in the long run? Haven't enough of them told me so for me to believe?

In one school on the edge of the city, students kept bees, bottled honey. Muslim girls in headscarfs stood in front of a large group and discussed the positive aspects of being "singled out as different." It felt refreshing, unexpected. Muslim girls, speaking fluent German, switched into English for me. They said there was power in difference—if everyone looked at you as "another kind" of person, then you were noticed, had an easier chance to shine. It reminded me of a poet's comfort in unusual perception. Seeing things "differently" always opens up possibilities of seeing the world in more intriguing, less predictable ways. I felt immediately drawn to these girls and their confidence. Speaking about poetry to students who knew intricate details about worker bees and hives also felt natural and gracious—again, the layers of thinking that poetry offers, opening wide fields.

One day, at a literary center on a mysterious, stony backstreet of Berlin, I helped a group of teens (Afros, striped T-shirts, a bird tattooed on a wrist) arrange wooden chairs around a big table. For hours we talked, wrote, shared entries from notebooks and sections from favorite poems, grieved, and celebrated. The words of Bertolt Brecht, who had lived only blocks from where we gathered, stitched a seam joining us all. He wrote about doubting; going this way and that way, all at once; the inevitability of doubting; the precious legacy of doubting, which has united all artists in all places since ancient days. In our circle, we had students of many backgrounds—a German-Swiss girl with thoughtful grief etched into her face, some shy recent immigrant students from Turkey, a young man wearing a Star of David necklace, a comic French-German PUBLIC POET! (handmade T-shirt in three languages) encouraging quieter students to offer opinions too. Anyone could witness the rich sense of community possible around a table when people share poetry's immediate exchange. Later, a boy who identified himself only as "J" wrote to me, referring to that day:

> I can't tell you what happened exactly. I can't tell you who said what, or which poem flipped the switch. But our time together at the lit. center gave me what I will need to live my life. And that is a big thing. Thanks.

A big thing.
A tiny, transportable thing.
What poetry does for us all the time.

On a crowded midnight subway in Berlin, an elderly Arab man in a baggy brown suit coat stared at me, looking startlingly familiar. We were both standing, gripping silver poles. He raised his hand and pushed across to my side of the train. "I knew your father," he said. "I am sorry he died." It seemed incredible to me. In a city of millions, running into an unnamed friend? And he handed me from his coat pocket a collection of poems by the great Iraqi poet Sargon Boulus, who, I would realize when I began reading, had died exactly the same day as my father. In exile, in Berlin.

Those about whom we hear no news
Those who are remembered by none:
What wind has swept their traces
as if they never were?
My father and the others
Where are they?
Where?

—Sargon Boulus, translated by Sinan Antoon

They are in poems still forming, bubbling in the mist that hangs over the street right before one year slides into another, another we will have to live without him, on Earth, full of him, thanks to voices and memory.

And who was that man on the train?

The more we travel, the more it seems that our family members are everywhere, our poetry replete with their presences. We write out of everything we have ever read or encountered. The music is in us. The ghost signs from the sides of ruined buildings in small towns we passed through only once float in us. The succinct phrases from gravestones in the Chinese cemetery in Manoa Valley, Honolulu, are carved in us. The lilting voices of children, their pride and uncertainty, their held-out questions, are etched forever in us.

I met Mahmoud Darwish in a Philadelphia hotel lobby after years of reading his poems. I'd been carrying his voice for so long that an actual encounter seemed somehow surreal. He stared at me and said, "I thought you were much younger!"

"I was," I said. "Weren't you too?"

Tell me about your life.
It was all a bouquet.
In whose hand?
What would you be if you were not a poet?
Everything? Aren't we already?

No, I've replied to questions many times over, the greatest moment of a writer's life is not when a new book appears in print. The greatest moment of a writer's life is when he or she meets people like you. People in some place one never traveled to before, who wish to converse.

Called Home on the Road

Claudia Rankine

Though the house has been remodeled, the stairs, despite being car-peted, creak. What I imagined as a silent retreat from the party seems to sound through the house. By the fifth step I decide to sit down and on the wall next to me is a torn passport photo of half a woman's face blown up and framed as art. Where did you imagine you were going? I say aloud to her.

"The purpose of art," James Baldwin wrote, "is to lay bare the questions hidden by the answers." He might have been channeling Dostoyevsky's statement that "we have all the answers. It is the questions we do not know." Where did you imagine you were going, and when did travel's constant movement become an answer? My mother never tires of telling me, "Girl, you have to stop running." But even before my birth, for the colonized Jamaican, movement was de facto.

In the 1950s, before Jamaica's independence, my uncle, my moth-er's oldest brother, immigrated to Brixton, where he continues to live as he approaches ninety. In 1962, ten or so years after he immigrated, a year before I was born, Jamaica would become independent of the United Kingdom; two years later, American immigration laws toward Jamaicans would relax, and just like that, I would become an American, his American niece, his American poet.

My uncle is a carpenter. Once, when I was in my twenties, he drove me around London showing me all the houses he had rebuilt. It took him hours to find them, hours for us to see all the construction he had done. Sometimes we had to get out of the car and walk to the back of a building or look in through a side window or climb up stairs to see exactly how he had made London London.

His name obviously wasn't on any of his buildings, and I would not be able to take myself back to the places he showed me, but the brick-and-mortar concreteness of his life's work was enough to satisfy him (and my mother because I suspect he was speaking to her through me about some old forgotten argument they had had in another life) that this place—which had always been a destination, even when he was a boy in St. Ann's Parish in Jamaica—was now his place.

The Trinidadian theorist and essayist C.L.R. James says what matters is movement: "not where you are or what you have, but where you have come from, where you are going, and the rate at which you are getting there." Perhaps my uncle settled here one building at a time, one room at a time. Maybe like him, I make stanzas in order to construct a new house to live in, or I make stanzas to take apart the houses I was given. Where did you imagine you were going? I say to the torn-up girl.

When I lived in London at the end of the millennium, I sat at my desk on the second floor of a rented house on Whittlesey Street on the South Bank and thought about what being an American meant. George W. Bush was running for president against Al Gore at the time. I watched Bush's speeches on BBC One with increasing trepidation. Had I been in New York City, much of my frustration and fear would have been hashed out across restaurant tables in the East Village or on the Upper West Side. Conversations with my British friends on the Cut, the road with restaurants near our house, began first with explanations. No short cuts could be taken, and once everything was explained, I would go home and attempt to understand my irritations on the page.

Much of *Don't Let Me Be Lonely*, a book I think of as being concerned with the culture and politics of the United States, was conceived, in part, walking the streets of London. My connection to the United States while living abroad came through media—the papers, the television, and the Internet. The unceasing British interest in the political workings of its former colony not only kept me informed but perhaps also pushed me to close the Atlantic distance in my writing.

Our host tonight is a visual artist and a curator. He creates things in time and space, and as he is creating, he is curating; even this party is a kind of talking sculpture, and when he notices me sitting on the hallway steps, he wishes to engage me in the flow of the conversations. I allow myself to be guided back into the living room.

I don't know. I say that aloud because someone wants to know the name of the film shot in Ridley Road Market, which is just two blocks away and where I hear you can get "bush meat" if you go to the right stall. *Dirty Pretty Things*, someone says. *Dirty Pretty Things*, I repeat, as if the person asking is deaf.

Walking in the mist toward the party earlier, just before getting to the Ridley Road Market, I had come upon the Dalston C.L.R. James Library. James's seminal work, *The Black Jacobins*, sits in my library in Claremont, California, as a testament to my own membership in the African diaspora his work addresses. Seeing him commemorated on a public building in the Hackney borough of London was a bit like hearing my own name called out on the road. I still don't expect the Empire to memorialize its subjects, and I am surprised: I am, after all, not a stranger; these streets know I am here.

As if he can hear my thoughts, the BBC producer I am sitting next to on the very comfortable black leather sofa turns to me. Are you still living in New York? he asks. He and I had met more than twenty-five years earlier on the island of Grenada, two years after the US invasion, and it has been at least a decade since I've seen him. He produces films, so I ask if the BBC has done a documentary on C.L.R. James. He doesn't know but says the controversy around the Dalston C.L.R. James Library surprised him. The controversy? I repeat by way of an invitation. In 2010, the Hackney Council announced it was opening the first new library built in Hackney in the last twenty years. This new, modern, high-tech facility is to replace the Dalston C.L.R. James Library just blocks from where we sit. The announcement included the information that the new library would no longer be known as the Dalston C.L.R. James Library.

More than likely, the council didn't understand his significance to this community, my producer friend adds, with a wry smile that wings the lines bordering his eyes in such a way that he becomes both youthful and ancient in the same instant. It was a "no-you-didn't" moment, I say, and this makes him laugh outright. Do you think the new library and the desire to remove his name had something to do with the gentrification that is happening here in Hackney now? I ask. Do you think it will rain tomorrow? he counters by way of an answer. Now we are both laughing. Keep Britain tidy, he adds. You are quoting Banksy, the graffiti artist? I ask, wondering how he means it. The same, he says as he turns to a question being asked of him by someone who has recently arrived, and only then do I remember reading in the *Guardian* that morning that there's a new Banksy stenciled on the side of a building in North London: SORRY! THE LIFESTYLE YOU ORDERED IS CURRENTLY OUT OF STOCK.

The British poet Malika Booker, whom I met at Cave Canem in Pittsburgh a year previous, spoke about the importance of C.L.R. James to her as a poet; this memory makes me look around the room for her despite knowing she is not here. Even before she started writing, she said, she remembered reading an essay of James's in which he discussed the work of the writers Toni Morrison, Alice Walker, and Ntozake Shange. He ended the essay with a directive to write poetry. He wrote, "Write what you think—and maybe what you write about your day-to-day, everyday, commonplace, ordinary life will be some of the same problems that the people of the world are fighting out. You must be able to write what you have to say, and know that that is what matters." It seemed poetic justice that the very same, ordinary, everyday people would be the ones to insist that his legacy be continued on the face of their local library.

This house, the home of my hosts, is filled with art and sculpture. My gaze returns to what I believe to be the same spot, but always I see something I haven't noticed before. In the painting directly before me, which I'm sure has been there all evening though I am noticing it only now, the telephone lines are just visible as telephone lines. The black and white could easily blur back into atmosphere, lose all distinction. Most Turneresque, says the man sitting across from me. You are the American poet, no? Yes, I say.

This man has the face of the English sky—full of weather, always in response, constantly shifting, clouding over, and clearing briefly—though he is not British. He has written a memoir and, more recently, a novel. I have read neither, but his kind moodiness, his restlessness persuade me to make a mental note to read both as soon as I return to the United States. His wife joins us; how similar they are, how available they are to their emotions. Their immediacy is admirable, I am thinking, though we are talking about the recent riots in Hackney. He says he feels they were similar to the Rodney King–L.A. riots, but the media in the UK handled it very differently. The riots began at the end of the summer when Mark Duggan, a black man, a father, and a suspected drug dealer, was shot dead by officers from Scotland Yard's Operation Trident (a special operation addressing gun crime in black communities). As the rioting and looting continued, government officials labeled the violent outbreak "opportunism" and "sheer criminality," and the media picked up this language. Maybe the police let the looters continue their rampage so that those images could replace the fact of shooting an unarmed man. In the United States, Rodney King's beating, caught on video, trumped all other images. If there had been a video of Duggan being executed, things would have been very different, I hazard to say. Will you write about Duggan in your poetry?

the memoirist-turned-novelist wants to know. Probably not, I say. Why not? he asks, looking slightly irritated. I begin to think he does not like police, Duggan or no Duggan.

Why not? Well, because I read about it online in my study in the United States a few months ago and even as the story caught my attention, it felt both familiar and foreign. What felt familiar was an institutional body (the police) tied rhetorically to justice acting unjustly toward a young black man. Everything else felt specific to North London and the culture, the tensions, the recognitions, the disappointments, and the failures that exploded in the riots that followed the shooting. It is this same kind of accumulation and release that drove me to write about the forty-one shots fired by the four police officers who murdered Amadou Diallo in New York City in February of 1999. Before it happened, it had happened and happened. As a black body in that city, writing about Diallo was necessary if I was to hold on to the fiction that this was an event "wrongfully ordinary," so outside the ordinary. Though the moment had occurred and occurred again with the deaths of other random, unarmed black men, Diallo's forty-one shots somehow cut off air supply in the body politic by virtue of the excessive, blatant barrage. And though grief exists for Duggan as a black man gunned down, in my body was not the same overflow of compromises, deaths, and tempers specific to a place I woke to and went to sleep in most days.

The news of Duggan's death came to me in a different rhythm; as C.L.R. James wrote, "What do they know of cricket who only cricket know?" My writing comes out of relationships to subjects over time and not to any subject in theory. There is often, between my own body's rhythms and the subject, a simultaneity that has to do with "the war my presence has occasioned in the American soul," to quote Baldwin. I am full of my feelings, feelings shaped by the politics, history, and culture that have shaped me, and if I don't want to be drowned by these feelings, I need to take Baldwin's lead and at least attempt "to lay bare the questions hidden by the answers."

Rarely can I import the same level of heightened engagement when I travel, as I am filled with a brimming curiosity that presses up against a needling sense of not knowing. The traveling seems to cement my American citizenry and throws into relief my impatience, my expectations, my questioning, my pleasure, and my humor as informed by my hybrid American life. And though I recognize the similarities built into global cities, a body moving through moves through differently than the ones residing. "You're part of the misery and you can't make it more or less," says the Chinese artist Ai Weiwei. Mark Duggan, I am part of your misery, and I can't make it more or less. I know I won't write about the dynamics of your death because I don't understand the dynamics of your death though I believe I understand the dynamics of your death.

With my eyes closed, I consider how all of us at this party, a group of middle-aged artists, lawyers, filmmakers, writers, and journalists, in a house worth more than a million pounds, in a borough where half the people are immigrants from Africa and the Caribbean, situated around the corner from a market famous for selling "bush meat," might be implicated in the "sheer criminality" of the riots. The equation is too simple, simplistic, yet the rage, frustration, and dehumanizing drive to acquisition remain present, simmering always, occupying everyone. I won't write about Mark Duggan or the riots. And yet I am searching my conscience because there is an answer to find, a problem to solve.

I begin to move through the room, the talk of this other country, a country I am connected to by history and yet culturally ignorant of. I wish to hear. I want to see what this other body looks like. I wonder if my uncle had anything to do with the renovation of the houses on these streets. I could ask him. He would probably say yes on principle. I turn and turn, and then there is my host. This morning on the radio, he heard an interview with a poet—he can't recall the poet's name but perhaps I will help him remember. He thinks he would like to read this poet, though normally he doesn't read poetry, not much, but this poet claims to be inspired by a British comic actor my host likes very much. Knowing my poor memory for names, I don't place much hope in my ability to come up with the correct name, but it occurs to me that if I can offer up *any* name, attention will inevitably sift from me, leaving me to wander. To wonder.

Whoever this poet is, he has a prestigious appointment at Oxford. Is it a man? I ask. I don't ask if it is a white male but I am making this assumption, and out of nowhere arrives the name Geoffrey Hill. That's it, my host says cheerfully, happy that the poet knows of the poet. He has all good intentions in his affable embrace of me and keeps the conversation moving with his questions.

Hill has the reputation of being difficult because of what I like to think of as London street syntax, I say. A-to-zed syntax, my host counters with a chuckle. Remembering that I was first drawn to Hill's work because of Paul Celan's "Tenebrae," I recite the opening of the poem:

> We are near, Lord,
> near and at hand.
>
> Handled already, Lord,
> clawed and clawing as though
> the body of each of us were
> your body, Lord.
>
> Pray, Lord,
> pray to us,
> we are near....

I tell my host that Hill's "Tenebrae" turned out to have a Utopian wholeness starkly different from the reversals formed though genocide in Celan's poem of the same name. I was drawn nonetheless to Hill's work by its mental turns; the speaker is rarely stable but gains his footing with and against the movements of an other—often a "you"—in the

poem. Sometimes the other is a historical figure, sometimes a remem-
bered place:

And you, who with your soft but searching voice
drew me out of the sleep where I was lost,
who held me near your heart that I might rest
confiding in the darkness of your choice:
possessed by you I chose to have no choice,
fulfilled in you I sought no further quest....

Often enough in Hill's poetry, the internal world of his speaker is
adjusting to some external reality; the reality that makes internal nego-
tiations necessary regularly involves the British Empire—"... the life of
empire like the life of the mind / 'simple, sensuous, passionate', attuned /
to the clear theme of justice and order, gone"—a dynamic familiar to any-
one like myself, born with black skin in a former colony and reared in a
country built through slavery and still running on racism.

The more I read of Hill's work, the more his marriage of the personal
and historical makes sense to me. There is always, I think, a social con-
tract in his writing with the history of the place that informs the evolution
of the voice. I am interested in the way Hill's voice speaks to and from
and across history, as I am attempting to do in my own work. The dif-
ficulty is that imperialism, colonialism, capitalism, and some other isms
we probably don't know about yet have spent their histories attempting
to erase my voice. I know, in the same way I know my own name, that the
poetry of a place is inextricably tied to the politics of that place as occa-
sioned through its history. Only a thick-skinned kind of privilege would
allow me to ignore that. Still, as much as I am a stranger in London, being
here weeks before the fiftieth anniversary of Jamaica's independence
somehow brings me closer to Hill's own negotiations of empire. In any
case, I tell my host that "Tenebrae" is the title poem so he can always find
that collection, but I suggest *Mercian Hymns*, hymns of the borderers,

as a starter book. My host enters this into the notes app on his iPhone—
Mercian Hymns.

Getting to the bathroom means going up the creaky steps. Someone
has gone up, and now he is coming back. I listen to the low, dull sound
of each step. When the last dies away, I decide finally to leave the party,
leaving the torn-up girl to the country she landed in.

Somewhere I find my hosts: kiss, kiss. The streets are wet but the air
is dry, and in the night light, my internal hum seems externalized. I walk
through the market with all its security gates pulled down. Even deserted
it feels alive: "Three pounds, love; a pound fifty, love." Change *love* to
darling and I could be in Jamaica purchasing pretty much the same pro-
visions. Strip the endearments away completely and I would no doubt
be back in my naturalized home. A car stops at the light, and through
the open window, Eric Burdon sings, "When I think of all the good times
that I've wasted having good times." Down the road, only the KFC and
an Indian place remain open. Retracing my steps this time, I am looking
for the Dalston C.L.R. James Library as a landmark that will help me get
back to the hotel; as soon as it enters my line of sight, I make a run for it.

Solitary: Spending a Fulbright Year in South Africa

Susan Rich

I began working on my Fulbright application just three months after my father's death and a year after my mother's. My parents had just disappeared, and I had no idea how I would survive without them. I knew only that living one's desires was the only thing that mattered. I had only one life. One. That's not a very big number.

Fulbright: such an optimistic word. I imagined *Ful* and *bright* as an enlivened state of mind, hopeful and wildly idealistic. "Our future is not in the stars but in our own minds and hearts," stated Senator J. William Fulbright when he introduced legislation to Congress. Begun shortly after World War II, the Fulbright Program started as a way to encourage mutual respect among countries through educational and cultural endeavors; the senator believed it was a crucial first step to creating an alternative to armed conflict. From one good idea came a global community of artists, scientists, and poets crisscrossing boundaries of ethnicity and race, economic and religious beliefs.

When the time came for me to apply for a fellowship, I felt as if I were writing a tired film noir instead of developing a plan that would enable me to cross cultural borders. Working on the Fulbright application almost overwhelmed me. My nonexistent personal ad would have read "Single woman, 37 years old; has little idea what she wants out of life." I was lost.

Traveling to South Africa *sounded* exciting; it seemed as good a plan as any. Why not interview poets continents away? Why not study another culture's poetry of commitment? The truth was I didn't know what else to do. Two years earlier, I had quit my job with Amnesty International to pursue an MFA in poetry at the University of Oregon. I was still adjusting to the idea that my parents had just left me. For good. Now that I was going to receive my degree, there seemed no clear career path to follow. I had no set geography or sense of myself. A year in a new country and, I presumed, in a new skin, sounded right.

I had never won a fellowship of any kind. I had no fancy credentials other than a soon-to-be-completed MFA. I applied for the Fulbright Fellowship believing it was a long shot. And it was.

The University of Oregon made a point of assisting students with the Fulbright process. The folks in the Office of International Affairs emphasized the importance of a strong proposal that could realistically be enacted. The *real* over the fantastical, they reminded us. The advice paid off: University of Oregon students have often earned the most Fulbright awards in the Pacific Northwest. I'd learned this from the Creative Writing Program director before deciding to move across the country to Oregon from Massachusetts. He'd used the lure of a Fulbright year as a recruiting tool. The Office of International Affairs assigned an administrator to mentor me as I worked on my application. Every other Friday at four p.m., I met with Maggie Morris, assistant vice provost for research and graduate education, in her office, which smelled of oranges. I took a new draft of my essay, which often bore no resemblance to what I had shown her two weeks earlier. She was gentle with my fickleness, and I got the sense that she enjoyed finishing her week imagining South African poets with me.

It took me time to understand that creating grant proposals is by definition a kind of speculative writing. Though I researched every South

African poet I could find and every South African university that might offer to sponsor me, my initial project of interviewing South African poets ultimately was going to succeed only if I could meet the writers and win their trust. Maggie Morris assured me that no one expected that the project would crystallize as I had planned it; the key was to design a good plan.

As with the Fulbright application, I wrote my proposal as if my life depended on it. That summer, as I took every book out of the library that made even a passing reference to African poetry, I honestly believed my very existence hinged on obtaining the fellowship. As contrary as this was to my life experience (I had never won so much as a ballpoint pen), I knew I needed to will this Fulbright year into existence.

After many weeks of not being able to write, the first paragraph of my proposal emerged fully formed. The words provided a map for where I needed to go:

> Poetry is manna, is revolution, is lifeblood that pulses through the body to the pen, to the paper, through memory to metaphor, from a life to a community, from pain to redemption. Poetry is witness. Nelson Mandela writes, "Poetry cannot block a bullet or still a sjambok [whip], but it can bear witness to brutality—thereby cultivating a flower in a graveyard." Writing poetry is a conscious act, an act of taking responsibility. It is neither political nor leftist propaganda to say poetry must be of this world.

After two months of writing and rewriting my proposal, I was interviewed on an early October day. Professors of music, mathematics, biology, and business all convened. Most major universities have a local Fulbright committee, composed of faculty from across the disciplines, that meets with candidates and eventually ranks each one.

As the committee began its work, the director of the Office of International Affairs, Tom Mills, an exceptionally warm and astute man, immediately put me at ease. The committee's questions ranged from the practical (Would I be able to manage on my own in a country I had never visited?) to the more project-based (How would my work with South African poets connect to my professional goals?). I read my poem "Nomadic Life" as part of the interview. Tom had suggested I take some of my poems along. He thought the committee might want to hear my work. It did. I read my poem honoring the Fulani nomads I had known during my time as a Peace Corps volunteer in the Republic of Niger (West Africa). Here's what I learned during my interview: an element of surprise—catching one's audience off guard, igniting imaginations—helps one's project succeed. I'd been hesitant about reading my own poem, but Tom had insisted, reminding me that my work as a poet would inform my entire Fulbright experience.

The day I received the letter congratulating me on my acceptance, May 20, would have been my father's seventy-fourth birthday. It seemed like a sign from the other side of the grave saying, "Go!" Nevertheless, how wrong it seemed not to telephone him to share the news.

As I slipped out of my life in Eugene, Oregon, I had two suitcases so big that I could have fit several bodies inside each of them. They were the height and depth of bags I had seen in airports, zipped up by families moving from one country to the next, taking only what they could wheel. My situation was similar. I left for South Africa with no notion of when or how I would return home because I had no home. My parents' deaths had absolved me of belonging to any singular place. Home was a house in Brookline, Massachusetts, sold to the highest bidder, my permanent address gone in a storm of legalese.

I remember a freak hailstorm in Portland that closed the airport. I remember learning that "act of God" was a legal term and that the airline wasn't responsible for my two-day wait for the next plane to Cape Town.

I remember a day in LAX, when, out of boredom, I dialed my high-school sweetheart's phone number and talked briefly with his lonely wife.

Finally, I boarded a flight that took more hours (and days) than I could account for. This had something to do with crossing the international date line. I remember a twelve-hour stay in Kuala Lumpur, a beautiful city of dust and donkeys. I remember a five-star hotel scented with bougainvillea blossoms, thanks to a voucher from Malaysian Airlines. Oddly, this was the very cheapest fare one could buy. The route I chose was known as "the wrong way round" because it took an extra day. All this lent a heavy dose of surrealism to my journey.

My one South African friend, whom I had met in Boston a decade before, picked me up at the airport and drove me to my new home at Festival Court, which was festive only in the way that funerals are festive: not at all. I'd arranged to take over the one-bedroom unit complete with bed, sofa, two chairs, and kitchen table sight unseen. I had refused to buy the love seat, irking the former tenant, who sent multiple e-mails trying to convince me of its floral beauty. Because this was 1997, and smartphones with digital cameras did not yet exist, I had taken the place on faith. What I found: two tiny rooms in white and tan. My flat looked onto Table Mountain—so close it seemed I could kiss the rock face from the bed. From my angle of vision, this seemed the largest and saddest peak I had ever seen.

In South Africa, place took on enormous meaning. One journalist explained to me in a confidential tone that South Africans have more attachment to the land than any other people. She said this as we climbed Lion's Head, a small mountain in the center of Cape Town. She and I were not alone on our midnight pilgrimage. More than a hundred partiers were there, carrying picnic baskets and bottles of wine. There is a tradition of climbing Lion's Head on nights when the moon is full. Even the set of hand chains drilled into the final rocks did not deter the crowd. In a city where people afraid of house burglars literally run from car to front door, a midnight mountain sojourn seemed almost supernatural.

The hikers helped one another transition from scree to mountaintop. Although the crowd of partiers was mostly white, mostly middle class, it was racially mixed. On top of Lion's Head, I felt that the new South Africa might have a chance of success. At least for those who love to look at the moon.

In Cape Town, white people in my neighborhood rarely walked the streets. No warm evening strolls to the corner market, no walking the dog after dinner. The only South Africans I saw on my walks to and from the university were the black women who cooked, cleaned, and took care of the children of white families. Never before had I visited modest apartments that sparkled so! Never before had I had a lease that included rules governing the use of the storage locker—more often used as the servants' quarters. Even after the end of apartheid, even with Nelson Mandela as president, some black workers lived behind the garage in a lower-middle-class apartment block. What did I condone as I signed my lease, paid my rent, walked past the men outside their storage units, drying their clothes on the same frayed line as my own?

One of the things about living in a country that is not one's own is the constant state of not knowing. Each day, I carried with me a basket of ever-shifting questions—painful to ask and even more impossible to answer. Was it better to hire someone to scrub my two rooms and help alleviate the high unemployment rate, or was it best not to participate in a corrupt vestige from the past regime? Was it morally complicated to go hiking in the mountains if the National Party had constructed the overnight huts and long pathways under the apartheid system? Was I guilty by virtue of the air I breathed? I muddled my way through these questions as I walked past poinsettia and oleander trees to my university office. And on some visceral level, I believed I was guilty. Although I still enjoyed the delicate trees.

At least once a day, in the early morning as I climbed the hill to the campus or at dusk when I returned home, I passed a quiet young man who lived under the eaves of the corner market. Often, he greeted me with a rock-star smile, his eyes soft and appealing. At other times, he was entrenched in his own world, singing or weeping under his breath. Over the course of several months of daily walks, I often thought about this man, wondering why he chose to spread his blue blanket near my house instead of in one of the townships, where most black citizens still lived. How did he endure his solitude day after day? I identified deeply with this man whose name I never learned.

With few exceptions, the poems I wrote during my time in Cape Town focused on the men, women, and children who lived on the busy streets and roundabouts of the city. Although I had previously lived in Zinder, Niger, and Cambridge, Massachusetts—both places where street people were ever present in my daily life—in Cape Town, the stark contrast of rich and poor struck a harsher note. Young children no more than six or seven years old were sent into the street to knock on car windows, their mothers standing in the shadows. And in the celebration of the new idealistic and democratic South Africa, the legions of homeless people at red lights, shopping centers, restaurants, apartment blocks, bars, and beaches showed up the facts of a different South African narrative.

And the beautiful man I saw each evening? His presence took up a larger-than-life residence in my interior world. As a woman who had just been orphaned, who no longer had a home, I of course connected to this man. Something I could barely put into words. In a country where the idea of transformation was ubiquitous, this man still lived on the street alone. The truth was that for the majority of black South Africans, life did not improve economically in the first years after the dismantling of apartheid. My poem for him, "Change," ends with

This man who nests
underneath the café eaves

tonight looks up and almost
nods to me—to me, not the stranger
from a distant country.

I still picture him in my mind's eye, bedding down for the night as I walk past with my carton of milk and bottles of ginger beer. What might have happened if I had done something more than pour a few coins into his cupped hands? What if I'd learned his name?

As an outsider in a country that had had very few "cultural" visitors in the decades since the United Nations had called for a cultural boycott requesting that all academic and cultural institutions terminate ties to South Africa, I was in a strange position socially. The English faculty was certainly kind to me, if from a distance. My colleagues were happy enough to take me to a movie or a play, but they rarely moved beyond the one obligatory date. This was understandable in a country the outside world often condemned.

During my Fulbright year in South Africa, political poetry took front and center stage in my life. I met with men and women who had been jailed for their beliefs. I met poets who had gone to prison for their poetry, professors who had been jailed for doing nothing more than writing a pamphlet, editing a speech. One such poet and former philosophy professor I met, Jeremy Cronin, a man who had once contemplated the priesthood, now works for the South African government as deputy minister for transportation.

In a 2001 interview with Irish scholar Dr. Helena Sheehan, Cronin mentioned the odd trajectory that had led him to move from his position as a University of Cape Town lecturer in philosophy to political prisoner. His lack of political activism before imprisonment is a common enough story but in his case struck me as extreme. Cronin stated,

"So I ended up in prison as an ANC/SACP [African National Congress/ South African Communist Party] prisoner, but I'd never been to an ANC meeting in my life. I'd never seen an ANC flag. I'd never sung an ANC song, not that I can sing...."

During some of the toughest years (1976–1983) of the apartheid struggle, Cronin was imprisoned, spending a portion of his time in solitary confinement. He was arrested under the Terrorism and Internal Security Act and tried in Cape Town Superior Court. At the beginning of his seven-year term, his young wife, Anne Marie, died of a brain hemorrhage. Now his love poems to her are taught to schoolchildren across the nation.

A man in his middle years, Cronin retains schoolboy good looks. His brown eyes smile at the edges; his hair looks thick and well combed. A pinstriped shirt and worn sports jacket are casual reminders of his years lecturing in college classrooms. Cronin told me that for his first book, *Inside*, he composed the poems inside a cell—literally. He needed to memorize his work and then write the poems down, revising them only after his release from prison.

One signature poem, "Motho Ke Motho Ka Batho Babang," details a communication between two prisoners who can see each other only in the reflection of one handheld mirror. This seems an apt metaphor for how difficult it is to look at any life except indirectly. The poem's title references a common African concept: ubuntu, a belief in a healthy community as central to society; the individual is not as crucial, culturally, as in Western belief systems.

"Motho Ke Motho Ka Batho Babang
(A Person Is a Person Because of Other People)"

By holding my mirror out of the window I see
Clear to the end of the passage.
There's a person down there.

A prisoner polishing a doorhandle.
In the mirror I see him see
My face in the mirror,
I see the fingertips of his free hand
Bunch together, as if to make
An object the size of a badge
Which travels up to his forehead
The place of an imaginary cap.
    (This means: *A warder*.)
Two fingers are extended in a vee
And wiggle like two antennae.
    (He's being watched.)
A finger of his free hand makes a watch-hand's arc
On the wrist of his polishing arm without
Disrupting the slow-slow rhythm of his work.
    (*Later*. Maybe, later we can speak.)
Hey! Wat maak jy daar?
    —a voice from around the corner.
No. Just polishing baas.
He turns his back to me, now watch
His free hand, the talkative one,
Slips quietly behind
    —*Strength brother*, it says,
In my mirror,
    A black fist.

I've read this poem with groups of students from Buffalo to San Diego, each time asking everyone to shout out together this universal African saying: *Motho ke motho ka batho babang*. The cinematic feel of the piece, the unspooling of sound and meaning until readers are left with the iconic symbol of the black fist, makes real the human connection across prison cell and color line.

When Cronin and I met at an outdoor restaurant outside Johannes-
burg, *Even the Dead* had just been released, and the cover art featured
an extreme close-up of his handsome face. The publisher had made this
picture a prerequisite for publishing Cronin's collection of poems. As a
deputy minister in the new South African government, Cronin was well
known. As a poet, well, no one was really known for writing poetry in
South Africa. Instead, the country was in love with its new political and
social freedoms; poetry had yet to find its place.

What gripped the public consciousness during my time in South
Africa were the Truth and Reconciliation Commission hearings (TRC)
happening in different locations across the country. The TRC was a court-
appointed body that focused on uncovering the victims of gross human
rights violations and provided a legally sanctioned forum for people to
tell their stories. Perpetrators of crimes could also come forward and
recount their stories in exchange for amnesty, meaning they could not be
charged for their crimes later. As with most human rights commissions,
the system was complex and, by its very nature, imperfect.

I attended hearings outside Cape Town and watched *Special Report*,
the Sunday-night television show that provided TRC updates each week.
In South Africa, the name of the game was a visual and often disingenu-
ous view of forgiveness. Grieving mothers met with the Afrikaner men
who had tortured their sons and were expected to accept the mise-en-
scène of apology. It went something like this: a thick-necked white man
rides through the village that he terrorized as a soldier in the South
African army, only now he's on the back of a flatbed truck, waving
and smiling to the people. Eventually, the truck and the gang of South
African Broadcasting Channel (SABC) cameramen pause on key, and the
man (these white men *do* look alike) delivers a speech that covers three
points: I am sorry for what I did; I hope you can forgive me; I have no
money or anything of value for the community except a few moments on
TV. Oddly, many people did seem to feel that a TV crew's filming in the
village was payment enough—but not everyone.

From "Special Reports"

With a lop-sided stride, she finds her way
to the visitor, steps up proudly, fires

saliva spitting dead
straight in the eyes of forgiveness;

one widow fine-boned and lean,
bows to the cameras of the SABC.

—Susan Rich

My poem ends with this woman's interrupting the narrative of the all-forgiving mother. But as with many of the poems I wrote about my time in South Africa, the work feels weak when compared with the complexities of its subject. South Africa didn't fit neatly into file boxes; I needed a new vocabulary for my experiences, and I'm not sure I ever exactly found it.

Teaching at the University of Cape Town afforded me opportunities to interact with South African students and faculty. I sat in my little room at Festival Court with the big view of Table Mountain, composing lesson plans for creative writing in the first term and American poetry in the second. It was in South Africa that I first taught the poetry of Elizabeth Bishop, Naomi Shihab Nye, and Yusef Komunyakaa. It was in South Africa that I attended my first MLA-style academic conference and published my first (and only!) academic paper.

I met Mazisi Kunene, a former Angeleno who taught for nearly twenty years at UCLA, at the same conference. He left South Africa in 1959 to help lead the antiapartheid movement in the UK. A member of the ANC, he became its main representative in Europe. In his long life, he worked as an academic and a political activist.

Kunene and I met at an academic conference of English professors, at which the number of carjackings tallied during the week was often the key subject during the Q & A. For a few mornings in a leafy suburb of Johannesburg, we sat together talking poetry over eggs and coffee. Together with the Shakespearean scholar David Schalkwyk, we created a multicultural society of three. Kunene seemed amused by the fact that Schalkwyk came to the table each morning with a poem he'd worked on throughout the night. Fifteen years have passed since those generous mornings of breakfast and combustible laughter, but my sense of the quiet utopia we created there has not diminished.

A decade after our meeting, Kunene became Africa's (and South Africa's) first poet laureate. A year later, in 2006, he was dead at seventy-six.

From "Tribute to Mshongweni"

Your dreams shall invade our earth
Creating an endless line of horizons
We too shall follow the song of the night-bird to the hill
The whole earth shall see the falling star

—Mazisi Kunene

I am glad to have known him, if only across the breakfast table. I keep this small table in my mind's eye as another reminder that South Africa might transform into a place where poets, scholars, and even young Americans can come together.

In South Africa, poets were granted little attention. Especially young poets. In 1997 there was only one graduate degree program in creative writing and just a handful of annual literary events. However, I met one poet whose work I admired very much: Mxolisi Nyezwa, a man from Port Elizabeth. When we were introduced, because he was very shy and I was very shy, not much—if any—conversation took place. We stared at each other. I smiled; he looked down. Still, I found his poetry compelling. He had started the bilingual magazine *Kotaz* while living in the township where he had been born. I took this as a good omen for South African poetry; if Nyezwa was staying in the township, it meant he was making a commitment to live and document the new South Africa. Later, I sent him poems and was very thankful that he published them. Through letters, we were able to correspond. Today *Kotaz* is still going strong, and Nyezwa has published three collections of poems: *Song Trials*, *New Country*, and *Malikhanye*. A participant at the Poetry Africa festival sponsored by the University of KwaZulu Natal, Nyezwa wrote,

"Poetry is a simple way to remind us of our humanity. It guards against placing blind faith in the sciences, which are constricting to the human spirit. In poetry we discover our basic selves."

Nyezwa's style of poetry is deceptively simple. His images and obsessions contain echoes of Pablo Neruda's work. It makes sense to me that when living in extremity, in conditions that the human heart can barely comprehend, a poetry of the surreal becomes necessary.

From "I Cannot Think of All the Pains"

i cannot think of all the pains that have come
and gone, pains in men's waists
and in men's shoes—
i cannot have relief proper, wearing a neat tie.

But it was Ingrid de Kok, a South African poet who had gone into self-imposed exile in Canada and whose poems I had discovered while I was at the University of Oregon, whose work most compelled me. In a speech she gave at Northwestern University, de Kok explained the double bind South African poets find themselves in. "It's impossible to write poetry in South Africa without confronting the experience people have had of language and the expectations they therefore have of writers, whose ambiguous function is to undo the word while using the word." I found de Kok's questioning of her "right" to write a lyric of South Africa central to the question of poetry in South Africa: "Why do I write, what may I write, and for whom do I write?" she asks herself. In "Mending," de Kok imagines a woman sewing as a metaphor for the new South Africa— the scene is damaged, with a "trail of red" and "a histogram of welts and weals."

"Mending"

In and out, behind, across.
The formal gesture binds the cloth.
The stitchery's a surgeon's rhyme,
a Chinese stamp, a pantomime

of print. Then spoor. Then trail of red.
Scabs rise, stigmata from the thread.
A cotton chronicle congealed.
A histogram of welts and weals.

The woman plies her ancient art.
Her needle sutures as it darts,
scoring, scripting, scarring, stitching
the invisible mending of the heart.

Elizabeth Bishop's "One Art" lives quietly underneath this poem. The poems share a similar sense of loss in the face of history—whether personal or political. Both pieces require a formal vessel to contain the enormity of emotion. And, as de Kok told me in conversation, the poem is telling not only the story of South Africa but also the story of a woman struggling with the loss of her lover. Perhaps this poem answers, in part, de Kok's question of how to write a South African poetry—a poetry that contends with both personal and national urgencies.

De Kok was the reason I chose South Africa as the country for my Fulbright. I was just as intrigued with her as a person as I had been with her poems. She took a great interest in my life and work—in a way no one had done before. She treated me as a fellow poet and, in time, we became close friends.

Many young writers keep journals while traveling, and I was no different. As I wrote, I often worried about whether my experience was authentic enough. Was I seeing the real South Africa? Did I spend enough time in the churches, the museums, the bars? I wrote about the electrical sockets in the country—that they too were undergoing a transition—the old table lamps unusable with the newfangled three-pronged outlets. I wrote about the color of lemons—that they were a mottled green, never ripe enough.

Looking back at these journals, I understand the difficulty of being in a place and time shot through with contradictions. The poetry of South Africa was changing and in the immediate aftermath of apartheid, it was perhaps too early to tell what change might mean for the country, let alone for poetry. Writers, business people, and arts educators were all searching for new ways to tell the nation's stories—and to lay the foundation for creating new ones.

Every person who worked at the South African Museum—from museum guard to secretary, kitchen staffer to executive director—chose a favorite piece for this inclusive exhibit and wrote a curatorial note concerning why it was the piece he or she related to most. Ingrid de Kok took me to the museum in Cape Town early on in my stay; she insisted that I examine each piece in the show. I now suspect she wanted me to understand how South Africa was changing, that soon black men would not live behind apartment blocks in storage units, that a new democracy was forming. It was at this same museum, downstairs in the tearoom, that I first interviewed de Kok. My tape recorder captured her intense voice: a woman with confidence, committed to a changing nation. In some ways, my time in South Africa paralleled that art exhibit. I recall a series of experiences—midnight climbs, street people, Truth and Reconciliation Commission rallies, classes at the university—that were "chosen" by the various selves at work in me at the time.

In the year leading up to my Fulbright Fellowship, grief and change permeated each interaction, every space that opened to me. The dislocation of losing parents is not analogous to a country's gaining its freedom, but in an illogical way, the experiences matched up. South Africa underwent a total sea change in the 1990s; Nelson Mandela, once the world's most famous political prisoner, became the first black president of a country where, because of his skin color, he formerly had not been legally allowed to vote. The new South African constitution, compiled by working groups of lawyers, nongovernmental organizations, and community groups, became a model for progressives everywhere.

After my Fulbright year ended, I stayed on in South Africa for six more months, working for the United States Information Service and teaching at another South African university. Then suddenly I knew it was time to go home. I packed up my Festival Court apartment—passing it on to the next American, an African-American sociologist from Indiana—and returned to my old Toyota station wagon parked in the lot of my neighbor's auto-repair business in Eugene, Oregon.

It must sound like living in South Africa was a struggle—and it was. Triple locks on the doors and a telephone that rarely rang. But struggle is where I discovered what I could endure; struggle is how I learned to trust my instincts and push beyond my self-imposed boundaries. What I have not stressed enough about my time in South Africa are the close friends I made, the experiences I wouldn't trade away. The long walks home with Rustum, who suggested the title of my first book, the spiraling talks with Lisa as we tried to unpack the nature of our lives, everything enlivened by the newness of another continent.

My connection to Africa, if not strictly South Africa, remains alive in the poems I write and the students I teach. I am on the faculty at Highline Community College, which has the most diverse student population in Washington State. Sometimes international students join my classes having left their homes in Cameroon or Kenya five days earlier.

To better understand their sense of dislocation, it helps that I know firsthand what it is like to be seen as "other" by everyone around me and at the same time to have my own expectations of who I am shift as if I were standing on tectonic plates. Only in a country not my own would I be interviewed as an "American writer" on national radio or be invited to teach "American poetry" at a prestigious university. I was a recent MFA graduate without a book, and these opportunities were not available to me at home. Yet this dislocation, this insecurity bred from never understanding the expectations of those around me, made these experiences otherworldly. I suspect my African students have similar feelings when they are expected to share their ideas in front of the class or are required to write a five-page critical analysis of New American Cinema.

Today, time alone comes to me infrequently. An hour after midnight with a book or an afternoon working on a poem amplifies the moments I can keep to myself. Small crumbs compared to a Fulbright year. Sometimes I wish I could return to that year, to days spent in solitary, more aware now of how crucial the time was for my development as a writer and as a person. Who was that young woman who was curious enough to dive headfirst into the experience of otherness? I've come up with more questions than answers. Questions of authenticity and dislocation, of dealing with grief and transformation, most of all of learning what it is to travel this one curious life as a writer, a Fulbrighter who stays suspended in an enlivened state of mind—singing or perhaps weeping under her breath.

By Touch

Alissa Valles

If you set out on a journey pray that the road is long
a wandering without apparent aim a blind groping
so you come to know earth's harshness not just by sight but by touch
so that you measure yourself against the world with your whole skin

—Zbigniew Herbert, "Journey"

My Kraków studio was on the sixth floor of an old apartment building just outside the Planty, the strip of gardens wrapped around the old city center. From my window, I looked out over a convent garden where Sisters of the Visitation often wandered in their magpie habits, chatting with the gardener. When I arrived from John Paul II International Airport, Jan, my landlord, carried my large suitcase all the way to the top. "*Ciężko być poetą!* (Being a poet is so tough!)" he joked. I'd taken a leave of absence from doctoral drudgery. A Kosciuszko fellowship I'd been awarded the previous year and deferred never came through, and by the time the gardener of the Visitation was climbing a ladder to pick apples, I had to scramble for work. That turned out to be a good thing. It meant I met a wild variety of people outside the university, where I was studying advanced tongue twisting and auditing philosophy seminars.

Jan, a geologist, and his wife, Aka, often invited me down to the second floor for tea and metaphysics during the time I was there, even when my rent was late.

My pretext for fleeing school was translation work for an American anthology of Polish prose the poet Adam Zagajewski was editing. Adam conjured a modest grant for me from a mysterious foundation that I still suspect he invented himself and surreptitiously funded. He also introduced me to Jan and Aka and to many others in Kraków, a graceful but conservative and clique-ish city. During the fall of 2004, Adam and I met regularly to discuss (and argue over) the anthology and whatever else came up. Czesław Miłosz had died in August of that year, and after an absurd national controversy over his burial site, Polish letters began to settle around a vast empty space with Gothic eyebrows. Translating essays, letters, and diary entries by more than a dozen writers, including Aleksander Wat, Tadeusz Różewicz, and Miron Białoszewski, along with interviews and a few poems for the anthology, meant struggling to carry a wide variety of idioms into English. It also meant learning to distinguish between aesthetic and political arguments specific to their time and place and arguments that were part of what I think George Steiner called the gossip of eternity. It was more difficult and rewarding than anything I'd done in school.

I was finishing my first book of poems. Insomnia was fertile. The convent bells woke me early in the morning, and I would swear, stagger to the stove to make coffee, translate for a few hours, then go out to classes or meetings, eat something, take a walk, and then climb back to the sixth floor to take a nap and return to my desk after dark. I did some English tutoring and editing; there was such demand for both at the university that students and faculty approached me, sometimes even on the street, with queries about my rates (which I made up on the spot according to how wealthy the asker looked). I even tutored a few prostitutes looking to get out of the game, one of whom went on to work for the city tourist office. In return for the chaste English I gave her, she greatly enriched my Polish sex slang. The Book Institute charged with promoting Polish literature abroad was seemingly always on the lookout for native speakers of various languages to do translations and editing. I started to write articles and reviews for magazines in both Europe and the United States, the first ones on spec, eventually on commission.

I got occasional editing or writing jobs from the Institute for War Documentation in Amsterdam and the BBC World Service, where I had worked after college. Even a small payment in euros or pounds went a long way in Poland. Off the central square, an *obwarzanek* (a proto-bagel) cost only fifty groszy—about fifteen cents—and friends would visit with bouquets of vegetables from their allotment gardens. Adam lent me dictionaries and reference books, and if I went to see a publisher or writer, I'd come home with an armful of books. When I needed a prescribing doctor, a friend put me in contact with a Dr. Bomb, who treated me *pro bono lyrico*, as he put it. Without the generosity of these people, I would have been obliged to go back to school with my tail between my legs, which seemed to me at that time a kind of perdition.

I worked on several translation projects alongside the anthology. I'd felt an instant affinity for Zagajewski's contemporary, Ryszard Krynicki, when I'd started to read him as a Slavics student in England. It was my great luck that Krynicki did not speak—or at least did not admit to speaking—English and felt at home in excruciating silences. My errors of syntax and pronunciation immediately became language games. Unlike most poets, he didn't like to talk about himself, and we mostly talked about other writers, especially Paul Celan, whom he loved, honored, and translated, and Zbigniew Herbert, with whom I was in love. Herbert had dedicated one of his greatest poems to Krynicki: "To Ryszard Krynicki—A Letter." Now Krynicki was the publisher responsible for Herbert's poetry.

I'd started translating Herbert—on whom I was planning a dissertation—at the University of Chicago, in an independent study with J.M. Coetzee, not expecting ever to publish my versions. Translation is an intimate and risky form of associating with a writer you love: you have to serve another voice selflessly and yet be faithful to your own language. This is difficult enough when the writer can argue and explain. When the writer is no longer alive, there is a powerful sense of courting a ghost. Tracking down family, friends, belongings is an occult part of what Walter Benjamin called the "task of the translator." By the special logic of the Eastern European intelligentsia, once I had talked to one or two people about my projects, I was instantly put in touch with others who wished to help or encourage me. I visited Herbert's widow, Katarzyna, in Warsaw and sat in Herbert's old study, surrounded by his books and papers, leafing through his sketchbooks. Szu-szu, a plump white cat I knew from Herbert's poems, known to empty glasses of vodka left on the table, was still padding around.

Krynicki introduced me to a gaggle of younger Polish poets he published. These guys, almost all of them called Marcin, scorned the patriarchs I adored (Miłosz, Herbert) and worshipped instead the puffed-up daddies I had impatiently rejected (O'Hara and Ashbery). There should be a Freudian term describing lust for someone else's parent. The younger poets were trying to free themselves from the political burden Polish poetry carried. What they wrote seemed to me an unprecedented hybrid of Europe and the United States and because that was the kind of thing I was looking to do myself, it had a wicked appeal for me. To be surrounded by poets who spurned Herbert just as I was making my own versions of his poems was bracing. Herbert's nature was to work against his immediate surroundings, to find his feet in confrontation and controversy. Traction sparks energy, and as Herbert says, only garbage flows with the stream.

After a year I gravitated from Kraków to Warsaw—an infinitely uglier but much more liberal city—and decided to leave graduate school. I found two jobs, both by word of mouth: one at the Jewish Historical Institute, where I translated and edited texts from the World War II archive, and another at the antitrafficking organization La Strada International, tutoring and mentoring young women who had been forced into prostitution.

I rented an apartment from a feminist writer, Agnieszka Graff, who was one of a startling number of inspiring and independent women I met in Warsaw. Pani Herbert took me to a Pani Kafka who provided me with black kittens. The following years were thick with Herbert, with syntax and simile, with rebellions and reconciliations, with blood, ink, and tears. I left the United States in the year of Abu Ghraib and the sickening stench of official lies. I returned in the year it transpired that the US government had "rendered" prisoners to Poland. You can't escape from home, but you can learn to tie new knots, love foreign princes, grow a new tongue, eyes, skin, scars.

Beyond the Page

A Glance Back

Elizabeth Bishop in Brazil[1]

Ashley Brown

Future biographers will probably make a great deal of Elizabeth Bishop's twenty years in Brazil. This was the country of her middle age and her full maturity as a poet, and it continues to provide a background for her years in Boston. As I stood recently on her balcony looking at the water-life on Boston Harbor, I thought back easily to the first time I met her in an apartment high above Guanabara Bay at Rio de Janeiro, and then I thought: she always has the most spectacular views! I hope she doesn't mind my stating in print that she is farsighted; I rather envy her that. When I, quite myopic, could barely see a freighter steaming across the bay, Elizabeth was already describing the activity on deck. Brazil is a good place for the keen observer. It is teeming with particularities, and when I first lived there I (a former philosophy major) thought that the easy way out was to become a complete nominalist; one had to keep one's head. But Elizabeth seemed perfectly in harmony with this barrage of sights, sounds, and smells that awaited one at every hand. She was staying then in a section called Leme, and over the telephone she

---

1. Ashley Brown, "Elizabeth Bishop in Brazil" from *Elizabeth Bishop and Her Art*, edited by Lloyd Schwartz and Sybil P. Estess (Ann Arbor: The University of Michigan Press, 1983). Originally appeared in *Southern Review* (October 1977).

explained, before I went there the first time, that the way to remember it was to recite "Now I lay me down to sleep" in the taxi.

The time was 1964. I had with me a letter of introduction from Flannery O'Connor, an old friend, who had written: "I'm up here in the hospital else I would send you some peafowl feathers to take her from me. She sent me an altar in a bottle." This was Flannery's last letter to me; I did not realize then how close to death she was, but later that summer I read about it in the *Jornal do Brasil*. Flannery and Elizabeth had never met; they had spoken only once by long-distance telephone, but they had corresponded for some years and formed a friendship based on a wonderful sense of humor as well as a mutual respect for each other's literary worth. The altar in the bottle I had admired on Flannery's bookshelves in the parlor at Andalusia Farm. Actually it was a wooden cross with bits of paper and tinfoil and a rooster at the top (reminiscent of Elizabeth's poem "Roosters"?). It probably came from the Northeastern state of Bahïa, which is especially rich in folklore. I always thought it was a kind of emblem of some artistic trait that these two writers shared— perhaps their unusual unsentimental love of the beauty to be found in common life.

Much of the time in those days Elizabeth lived with a friend, Lota de Macedo Soares, in a really handsome modern house in the mountains above Petrópolis. Another spectacular view. Petrópolis, a couple of hours' drive from Rio, is the old imperial summer capital, and Rio society still repairs there during the hot season. The house was called "Samambaia," after a fern with rather coarse leaves that grows in many parts of Brazil. It was long and low but went off in several directions from a room, open much of the time, where people breakfasted or dined. Indeed, most of the house could be open, and I remember with delight the hummingbirds that darted through. Elizabeth, an amateur ornithologist, said that there were two hundred species in Brazil. Was that possible? But she lived in the house week in and week out, and in a lovely poem called "Song for the Rainy Season" (1960) she gives us the scene that the casual visitor might overlook:

> House, open house
> to the white dew
> and the milk-white sunrise
> kind to the eyes,
> to membership
> of silverfish, mouse,
> bookworms,
> big moths; with a wall
> for the mildew's
> ignorant map;
>
> darkened and tarnished
> by the warm touch
> of the warm breath,
> maculate, cherished,
> rejoice!

"Samambaia" is the setting for several other poems: "Electrical Storm," which immortalizes Tobias the cat; "The Armadillo"; and the somewhat later "Rainy Season; Sub-Tropics." "The Armadillo" takes place during a festive season that is celebrated in June—the feast of São João, which comes at the winter solstice there. The fire balloons in the poem are illegal with good reason:

> With a wind,
> they flare and falter, wobble and toss;
> but if it's still they steer between
> the kite sticks of the Southern Cross,
>
> receding, dwindling, solemnly

and steadily forsaking us,
or, in the downdraft from a peak,
suddenly turning dangerous.

This poem, one of the finest, is absolutely sensitive to every nuance of movement. Although it is contained within a pictorial setting (all can be visualized), Miss Bishop's rhythmic control largely accounts for the *pretty, dreamlike mimicry* that prepares the way for the final moral statement.

"Rainy Season; Sub-Tropics" (1967) might be regarded as a companion piece to "Song for the Rainy Season" if you shifted your attention to the animal life outside the house. It turns on the theme of self-pity that Elizabeth Bishop has often dealt with in various subtle forms. I suspect that it is the human quality she most dislikes, though she sometimes presents it in a good-natured way, as in "Crusoe in England," where she has her hero reminisce:

I told myself
"Pity should begin at home." So the more
pity I felt, the more I felt at home.

"Rainy Season" is a triptych of prose-poems with these speakers: a giant toad, a strayed crab, and a giant snail (the lesser orders of nature come very large in Brazil). They are all displaced; they all embody human feelings (vanity, aggression, envy, fear, longing for repose, and so on) in a disconcerting way; and their reactions to each other in the three monologues compose a scenario. The brilliance of the description cannot be conveyed in a brief quotation. About the time that I first read this I saw Beckett's *Play* (1964), with its three characters in urns up to their necks, each lit in turn by a spotlight as he blames the others for his plight. (The situation that is being recollected in a kind of purgatory is a tawdry adultery.) I thought: how interesting that Elizabeth's characters with their density of concrete life and Beckett's with their babble of clichés should come so close together in one's mind. "Pity me," says the toad in his first line. "Pity me," says the snail near the end. "Pity them," says Beckett's Man halfway through, and his sad trio run the same gamut of feelings as the poor rain-creatures.

At "Samambaia" you could go forward onto a great stone terrace that overlooked the valley towards Petrópolis. This, however, could be dangerous for the acrophobic, and I gathered that Aldous Huxley, a visitor a few years earlier, had almost pitched over the edge. If you walked up from the house you came to Elizabeth's study, a small cottage. This was situated above a waterfall that rushed down the mountainside. (Her snail says, "The waterfall below will vibrate through my shell and body all night long. In that steady pulsing I can rest.") Elizabeth had the splendid idea of having the cascade dammed, just momentarily, to make a tiny swimming pool, and you could descend there from the study through a clump of bamboos. The study itself was comfortable and clearly the working-place for a serious writer and reader with a large eclectic taste; nothing formal about it. Photographs of Baudelaire and Marianne Moore and Lowell were tacked to the wall. Here and in the main house were superb artistic objects from various parts of Brazil, where by this time Elizabeth had travelled extensively. She has always liked simple things that most people would reject. I remember a dishpan made of colorful flattened-out cans that had contained soybean oil or peas or perhaps cheese; they had been soldered together. (This brief phase of industrial folk-art is over in the 1970s, and now housewives along the Amazon use plastic dishpans like everyone else's.) I mention these details, trivial as they may seem, because they suggest the human scale of Elizabeth's poetry. A poem like "Jerónimo's House" is composed almost entirely of such details, and in its quiet way it bears out a "rage for order" as much as any poem by Stevens.

Elizabeth landed in Brazil somewhat by accident in late November, 1951. She had actually intended to land there, but only to stop during a voyage round South America. This incident is amusingly recalled in "Arrival at Santos," done from the tourist's point of view. Miss Breen, Elizabeth's fellow passenger, the retired police lieutenant, really existed, and she rather liked being put in the poem. One curious textual matter: in the original version the author was taking Scotch through the customs; when the poem was reprinted in *Questions of Travel* it became bourbon. Which *was* it? Then Elizabeth ate some item of fruit (a *cajú*, I believe) that disagreed horribly with her; she was laid up for an extended recovery; and her ship sailed on without her. But she had friends in Brazil whom she had known in New York during an earlier period; she liked the country, and she stayed.

The poems in *Questions of Travel* are the chief literary legacy of Elizabeth Bishop's Brazilian years, but as a professional writer she occasionally turned her hand to other things, and eventually she became an important translator and an intermediary between Brazilian and American culture. The Brazilian government awarded her the Order of Rio Branco in 1971. In a conversation piece published some years ago in *Shenandoah* (Winter 1966) I asked her whether she had been able to get anything from the country except its appearances, and she replied:

> Living in the way I have happened to live here, knowing Brazilians, has made a great difference. The general life I have known here has of course had an impact on me. I think I've learned a great deal. Most New York intellectuals' ideas about "underdeveloped countries" are partly mistaken, and living among people of a completely different culture has changed a lot of my old stereotyped ideas.

Elizabeth managed to put some of her knowledge into an illustrated book commissioned by Time Incorporated in 1962. Her text was no doubt "edited" to some extent in New York, but I can detect scarcely a trace of *Time*-style, and in fact, the book is still the best introduction to the subject. This is because the author is very close to the rich popular life around her; unlike so many of her compatriots, she is not blinkered by statistics and theories about economic "take-off." Much that she observed only twenty years ago is already passing into oblivion as the Brazilian population moves into the big cities. Not many North Americans could have written this:

> In the field of popular culture, however, undoubtedly the greatest achievement is the creation of the figureheads used on boats on the Rio São Francisco. Called *carrancas*, the figureheads depict animals, women and characters from Afro-Brazilian folklore, but one of the favorites is always the "Great Worm," the most dreadful of the spirits that live in the river. Some of these figureheads are very fine, towering several feet above the bow of the boat and carved in strong and simple style reminiscent of Romanesque sculpture. Unfortunately, *carrancas* are being used less and less today, and the art of carving them is dying out.

One evening in Rio we were invited to the house of a rich man who had collected a number of *carrancas* and placed them round his garden and swimming pool; they *were* impressive looming out of the dark, almost theatrical in this setting with its expensive lighting effects. What would they have looked like on the river? Very few people in Brazil could have seen them. Elizabeth, an indefatigable traveller, finally went down the Rio São Francisco on an endless trip in 1967. But it was a mixed experience; her immediate reaction came on a postcard:

> ... in retrospect I'm glad I did it + some of the worst will no doubt seem funny as time goes on—but never never the hideous poverty. The boat a very quaint stern-wheeler made in the U S A 70 years ago—everyone nice and polite,

but each and every one asked if I had a "family" and when I said no, they all commiserated with me, but also, I felt, rather avoided me as being not quite all there.

This, I think, records her *un*sentimental love of common life.

Elizabeth, who already had Spanish (from a period in Mexico during the 1940s) and French (from an even earlier period in Paris), learned Portuguese soon enough during her first years in Rio. In any case, nearly all of her friends were Brazilians. About this time she was introduced to an elderly lady, Sra. Alice Brant, who had grown up in Diamantina, a somewhat remote town in the state of Minas Gerais (General Mines). Alice Brant was half English by descent; her grandfather had gone out as a doctor with a mining company and remained; but she was brought up as a Brazilian. As a young girl in the 1890s she wrote a diary that she later called *Minha Vida de Menina* (*My Life as a Little Girl*). It was not till 1942, when she was living in Rio, that she had any idea of publishing it; her husband, the president of the Bank of Brazil, made the suggestion. She used the pseudonym "Helena Morley." Although the Diary was only intended to amuse her family and friends, it was recommended to the public by the French novelist Georges Bernanos, who was in wartime exile in Brazil, and it has had a kind of classic status ever since; one can often find a copy in the stationery shops.

Elizabeth proposed to translate the Diary and immersed herself in the subject. It was a good excuse for another journey, this time to Diamantina, which was not easy to reach twenty-five years ago. Nowadays the town, with its fine old houses, is rather famous among connoisseurs of architecture, and one can drive there on an excellent road. The Diary is, among other things, an authentic record of provincial life at a moment when Brazil was moving into another epoch of its history. (Slavery had been abolished in 1888 and the Empire succeeded by the first Republic the following year.) But its main interest lies in its loving but candid account of a family, a theme to which Elizabeth would return. Her introduction to the translation is one of her best pieces of prose, and, as Marianne Moore said in a review (*Poetry*, July 1959), "The attitude of life revealed by the Diary, Helena's apperceptiveness, and innate accuracy, seem a double portrait; the exactness of observation in the introduction being an extension, in manner, of Miss Bishop's verse and other writing...." The Diary in fact occupies an important place in Elizabeth Bishop's canon.

The Brazilian poems in *Questions of Travel* are not arranged according to their date of composition, but they do compose a set of related responses to a scene. All of them were retained by the author in the Chatto and Windus *Selected Poems* of 1967. Needless to say, they exemplify a wide range of style; Miss Bishop, as her readers know, has large resources of poetic "attack." "Arrival at Santos," which originally came near the end of *A Cold Spring*, looks just right when it is reprinted as the opening poem in *Questions of Travel*. Then comes "Brazil, January 1, 1502," which was first printed in the *New Yorker*'s number for the New Year in 1960, after the poet had lived in Brazil for eight years and assimilated a great deal of its history as well as its landscape. New Year's Day of 1502 was the date on which the Portuguese caravels arrived at Guanabara Bay, which they mistakenly thought was the mouth of a great river—hence Rio de Janeiro (January). This is a poem of wonder, however; the poet assumes the vision of the Portuguese discoverers, and the texture of the verse could not be more different from that of "Arrival at Santos." Indeed, the word *texture* is appropriate here, because this is a verbal tapestry, and we move in and out of the setting as though we still had the allegorical sense of the sixteenth century. ("Still in the foreground there is Sin: / five sooty dragons near some massy rocks.") The historical theme shouldn't be overlooked. In her text for the *Time* book Miss Bishop observes that "the Portuguese lacked the bloodthirsty missionary zeal of the Spaniards," but the Christians of her poem are "hard as nails"; and at least a century of Brazil's early history comes out in this passage:

Directly after Mass, humming perhaps
L'Homme armé or some such tune,
they ripped away into the hanging fabric,
each out to catch an Indian for himself—
those maddening little women who kept calling,
calling to each other (or had the birds waked up?)
and retreating, always retreating, behind it.

For a decade or so I have thought this poem fascinating as an act of perception: That is, on what terms does the mind approach a scene, and with what preconceptions? And how can one recover the sense of any earlier period? The author briefly quotes Kenneth Clark's *Landscape into Art* as an epigraph. I would suggest E.H. Gombrich's *Art and Illusion* as being even more useful for speculating on this theme.

The title poem, "Questions of Travel," was first published in 1956, about four years after Elizabeth had taken up residence in Brazil. The tourist has now become the passionate observer and, in a sense, has lost her innocence. The poem is a wonderful mosaic of things that one can see and hear along a Brazilian highway—say, along the road to Petrópolis. (Some of these phenomena are, I fear, doomed as highway culture in Brazil resembles ours more and more.) The mechanic's wooden clogs "carelessly clacking" over the floor of the filling-station, the bird in its fancy bamboo cage above the broken gasoline pump—what a pity, says the poet, to have missed these things in all their particularity. And what random historical causes lay behind them? The poem builds up in a seemingly (but only seemingly) casual way to the two formal stanzas in italics at the end, where the traveller asks herself:

Continent, city, country, society:
the choice is never wide and never free.
And here, or there...No. Should we have stayed at home,
wherever that may be?

But she has already answered her question in the poem, where, for me at any rate, a whole phase of lost experience has been transmuted into something permanent. The English poet Charles Tomlinson took her to task in his review of *Questions of Travel* (*Shenandoah*, Winter 1966), in which he said, "For the fact of the matter is, Miss Bishop travels because she likes it, not because she is homeless in the way that Lawrence or Schoenberg were." But is it really necessary to insist on this kind of "radical homelessness?" It seems to me perfectly obvious that Elizabeth Bishop has followed Henry James, Katherine Anne Porter, and certain other Americans who have gone out into the world, and these are the names to mention. She knows very well who she is. Again, speaking for myself, I have often wondered about the accidents of history that have made my Brazilian friends different from me—they come from a country as old and large and diverse as ours, they had slavery twenty-five years after we did, they too are apt to make exaggerated claims. Elizabeth's poems have more of the "feel" of life in Brazil than anything else written by a North American because they undercut the large generalizations that we all have when we approach a subject on this scale.

The remaining poems in *Questions of Travel* are about poor people in various parts of Brazil, and I think that Mr. Tomlinson misses the point again when he says that "the better-off have always preferred their poor processed by style." I suppose one could turn that remark against Wordsworth in "Resolution and Independence," but surely his old leech-gatherer is *dignified* by being put into *rime royale*. One could hardly think that Wordsworth knew his poor more intimately than Miss Bishop, and he is the master of this kind of experience in English poetry. Miss Bishop in fact has often chosen to write about the humble for reasons of her own—and poems like "Jerónimo's House," "Songs for a Colored Singer," "At the Fishhouses," and "Faustina, or Rock Roses" are among her most assured successes. I don't think she would have done better with intellectuals or diplomats' wives as subjects.

"Manuelzinho" and "Squatter's Children," which were written

around the same time as "Questions of Travel," are about people who might be found on the hillside leading to "Samambaia." (A group of three "Samambaia" poems that I already mentioned comes next in the collection.) Flannery O'Connor would have regarded them with the same steady humorous gaze (though she would have put them in more drastic situations), and I could easily imagine Manuelzinho with a change of name at Andalusia Farm. His poem is one of Elizabeth Bishop's most developed works of portraiture—an elusive maddening figure seen in the round, at different seasons, in different lights. Quotation hardly does it justice; the effect is unusually cumulative, and much lies behind this wry conclusion:

> You helpless, foolish man,
> I love you all I can,
> I think. Or do I?
> I take off my hat, unpainted
> and figurative, to you.
> Again I promise to try.

The remaining poems take us to different parts of Brazil where Elizabeth lived or travelled. "Twelfth Morning; or What You Will" is set at Cabo Frio (Cold Cape), which is east along the coast from Rio. This is another poem that radiates a "sense of glory" (I borrow the phrase from Herbert Read). The black boy Balthazár, coming out of the mist, over the "shopworn" dunes and debris and the rusted wire, is like a young prince, the four-gallon can on his head notwithstanding:

> You can hear the water now,
> inside, slap-slapping. Balthazár is singing.
> "Today's my Anniversary," he sings,
> "the Day of Kings."

And here at the end of the poem the rhymes finally emerge, the sense of glory is complete. One of Elizabeth Bishop's favorite poets is George Herbert; perhaps the naturalness of tone and the craftsmanship owe something to him. Placed between two longer, more ambitious poems, her own celebration of Epiphany (called "The Day of Kings" in Brazil) is modest but a delight.

"The Riverman" is so long that one could easily devote an essay to it. But perhaps this is unnecessary. It is partly worked up from *Amazon Town*, a book by the anthropologist Charles Wagley, as Miss Bishop acknowledges in her headnote. The book was published in 1958; she was writing her poem the next year. *Amazon Town* is admired in professional circles as a work of scholarship, and I should say that it is a work of considerable literary merit as well. There is no need to trace the prose passages that Miss Bishop has used; the important thing is the transmutation into poetry, and here James Merrill has made the right comment: "Wonderful, fluid, pulsing lines—you hardly feel the meter at all." (*Shenandoah*, Summer 1968). This poem of the river runs through 158 lines based on three stresses in each line: a constant undercurrent, as it were, for the action. (For comparison one might turn to Eliot's adaptation of the first paragraphs of *The Heart of Darkness* in *The Waste Land*, III.) An even more important matter is this: for the poet, the experience of reading Charles Wagley's book meshes with her own experience along the Amazon. It is like the case of Wordsworth's "Solitary Reaper"; we know he took the poem out of someone's travel-book, but he could not have brought it off without his excursions through the Lake District.

"The Burglar of Babylon" returns us to Rio and the apartment in Leme, which lies below the hill of Babylon. The *favelas*, or hillside slums, are now almost gone in this section, but fifteen years ago they were very much in evidence. This is Elizabeth Bishop's longest narrative. The subject was at hand; it was reported at length in the newspapers; and from the terrace of the apartment she could see the soldiers hunting down the young criminal Micuçú. How was this to be presented, given the possibilities? Elizabeth instinctively used the modern ballad, which for some readers means Auden's poems in this form, the ones about Miss Gee and Victor. (The latter, I should think, is more successful in its tragicomic treatment of a stereotyped subject.) "The Burglar of Babylon" also owes something to cinematic technique in its camera angles, its "cutting" from one shot to another. But its perspectives are finally verbal. Not only the echoes of the old ballad idiom, but the conversation of the people in the bar, Micuçú's auntie, the soldiers, Micuçú himself—all of this goes perfectly into traditional quatrains. The poem was first published in *The New Yorker* in November, 1964; simultaneously a remarkable translation by Flávio Macedo Soares appeared in the literary review *Cadernos Brasileiros* in Rio. The translation in fact testifies to the success of the original, as though the English and the Portuguese were descended from the same source:

> Nos morros verdes do Rio
> uma mancha temĭvel cresce:
> os pobres que vêm para o Rio
> e não têm como regresse.

All things considered, this is the best as well as the most humane of modern ballads.

Two more poems from Leme are included in the last section of *The Complete Poems*: "House Guest" and "Going to the Bakery." These are slighter than the Brazilian pieces in *Questions of Travel*. The details are sharply etched, especially in the latter poem (Flaubert himself would be impressed by the *progression d'effet*), but the sense of wonder, always one of Elizabeth Bishop's strong points, has diminished. The last of *The Complete Poems* (but far from the last of Elizabeth's poems, I'm glad to say) is "Under the Window: Ouro Preto." This is an affectionate tribute to a town in the mountains of Minas Gerais that has survived from the eighteenth century. Ouro Preto (Black Gold) was the capital of the state till about 1900, then abandoned and difficult to reach, then rediscovered during the last generation. It is a splendid repository of late-Portuguese baroque built during a period of wealth, much of it designed and executed by the legendary Aleijadinho, a poor crippled mulatto who became his country's greatest artist. Elizabeth, who had often visited Ouro Preto, even when the going was rough, finally succumbed to its charms in 1965 and bought an old house, which she proceeded to restore. It dated from about 1730. When the work began, she discovered that the *pau-a-pique*, the thick wall of wattle and mud, was actually tied together with rawhide in some places, and a bit of this architectural oddity was preserved under glass when the restoration was finished. And as usual a balcony, in this case overlooking the whole range of Ouro Preto on its steep hills. Although the trucks from the bauxite mines hurtled alarmingly close to the front door, a certain order prevailed inside. "Under the Window" is a low-keyed, amusing rendition of Brazilian life, so much of which is spent out-of-doors, and another demonstration of how a poem can be made out of the most unlikely materials.

[...]

I think that Elizabeth has lived through this experience many times; her translation is deeply felt. More recently she has filled out the picture, as it were, with three shorter poems from Carlos Drummond in the anthology of Brazilian poetry that she edited with Emanuel Brasil in 1972, and taken together, her versions of this poet's work are a considerable achievement.

This brief account of Elizabeth Bishop at a certain period of her career of course omits a great deal. For instance, she wrote several of her Nova Scotia poems during these years, and this is a locale to which she has returned imaginatively if not actually many times. The world of her poetry is large. Although it differs from that of Wallace Stevens in some ways, I think that she, more than anyone else today, has the same humanist vision of north and south, the seasonal round, the imagination creating its order sometimes in most discouraging circumstances.

An Interview with Elizabeth Bishop[1]

Ashley Brown

Brazil: Elizabeth Bishop's study is a small house which lies up the hill from her home in the mountains near Petrópolis, the old imperial summer capital. The study is perched above a waterfall. One looks through the windows at a clump of bamboos which descend to a tiny swimming pool, momentary repose in the course of the cascading water. The room is filled with books, comfortable armchairs, piles of old literary quarterlies. An exquisite oratório *from Minas Gerais and other small miscellaneous objects stand on the bookcases. A literary visitor will notice photographs of Baudelaire, Marianne Moore, and Robert Lowell near the poet's work-table. Tobias, an elderly cat, and Suzuki, his younger Siamese companion, reluctantly move from the vicinity of the typewriter.*

INTERVIEWER: I think you have one of the handsomest settings in the world. What poet could ask for more? Do you find that a dazzling

---

1. *Shenandoah* 17, no 2. (Winter 1966), 3–19.

Editor's Note: Ashley Brown, "An Interview with Elizabeth Bishop" from *Elizabeth Bishop and Her Art*, edited by Lloyd Schwartz and Sybil P. Estess (Ann Arbor: The University of Michigan Press, 1983).

landscape like this is an incentive to write, or do you prefer to shut yourself off from visual distractions when you are working?

MISS BISHOP: You will notice that the study turns its back on the view of the mountains—that's too distracting! But I have the intimate view to look at; the bamboo leaves are very close. Everybody who comes here asks about the view: is it inspiring? I think I'll put a little sign saying "Inspiration" on those bamboos! Ideally, I suppose any writer prefers a hotel room completely shut away from distractions.

INTERVIEWER: You have been living in Brazil since about 1952, haven't you?

MISS BISHOP: Yes, it was the end of November, 1951, when I came here; you remember my poem, "Arrival at Santos."

INTERVIEWER: As far as your poetry goes, have you been able to get anything from Brazil except its appearances? I mean, can you draw on the social and literary traditions here?

MISS BISHOP: Living in the way I have happened to live here, knowing Brazilians, has made a great difference. The general life I have known here has of course had an impact on me. I think I've learned a great deal. Most New York intellectuals' ideas about "underdeveloped countries" are partly mistaken, and living among people of a completely different culture has changed a lot of my old stereotyped ideas.

As for the literary milieu in Brazil, it is so remote from ours. In Rio for example, the French influence is still powerful. I find the poetry very interesting, but it hasn't much to do with contemporary poetry in English. Our poetry went off in a different direction much earlier.

INTERVIEWER: When you say our poetry went off in a different direction, what do you mean?

MISS BISHOP: What happened with Eliot and Pound as early as 1910—modernism. The Brazilians' poetry is still more formal than ours—it's farther from the demotic. It is true, of course, that they had a *modernismo* movement in 1922, led by Mario de Andrade and others. But they still don't write the way they speak. And I suppose they have still never quite escaped from romanticism. It's an interesting fact that there is no word in Portuguese for "understatement." Marianne Moore's poetry is nearly all understatement. How can they understand us? So much of the English-American tradition consists of this. They have irony, but not understatement.

By the way, I lived in Mexico for a time twenty years ago and I knew Pablo Neruda there. I think I was influenced to some extent by him (as in my "Invitation to Miss Marianne Moore"), but he is still a rather "advanced" poet, compared with other South American poets.

To summarize: I just happened to come here, and I am influenced by Brazil certainly, but I am a completely American poet, nevertheless.

INTERVIEWER: What about the Portuguese language? Do you find that reading it and speaking it (and being surrounded by it) have increased your awareness of English?

MISS BISHOP: I don't read it habitually—just newspapers and some books. After all these years, I'm like a dog: I understand everything that's said to me, but I don't speak it very well. I don't really think that my awareness of English has been increased. I felt much the same when I lived in France before the war. What I really like best is silence! Up here in Petrópolis, in the mountains, it is very quiet.

INTERVIEWER: How would you describe Portuguese as a poetic language?

MISS BISHOP: From *our* point of view, it seems cumbersome—you just can't use colloquial speech in that way. Grammatically, it is a very difficult language. Even well-educated Brazilians worry about writing their own language; they don't speak their grammar, as it were. I imagine it's easier to write free verse in Portuguese—because it gets you away from the problem. They did take to free verse very quickly here.

INTERVIEWER: Now, if I may, I'd like to recall you to North America and your childhood. You actually spent your earliest years in Nova Scotia, didn't you? Did you live in the kind of house where people encouraged the children to read? Or did your literary interests come later?

MISS BISHOP: I didn't spend all of my childhood in Nova Scotia. I lived there from 1914 to 1917 during the First World War. After that I spent long summers there till I was thirteen. Since then I've made only occasional visits. My relatives were not literary in any way. But in my aunt's house we had quite a few books, and I drew heavily on them. In some ways the little village in Canada where I lived was more cultured than the suburbs of Boston where I lived later. As for the books in our house, we had Emerson, Carlyle, all the old poets. I learned to read very early, and later I used to spend all of my allowance on books. They were all I ever wanted to buy.

INTERVIEWER: What were some of your favorite books? Were you ever deeply impressed by something you read in those days?

MISS BISHOP: I was crazy about fairy tales—Anderson, Grimm, and so on. Like Jean-Paul Sartre (as he explains it in *Les Mots*), I also read all kind of things I didn't really understand. I tried almost anything. When I was thirteen, I discovered Whitman, and that was important to me at the time. About that time I started going to summer camp and met some more sophisticated girls who already knew Emily Dickinson and H.D.

and Conrad and Henry James. One of them gave me Harriet Monroe's anthology of modern poets. That was an important experience. (I had actually started reading poetry when I was eight.) I remember coming across Harriet Monroe's quotations from Hopkins, "God's Grandeur" for one. I quickly memorized these, and I thought, "I must get this man's work." In 1927 I saw the first edition of Hopkins. I also went through a Shelley phase, a Browning phase, and a brief Swinburne phase. But I missed a lot of school and my reading was sporadic.

INTERVIEWER: Did you write anything much before you went to Vassar? I remember your saying you had some exceptionally good teachers at Walnut Hill School in Natick.

MISS BISHOP: I wrote a good deal, starting at the age of eight. When I was twelve I won an American Legion prize (a five-dollar gold piece) for an essay on "Americanism." This was the beginning of my career. I can't imagine what I said on *this* subject! I was on the staff of the literary magazine at school and published some poems there. I had a good Latin teacher and a good English teacher at Walnut Hill. The teaching was of a very high quality. I only studied Latin then. I didn't take up Greek till I went to Vassar. I now wish I'd studied nothing but Latin and Greek in college. In fact I consider myself badly educated. Writing Latin prose and verse is still probably the best possible exercise for a poet.

INTERVIEWER: You were in what turned out to be a brilliant literary generation at Vassar—Mary McCarthy, Eleanor Clark, Muriel Rukeyser, besides yourself. Did your friends set a high standard of criticism even in those days?

MISS BISHOP: Actually I was a close friend only with Mary. Eleanor and I were friends, too, but she left for two years, and Muriel was there for just a year. Yes, they, we, were all terribly critical then. One big event for us was a little magazine we started. Mary has recently talked about this. This is the way I remember it: The regular literary magazine was dull and old-fashioned. Mary and Eleanor and I and several others decided to start one in competition. It was to be anonymous. We used to meet in a speakeasy and drink dreadful red wine and get slightly high. (Afterwards the college physician analyzed the wine and found it contained fifty per-cent alcohol, she said, but I can't believe that.) We called the magazine *Con Spirito*. We got out only three numbers, I think, but we prevailed. I published several poems and stories in *Con Spirito*. T.S. Eliot came to Vassar about this time. I was elected to interview him and I was abso-lutely terrified. But he was very gentle, and later he flattered us by saying he liked some of the things in our magazine.

INTERVIEWER: In those days did you think about becoming a poet or a novelist?

MISS BISHOP: I never *thought* much about it, but I believe I was only inter-ested in being a poet.

INTERVIEWER: You grew up in the Marxist '30s. Do you think this radical political experience was valuable for writers? Or did it blunt people's per-ceptions to be thinking in such exclusively political terms?

MISS BISHOP: I was always opposed to political thinking as such for writ-ers. What good writing came out of that period, really? Perhaps a few good poems; Kenneth Fearing wrote some. A great deal of it seemed to me very false. Politically I considered myself a socialist, but I disliked "social conscious" writing. I stood up for T.S. Eliot when everybody else was talking about James T. Farrell. The atmosphere in Vassar was left-wing; it was the popular thing. People were always asking me to be on a picket-line, or later to read poems to a John Reed Club. I felt that most of the college girls didn't know much about social conditions.

I was very aware of the Depression—some of my family were much affected by it. After all, anybody who went to New York and rode the Elevated could see that things were wrong. But I had lived with poor people and knew something of poverty at firsthand. About this time I took a walking-trip in Newfoundland and I saw much worse poverty there. I was all for being a socialist till I heard Norman Thomas speak; but he was *so* dull. Then I tried anarchism, briefly. I'm much more interested in social problems and politics now than I was in the '30s.

INTERVIEWER: What poets did you meet when you started moving around in the world? I believe you have known Marianne Moore for many years.

MISS BISHOP: I met Marianne Moore in 1934, the last year I was in college, through Fanny Borden, the college librarian, an old friend of the Moore family. (I had read a few of her poems in anthologies.) I asked Miss Borden why she didn't have *Observations* in the college library, and she said, "Are you interested in Marianne Moore? I've known her since she was a child!" And she introduced me to her shortly afterwards.

When I was a junior, *Hound and Horn* had a contest for students. I sent in a story and a poem and got honorable mention for both. I also had a story and a poem in a magazine called *The Magazine*, run by Howard Baker and his wife. Baker's friend Yvor Winters wrote me; I think he wanted to take me under his wing. But nothing came of that. He introduced me to a former student of his, Don Stanford, who was then at Harvard.

INTERVIEWER: Were you in any way affected by Auden during the '30s?

MISS BISHOP: Oh, yes! I started reading him in college. I bought all his books as they came out and read them a great deal. But he didn't affect my poetic practice. I think that Wallace Stevens was the contemporary who most affected my writing then. But I got more from Hopkins and the

Metaphysical poets than I did from Stevens or Hart Crane. I've always admired Herbert.

INTERVIEWER: What do you like especially about Herbert?

MISS BISHOP: To begin with, I like the absolute naturalness of tone. Coleridge has some good remarks on this, you remember. And some of Herbert's poems strike me as almost surrealistic, "Love Unknown" for instance. (I was much interested in surrealism in the '30s.) I also like Donne, of course, the love poems particularly, and Crashaw. But I find myself rereading Herbert a great deal.

INTERVIEWER: Do you owe any of your poems to Herbert?

MISS BISHOP: Yes, I think so. "The Weed" is modelled somewhat on "Love Unknown." There are probably others.

INTERVIEWER: Do you have any comments on the religious poetry of the '40s? I am referring especially to the long poems by Eliot and Auden, also to such books as Tate's *The Winter Sea* and Lowell's *Lord Weary's Castle*. In those days we seemed to be moving into something rather unexpected, a brilliant period of Christian poetry. But this has scarcely continued, has it?

MISS BISHOP: As far as Eliot and Auden are concerned, I find Eliot much easier to understand. He led up to the *Four Quartets* by a long process. Eliot is not very dogmatic, not in his poetry (the prose is another matter). Auden's later poetry is sometimes spoiled for me by his didacticism. I don't like modern religiosity in general; it always seems to lead to a tone of moral superiority. Of course I have the greatest admiration for Auden as a poet. As for religious poetry and this general subject, well, times have changed since Herbert's day. I'm not religious, but I read Herbert and Hopkins with the greatest pleasure.

INTERVIEWER: Do you think it is necessary for a poet to have a "myth"— Christian or otherwise—to sustain his work?

MISS BISHOP: It all depends—some poets do, some don't. You must have something to sustain you, but perhaps you needn't be conscious of it. Look at Robert Lowell: he's written just as good poetry since he left the Church. Look at Paul Klee: he had sixteen paintings going at once; *he* didn't have a formulated myth to look to, apparently, and his accomplishment was very considerable. The question, I must admit, doesn't interest me a great deal. I'm not interested in big-scale work as such. Something needn't be large to be good.

INTERVIEWER: But some poets and critics have been terribly concerned about this, haven't they?

MISS BISHOP: Some people crave organization more than others—the desire to get everything in its place. Auden really thinks this way, I suppose. Marianne Moore, on the other hand, has no particular "myth," but a remarkable set of beliefs appears over and over again, a sort of backbone of faith.

INTERVIEWER: I know you have a lively interest in the other arts—music and painting especially. Have your poems been much affected by these things?

MISS BISHOP: I think I'm more visual than most poets. Many years ago, around 1942 or 1943, somebody mentioned to me something that Meyer Shapiro, the art critic, said about me: "She writes poems with a painter's eye." I was very flattered. All my life I've been interested in painting. Some of my relatives painted. As a child I was dragged round the Boston

Museum of Fine Arts and Mrs. Gardner's museum and the Fogg. I'd love to be a painter.

INTERVIEWER: What about "Songs for a Colored Singer"? You didn't compose those to tunes, as it were?

MISS BISHOP: I was hoping somebody would compose the tunes for *them*. I think I had Billie Holiday in mind. I put in a couple of big words just because she sang big words well—"*conspiring* root" for instance. As for music in general: I'd love to be a composer! I studied counterpoint and the piano for years, and I suppose I'm still "musical." But I wanted to be a doctor, too, and I got myself enrolled at Cornell Medical School. I think Marianne Moore discouraged me from going on with that.

INTERVIEWER: I wonder if you sometimes "feel" your way into a poem with a sense of its rhythms even before the subject has declared itself— you know, the way in which "Le cimetière marin" was composed?

MISS BISHOP: Yes. A group of words, a phrase, may find its way into my head like something floating in the sea, and presently it attracts other things to it. I do tend to "feel" my way into a poem, as you suggest. One's mind works in unexpected ways. When I was writing "Roosters," I got hopelessly stuck; it just refused to get written. Then one day I was playing a record of Ralph Kirkpatrick performing Scarlatti: the rhythms of the sonata imposed themselves on me and I got the thing started again.

INTERVIEWER: In composing a poem like this, do you start from a kind of pleasure in the stanzaic arrangement as such, or do you let the experience dictate the form?

MISS BISHOP: In this case I couldn't say which came first. Sometimes the form, sometimes the subject, dominates the mind. All other poets I've ever talked to say pretty much the same thing. On this subject I rather like Housman's essay, *The Name and Nature of Poetry*. That's only one side of the question, but it's very well stated.

INTERVIEWER: I wonder if you could reveal the *donnée* for your sestina called "A Miracle for Breakfast." It has an attractive surrealist quality about it, but I'm curious about the kind of experience which brought the poem into being.

MISS BISHOP: Oh, that's my Depression poem. It was written shortly after the time of souplines and men selling apples, around 1936 or so. It was my "social conscious" poem, a poem about hunger.

INTERVIEWER: That was the heyday of surrealism, too, wasn't it?

MISS BISHOP: Yes, and I had just come back from my first year in France, where I had read a lot of surrealist poetry and prose.

INTERVIEWER: When I read the poem here in Brazil, my students keep asking, "Was she waiting for the ferry?" You remember that early in the poem you have one crossing the river.

To move on to something else: "At the Fishhouses" is my favorite in your second book. This seems to me a kind of Wordsworthian poem, something like "Resolution and Independence." But your poem is mostly in the present tense and is more immediate and "existentialist." Wordsworth really seems to mean "emotion recollected in tranquillity" and puts his poem mostly in the past tense. Do you have any comment on this comparison?

MISS BISHOP: I think it's a question of how poetry is written. There has been a great change in the knowledge of, or at any rate the attitude towards, poetic psychology. One of the great innovators here is

Hopkins. When I was in college I wrote a piece on him. While I was preparing it, I came across an essay on seventeenth century baroque prose. The author—I've forgotten who—tried to show that baroque sermons (Donne's for instance) attempted to dramatize the mind in action rather than in repose. Applying this to Hopkins in the paper I was writing, I used a phrase which impressed me in "The Wreck of the Deutschland," where he says, "Fancy, come faster." He breaks off and addresses himself. It's a baroque poem. Browning does something like this, but not so strikingly. In other words, the use of the present tense helps to convey this sense of the mind in action. Cummings does this in some poems. Of course poets in other languages (French especially) use the "historical present" more than we do. But that isn't really the same device. But switching tenses always gives effects of depth, space, foreground, background, and so on.

INTERVIEWER: Perhaps something like switching keys in music.

MISS BISHOP: Yes, indeed, very much so.

INTERVIEWER: What do you think about the dramatic monologue as a form—you know, when the poet assumes a rôle? This "poetry of experience" has been very attractive to a lot of poets. I believe you have done this two or three times—for instance in "Songs for a Colored Singer" and "Jerónimo's House."

MISS BISHOP: I haven't given it much thought. Robert Lowell and others have done brilliant things in this form. I suppose it should act as a sort of release. You can say all kinds of things you couldn't in a lyric. If you have scenery and costumes, you can get away with a lot. I'm writing one right now.

INTERVIEWER: I've just been reading a poem of yours called "A Summer's Dream." It's a wonderful miniature, an evocation of a dying seaside town.

Every detail counts. Did you reduce this from something longer?

MISS BISHOP: I went for the summer once to Cape Breton. This little vil-lage was very small indeed. I think in the poem I said the population contained a number of freaks. Actually there were a few more people. But some exceptional giants came from this region, and I think in the poem I conveyed some idea of what the people were like. No, I didn't compress the poem.

INTERVIEWER: Do you find yourself revising a poem like this?

MISS BISHOP: No. After a poem is published, I just change a word occa-sionally. Some poets like to rewrite, but I don't.

INTERVIEWER: How did you happen to go to Key West, where you wrote some beautiful things? Did you find it a good place for writing?

MISS BISHOP: In 1938, I believe, I was on the West Coast of Florida to fish. I went to Key West just for a couple of days to see what the fishing was like there. I liked the town and decided to go back there in 1939, after another eight months or so in Europe. Eventually I acquired a modest but beauti-ful old house. I can't say Key West offered any special advantages for a writer. But I liked living there. The light and blaze of colors made a good impression on me, and I loved the swimming. The town was absolutely broke then. Everybody lived on the W.P.A. I seemed to have a taste for impoverished places in those days. But my Key West period dwindled away. I went back for winters till 1949, but after the war it wasn't the same.

INTERVIEWER: While I'm mentioning Key West, would you say something about John Dewey, whom you knew so well there? I think you'd agree that his prose style, even in his book on aesthetics, can be rather clumsy and does his reputation no good. But he was a very sensitive man, wasn't he?

MISS BISHOP: Yes, very. I found him an adorable man. He could work under any conditions. Even at the age of eighty-five he missed no detail. He and Marianne Moore are the only people I have ever known who would talk to everyone, on all social levels, without the slightest change in their manner of speaking. I think this shows something important about Dewey and Marianne Moore—they have the kind of instinctive respect for other people which we all wish we could have but can only aspire to. No matter how foolish your question, he would always give you a complete and tactful answer. He loved little things, small plants and weeds and animals, and of course he was very generous in dealing with people. I remember when "Roosters" came out in *The New Republic*; he read it and said, "Well, E*liz*abeth, you've got these rhymes in threes very well. I wish I'd learned more about writing when *I* was young."

INTERVIEWER: Some people might be surprised to know that Flannery O'Connor admired Dewey. The last time I saw her, in 1963, she was reading two of his books.

MISS BISHOP: Well, I'm sure she knew more about his philosophy than I do!

INTERVIEWER: You've been a literary associate of Robert Lowell's for quite a few years, haven't you?

MISS BISHOP: I think, and I hope, we have been very good friends for twenty years. Both his life and his work have been of great importance to me. He is one of the few poets whose name in a table of contents or on the cover of a magazine gives me a sense of hopefulness and excitement even before I've read the poem.

INTERVIEWER: What do you think of the turn his poetry has taken in the last few years—beginning with *Life Studies*?

MISS BISHOP: One does miss the old trumpet blast of *Lord Weary's Castle*, but poets have to change, and possibly the more subdued magnificence of his later tone is more humane.

INTERVIEWER: I think I have you about up to 1950 now. This would be the period when you had the appointment at the Library of Congress. You were there shortly after the Bollingen Prize fiasco, weren't you?

MISS BISHOP: Léonie Adams was my predecessor, and she got the worst of that affair. MacLeish had a good idea about the job, and some of the poets fitted in rather well. I didn't really earn my keep—I didn't give lectures and readings, in fact never do. But for the only time in my life I saw bureaucracy functioning, and it certainly contributed to my education.

INTERVIEWER: Like many literary people, you visited Pound during the '50s. Do you have any prose comment, as it were, to make about him? You've already put yourself on record in verse in "Visits to St. Elizabeths."

MISS BISHOP: I think I've said all I want to in that poem. I admired his courage enormously; he proved his devotion to literature during those thirteen years.

INTERVIEWER: By the way, I'm rather interested in the formal scheme of that poem. How did you hit on it?

MISS BISHOP: It's the old nursery rhyme, "This was the house that Jack built." I've always liked nursery rhymes, and this one seemed to work here.

INTERVIEWER: Here in Brazil poets like Vinícius de Moraes have been writing lyrics for *bossa nova*. Have you ever wanted to do something like this in English?

MISS BISHOP: I've always wanted to write popular songs, and I've tried several times but never succeeded. I like some popular song lyrics very much, "Mean to Me" for instance.

INTERVIEWER: I think quite a few people have already seen and admired your new poem, the ballad called "The Burglar of Babylon." It's a knock-out. Did you have any trouble in finding a suitable medium for this poem? It's really worked up from some journalistic material, isn't it?

MISS BISHOP: No, I sat down and wrote it almost straight off, with a few additions and changes. Most of it was written in one day. It naturally seemed to present itself as a ballad. It's a true story, taken from the newspaper accounts; I made only two minor changes in the facts.

INTERVIEWER: Did you actually see Micuçú being hunted down on the *morro* of Babylon in Rio?

MISS BISHOP: No, but I saw the soldiers. We could watch them through binoculars from the terrace of the apartment house.

INTERVIEWER: With your new book of poems, *Questions of Travel*, about to come out, what are your immediate literary plans?

MISS BISHOP: Well, they are always the same, to write poems when I can. I'm also planning a book of prose about Brazil. It is tentatively called *Black Beans and Diamonds*. It's to be a combination of a travel book, a memoir, and a picture book. I am quite interested in photography. I'd like to make Brazil seem less remote and less an object of picturesque fancy. It's not really so far from New York. I think that since the great naturalists (Darwin, Wallace, Bruce, and so on) there hasn't been much close observation (at least by foreigners) of Brazil. Except perhaps for Lévi-Strauss.

INTERVIEWER: What do you think about the state of American poetry right now?

MISS BISHOP: Very good. We have lots of fine poets. Perhaps I'd better not mention any names, but I really admire and read with pleasure at least seven of my contemporaries. As far as poetry goes, although I am afraid that is not very far, this is a period that I enjoy.

Emergence[1]

Carolyn Forché

Infancy is what is eternal, and the rest,
all the rest is brevity, extreme brevity.

—Antonio Porchia

Inspiration is not the granting of a secret or of
words to someone already existing: it is the granting
of existence to someone who does not yet exist.

—Maurice Blanchot

I was five months pregnant with my first and only child when we arrived in Johannesburg for what was to have been two years. It was summer in the southern hemisphere, the sky poached by sun and fog, and my first impression was such that in letters home we would describe this place as a "California with slavery." We had come to document apartheid in photographs and text. Officially, my husband would work at the *Time* bureau, and I would accompany him as wife and expectant mother.

For a brief time, I was able to work with the Soweto parents of

---

1. Carolyn Forché, "Emergence" from *Salmagundi* #123 (Summer 1999).

detained children, who wanted information about international human rights organizations. Without the necessary police permits which were impossible to obtain, we were nevertheless able to enter townships and homelands, led by churchworkers who knew how to avoid police roadblocks, and as my womb swelled, I also grew invisible, no longer attracting police who would not wish to involve themselves with so pregnant a white woman. My husband concealed his cameras, passing me the exposed film to keep under my maternity dress. The images produced from this film would not often appear in the press, however, as the media tacitly respected much of South Africa's ban on "visual documentation of unrest." Those who defied this ban found their employees deported, or unable to renew their visas, as would eventually happen to us. These were the last years of apartheid, as destiny would disclose, and South Africa was living under what was then called a "state of emergency."

Emerge, I wrote, *emergence: to rise, to come into the light, to rise up out of a liquid in which the subject has been submerged.*

My notebooks filled, as they had in other parts of the world: vignettes, aperçus, bits of utterance. There was world and paper, and each could cross the surface of the other, marking it lightly but indelibly. Writing was my way of knowing what was for me otherwise unknowable, and like Ryszard Kapuściński whom I admired, I preferred to work "in the forest of things, on foot, in the world," which I hoped to participate in, rather than experience.

There was never a question of my giving birth in apartheid South Africa. The plan had been to drive overland to Zimbabwe when the time came. I'm not sure why I hadn't anticipated the arduousness of such a journey, nor recognized the risks incurred by a thirty-five-year-old "elderly *prima gravida*," electing to receive her prenatal care from obstetricians on three continents, but I had not yet experienced the sea-change of motherhood, holding rather to an image of life continuing much as it was, but with a sleeping baby tied to my back.

Suppressed perhaps were the labors of my childhood as the eldest daughter of seven, tri-folding clouds of diapers, running bed linens through the mangle, stirring Catholic school uniform shirts in pots of starch. Lost were the babies' cries, the slow-thickening puddings and white sauce, mounds of socks to be matched and toddlers watched never closely enough. Left behind me, Saturday mornings scrubbing foyer and bath tiles with Fels Naptha, taking pails of oil soap to the rows of wooden dining chairs. I made lunch for the "little ones" when I was six, and by seven baked my first loaf of bread. So standing evenings at the open window over foaming dishes I began subliminally to narrate a bearable selfhood. During endless hours of menial work, I spoke to God, who surrounded me, then to voices in books, and finally to fields and sky, where a presence was. Writing, I thought, formed itself elsewhere and passed through me, coming out of my hands. It was mysterious and foreign, but the experience of its making could not be compared to anything else. In the act of writing, there was heightened being, which could be remembered as ecstatic. There was, first, what could be said, and later, the way of saying, which was superior to the said.

My mother and I shared the arduous work of caring for the six children she bore in the ten years after my birth. She would bring the newborns home, wrapped in delicate "receiving" blankets, and I would steal into the darkness of my parents' room to gaze at a new one asleep in the straw basinette, pale-haired and fragile, having made an arduous journey from God's world. My mother was almost a child herself when she began, or so it seems to me now. For reasons that can never be disclosed, she was perhaps ill-prepared for her brood: she had *wanted* many children, but had pictured us all as sleeping infants, wingless, perfect and from heaven. She made *Novenas* to the Mother of God, sang to us, wept, took to her bed and told us we would understand when we were grown. At night, while I read and wrote by flashlight under my blankets, I heard the clacking of her Royal manual typewriter, and eventually discovered the silvery Christmas box of her poems and stories, some clipped from newspapers, hidden in her mysterious closet among evening clothes no longer worn.

"Join the convent," she would advise me above the din during some shared task or another. So it was not as if I hadn't known.

We left South Africa precipitously on March 17, 1986, a month to the day before my son was born because, among other reasons, we had broken unjust laws, and I was afraid to risk giving birth in jail. Specifically, we were accused of violating the restrictive "Group Areas Act" by having black houseguests, and it was suspected that we were also disseminating "images of unrest" to the outside world. Our arrest, fervently desired by our "Rhodesian" landlady, was considered by our lawyers unlikely but possible.

We left behind the tag-sale furniture we'd assembled into a service-able household, including the straw cradle with its bridal mosquito net. In my hurry I left some of my notebooks, but these contained indeci-pherable drafts of poems and so would pose a problem for no one. I don't know if those lines will return to me in a patient hour, but the cradle appeared often for a time in my dreams.

I remember not feeling certain we were safe until the wheels were tucked into the belly of the plane. My son leapt and fluttered through the night. I wrote notes toward poems as we refueled in Madagascar, notes which had become, I thought, a substitute for what I had once considered "finished poems." We were enroute to Paris, and as this was the last day of my pregnancy when I would be accepted as a passenger on a commer-cial carrier, my son would be born there. A French photographer, Gilles Peress, had offered us his place, as he would be returning to document "The Troubles" in Northern Ireland, and would not return to Paris again for some time.

So it was that we lived for a year at 11 rue Schoelcher, in an atelier identical to Simone de Beauvoir's, who lived beside us at 11 bis. until her death that April. The two-storey windows opened on a luminous fresco of clouds, and from the little *loggia*, it was possible to gaze out over the graves in the cemetery of Montparnasse. In the armoire, there were books, and little paper soldiers fighting the Franco-Prussian war. At the farm-table, I translated the poet Robert Desnos, many afternoons alone with the windows open, conjugating the *future perfect*, ivy shivering on the cemetery walls, waiting for the infant to come, a Desnos line revealing itself, and I thought: *how is it possible that I am living here*, as if a childhood dream had found an empty theatre in which to mount a small production of its hopes?

By proclivity and circumstance, I had in recent years often been in countries shattered by suffering and war. Why? I might have asked, or well might have, anticipating the birth of a child. Men and women came into my life, offering to teach me things I could not otherwise learn, and I said *yes* out of curiosity, ignorance, a need to please, and a desire to obey God, *for* whom language had first come, in the form of spontaneous prayer-songs spoken when I thought no one was listening.

During my childhood, the stars were more thickly clustered, and they whispered. I was not "by myself" often, but when I was, sometimes felt that my "self" opened and left, remaining near*by* as the phrase would have us imagine. If I were in the house at those times, the furniture swelled toward me or diminished as if moving away, accompanied by a crescendo of air against glass, my own breath, some mysterious hum of world. This was a state my sister also experienced and it terrified us both. I would later understand that objects remain where they are, and space dilates between them as time passes. If I were outside, however, in the woods or fields behind the house, this was not so disturbing, perhaps because one does not expect fixity in nature. God was there.

Despite the efforts of the Sisters of St. Dominic, Order of Preachers, to promote the idea of a carceral earth and a juridical cosmos, I imagined rather that the earth was a school, and that humans and other life forms were *already* burning, as light issued visibly from them, and the world, if saved at all, would be saved entire. If this were so, there was work to be done, and I hoped to comport myself well enough that God would give instructions in a form I could understand. Such was my spiritual pridefulness that I appended a request that this instruction not be given by an apparition, which would surely frighten me to death. After many years in the labyrinth of such expectations, it quite circuitously became clear to me that my instructions were to say *yes*.

Until now, until Paris, this *yes* had entailed what I *thought* had been an acceptance of mortality, a willingness to forego self-protection as circumstances required, and a faith in the luminous web of souls dedicated to what may have been simplistically conceived as a teleological endeavor. However, I was now an expectant mother, and what I imagined I was doing was about to change, utterly and for my ever, not in increments but as a whole, not by extension but in essence. This would also happen to my "work," a place-holding term for the labor of nurturing the self-propagation of language.

One writes inescapably out of one's obsessions—linguistic, philosophical, formal, cosmological. During my formative years as a poet (and in my educational *milieu*), "form" was regarded as a container rather than a force, examined for its features and flaws rather than the consequences of its use. The poem was, as Charles Simic once put it, "an antique pinball machine with metaphors instead of balls." It was to be read as expressive of the sensibility of the poet, whose "voice" it conjured, and as an unparaphrasable utterance of complex figural interplay and patterned sound. The reader installed herself in this poem, reading analytically or "closely," so as to discern the intricacies of its making, rather as a watchmaker approaches the works with spring-pin tool and dust-brush. Thus machined, the poem was regarded as a species of discourse, to be valued for itself and for its utility as communicator of feeling and thought.

My first two published poetry books were written during my teens and twenties, in the mode of the first-person, free-verse lyric, a writing which seemed to me very much to corroborate *le monde vécu*, the lived world. I thought of words as the crystalline precipitate of conscious attention: particular, precise, and resonant with as much "poetic" euphony as I could "hear." At first, mother's college English textbook provided models, and I wrote mostly rhymed quatrains in unvaried iambic pentameter. Later, the nuns assigned the writing of "paragraphs," and after a demonstration which persuaded them that I had not been plagiarizing from an unknown source, permitted me to dispense with the topic-sentence/body/conclusion format, whereupon I wrote elaborate descriptions of natural phenomena. In early adolescence, I was startled to read lined free verse for the first time, which I did not understand but tried to imitate with disappointing results. There were some years of this. When my first book, *Gathering the Tribes*, was chosen for the Yale Prize, I received a letter from its judge, Stanley Kunitz, asking about my poetics, and as I was unaware of *having* a poetics, I wrote of my upbringing, and in response to questions regarding influences, named my mother and grandmother.

In my twenties, God's presence receded, and even the radiant and shivering poplars of my childhood achieved apparent visual stability. The world changed and changed again. I had been translating Salvadoran poet Claribel Alegría, because I was her daughter's friend, and because she was an older woman poet whose work had not yet appeared in English. So it was that when her nephew, Leonel Gomez Vides, appeared at my door for an unexpected three-day visit, I invited him in, whereupon he invited me to spend my Guggenheim year in El Salvador, then still at "peace," a euphemism for the silence of misery endured. I became what was later called a "human rights worker," and this work partially informed my second book, *The Country Between Us*, written feverishly but without the remotest sense of its "political" character or utility. Critical reception in the US was unexpectedly intense and mixed, but my focus was then on the collective work of building a network opposed to military intervention in Central America. Toward that end, I traveled through the United States for three years; later, human rights work would bring me to Northern Ireland, Israel, the West Bank, Lebanon and South Africa. During that time, I didn't focus on poetics as such, but not for lack of interest.

The safe harbor of France was where my intellectual and poetical life resumed. We lived in that small, sparsely furnished atelier in a manner more conducive to work than I had ever previously known. Wind carried the scent of narcissus from the graves to our open casements. Mornings the knife-sharpener cried up from the street, and like the other women, I raced out to have the kitchen knives honed. Our supply of milk and cheese was kept for a time on the sill, to the amusement of our *quartier*, until we bought a small refrigerator. Daily I wheeled my basket to rue Daguerre market, where I bought unfamiliar species of fish, seasonal fruits and vegetables, aged cheese, young wines, and such things as I have never managed to replace: hard Normandy cider, fresh lavender from Grasse. My command of French was still provisional, however, and I once mistakenly tried to buy two and a half kilos of parsley, to the amusement of *le commerçant*.

Aside from domestic pursuits, I spent my days writing and reading (in those days Martin Buber, Emmanuel Lévinas, Jean-François Lyotard, Phillipe Lacou-Labarthes, Paul Celan, Francis Ponge and Edmond Jabès), while translating Desnos, because I thought this effort would revive and improve my French. On the day before my delivery I completed the work, discovering on the final page some lines I had inscribed in a notebook during my first trip to Paris in 1977, and thus finding a poet for whom I had searched in the intervening years:

> *J'ai rêvé tellement fort de toi*
> *J'ai tellement marché, tellement parlé*
> *Tellement aimé ton ombre*
> *Qu'il ne me reste plus rien de toi.*
> *Il me reste d'être l'ombre parmi les ombres*
> *D'être cent fois plus ombre que l'ombre*

D'être l'ombre qui viendra et reviendra
dans ta vie ensoleillée

[I have dreamed so strongly of you
I have walked so much, talked so much
So much I have loved your shadow
That there now remains for me nothing more of you.
It remains with me to be a shadow among shadows
To be a hundred times darker than the darkness
To be the shadow that will come and come again
into your sun-blessed life.]

The discovery seemed magical and auspicious, and the next morning my labor began, so lightly that I did not at first realize what it was, and regretted my lifelong fear. After twenty-six hours, my son was delivered by caesarean, something I had not anticipated, but that my husband and the doctor had known was likely for weeks. I chose to be awake. I remember surgical lights, instructions in French, the intelligence of the eyes above the masks, a pressure, a sense of being pulled apart without pain, and then a weakening, more oxygen, a rapid exchange among the physicians, then my son held above me, silent and white then suddenly rosy and crying. For a moment, they let me hold him, and when he heard my voice the crying stopped. "He knows who this is," my husband said. I told him that I was his mother, and that everything would be all right. A day later I was given an emergency transfusion of two liters of whole blood. For some reason still unknown to the hematologists, I had stopped making red cells after the birth. There were tense hours, waiting for my body to begin its necessary work again. My son was beside me in an incubator, quiet, alert. I was utterly there, and when I came back I was still there, in a small hospital in Paris with the windows open.

We called him Sean-Christophe, this little one, this Other, who now called me to responsibility, and whom I could neither evade, comprehend nor possess as a *knowledge*. "The child lives," Martin Buber wrote, "between sleep and sleep...in the lightning and counter-lightning of encounter." With him I experienced a radiant interdependence of sensation and thought: he was of me but he was not "mine." He was as yet "unknown" to me, even though the egg that had contributed life to him had been with me since my own birth.

On paper in the following months, the "I" of my previous writing receded, having become an emptiness, replaced by a polyphonic and Schoenbergian symphony of cacophonous utterance. Absent this *I*, whose selfhood the poems formerly served, words became material and translucent, no longer transparently communicative of the sensibility I no longer possessed. This movement did not entail a repudiation, but was marked by a radical sense of unfamiliarity. Each page began *mis en question*: white, open, each word in all its plenitude marked the site of a wound. Anxious at first, I returned to my notebooks filled with "notes toward poems," and discovered nascent versions of the same phenomenon. These were not notes but the work itself, begun during my pregnancy, and without my conscious collaboration.

This was a work happening *with* me which was not *about* me, having to do with attention rather than intention, a work which would eventually disclose itself as self-altering rather than self-expressive. Rather than writing discreet (individual) poems from beginning to end, and passing them through a sieve of revisionary practice, I found myself attending to the work's assemblage, aware that I was creating a reading-space to be explored rather than received, but in the manner of one caught in a web of consequence. The historical density of the language seemed to limit its play of signification, as the cry of suffering remains a cry. This poetry did not have the function of recording or representing, but rather of attending to the making of its utterance.

The poems I had previously written now seemed the graveyard of possibilities. Tedium had taught me to narrate a self-in-the-world to relieve tedium. *Writing*, older than glass, younger than music, was no longer for me merely the guardian of the past, but a way into the open and the future. During the milk-hours of earliest morning, my son nursed beside the two-storey windows filled with cloud islands of a forming world. He seemed to see something I did not see. The ancients thought that light traveled from the eye to the world and this seemed so with him. He was at the gates of language, where only the invisible is obvious. Or so it seems to me now.

The World Is Large and Full of Noises: Thoughts on Translation[1]

Jane Hirshfield

Translation it is that openeth the window, to let in the light;
that breaketh the shell, that we may eat the kernel...

—Preface to the King James Bible

Even the physical embodiment of a sacred text is numinous: it is wrapped in leather or silk, stored in a cupboard used for no other purpose, copied over only by special scribes. It may be raised in both hands as an offering before being opened; it may itself be offered fragrant incense and sweet milk. All written work retains some trace, however faint, of this initial sanctity of the Word: the breath inhabiting Logos and the breath of inspiration are the same, each bringing new life into the empty places of earth. It is no wonder, then, that many different cultural traditions share an ancient prohibition against translation. As George Steiner has

---

1. Jane Hirshfield, "The World Is Large and Full of Noises: Thoughts on Translation" from *Nine Gates: Entering the Mind of Poetry* (New York: HarperCollins, 1997).

pointed out in *After Babel*, if a sacred text has been given to us directly by its divine source, surely it must remain exactly as it first appeared, each word preserved intact for the meaning it may hold. Whether in a sacred text or a contemporary poem, any alteration risks unwittingly discarding some mystery not yet penetrated.

Unease about translation does not just cover the exporting of texts into another language; their importation too can be problematic. Translation's very existence challenges our understanding of what a literary text is. Further, by asserting that things worth knowing exist outside the home culture's boundaries, translation challenges society as a whole. Translated works are Trojan horses, carriers of secret invasion. They open the imagination to new images and beliefs, new modes of thought, new sounds. Mistrust of translation is part of the instinctive immune reaction by which every community attempts to preserve its particular heritage and flavor: to control language is to control thought. The realization lends an extra dimension to the well-known Italian saying, "Traduttore, traditore" (Translator, traitor).

And still, translation occurs, playing an essential role in the innumerable conversations between familiar and strange, native and import, past and future, by which history and culture are made. It is integral to the way seed ideas and language strategies move out into the world, the new contending with the old until the translated works and forms are either rejected or naturalized. After sufficient time, shapes of thought and sound originally alien may themselves become the revered heritage, as certain exotic trees have come to be treasured in their new countries. Consider English literature, built almost entirely on the adopted powers of other traditions. Before the eleventh century's Norman invasion, English poetry relied on alliteration, not rhyme, for its binding sound, and the number of syllables within each metrical foot could vary freely. Yet what English speaker today would call iambic pentameter an imported meter, or think of the sonnet as an Italian form?

The desire to learn what lives within the incomprehensible speech of others is part of the deep-rooted human desire to know always more than we do. Such curiosity will overcome external limits, whatever the authority behind them—that is one lesson of Eden. And if the tale of the apple tells us the cost of such knowledge is death, and the story of Babel says that the price for pride of knowledge is a multiplicity of tongues, both offer no simple punishment. From each story's loss comes a gain: a sorrow, yes, but one that also gives birth to the continuing fertility and richness of this world.

What do poets themselves have to say of translation? On the fifteenth of February, 1924, Rilke inscribed these lines on the copy of *The Duino Elegies* he gave his Polish translator:

Happy are those who know:
Behind all words, the Unsayable stands;
And from that source alone, the Infinite
Crosses over to gladness, and us—

Free of our bridges,
Built with the stone of distinctions;
So that always, within each delight,
We gaze at what is purely single and joined.

With the gift of this poem about words' relationship to the Absolute, Rilke attempted to free his translator from the curse of "traitor." The Infinite comes into being only through the divided world of the particular, the poem says; while lesser, this realm of distinctions remains a realm of gladness, both necessary and good. By acknowledging that every word is both a reflection of his work's original mind and a path toward it, Rilke gave his translator his blessing to do whatever was needed. He offered his full trust that whatever the Polish words, the *Elegies* would remain alive.

The ontological issue at the center of Rilke's poem is this: where does a poem's true being reside? Surely poetry lives in the body of its words, as we live in our human bodies of bone and nerve, muscle and blood. Yet even in writing a poem's first draft, it often seems as if something were already there, which we hunt with words—something like the poem's soul. What else to call that magnetic pull of a destination unknown yet nonetheless present and calling, which causes a writer to accept one arising phrase and reject another, or to delete or alter or expand during revision?

The act of writing is a making, but also a following: of the mystery of source as it emerges into form; of the wisdom of the heart-mind as it encounters the wisdom of language. Translation asks a similar leap of faith. It becomes possible only if we trust that poetry lives both in its words and beyond them, and that at least some portion of this ur-poem can cross the abyss between one verbal body and another.

The Sung dynasty poet Yang Wan-li wrote on this subject as well:

> Now, what is poetry?
> If you say it is simply a matter of words,
> I will say a good poet gets rid of words.
> If you say it is simply a matter of meaning,
> I will say a good poet gets rid of meaning.
> "But," you ask, "without words and without meaning,
>   where is the poetry?"
> To this I reply: "Get rid of words and get rid of meaning,
>   and there is still poetry."
>
> (trans. Jonathan Chaves)

Yang argues against any idea of poetry that is unchangeable, unchallengeable, or fixed. In his use of meaning to urge us to pass beyond meaning, in his use of words to pass beyond words, he points to the mode of knowledge described in the Heart Sutra, the central text of Zen: "no eyes, no ears, no nose, no tongue, no body, no mind, no consciousness." The description does not mean that an awakened person is blind, struck deaf, numb to the world, and dumb. Rather, such a person is one who knows the world directly, without mediation, and knows the self in its widest existence, reflected in all things. The poet, too, is free to see with no eyes, to speak with no tongue. Poetry will continue on its own path, untroubled.

From the open spirit of these two passages, translators may take heart. Though I only encountered their words years after undertaking a cotranslation of the work of two classical-era Japanese women poets, I nonetheless found in them a retrospective reassurance, and also a kind of blessing. The old prohibitions live on as a useful self-doubt in the translator, ensuring that original texts be approached with due care. But still the silk ribbons of the home language must be cut, for the work to be read by others.

Knowledge is erotic. We see this not only in the Bible's dual use of the term "to know," but also, as classicist Anne Carson has pointed out, in the Homeric verb *mnaomai*, which means both "to hold in attention" and "to woo." What we regard must seduce us, and we it, if we are to continue looking. A great poem creates in its readers the desire to know it more thoroughly, to live with it in intimacy, to join its speaking to their own as fully as possible. We memorize it, recite it over and over, reawaken it with tongue and mind and heart. Many translators describe their first encounter with their chosen authors as a helpless falling in love: a glimpse of a few translated fragments can lead to years of language study in order to hear directly the work's own voice. And in matters of art, it seems, Eros is generous rather than possessive: the translator wants to reciprocate this gift received, to pass the new love on to others—and thus the work of translation begins.

A writer may turn to translating for therapeutic reasons as well, at times for self-cure, at times in the spirit of a physician prescribing for others. The translator-as-patient hopes some power of the original will enter her own work, or else uses translation as a way to keep fit during periods of nonwriting. Robert Lowell names both motivations in his introduction to *Imitations*; it isn't hard to see how the work of that book helped him both develop his range and, at the same time, step a little free of his own preoccupations. Kenneth Rexroth, another poet-translator, describes the curative aspect of translation at its best in his essay "The Poet as Translator": "The writer who can project himself into the exultation of another learns more than the craft of words. He learns the stuff of poetry. It is not just his prosody he keeps alert, it is his heart."

The translator-as-physician, on the other hand, hopes the new work will correct some misdirection or gap he perceives in the literature of his own time and language. Ezra Pound put forward both the troubadours of medieval France and the classical poets of China as good medicine for the lack of vigor he saw in English-language poetry in the early decades of this century. More recently, Robert Bly insisted that American writers attend to the Spanish and South American poets of the "deep image" in order to open themselves to the less-tamed realms of imagination. Each successfully altered the literary practice of his contemporaries. William Tyndale, who also translated in the spirit of correction, offers a more cautionary example. Hoping to bring greater accuracy to the scriptures in English, he published the first Biblical translation made from earlier Hebrew and Greek texts rather than from the then-standard Latin— and was burned at the stake in 1536. His Catholic accusers found too Protestant a cast in his "untrue translations."

For me, the decision to enter into the realm of translation came about through the meeting of accidental opportunity and long-standing desire, under circumstances I will relate a little later. I have translated as an amateur, almost always in collaboration, and always because there was something I had encountered in a brief sampling and wanted to read more fully. I have translated, then, for perhaps the most selfish of motives: simple greed. There were poems I wanted to read, but they lived in another tongue.

Once the process of translation begins, the translator enters into an erotic engagement with the chosen text, reading the poem again and again for its meaning, its resonance, its kinetic and musical bodies, its ambiguities, rhetoric, grammar, images, and tropes—for all the rustling of its many leaves and for the silences at its roots as well. The translator reads in the desire to join with what she reads, placing the life of the poem thoroughly within her own, discovering how each entering word modifies that life. As with any engagement, there are the families to consider as well: the translator's knowledge of the historical and cultural context of a poem, its religious background and its intentions, and the translator's own development as poet and as person—all these will contribute to the outcome.

In the midst of this interchange, both translator and poem change their natures. The poem that in its original form may contain a multitude of possible readings becomes in translation a poem in which a particular interpretation is more likely to predominate—though if the translation is a good one, the new poem will also have its resonance and overtones, its unconsciously preserved wisdom. The translator is changed in the way any important encounter changes a person: taking in a new vision of being, our own grows to include it. Eventually, the efforts and pleasures of courtship come to their natural conclusion—there is the leap, the moment of union when the translator joins with a poem so intimately that there is no longer a sense of "self" and "other," and the poem emerges, as if for the first time, within one's own heart and tongue.

At times in this process, the translator may feel not only a union of self with poem, but also a kind of identity with the translated author. Paul Valéry describes this sense of merging well in his essay in *The Art of Poetry* on translating Virgil, "Variations on the 'Eclogues'":

Faced with my Virgil, I had the sensation (well known to me) of a poet at work. From time to time I argued absently with myself about this famous book, set in its millennial fame, with as much freedom as if it had been a poem of my own on the table before me. At moments, as I fiddled with my translation, I caught myself wanting to change something in the venerable text.... "Why not?" I said to myself, returning from this short absence. Why not?

(trans. Denise Folliot)

Freedom from the words of the original combined with a deep love of its words lies at the heart of translation. In the act of true translation, as opposed to the act of parsing out meaning, there is a moment when all prior knowledge of a poem dissolves, when the words that *were* are shed as a snake sheds its skin and the words that *are* take on their own life. Some part of the poem's essential life, its way of traveling through the world, must pass through the emptiness that runs like a broad river-gorge between languages: the impossibility of any word, even the simplest, remaining the same in a different tongue. Think of *bread, panne, brot*— their entirely different flavors.

Translation occurs precisely in that moment of forgetfulness and dissolving, when everything already comprehended through great effort—grammar, vocabulary, meaning, background—falls away. In that surrendering instant, the translator turns from the known shore of the original to look into that emptiness where the outlines of the new poem begin to resolve, a changed landscape appearing through mist. This experience, as Valéry wrote, is almost indistinguishable from the experience of writing itself: the sense of active creative discovery is the same. Yet somehow, the original ur-poem is also there, crossing along with the translator the waters that surge between Rilke's Unsayable source and words.

If a certain sense of freedom is essential to translation, that is because fidelity's claims are so strong. Yet fidelity is in this realm a chimera. A literal word-for-word trot is not a translation. The attempt to recreate qualities of sound is not a translation. The simple conveyance of meaning is not a translation. What then can fidelity—even a fidelity already recognized as failure—mean?

Every translator can offer principles and explanations for having been more or less literal at this point, choosing one nuance of meaning over another at that, omitting "the untranslatable" here or adding there some information commonly understood within a poem's home culture. In my experience, though, these are after-the-fact descriptions of a process of choice-making as mysterious and intuitive as writing itself. Fidelity's multifaceted nature, impossible to define in the abstract, reveals itself only in practice. The attentiveness and flexibility required are as individual as those that make for a good marriage.

Writers and critics have nonetheless long debated the nature of translation, its possibilities, philosophies, and practice. Samuel Johnson, for instance, offered the oft-quoted opinion that the true test of a translation is whether it makes a good poem in English—a statement that holds myriad assumptions within its scope. Robert Frost, however, made clear that for him the original music was all—and unreproducible—in his famous assertion that "the poetry is what gets lost in translation." But "the poetry is what gets transformed" is Octavio Paz's response to Frost:

> After all, poetry is not merely the text. The text produces the poem: a set of sensations and meanings.... With different means, but playing a similar role, you can produce similar results. I say similar, but not identical: translation is an art of analogy, the art of finding correspondences. An art of shadows and echoes...of producing, with a different

text, a poem similar to the original.

Most poets who translate share Paz's sense of the process, though the ways they interpret it vary. The quest to reproduce the original poem's effects as much as its words—an idea Valéry also expressed—permits the issue of "fidelity" and "license" to dissolve on the tongue. Only such an understanding allows the impossible work to go on at all.

Walter Benjamin, in the classic essay "The Task of the Translator," raises the issue of another kind of fidelity. Benjamin suggests that a poem should not read entirely as though it were written in the new language but should preserve some flavor of the syntax and grammar of the original. To convey this idea, Benjamin quotes Rudolf Pannwitz:

> Our translations, even the best ones, proceed from a wrong premise. They want to turn Hindi, Greek, English into German instead of turning German into Hindi, Greek, English.... The basic error of the translator is that he preserves the state in which his own language happens to be instead of allowing his language to be powerfully affected by the foreign tongue.... He must go back to the primal elements of language itself and penetrate to the point where work, image, and tone converge. He must expand and deepen his language by means of the foreign language. It is not generally realized to what extent this is possible...

The proposal intrigues. Robert Fitzgerald, however, has responded to it by saying: "So to make something that is strange to our ears would not be doing justice to the work that was not strange to theirs." Fitzgerald's fidelity is to the work as it affects us, Pannwitz's to the various nature of thought in different languages. Each practice brings its gifts, though my own inclination is closer to Fitzgerald's: to seek an English-language style that reflects the language qualities of the specific work rather than those of the home language as a whole.

Almost all translators face the question of whether or how to retain a poem's formal structure. The main philosophies closely mirror those we have just seen: some translators attempt to replicate the formal qualities of the original, others try instead to convey the underlying effect without reference to prosodic form. The fundamental issue is not merely if form should be translated, but whether it can be.

It is worth remembering that in formal poems, as much as free verse, the subtle parts are where the real musical power is likely to lie. Occasionally, both form and content can flourish in the new version; Richard Wilbur's translations from the French are examples of what is possible when a poet, linguist, and translator of genius hold one pen. But in lesser hands, a coarsely mechanical reproduction of outer form can be more a disservice to a work's nature than the decision to turn to free verse. Form ill-married to meaning and breath places over the translated words a badly painted mask, a parody of their original grace.

Yet free-verse translation may seem a kind of surrender. Still, what is lost in that choice can be remedied at least a little with information about the original's form. Once the reader knows a poem was originally in rhymed couplets, those effects can be intuited; it is less easy to guess what else has been altered in order to reproduce rhyme-scheme and meter in a poorly done formal translation.

Best are bilingual editions, put into the Roman alphabet if necessary, along with a guide to pronunciation. Given this help, even a reader wholly ignorant of a language can sound a work out, while those with some familiarity can use the translation to gain better entry to the original, as well as to judge for themselves the choices that have been made. Still another method can be found in the many Penguin Books anthologies where the original appears accompanied only by a prose trot. If the reader is lucky, a work will exist in multiple translations—in their points of overlap and divergence, the hands of translators and author may be distinguished, though the original music remains out of reach.

Free-verse translation can still honor the essential movement of a poem. The parallelism of Chinese poetry is an indispensable and anchoring part of its nature, for example; though that language's tonal parallels cannot be brought into English, parallel sentence constructions can be kept. Their shapeliness holds part of the poem's information, subtly communicating its relationship to order, balance, and form itself.

To take another case, the alternating five and seven syllables of Japanese poetry are something most American ears fail to perceive, and so my own choice as a translator was to forego the original meter. But I held to the number of lines: to render a three-line haiku as a couplet, or a five-line *tanka* as a quatrain, for me would mask the asymmetrical unfolding of the originals, making them seem less different in aesthetic and worldview than they are. Yet many translators—from both ends of the spectrum of freedom and form—have chosen differently.

A translator's first obligation is to convey each poem's particular strengths. If music and intricacy of form are the greatest pleasures in the original, this is what the translator should try to capture; if a startling directness of language is at the heart of a work, then straightforwardness should govern the new version as well. Imagery, sensibility, feeling, sound, ideas—any of these can become the through-line of a poem's unfolding. One cannot perform vivisection on a living being; some mix of these elements will be present in any well-realized poem, and equally present in any translation. The issue, though, is to what extent a new version can mirror the original, to what extent it must find some differing path toward the same destination, "So that always, within each delight, / We gaze at what is purely single and joined."

Every poet leaves the landscape of poetry altered by his or her passage through it. One way this alteration occurs is when a writer comes to a new mode of vision through either making or reading translations;

Whitman's *Leaves of Grass*, with its King James Bible influenced rhythms and lists, is a good example of that process. The strengths of a great poem or tradition are only truly *translated* if they come into the language in a way that can then be used. Just as English takes in foreign words (*tao, zeitgeist, anima*) when no native one will do, so forms of poetic thought discovered in translation can work to expand what may be said.

"Unless there is a new mind, there cannot be a new line," William Carlos Williams wrote. The converse is true as well. When there *is* a new mind, or a new line, American poetry has shown a spongelike ability to absorb it. The imagist movement, of which Williams was part, brought to American poets some of the strategies of classical Chinese and Japanese poetry. A more recent example is the adoption of the *ghazal*. An Urdu form consisting of long-lined couplets linked in the original primarily by sound, it ends with a "signature" couplet in which the poet includes his or her name. In 1970, a scholar of Urdu, Aijaz Ahmad, invited seven American poets to help translate a collection of ghazals by the poet Ghalib. Some were translators as well as poets, others not. Several went on to use the form in their own writing; Adrienne Rich in particular included a number of haunting ghazals in her subsequent collections. From that beginning, the ghazal has entered contemporary poetry as a mode of writing marked more by a disconnectedness between thoughts and stanzas than by the intricate prosodic rules of the original form. But this oblique adoption is precisely how translation transforms: not by exact imitation but through a kind of hybridization, in which some kernel of the original's power is both preserved and changed.

Translation is one way the poetic mind refreshes itself, old forms of thought-making opening themselves to new ones. It is also a way the old is itself made new: one side-effect of translation (unless the work is also contemporary) is the recasting of a poem's relationship to time. This happens because translations are virtually always placed into the language of the present.

When an original grows old, its dated words and syntax serve as a kind of watermark. Age in itself gives substance—what has lasted becomes a thing worth keeping. An older poem's increasing strangeness of language is part of its beauty, in the same way that the cracks and darkening of an old painting become part of its luminosity in the viewer's mind: they enter not only the physical painting, but our vision of it as well. This is why seeing an old painting suddenly "restored" can be unnerving— we recognize a tampering with its relationship to time, miss the scented smoke of the centuries' passage. For just this reason, seminal works such as Chaucer's *Canterbury Tales* in English or *The Tale of Genji* in Japanese are "translated" from archaic into contemporary language only when they have become almost unintelligible to general readers (and even then, students continue to memorize a passage or two in the original form). But in bringing a work from one language into another, translators must decide whether to attempt to instill in their work a false patina of age or to recreate the freshness of diction the piece would have had in its own time. Usually, the second approach is chosen.

Older translations can become works of interest in their own right. People turn to Pope's Homer not to know Homer, but to know Pope's vision of him; most who now read Chapman's version have been sent there by Keats. Pound's versions of Rihaku (Li Po), called the best existing translation from the Chinese when they were made, are still thought that by some; they are also thoroughly Pound's. In his work we can see the American poet—thoroughly the product of his own time and tradition— suffusing and being suffused by the Chinese. The translations mark the tangible joining of two great tributaries of poetry's river.

For the most part, though, translations are ephemeral: each time current diction changes or the culture's idea of what constitutes a poem shifts, new translations are made. Victorian-era translators of Japanese haiku commonly put the unrhymed originals into rhyme—a poetry without rhyme was not, for many of these scholar-translators, poetry at all. We can see how such older translations reflect the aesthetic expectations of their makers in unconscious as well as conscious ways, yet it is virtually impossible to see the biases of one's own age. The continual remaking of translations may seem like a movement further and further from the original; it can be seen also as a way of returning a work to the perennial freshness of its original state.

As George Steiner has pointed out, the practice of choosing archaic language when translating ancient texts, while now rare, can serve a useful purpose, helping to ground the new version within the linguistic history of its new culture. A reader encountering a style of language he had come to expect in literature from the past would feel immediately and strongly "at home" in the new work, particularly if the work in question was already part of his cultural tradition. The King James Bible, surely the greatest translation English has seen, was put into a diction several generations older than that spoken at the time it was made. Creative accident, rather than conscious decision, may have played a part in this—the King James translators had been instructed to retain the best of earlier versions. But however it happened, the result was a translation whose clarity, beauty, and power so overwhelm that its language forms remain, four centuries later, a living force.

My own experience as a translator dates from 1985, when during a year as a Guggenheim fellow I started collaborating with Mariko Aratani on a translation of the poetry of Ono no Komachi and Izumi Shikibu, the two foremost women poets of Japan's classical period. I had first encountered a handful of their tanka in English as an undergraduate taking courses in Japanese literature in translation. The Japanese women's concerns—love and transience—paralleled my own, and despite the passage of a millennium since its composition, their poetry held for me an immediacy and power that was life-altering. Not only did it affect my own writing, it led me three years later to undertake the study of Buddhism; in 1979 I was lay-ordained in the lineage of Sōtō Zen.

I first realized the need for a larger selection of Komachi's work in 1971, and I waited almost fifteen years for someone to make it possible for me to read more. Then a fortunate introduction to Mariko—a weaver, jazz pianist, and native speaker of Japanese who also loved the classical-period poets—led to our translating a dozen poems together for a journal. We quickly decided to continue working toward a book-length selection of the two poets' work, eventually titled *The Ink Dark Moon*. Although in this account I will say "I" in describing the way a few poems from that book traveled from literal to final versions, Mariko Aratani's contribution at every stage was indispensible to the finished work. Her expertise went far beyond skills of language.

The poems appear here first as they did on the worksheet Mariko and I devised. During weekly meetings over the course of a year, we created such a sheet for each poem we considered for the book. Along with the original and rough translations were Mariko's comments covering background information, grammatical uncertainties, the nuances of certain words, and so on. I wrote down each Japanese poem in *romaji* (the Roman alphabet transliteration of spoken Japanese). The core English meaning (or meanings, if more than one were possible) appeared below each corresponding word, and the metrical line-units of the Japanese were separated by a slash mark. Through this system Mariko could give me access to both the sound of the original poem and its original syntax, something that even the most literal rough translation cannot do. I would then take the sheets away and work toward finished translations, returning them always to her for rechecking.

Here is a first poem, relatively straightforward to translate, by Izumi Shikibu, the greatest of Japan's women poets:

NADOTE	KIMI /	MUNASHIKI	SORA	NI /	KIENIKEMU /
why	you	empty	sky	in	disappear did (?)

AWAYUKI	DANI	MO /		FUREBA	FURU	YO	NI
Frail snow	even	!		when falling	falling	world	in

A prose headnote—not uncommon in Japanese poetry—offers more information about the poem's background: "Around the time Naishi [Shikibu's daughter] died, snow fell, then melted away."

Why did you vanish
into empty sky?
Even the fragile snow,
when it falls,
falls in this world.

The finished translation is quite close to the literal, with only minor adjustments of word order and a few changes of word choice: "vanish" for "disappear," "fragile" for "frail." Japanese does not use articles before nouns, and so in bringing the poem into English, I might have also chosen to say, "Why did you vanish / into *the* empty sky?" Why didn't I? One reason was rhythmic—the extra syllable seemed to my ear to clutter the poem. But more important, there was the difference in meaning. Without the article, Shikibu's daughter not only rises amid her cremation smoke into the sky, she also becomes that emptiness and absence—an effect that the inclusion of the article *the* would have diluted.

The five-line free-verse translation reflects but is not identical to the formal structure of the original. Japanese poetry's conventions for transcription onto the page are unlike those of English. Its vertical columns do not use visual breaks to mark each metrical unit, and at least one translator from the Japanese, Hiroaki Sato, advocates forgoing them entirely. My own feeling, however, is that for Western readers the line break is the fundamental signal that they are encountering a poem: words to be met with the mind and expectations of poetry. Even had I followed strictly the Japanese tanka's syllabic pattern of 5-7-5-7-7, the translation's fundamental "poem-ness" would not have been clear to American readers: English verse speaks a language of stresses rather than count, and American ears do not hear the pattern. Further, the two languages differ enough that metrically exact translations often are forced either to leave out parts of a poem's meaning or else add unnecessary words to fill the count. Both reasons affected my choice of form.

Another poem, one of Shikibu's most famous, required more extensive changes to bring the Japanese into English:

KUROKAMI NO /   MIDARE   MO   SHIRAZU /

Black hair   's   messiness, tangling (obj)   without knowing
                                                without caring

UCHIFUSEBA /   MAZU   KAKIYARISHI /

when lying prone   first   stroked
                  clear

HITO   ZO   KOISHIKI

person   !   longing

This poem is one continuous sentence, and the first task in approaching it is to determine the grammatical clauses governing meaning. In Japanese, word order is often the reverse of that in English and a syntactical break often appears after the first two or three line-units in a tanka. Using these principles, the poem's basic meaning quickly resolves itself: "While lying down without caring about black hair's tangling, longing for the person who stroked it first." This then became:

Lying alone,
my black hair tangled,
uncombed,

I long for the one
who touched it first.

The largest change between the original and the translation is that the poem has been placed into a grammatical voice, the first person. Many tanka, like this one, do not specify their speaker or point of view. This reflects not only Japanese grammar but also a culture in which experience itself, not the subjective frame around it, is felt to be important; a few lightly sketched phrases evoke a situation in which the reader becomes an equal participant. English, however, demands grounding. To follow the original grammar too closely would only mute the impact and emotional immediacy the poem carries in its own language.

A second departure from the literal is the word *alone*. My after-the-fact explanation (in actual practice, this is simply how the poem spoke itself after studying, joining, and forgetting earlier described) is that it rises out of *shirazu*—"without knowing or caring." This woman neglecting her hair is surely in the solitary aftermath of a love affair. Finding herself alone, she has no reason now to attend to her physical beauty; but she remembers such a time—not the recent love, but her first.

Shikibu, we know, was disowned by her family and divorced by her husband (Naishi's father) after she began a love affair with an imperial prince, who soon died. Later in life she took many lovers, and the reputation of "floating woman" came to accompany her reputation as a poet of surpassing insight and lyrical skill. Shikibu apparently tried to reestablish communication with her husband many times; though he never replied to her letters, he is almost certainly the early love she recalls in this poem.

A last change from the literal is that for the one word *midare* I used two: "tangled, uncombed." "Uncombed" and the earlier "alone" probably arose together, the near-rhyme giving the poem a music satisfying to my ear and the sound of the long *o* holding the poem's resonant grief; the word also reflects the indifference to self contained in *shirazu*,

201

"without caring." The textured physicality of the word works as well to bring Shikibu's presence vividly into the poem. This is true to the original's spirit: Japanese critics have long pointed out that Shikibu's tangled black hair is one of very few references to the details of physical life in all Japanese poetry.

I took more liberty still with this poem by Ono no Komachi, written around the year 850:

ITO	SEMETE /	KOISHIKI	TOKI	WA /
very	extremely	longing	time	—

UBATAMA	NO /	YORU	NO	KOROMO	O /
hiougi nut	's	night	's	clothing	(obj)

KAESHITE	ZO	KIRU
turned inside out	!	wear

Born roughly one hundred fifty years before Shikibu, Komachi was one of the first women members of the court culture to benefit from a newly developed system for transcribing spoken Japanese using Chinese characters. During this period Chinese served the Japanese court as the language of both writing and government, much as Latin functioned as the learned language of medieval Europe. Education in Chinese was reserved for men, however, so only with this new writing system could women participate fully in the literary life of a culture in which artistic skill was becoming a paramount value, and the exchange of poetry a central mode of communication.

Poems were written to express private feeling, but also to conduct a courtship, convey condolences, or demonstrate publicly (in frequently held official competitions) one's talent, learning, and refined sensibilities. Because the imperial court's women, unlike the men, wrote solely in the vernacular, they became primary creators of the great literary flowering of that age. Komachi in particular, living at the start of the era, brought to the writing of tanka a fiercely passionate nature, technical mastery as a poet, and, at times, a profound insight into Buddhist teachings.

The poem above shows Komachi's explicit revelation of passion. It also makes use of a technical device specific to Japanese poetry, the *makurakotoba*, or pillow word. A pillow word, much like a Homeric epithet, is an image that regularly accompanies its noun—the *wine-dark* sea is one familiar Homeric example. Like the cushion on which the round bowl of a temple bell is placed, a pillow word worked both to elevate a poem and to increase its resonance. And as with the wine-dark sea, the meaning of pillow words are often so archaic as to be baffling, unless one somehow discovers that the ancient Greeks did in fact make a wine whose color was closer to purple-blue than red.

The poem shows Komachi alone and missing an unnamed lover. Many of her poems are responses to seeing her absent lover in a dream. In one, she wishes she had never wakened; in another, she determines to commit herself to a life of dreaming; in a third, she mourns the cruel fact that even in their dream-meetings she and her beloved meet in the fear of being seen. In this poem, however, we see Komachi before sleep, turning her nightgown inside out—a folk custom believed to make one dream of one's love.

Here is the version appearing in *The Ink Dark Moon*:

When my desire
grows too fierce
I wear my bedclothes
inside out,
dark as the night's rough husk.

To American ears, the opening phrase of the original might seem abstract rather than emotional, but the phrase *ito semete* ("very extremely") is rare in tanka and would have stood out; later in the poem, the word *zo* also functions as an intensifier. My response was to replace the usual translation of *koishiki*, "longing," with the stronger "fierce desire." Because Japanese readers would at least be aware of the folk custom explaining why one might reverse one's nightgown when feeling longing, I chose to begin the poem with "When," to indicate that a causal connection exists. I also tried to give my translation of the pillow word, "hiougi-nut," an extra imagistic vividness and weight. Researching this pillow word for "night," I learned that the nut has a virtually black shell; I then made rather free with the image to create the last line of my version.

One thing translation teaches is that other choices may always be made. Here is an alternative translation of mine, closer to the original in one way, more free in another:

Longing,
fiercely longing—
To dream of him
I turn my bedclothes inside out
this dark-husked night.

For a final example of my own experience as a translator, here is another poem by Komachi. One of her most famous, it illustrates a different technical device of Japanese poetry, the *kakekotoba*, or pivot word: a word that can be read in two different ways, both intended to be part of the poem. (The pivot words below are indicated by an asterisk between the alternative meanings in English.)

HANO	NO	IRO	WA /	UTSURI	NI	KERI NA /
flower	's	color	(subj)	faded	has	alas

ITAZURI   NI /   WAGA   MI   YO   NI   FURU /
uselessly   my   body   world   in   aging
                                                     *
                                                 falling

NAGAME   SESHI   MA   NI
long rains   doing   while
  *
watching

Komachi here confronts transience in a manner quite different from that of Shikibu in her poem mourning her daughter. When she wrote these words, Komachi most likely was still in the midst of her life at court but would have been realizing that time must be nearing its end. A single woman would not be welcome in that world so centered on love and beauty once her own beauty was gone.

> While watching
> the long rains falling on this world,
> my heart, too, fades
> with the unseen color
> of the spring flowers.

The heart of the poem is its complex and skilled interweaving of its various images of passing time. No translation can convey kakekotoba with justice, and it is possible that no one from a different culture can fully appreciate the depth of regret expressed in Komachi's image of uselessly fading spring flowers. Where a poet of ancient Rome responded to transience and mortality with the proud attitude of *carpe diem*, the poet of classical-era Japan acquiesced with a heart full of sorrow, believing that such deep feeling was the mark of being human. The adjacent pivot words *furu* and *nagame*, with their multiple readings, create between themselves a kind of harmonic resonance. The poet is watching her own aging, the long rains are falling, she looks out of her window upon a rain that causes flowers to fade without being viewed, she herself grows older without being known by her lover. It is the other side of Komachi's passionate dream-life we see in this poem: the long hours of waking and solitude, the realization that human life is fleeting and the pleasures of youth and beauty even more fleeting.

Unlike most of the poems Mariko Aratani and I translated, this one exists in many different English versions; it was one of the poems that had first aroused my interest in Komachi and her work. Because it is much translated, and well, I felt a certain freedom (and a certain responsibility) to make it my own. In this version—one of eight or ten quite different drafts that I made—the idea of "aging" is implied by the fading spring flowers rather than stated, "uselessly" is clarified for the Western reader with "unseen," and the word for "body" became "heart" in an effort to make a poetic statement that flowed as seamlessly as possible. A "heart," I think, can both "watch" and "fade"; for a "body" to do so would seem incongruous. I could as easily have simply used the pronoun *I*, since the phrase *my body* is often used simply to indicate the grammatical first person. That is the choice made by Kenneth Rexroth, in his concise translation of this poem, and also by Burton Watson:

The colors of the flower fade
as the long rains fall,
as lost in thought,
I grow older.
(trans. Kenneth Rexroth)

The beauty of the flowers faded—
no one cared—
and I watched myself
grow old in the world

as the long rains were falling.

(trans. Burton Watson)

From even this small sampling, it is easy to see the range of possible choices in bringing these thirty-one syllables into English. In yet another version, Rexroth allowed himself almost complete freedom:

As certain as color
Passes from the petal,
Irrevocable as flesh,
The gazing eye falls through the world.

(trans. Kenneth Rexroth)

Though Japanese tanka are unrhymed, the varying sound of the words is part of their effect—much as it is in American free verse—and I would not want to close my description of working with these poems without touching on that part of the task. In my own version of Komachi's poem, the consonants and vowels shift as it progresses, culminating in the final "flowers," which contains most of the recurring sound elements of the poem; as in the opening line, especially, of the Japanese, the sounds of *o* and *a* preside. Japanese and English prosody are quite different, but my hope was that at least some of the effects of Komachi's music had found its way into the translation.

Translation is one way of learning what delicate clockwork causes a poem to keep accurate faith with music, meaning, and time. But even beyond this, translated poetry brings new realms of being. For me, encountering Komachi's and Shikibu's poetry at the age of eighteen wasn't simply an introduction to new ways of making poems that were moving and beautiful—their work taught me to see and feel differently, introduced to my life a new vocabulary of responses.

The twentieth century's flowering of translation brings with it the richness good poetry always brings: new spiritual and emotional and ethical understandings, new ways of seeing, new tools of knowledge as significant for an increase of inner life as radio telescopes are for an increased knowledge of the spiraling arms of distant space. If translators have an overriding responsibility, it is to carry these new powers in English as fully as possible, by understanding what may serve as a means of perception, what must remain in the ground of the original language, untranslatable and beyond reach. Our desire as readers remains the same as that expressed by the translators of the King James Bible—to break open the shell, that we may eat the kernel.

Translation that serves truly will widen our knowledge of what poetry—what humanness—is. When I read, as one still can, some spirited defense of English iambic meter as a basic expression of human nature, I despair. How can the authors of such essays not acknowledge that great literatures have been made of other meters than our binary or triple ones? That not all languages are stressed? That English-language forms, though they may be full of strengths and powers to our ears, are not the only possible forms? We should know these things not to reject the powers of our own linguistic history, but to welcome the powers of others. Poetry's task is to increase the available stock of reality, R.P. Blackmur said. It does this by reflecting for us our many human faces, our animal faces, our face of insect wings, our face of ocean and cliff. The world is large and, like Caliban's island, full of noises; a true poem reflects this, whether in the original or in translation. To try to encompass such knowledge, to be willing to fail, to prepare as fully as possible the work of poetry, to make the attempt in the recognition that any understanding is one among many—this is all we can do, as translators or as readers.

Many writers describe the attempt to bring the world into language as itself an act of translation. It is an attempt that must always fall short, and still the effort is made. One depiction of why appears in the inner dialogue captured in Robinson Jeffers's sonnet "Love the Wild Swan." The sonnet progresses by straightforward rhyme until the final three lines, which move into eye-rhymes that are not ear-rhymes. Then the poem, like the wild swan it describes, begins to escape our human forms, though not our lives.

Love the Wild Swan

"I hate my verses, every line, every word.
Oh pale and brittle pencils ever to try
One grass-blade's curve, or the throat of one bird
That clings to twig, ruffled against white sky.
Oh cracked and twilight mirrors ever to catch
One color, one glinting flash, of the splendor of things.
Unlucky hunter, Oh bullets of wax,
The lion beauty, the wild-swan wings, the storm of the wings."
—This wild swan of a world is no hunter's game.
Better bullets than yours would miss the white breast,
Better mirrors than yours would crack in the flame.
Does it matter whether you hate your...self? At least
Love your eyes that can see, your mind that can
Hear the music, the thunder of the wings. Love the wild swan.

This last, brief poem is by the ninth-century poet Kūkai—the Japanese Buddhist monk who, according to legend, developed the system for using Chinese characters to write Japanese words. Like the poem by Rilke at this chapter's beginning, it describes the relationship of source and manifestation; of word and Mind and the manifest, multiple world.

Singing Image of Fire

A hand moves, and the fire's whirling takes different shapes,

Triangles, squares: all things change when we do.
The first word, "Ah," blossomed into all others.
Each of them is true.

Glimpses of Vietnamese Life[1]

Denise Levertov

Part I

The overwhelming impression I brought back from my visit to North Vietnam two months ago was of a people who were not only unalienated from their society but who enthusiastically identified with it; a people whose striking grace and gentleness is both a characteristic shared with other peoples of Southeast Asia and a result of the sense of security given them by their genuine revolutionary solidarity.

I have spent the last few days typing page after page of factual material accumulated during my stay. I was beginning to feel I would never get it all down and to despair of conveying a feeling of the place, even with all my facts, or perhaps just because I had too many facts. So I began over, reliving impressions.

---

1. Published in *American Report* (Part I, February 26, 1973; Part II, March 12, 1973), and written follow-ing my visit to Hanoi, together with fellow poet Muriel Rukeyser and Jane Hart, war-resister and wife of US Senator Philip Hart (D-Mich.), just before Nixon's re-election.

Editor's Note: Denise Levertov, "Glimpses of Vietnamese Life" from *The Poet in the World* (New York: New Directions Publishing Corporation, 1973).

Flying in from Vientiane, looking down at the great range of thickly forested mountains, relieved to see they were not pocked with craters but seemed endlessly green and impenetrable. Then the descent, green, lakelike rice paddies, little thatched houses, the broad curve of the river—and at last after our three-day journey stepping out into the Vietnam that has been in our thoughts daily for years now, but has seemed almost mythical in its remoteness.

Brilliant sunshine, smiling faces, and flowers at the barrier—yes, for us, from our hosts, the Union of Women and the Committee for Solidarity with the American People, and three young interpreters. We all hug each other, there is laughter, and a few tears of excitement.

While a young administrative assistant from the Solidarity Committee, who has one of the most memorable warm smiles I've ever seen, goes to see to our luggage, we all repair to a little waiting room where we are served the first of the innumerable cups of delicious green tea we drank that week. As we walked to the waiting room I found myself next to Lien, one of the interpreters. My arm around her, I felt the silkiness of her long black hair and her fragile, almost childlike shoulders. All three of us feel huge all the time we are in Vietnam.

With free use of the horn to warn the many bicyclists, the water buffaloes, and oxen, the people with one-shoulder yokes moving with the swift balancing step that reminds me of Mexican tortilla sellers coming down into Oaxaca from San Felipe, we drive into the city of Hanoi. (Now, in January 1973, I shudder as I think how that whole across-the-river district, half urban, half rural, has been blown to smithereens. How many of those very people, the first passers-by I saw in Vietnam, died among those ruins?) It is not only the gait of the people carrying goods to market that reminds me of Mexico, but the thatched small dwellings, the banana, jacaranda, palm, and *tabachin* trees, red-blossomed with feathery leaves.

On arriving at the hotel, what joy! I find my "brother," Nguyen Cong Hoan, waiting to greet me and meet my companions. He is the elderly novelist I met in Moscow in December 1971. He was there to visit a granddaughter studying (as many Vietnamese students do) at a Soviet university. I had been invited to Russia to meet some poets.

We made friends quickly and deeply, and he honored me by saying we were henceforth brother and sister. There were tears at our parting; he was not young, and was going back to the air raids, and at that time it had seemed unlikely I would have the chance to visit Hanoi in the foreseeable future.

Now we meet joyfully. I find that he is very famous and revered, and is loved above all as a humorist. Other members of our third host organization, the Writers' Union, who are at the hotel to welcome us, tell me this and add that he is considered a "national treasure."

The hotel rooms: very clean, simple, well-equipped, each with bathroom and balcony. There are rubber sandals by each bed. The style of the room reminds me of Italian moderate-priced provincial hotels. There are *jalousies* at the balcony doors and mosquito nets on the bed, which make a curious kind of little tent when unfurled. However, there don't seem to be any mosquitos.

A feature of the rooms—and nearly all Vietnamese rooms I was in—is a table set with a teapot, two small teacups, a tea caddy full of green tea, and a thermos full of hot water! Brought up to believe tea-water must be at a rolling boil, I am amazed.

Sensitive to our possible travel fatigue, which we are too excited to feel, they have arranged that our first outing be to peaceful lakes and parks. There is some bomb damage visible on the way. We are embarrassed at being VIPs driving fast through the almost carless, bicycle-filled streets of a country that *our* country is blasting. But there is no other way for us to see all that we are to see in a week, and we come to accept it.

It seems strange to be strolling by the shore of one of several lakes within city limits (among them the legendary lake in which a hero of old found the golden sword by which he put the Chinese to flight—a sword which, when he later returned it with gratitude to the water spirit, changed to a jade-green dragon and vanished beneath the waters).

Yes, it seems strange, watching men and boys fishing, children at play in the late-afternoon amber light, to be experiencing so much peace here, where I expected to share in some of the physical struggle of a land that has indirectly changed my life. The peace we experienced in Vietnam, not only this day but also in so many moments and hours during our stay, was the peace at the heart of the storm.

An apricot sunset, relaxed, slightly hazy dusk, mild air. Temples, pagodas. Superb topiary—tamarisk bushes cut into elephants, lions, birds. And everywhere the man-sized cylindrical holes, lined with concrete, that are the highly effective air-raid shelters we have seen in photographs. There is a little water in the bottom of them; gardeners have been sprinkling the grass and flowers. Lids lie ready by the holes.

All this relaxation is of course because no raids have occurred in over two weeks. Many children have been temporarily brought back to the city from the rural areas to which they were evacuated, though no schools at any level up through university are open in Hanoi. "We missed them so," some parents say to us.

Vigorous cockcrows in the center of town wake us in plenty of time for early Sunday Mass. Our hosts want us to see that religious observances are not suppressed here.

The large cathedral is full. The congregation is divided, men on the left, women on the right, and the men's side is as full as the women's. Moreover, there is a surprisingly high proportion of young people. Also a few gray-habited nuns.

The music is European. We are late, and stand near the back, so I don't hear if Mass is said in Latin; a hymn is sung in Vietnamese.

Coming out into the square before the cathedral with the rest of the congregation, we find others waiting to come in to the next Mass. Near the church doors, at the tops of the steps leading down to the square, were the only two beggars we saw the whole time we were in Vietnam, old men with "mandarin" beards like Ho Chi Minh's beard in his later years. People over sixty-five are pensioned, but some few, I was told, who had always been beggars—perhaps since childhood—still beg out of habit. I did not see anyone give to them.

Ho Chi Minh's picture hangs in all official buildings and public places such as the hotel lobby, and in people's homes too. But there are no giant-sized posters of him, like the representations of Mao one sees in pictures of China, or of other leaders elsewhere. These pictures, usually photos, not idealized representations, are never larger than the pictures one sees in America of John Kennedy for instance; and they don't show him in heroic poses but as Uncle Ho, very human, no taller than anyone else, often with others beside him, often with children.

Similarly, there is no equivalent of the Little Red Book or of North Korea's similar book; when the words of Uncle Ho are quoted, they are lines from his poems, or sometimes ancient proverbs he liked to use. No heavy leadership cult, but pride and affection, personal as if he were each person's beloved uncle.

I go with Muriel to the St. Paul Hospital, where she has to get a foot infection treated. The nurse in charge is very gentle. In the visitors' book in the waiting room I read notes of thanks, in French and English, from various foreign visitors who have been treated there.

In the treatment room I watch the witty, patient, French-speaking doctor, a man I'd love to talk with longer, carefully scrub up and attend to the infection on Muriel's foot, and I note that student nurses as well as the head nurse address the doctor directly and without the fear of authority that is traditionally instilled in the minds of "probationers" (as they are called in England, where I was once one myself).

Later we are at the Bach Mai Hospital (yes, the same one on whose very existence the despicable Jerry Friedheim of the Pentagon cast doubt—before he had to admit grudgingly it had indeed been hit). The tall thin director—recently described in a French journalist's report after the terror bombing as running desperately from area to area of what had been his hospital, organizing the digging out of whoever was still alive under the rubble—escorted us on a tour that included those parts of the hospital that had already been bombed before our visit (late October) and the busy wards in full use. Even in these there are signs of damage—cracked plaster is being repaired by groups of workers, male and female, and there's a sound of hammering and sawing.

We are stunned by the encounter with two patients' cases in particular. One is never fully prepared for the sight of suffering. These are two children, boys, each in small separate rooms, each with a silent, stony-faced mother sitting by his bedside.

One has lost both legs from just below the knee. His left arm and his body are bandaged, too. He lies on his back, expressionless, toying and toying with a little spool of some kind he holds in his hands. The nurse tells us it is good he exercises his fingers—the arm injury has partly paralyzed the arm but the full use of it may return. We think of how his feet will never return, and even if he can be fitted with artificial legs eventually, he will never run and jump again. He is only eight years old.

The other is a couple of years older. Bomb fragments[2] have lodged in his brain, as well as elsewhere in his body. His head is swathed in bandages—his face looks out of its turban with a strange expression, disoriented. It is probable the brain damage is irreversible. We cannot speak. Going out into the sunlight again, we take photos of bomb craters in the gardens.

At the Writers' Union we read poems to each other in our own languages, then our wonderful chief interpreter Quoc, who is twenty-eight and has a

---

2. I.e., pellets from an antipersonnel weapon, of the type which has over three hundred pellets to a "bomblet" and over six hundred "bomblets" to each "mother bomb." Formerly made of metal, these pellets were "improved"; that is, are now made of a plastic undetectable in the victim's flesh by X-ray.

wife and two young children but looks about sixteen, gives instant paraphrases of them, which from Vietnamese into English, at any rate, are remarkably poetic. Those of us, both Vietnamese and American, who speak French amplify his versions. Mr. Quat of the Solidarity Committee, who speaks English well, is there to help out also.

A marvelous atmosphere of good fellowship, not only from them toward us but *between* them. None of the rivalry one can too often feel at writers' gatherings.

Huy Can reads a poem about the messages hastily scrawled on the walls of his home town of Haiphong after the bombardment—"I have the baby safely and have gone to Tu's house," or "Our son was hurt and I have gone to the hospital. Look for us there," or "Don't go into what's left of the house. It's dangerous."

I'm reminded, by his use of the vernacular, his collage—but more than collage—of things actually seen and heard, of the spirit and practice of William Carlos Williams, and I tell them a bit about him. (Later I find a French translation of "An Ode to Whitman" by Huy Can.) They listen with close attention. They don't want to hear as much about the politics and the antiwar efforts and "protest poetry" of American poets as about poetry itself.

There are more men than women at these gatherings at the Writers' Union, but women are represented, too. One of the women poets is very young and pretty. She brings her little boy with her and I draw him a picture. Later she brings me a gift—a large earthenware pig and piglets, symbol of many good things.

Secretary General of the Union is Nguyen Dinh Thi, poet and novelist, born in 1924, whose first books were printed on jungle presses during the struggle against the French. He was twice imprisoned, and commanded a battalion of the Liberation Army.

He's a man whose physical beauty and grace of presence are inseparable from his moral and spiritual beauty and grace. He speaks to us of how he sees the war not only as the clash of forces, two national identities, but as an experience that reveals clearly the worst and the best on both sides.

Like a storm, he said, it blows the lid off things, it reveals the garbage of bestiality hidden by the cloak of civilization. The horror of uncontrolled technology has been shown us, technology in the service of immoral men. "And," he told us, "we in Vietnam can understand your shame because we have *our* shame too, that people like Thieu, going further than any other puppets, actually invite the US to come and bomb their own country." He said this is not only because it was true but because in the kindness of his heart he wanted to alleviate our burden of shame at being members of what has become the Monster Race.

That same storm, he continued, has also revealed the best—in America as well as in Vietnam. It was interesting to me that he cited Norman Morrison as a paradigm of that best. Communism in the DRVN is characterized by its humanity, exemplified in this instance by the reverence in which Morrison, a Quaker, a pacifist, whose political action took the ultimate Buddhist form of self-immolation, is held, and not by Thi alone but by many people. Later we were to hear a poem famous in Vietnam, written by To Huu, one of the best-known poets, born in 1920, which is a monologue spoken by Morrison to his baby daughter. And I find his name in other poems too. His life sacrifice burns on in Vietnamese hearts.

The goodness of America, Thi went on, is not in the ascendant; yet the catalyst of the war has brought about the coming together for a common goal of many people of different backgrounds. "Don't think all your actions are in vain. Your support is important to our morale. And we have a proverb, *Many breezes make a big storm*. If peace comes, we will thank not whoever is in power in America, but the steadfast peace movement. The green bud has more potential than the yellow leaf."

Thi speaks of the ancientness of Vietnam. Pottery has been found there two thousand years older than any from India and China. There is evidence that rice was first cultivated in the Red River and Mekong

Delta. He speaks of how, always under pressure from large and oppressive foreign powers, the Vietnamese survived as a people, retained and developed their identity, by developing a strong sense of mutual aid, of personal relations. "We can sacrifice all for independence, but we are also an open-hearted people. We cherish life but are fearless of death." As I listen to him I realize that profound truth is being spoken, not a rhetorical statement:

The American fear of death, with America's resulting funeral industry, America's obsession with the "new," even America's racism which ties in with the Western equation "white equals purity, light, and life; black equals corruption (sin), darkness (of the grave), and death," (followed by "black as hell")—surely, I remind myself (for it is not an original idea) this is the same fear that erupts in American violence and—ultimately—genocide.

And conversely, the amazing ability of the Vietnamese not merely to fight on under such material odds but to be so generous, so discriminating between culprits and victims, between one American and another, and to be so cheerful and kindly in their relations with each other— surely it does indeed stem from their simply not having the obsessive fear of death.

They don't *court* death but they accept it, and *thereby* are able to truly "cherish life." "My people," says Thi in his soft but clear voice, "are gentle and merry." And later, "As a writer, I don't find the regime a *perfect model*, I see it rather as a slow accretion that is *in process*. As a poet, that is a joy to me—to witness and participate in that process. We are *finding the way*. Each day must be a new invention."

This is the life that our government, in our name, has been attempting to pulverize.

Part II

I begin the writing of this second group of recollections of my fall visit to North Vietnam after the cease-fire has been announced. Though there is relief in knowing that, for the moment at least, the people and scenes I am describing are not subject to constant threat, nevertheless with each word, with each face or field that comes into the mind's eye, comes the thought, "Are they still there? Did they survive the December terror bombings?"

We drive in a jeep, followed by two others, south from Hanoi. Jane Hart and I are in different jeeps, each with guides and interpreters.[3] In the third jeep ride our accompanying photographer and some aides. We are soon out of the city and into a landscape of tender, moist shades of green, full of the "water-mirrors" I had imagined in a poem, "What Were They Like?," written in 1966.

The growing of rice is staggered so that one sees it concurrently in many different stages of development: some fields are flooded, with no shoots visible above the water, in others the vivid young rice looks quite short, and in others it grew taller than I had realized; it looks similar to other grains, high and tasseled.

The roads are fairly straight in this flat country, and not dusty even when unpaved, for the soil seems to be a wettish red clay. Indeed the colors are reminiscent of Devonshire or parts of North Carolina, but with the luxurious vegetation of these latitudes. Many clusters of banana and other fruit trees and lines of palm trees give variety to the wide terrain. Sometimes we see a range of mountains on the horizon, clear-cut, manifold. The sky's light, joyful blue deepens as the sun mounts; two or three indolent clouds are reflected in the rice paddies, again giving me a feeling of *déjà vu.*

Buffalo, slow as clouds, ruminate here and there by the roadside; others, with their masters, plunge vigorously through the watery fields;

---

3. Muriel Rukeyser remained in Hanoi during this excursion.

sometimes both man and beast are under water up to their chests, but one of my guides tells me land that is this wet is not desirable. Along the roads go pedestrians and cyclists—men and women and sometimes children—some not riding but pushing the bicycle, loaded with heavy but manageable sacks of produce or other materials, tied to a central pole.

Every now and then an oxcart passes; more rarely, carts drawn by small horses—or an army vehicle, camouflaged not with paint but with real branches. Many of the military personnel we see, even in Hanoi, wear wreaths of green branches around their helmets—perhaps for coolness rather than for camouflage. It gives them a bucolic appearance eminently suitable to soldiers who are basically and deeply attached to rural areas.

As we pass through hamlets strung out by the roadside we often notice families eating just outside their small thatched houses, sitting at tables placed under a tree or a palm-leaf shelter. Sometimes we see little restaurants in the same style, and shops. For some reason there are an enormous number of barbershops, all thriving. I laugh with my interpreters and guides about this. We are very gay.

Even as we laugh I think to myself how strange it is to be having such a good time in this war-scarred country, the idea of which has been like a heavy lump in my chest day and night for years. But not just this day in the country, *every* day I experienced from my Vietnamese friends the swift-flowing movement of feeling from laughter to tears, from grief to joy, and back again. And I came to feel that while I personally may be volatile, that is not what the Vietnamese are: it was not anything shallow or easy I was witnessing but the free play of genuine emotion possible only to a people with deep roots in their culture, their soil, and at the same time with the abundant flowering branches of security and hope that their revolution has given them.

With the same companions in laughter I share the tears of extremely painful experiences. I have a photograph that commemorates the first:

it shows me holding hands with a woman who looks at me sorrowfully. Sunglasses hide my own expression, but in fact I was crying. Around us, looking concerned, are other people—some of my companions, some of her neighbors. We had just come out of her tiny house built on a dike, its floors beaten earth but all within immaculate.

Much of its space was occupied by two large platform beds, plain but solid-looking. And on one of them sat her eleven-year-old daughter. The father had ushered me in, graciously but humbly. The little girl, silent, patient, and otherwise perfectly formed, had had a foot blown off by yet another antipersonnel bomb. Nothing, nothing to say. I stumble out into the noon heat, the mother follows. We stand there gripping each others' hands tightly. Her neighbors crowd around—a murmur does not alter the basic silence. And at last we unclasp our hands and I depart. Three months have gone by since that day, but I feel I am still standing there within that moment.

We are crossing a river on a ferryboat. Mme. Bé, of the Union of Women, and I get out of our jeep and stand gazing downstream. Mme. Bé is conversing with one of the many other ferry passengers—most of them pedestrians. When we get back in and drive on, up the dike on the far shore and over onto the ongoing road, Bé tells me of what had passed between her and the old woman with whom she had spoken.

"Who are the women from the distant place with whom you are traveling?" inquired the old lady—dressed in blouse and trousers dyed to a shade of powdery brick red, a color much worn in the Delta, the very color of its earth.

"They are Americans—visitors from America," Bé told her. "Americans! Yanquis!" exclaimed the old lady, horrified, shifting the weight of the carrying pole balanced on her shoulder, a bundle or basket dangling from each end of it. "Why do you want to bring such evil people here?" "But these are friends—friendly Americans, not those who come to kill us."

"Ah, good then; it is good that they come."

Immediately appeased, immediately ready to believe we are indeed friends, not the enemy. Mme. Bé laughs as she tells the tale—but I can't laugh. It seems to me too important, too moving, not funny at all. The old lady is probably illiterate—one of the small minority, all in the over-sixty age group, to whom the revolution's work in education, which reversed the literate/illiterate ratio, came too late.

Her reactions are direct, not filtered through any medium but her own experience. She has seen the cruel and rapacious landlords go, justice and self-improvement and mutual aid established in village life, the tragic, arranged marriages of her younger days become history, along with famines, diseases, and the high rate of infant mortality.

She has seen the growth of the Women's Union, which promotes and safeguards the rights of all women, young and old, married and single, and which has a branch in every town and village of the North. She has seen happy children going to schools that simply did not exist except for a tiny elite when she was young, and students returning from the universities to share their knowledge—as nurses, doctors, agronomists, teachers—with the people of their home villages.

And she has seen the huge bombers from a country half the world away fly over implacably, wave after wave, year after year, attempting to smash all this happy activity with mysterious, inexplicable brutality. Yet when these strange, tall, pink-faced women appear out of nowhere and she is told they are Americans, how quickly and how trustingly her initial horror is succeeded by a friendly acceptance of their being some other kind of American, not the destroyers.

This generosity of spirit, typical of what I observed, results from what I so frequently felt was an embarrassing overestimation, on their part, not only of the strength and dedication and size of the antiwar movement in America but of the degree of general good will existing among the mass of people in the US toward the people of Vietnam.

At the village guesthouse where we spend the night, we sleep in one spacious room. The large platform beds, two on each side, are almost like separate rooms once the mosquito nets are drawn down. The beams of the high roof are beautifully carved. This was once part of a Buddhist temple. The sleeping room is entered through a large living and dining room, where we were served a delicious supper and breakfast. Outside, a long veranda runs the length of the building (the men in our party sleep in an identical set of rooms further along it) and on the veranda, flanked by flowerbeds and potted plants, are washstands with jugs of water, towels, and soap.

In back of the building is a set of outhouses. Returning to the main building from the outhouse early in the morning, I stop to watch the mist rising over a nearby pond. Across the water, beyond the water lilies, a path adjoins the bank. I glimpse children leading water buffaloes out for the day, an older schoolboy with books and bicycle, women with baskets talking to each other. Smoke from morning cooking fires rises with the mist. Birds are singing.

Last night an air-raid siren had sounded in the far distance, but this morning there are only pleasant, mild, life-sounds in the quietness. Someone is playing a bamboo flute under the persimmon trees. This is a glimpse of the immemorial village life so many Vietnamese poems and stories celebrate—what Thi, our poet friend in Hanoi, hoped we would see, calling it the root, the core of all things Vietnamese.

"Explain to the American people," said a worker at the Collective Farm later that day, "that life here is not turned upside down: the bombing is useless as well as savage."

Mr. Quat (Chairman of the Committee for Solidarity with the American People): "As long as the war goes on we are neither happy nor sad. Revolutionaries are simply people who want a better society and try to create it. When one has walked ten thousand miles one does not turn back before the last one hundred."

A wonderful concert had been prepared for us on our last day. Thi has arranged it, and it takes place in a large reception room at the Writers' Union. The folk and traditional music is enchanting, including such instruments as the monochord (which weeks later in Boston I look up in my 1885 Grove's *Dictionary of Music*, and find that it is reputed to have been invented by Pythagoras, but that he probably learned of it from the Egyptians, and that Euclid wrote of it in defining the intervals of the ancient Greek scale!), the bamboo flute, a bamboo xylophone or marimba, and a most ingenious kind of rattle the use of which involves dancelike movements of arm and wrist.

European-style music is performed well also, and poems are recited. Perhaps the most memorable of all the pleasures of this concert, and the most difficult for me to describe, is a skit performed by two little girls, daughters of a famous theatrical couple. Their older sister acted as announcer for the whole concert. Dressed as Saigon street boys, they mock the clumsy GIs whose shoes they shine. Their sense of comedy, their expressive and charming little faces, their professionalism, and at the same time the fun they were obviously having, are beyond my skill to describe.

Mme. Nguyen Khanh Phuong, of the PRG delegation in Hanoi—a beautiful woman who suffered unspeakable tortures in Diem's prisons and does not know the fate of her husband, arrested in 1959, nor has she seen her daughter since she was wrenched away from the year-old child in 1955—tells us how she survived "only thanks to the care and love of my comrades in the NLF."

We sit around a long coffee table in an elegant room at the delegation's house in the area of Hanoi where the embassies are clustered and where the well-to-do French once lived in luxury. Two young women from the South, brought to Hanoi for medical treatment of unhealing wounds and other results of torture under the Thieu regime, tell us their terrible stories. They don't weep. But they are deeply angry, and hurt as much emotionally as physically. Mme. Phuong rises from time to time to replenish our cups and plates with tea and fruit.

I slip a paper napkin she hands me into my notebook to keep as a memento. "After twenty years of struggle," she says, "who could imagine we could give up? We are sustained by our deep belief in the justice of our cause. We suffer and fight in order to bring a time of happiness."

The two young women—who were not political when they were first arrested—sip tea and sit proudly upright. One has a colostomy, the other a complicated and painful hernia requiring a series of operations. Mme. Phuong, dressed in the long silk tunic worn for occasions of ceremony or festival, smiles at us with her sad eyes, a smile of pride and hope.

As we leave, each woman takes our hands in both of hers and holds them a long moment—and at the last minute I venture to embrace them, and each returns the embrace with warm sisterliness. They come out to wave to us as we drive away.

I write in my notebook, "All that we have known about and have been trying to spread among other people seems unreal compared to seeing mothers at the bedsides of their half-destroyed children, or hearing the stories of women like these. I cling to the need for revolutionary optimism, I yearn for it; and we *see* it, we feel inspired by it—but we have a long struggle before us in order to really *share* it. It seems to me such hope, faith, charity, can only emerge out of a suffering we have yet to experience."

Epilogue

I feel this is an appropriate place to end, because it will serve to remind readers and myself of the ongoing struggle, both in Vietnam—where at this very moment, despite Nixon's vaunted "peace," political prisoners are being murdered by America's puppet Thieu and his henchmen, and in the US where we who do want true peace and justice for all, and who do at least *try* to work for it, have so much to learn and so far to go before we can offer any effective resistance to the continuing outrages our country perpetrates (and the US is bombing Laos even as I write[4]) or

---

4. And now (April 1973) Cambodia.

any strategy for dealing with the next major outbreak of US aggression, wherever it occurs.

Self-reproach can be a form of self-indulgence. That was something I began to learn in Vietnam, even though I experienced more self-reproach there than I ever had before: not because we do nothing, but because we don't push ourselves to do just a little bit more. I came to see, during that week, that revolutionary optimism is the *fruit* of serious struggle; that for us—at such a different point of moral and political development, and so deeply enmeshed and confused among the gross material and technological manifestations that surround us from birth—there is possibly far more strength and impetus to be drawn from contemplation of the *positive* quality of life in the Democratic Republic of Vietnam than from contemplation of the sufferings its people have endured.

In other words, the impetus to our own development toward the social change which alone can bring peace, can come more strongly from the knowledge of how humane, kindly, joyful, and constructive it is, after all, possible for human beings to be, than from grief, anger, and remorse when these emotions are separated from such positive knowledge.

Courage is patient.

Living in Machado[1]

Philip Levine

The village of Castelldefels is less than twelve miles south of Barcelona. I took my family to live there after my wife and I discovered it possessed an Anglo-American school that was first class and inexpensive and that it cost far less to live there than in Barcelona. A woman at the American consulate had given me elaborate and very exact instructions as to how to locate a particular Dutch realtor who could rent me a *torres* (the term used in Catalunya to denote a detached house) for far less than such space would cost in Barcelona where, I was assured, I would have to bribe several people before I could get anything at a reasonable price; apartments stayed in the same family for generations, and no one would rent anything remotely affordable before cleaning out an American, all of whom were rich.

The Dutch realtor, who described himself as an agent (not a secret agent or a commercial agent or even a real-estate agent—merely an agent) turned out to be a wonderfully civilized and witty man as well as an honest one; he spoke every known language with a made-in-Holly-wood accent and a vocabulary that suggested he'd learned by reading

---

1. Philip Levine, "Living in Machado" from *The Bread of Time: Toward an Autobiography* (New York: Alfred A. Knopf, 1994).

nineteenth century fiction. (To make the point that French food was better tasting and more reliable than Spanish he would say, "The Spanish kitchen is not so fine, I think, as the French, you think?") His name was Hans Breen, and within a few days he had my family of five installed in a spacious and crude dwelling directly across the way from his own, which was an identical twin to ours but fixed up to resemble a habitation, whereas ours was barren enough to suggest a cavalry barracks. Once my kids were properly enrolled in school, my goods from America collected at the main post office in Barcelona, and extra blankets and two butane heaters loaned for the coming cold weather, Sr. Breen felt it was responsible for him to take off on his annual vacation, which this time was to include Rome, Florence, Paris, and two weeks in his native country visiting old friends in the publishing business, which had once been his own business after a hitch in the former Dutch East Indies. He waved goodbye gaily at us from the front seat of his tiny Renault, which he drove with an élan and abandon suggesting that underneath his proper exterior he was actually a Brazilian baby millionaire sowing his wild oats.

The departure of Breen meant that our only link with the Spanish language was broken. I decided it was my duty to rectify this problem, and I set about spending two hours a day after lunch studying Spanish by means of a textbook given to me by a colleague at Fresno State. Why the book began with a study of the subjunctive I had no idea. I began searching for occasions on which I might employ it; I would say, "If that were a loaf of bread how much would it cost?" or "If this were a *bodega* what sort of wines would you be likely to offer for sale?" My wife suggested, slyly, that there had to be a better way of learning the language and the sooner I hit upon it the better. I had already noticed that my oldest son could, when we went to our favorite local restaurant, employ the simple present tense in ordering a four-course meal and wine for his parents, a liter of white for mama, a liter of red for papa, and he could be polite and effortless about it and win smiles from the dour waiter, who preferred to watch "Voyage to the Bottom of the Sea" undisturbed by the requests of customers. Mark had the meal underway, the bread on the table, the simple green salad oiled and soured, while I was still formulating my opening remarks: "If you had a paella today, would it be possible for the five of us to receive it this evening?"

This was late summer of 1965, the first time I'd been out of the country since my bachelor days and the only time I'd traveled any distance with the responsibility of a family of five. I was on a sabbatical leave from Fresno State, which gave me the munificent sum of half my annual salary of $9,800 for the year. I had picked up another thousand by teaching summer school for the first time in my life and still another by teaching two summer poetry workshops. A friend and patron had also added some thousands to this, but we had spent almost a third of our total in getting to Spain by means of a long trip through Europe in a VW Squareback sedan we'd purchased in Wolfsburg, where it was manufactured. Although our rent was less than $65 a month including utilities, and food was cheap and good, and wine was next to nothing, I was worried about money. I wasn't sure how I might earn some, but no matter what I did I'd have to learn Spanish. The few Americans I'd met at the Institute for North American Studies in Barcelona all spoke wonderful Spanish and struck me as unaccountably cheerful, as though they would rather be living here than in any other city in the world, while I longed—secretly—for Detroit, New York, even Fresno. I was homesick for the first time since I'd moved to Fresno in '58. I wrote a great many letters to friends back in the States and received almost nothing in return. These were loyal friends, but most of them were employed and lacked the time to sit down immediately and respond in spite of whatever note of urgency they might pick up in my letters. In fact I was doing my best to disguise my need. I wanted this first foreign family venture to appear to be a success. I had pushed it hard in spite of the advice of many people who'd insisted I couldn't afford it.

In Spain postage stamps are sold at the post office and also in tobacco stores, all of which are controlled (or were under the Franco government) by a national monopoly. Often these little tobacco shops also sell stationery items, note books, airmail envelopes, pads of writing paper, pens of all kinds, ink in bottles and cartridges, pencils. The lines at the post office are usually formidable and the senior clerks behave like vice admirals of a defeated armada, so most people take their personal letters to these little tobacco shops. Exiting the nicer of the two in the center of Castelldefels, I noticed a small sign next to the Pelikan fountain pen I had been admiring. It read in English, "Spanish Lessons Given," though "lessons" was spelled with only one "s," which did not inspire confidence. I went back in the shop and in my Spanish asked the young, dark-haired woman if I might inquire about the lessons. (It was perhaps the first occasion on which the subjunctive seemed appropriate.) She stared at me uncomprehendingly, so I reached inside the display case and plucked out the little hand-made sign. "Ah," she said in English, "you want my brudder. After one," she said, pointing at her wrist, "he is here."

Thus it was that afternoon I met Sr. Juan Rusiñol, a tall, long-faced Catalan gentleman, who indeed offered private Spanish lessons at his own *torres*, which was less than a mile from mine, for one hundred *pesetas* an hour, or $1.67 US. Since I was spending almost $100 a month on my children's education, I thought it reasonable to spend a few dollars on my own. We arranged for an initial lesson on the following afternoon, commencing at four p.m., when his stint at the store was complete.

It's impossible to explain by what magical process I believed the Spanish of Sr. Rusiñol would become my own. Somehow I did not envision hard work, hours of memorizing, and the writing of lessons, and thus it was I arrived at his *torres* the following day in a state of considerable excitement, akin to the excitement one feels when one is about to encounter the psychiatrist who will rid one of all his or her phobias by means of the right word or the right pill. Seated in his little upstairs study that looked out on a dismal display of brown-stained trees, and equipped with pencil and note pad on which to inscribe the phrases I needed to memorize, my hopes began to sag. It was not until later in the hour when the sun had dropped behind the western hills and the evening came on with a suddenness I was unused to, that things began to brighten. Sr. Rusiñol asked what I was by profession. I answered with as much simplicity and dignity as I could muster, "*Yo soy poeta.*"

Thus there began what was probably the first course ever offered in the village of Castelldefels on the subject of modern American poetry, taught by one young American poet to one not-quite-so-young Catalan poet, for the moment after I had uttered one of my first declarative sentences in simple present tense in Spanish, "*Yo soy poeta,*" Sr. Rusiñol switched adroitly to English and responded, "I too am a poet." "*En Español?*" I asked. "No," he said, "in my native language, Catalan," at which point he opened the door to his study and called to his nephew who had been studying in the next room. A tall, slender boy of perhaps ten years appeared at the door; he seemed in no way abashed by the presence of a stranger. In Spanish Sr. Rusiñol asked the lad how the school day had gone. The boy's response was incomprehensible to me. They exchanged a few more brief remarks and the boy went back to his room. "Could you understand what he was saying?" asked Sr. Rusiñol. I confessed I hadn't caught a word. To my relief I discovered he had not been speaking Spanish; all day he worked at school in Spanish, and the moment he returned home he reverted to his own language, which was Catalan. "You wonder why this country is insane?" he asked. (Actually I had never wondered, for Spain under Franco made just as much sense as California under Reagan.) "We go to school in one language and think in another, a language it is no longer legal to publish in, to debate in, to speak at a gathering of more than five people."

Before I could formulate a Spanish sentence in which I could pose a question regarding the nature of Sr. Rusiñol's poetry, he asked me in English whose poetry I thought larger, that of T.S. Eliot or that of Walt Whitman. As I struggled for the vocabulary to express my sense of the immensity of Whitman, Sr. Rusiñol switched the focus of our discourse one more time in his favor. "If you are more comfortable speaking your own language, please do so, as I comprehend it." That my desire to speak one of his other languages had brought me to this room in the first place seemed suddenly unimportant in comparison to the overwhelming urge for the two poets to reach an accord in this village that seemed at best indifferent to poetry. The rest of our time seemed to rush by as I spoke on my differing loyalties to these two great American poets. Almost two hours passed before my mentor rose to let me know our session had come to an end. Before I left he handed me a dog-eared copy of a lesson book entitled *Spanish Made Simple* and instructed me to master the first three lessons before our next meeting. As we shook hands, Sr. Rusiñol told his first and only lie in my presence. "Your accent is very good," he said.

Barcelona in 1965 was a raw, sprawling industrial town which on most days brooded under an enormous cloud of gray smog so heavy that for months I thought it was about to rain. Spain's burgeoning automobile and motorcycle industries were located in the western and northern suburbs of the great city, which spread out for ten miles or so in each direction save the east, where the sea stopped it abruptly. Barcelona's great modern architect, Gaudí, had not yet been discovered by the non-Catalan public, and thus most of his buildings were encrusted with industrial filth and several were misplaced on the maps the state tourist agency handed out. Actually tourists were rare, although tourism was the nation's greatest supplier of foreign capital. The millions of northern European visitors came mainly for sun and sea; in summer they drowsed along the beaches of the Costa Brava north of Barcelona, and in autumn and winter they headed directly toward the warmer coasts of Andalusia. One had little doubt one lived in a police state: heavily armed cops were everywhere, almost always in pairs. (The story was these "twins" spied on each other and thus were unbribable.)

Still, something anarchic from the city's past clung to the place. Although Antoni Gaudí was a religious mystic and his art was meant to pay homage to the Catholic God of his upbringing, the buildings them-selves were wild and totally unpredictable, made up as they were of beams shaped like bones, rooms without corners, windows suggesting the eyes of sea creatures, metal railings that undulated like the waves of the ocean, and from the niches of his great unfinished cathedral, *La Sagrada Familia*, peeped the stone eyes of snails and turtles. The project was approaching its hundredth anniversary and the citizens spoke of it as soon reaching completion although the whole roofless jumble lacked more towers than it possessed, and only a dozen or so stone cutters were on the job. Even the cardboard scale model in the tiny museum next door was unfinished, though I was assured the drawings for it—in Gaudí's own hand—were extant. In the older quarters of the town near the port there were Renaissance palaces of great beauty cheek by jowl with the tenements of the workers. In the ancient, narrow streets the noise was unimaginable as the two-stroke *motos* tore past. The people themselves seemed to have forgotten how to talk outdoors, and conversations were conducted in a series of outbursts and harsh shouts. The anger of this repressed working class—once so thoroughly politicized and union-ized—burst out constantly in unrehearsed moments of street theater. Anything approaching significant political action was outlawed, and the various police forces included a special political police nicknamed the *gris* because of their heavy gray serge uniforms. State cops were every-where toting their tommy guns and taking notes on the least departure from the ordinary: a foreign license plate, a late party, a new house guest, an especially aggressive dog. Up and down the streets they went at all hours with their little notebooks, writing in what I imagined a terribly efficient script. My neighbors ignored them and went about their lives with noise and abandon. A mile from our *torres* a camp full of Gypsies lived in a small clearing under a railroad viaduct. I would see the men in town in their wide-brimmed Cordovan hats strutting like peacocks. Everyone assured me their plans called for theft and I must never leave my house unguarded for long. As far as I could tell the police pretended they did not exist, and their women begged shamelessly, screwing their heads to one side as though they were simple or deformed. I walked a wide circle around them.

My second lesson with Sr. Rusiñol began in Spanish. I had pored over the first five lessons in *Spanish Made Simple* and was prepared to discuss the objects in a typical Spanish living room (although as yet I hadn't seen one) or enumerate the various members of a family, but my maestro asked me to describe the landscape of New England and contrast it with that of the Great West. Before I could see what was coming he requested my opinion on the part those landscapes had played in the work of Ralph Waldo Emerson and Robinson Jeffers, whose reputation was clearly larger in Catalunya than it was in Fresno. I explained as best I could that other poets had replaced Emerson and Jeffers, though the former was still an extraordinarily influential essayist and moral thinker. "Americans no longer read Robinson Jeffers?" he asked in English. "Then whom do they read?" I made mention of Wallace Stevens and William Carlos Williams, and in my faltering Spanish described them as the two great mountain peaks under which the rest of us wrote. Neither name meant anything to him, and he seemed utterly puzzled and more than a little saddened at the passing of Jeffers, who he assured me had made an indelible impression on him. I assured him that Jeffers had made an indelible impression on me as well, but the young were looking for something less spectacular, less orgiastic, less operatic. Of course I was speaking in English now. "Less operatic?" he said. "Do you mean less like Mozart or less like Wagner?" We were communicating. "Less like Wagner," I said. "Would you also say they want a poet who is less Spanish?" For some reason he thought of Jeffers as Spanish in character. Here I confessed my puzzlement, for while certain Hispanic poets were well known in the United States, García Lorca and Neruda, we knew almost nothing about the rest of their poetry and absolutely nothing about the nature of Spanish life.

After a brief silence during which he seemed to be considering my remarks, I asked if we might continue in Spanish. He bowed his head in a courtly manner and asked me to count to a hundred, to name the days of the week, the months of the year, the various trees outside his window, the colors of the sea and sky, the parts of the body, the features of the face, the reasons for living.

How Sr. Rusiñol located a copy of the old New Directions *Selected Poems of William Carlos Williams* edited by Randall Jarrell I have no idea. The stationery store offered a selection of new and used paperbacks for sale, but I'd never spotted a book of poems among them. Most of the books covered the range from English editions of James Bond thrillers all the way to English editions of John le Carré. At the next lesson my teacher informed me, in Spanish, that he had read the entire volume and was puzzled as to why it was regarded as poetry. I leafed through the familiar pages wishing I'd brought a copy from home, and then remarked without thinking that perhaps there were certain poets who didn't translate well. I had heard that the French, for example, hadn't the least idea why Wordsworth was regarded as a major poet. Sr. Rusiñol remarked quietly, so quietly in fact, that I immediately realized my tactlessness: he had read the poems in the original. "Yes, of course," I said, "but perhaps one has to be an American to 'hear' Williams. I'm told the English find nothing in his poems." The latter was a spur-of-the-moment invention; I had no idea how the English responded to Williams aside from the fact that Levertov, Thom Gunn, and Charles Tomlinson had all responded to him as ardently as anyone.

By this time we were conducting whatever lesson was going on in English. I offered to read him one of the poems to demonstrate its musicality, and he indicated with a nod of his head that I should proceed. I chose one of my early favorites, "Dedication for a Plot of Ground," which for me possesses an enormous rhythmic drive. I looked up after what I'd thought was an impressive and passionate rendering to find Sr. Rusiñol looking thoroughly befuddled. "I do not hear poetry," he said, and so I began to quote Frost's remark about poetry being what gets lost in translation, but this time hearing my error I veered off into an irrelevant paragraph about the greatness of Frost, whom the English also could not hear, knowing perfectly well that the English poet Edward Thomas was one of the first important writers to properly measure the true greatness of Frost.

Sr. Rusiñol took the book from my hands and, holding it tenderly, leafed through the introduction and stopped at an early poem, which I could see he was rereading to himself. He looked up with a wry smile on his face and said, "Tell me, in your own language please, why Mark Anthony is in heaven."

I started to talk about Williams's belief that our failure could be traced to the failure of our first European ancestors to submit to our hemisphere; they had fled the Old World in order to find a new world to locate their minds and imaginations, but instead of abandoning the garbage they brought with them, they imposed its order on America. He interrupted me. "Is this the Catholic heaven Mr. Williams is referring to? Does he put an adulterer into heaven as an insult to the Catholic church?"

"I don't think in this poem," I said, "he really cares about the Catholic heaven. Of course being a pagan Mark Anthony couldn't go to the Catholic heaven, and Williams was not a Catholic anyway. He means heaven to be a place of final reward for living as one should, for committing oneself totally to the passions that he, Williams, had committed himself to. It's Williams's own version of heaven." At last I was warming to the task.

Sr. Rusiñol looked once again at the book he so gently held in both hands and this time read aloud.

...how many times
from grass and trees and clouds
enters my north room
touching the walls with
grass and clouds and trees.
Anthony,
trees and grass and clouds.

For a long moment he sat in silence, and then he looked up at me and asked, "Did I read that properly?"

"Yes, of course."

"Do you hear poetry in what I read?"

"Yes, to me that whole poem is very beautiful."

"Perhaps," he said, "your Williams is like our good Machado, for in our Machado there is something that only we Spaniards can hear, some nuance that crosses no border. The French also do not acknowledge him, though like Americans they have regard for our Lorca and even Juan Ramón. For us the good Machado is the pinnacle, the apex, the Alp that looks down on all the rest of our great modern poets."

What American "high culture" there was in Barcelona collected around the institute for North America Studies on the Via Augusta in one of the posher neighborhoods some miles up the great sloping hillside on which the city is built. In 1965 there weren't enough cars in Barcelona to make parking a problem, so quite often I'd stop off at the *Instituto* to check out books, for they had been kind enough to grant me the use of their library. I, in turn, had given them a poetry reading, for which the director, Dr. Frauenfelder, rewarded me with the largest bottle of Johnnie Walker I had ever seen.

One day, spotting me poking around the library, Frauenfelder asked me to come upstairs to his office and meet someone who shared my passion for poetry. It was thus I met Hardie St. Martin, who had only recently embarked on his monumental anthology, *Roots and Wings*, a collection of modern Spanish poetry translated into English largely by American poets. He had already enlisted the cooperation of Kinnell, Merwin, Haines, Stafford, Wright, and Bly. He asked me if I was interested in contributing, and I assured him I was, although as yet my Spanish was almost non-existent. It didn't matter, he remarked, Bly couldn't order a glass of water in Spanish, but he had a genius for translating the poetry.

Sitting in Frauenfelder's cramped office, I was immediately drawn to this little man in a gray striped suit and red tie. Hardie sat bolt upright, his delicate hands together in his lap, and laughed frequently. His speech, which was produced almost entirely in the front of his mouth, was at first difficult to grasp, for he did not so much speak as chant. He had wonderfully white, gleaming teeth which one saw a great deal of because his mouth was never closed. He took so much pleasure in all he said that I found I took pleasure from it myself. The names of Spanish poets peppered his conversation, all pronounced in a manner unfamiliar to me. I took his accent to be authoritative, for José Hierro was to him Pepe Hierro and sometimes merely Pepe, and Francisco Brines was Paco, and there was a great salad of others whom he hoped to include in his project, poets whose names were utterly new to me, Gloria Fuertes, Gil de Biedma, Claudio Rodriguez, all of whom he seemed to know on a first-name basis.

In a few hours he was off by train to Madrid, which he assured me was a far more exciting and international city than Barcelona, for the citizens stayed up until the small hours of the morning talking poetry and philosophy and drinking brandy, whereas the dour Catalans were asleep before midnight so as to be prepared for the following day's commercial labors. Why he had chosen to live here and not in Madrid went unexplained. With his olive skin, close-cropped curly graying hair, and odd oval-shaped skull, Hardie looked like the embodiment of all things

Mayan. (I later learned he was born in British Honduras, the child of a Venezuelan mother and a father from the States.) When he switched into Spanish, which he did every few minutes, I found him incomprehensible, for he failed to end one word or begin another; it was one seamless stream of watery sounds upon which the emphasis fell everywhere and nowhere. Still, his delight in poetry was exciting for me.

Our second meeting was at our *torres*. Hardie arrived unannounced and unexpected one Sunday afternoon with two Spanish friends, only one of whom spoke any English at all. Antonio, a big horse-faced man, sat in a chair nursing a glass of red wine as he prepared himself for his voyage into English. He had one of the harshest voices I'd ever heard, and he used it to drop his pearl: "Kirk Douglas," he said. I'm afraid I was less impressed than I should have been. He gathered his breath and took a second chance: "Burt Lancaster." But since he didn't pronounce his "t's" it came out "Boor Lancasser." He was by trade a construction worker in Barcelona, an Andalusian originally, who like so many of his *lansmen* had come up to Barcelona when only a teenager to find work and, finding it, had settled in. The other fellow was a small, morose man who frowned a great deal, refused to sit, and downed glass after glass of red wine without thanking his hosts. They were killing time while they waited to meet a third friend, José Maria, in a bar. In spite of the din Antonio created, Hardie did his best to keep the attention on things poetic. He had the day before received some translations of Machado from Bly; they were remarkable, and he wanted to share them with me as soon as possible. He recounted a tale of Bly's adventures in England, and how without effort Robert had appalled the Brits with his pronouncements on the ultimate nature of poetry. It was clear that Hardie was under the sway of this great romantic figure who was Bly or some creation of Hardie's he called Bly. At one moment out of the corner of my eye I caught the morose fellow fondling himself as he stared at my wife. Hardie caught my glance and quickly looked over his shoulder. The man laughed in Hardie's face and shouted something unintelligible. Hardie leaped to his feet and confronted him. The man shouted back, and then Hardie slapped him across the face. Antonio rose from his chair and ordered the man out. A few minutes later Hardie and Antonio left to keep their appointment.

Spanish Made Simple is a book designed to aid the commercial traveler who wanders into the uncharted regions of Mexico without a native guide. It teaches one how to ask for the prices of *serapes* and *rebozos* and even *retratos*, it helps one order a meal or locate a bus stop or call for a taxi. Mastered, it would also allow one to spend a cordial evening in the company of a Mexican *comerciante* and his *esposa* and *niños*. It is remarkably mum on the subject of prosody and seems to have no opinions whatever on the entire dramatic unfolding of poetry in Spanish from Góngora to Blas de Otero. Thus I was severely handicapped during my hours with Sr. Rusiñol, for he kept veering away from the language of daily intercourse to speak of Miguel Hernandez, Juan Ramón, and his favorite, the good Machado. It was actually some weeks before I discovered that Juan Ramón, whom I pretended to have read, for he had assured me that everyone had read him, and Juan Ramón Jiménez were one and the same person. Once, when I had the temerity to ask if he admired the shorter lyrics of Jiménez, he stared at me in puzzlement. I repeated the name and when he remained silent wrote it carefully on my notebook, which I turned so he might read the name I was sure he knew. "Do you mean Juan Ramón Jiménez?" he said in English. Of course I did. Ah, Spaniards did not refer to him as Jiménez but rather by his "real" name, Juan Ramón. I was slightly puzzled, and he saw it immediately and assured me this was a fact.

"Why do you not say 'Federico García' instead of García Lorca or simply Lorca?" I asked.

"Aha," he said, "because half the country is García and only Lorca is Lorca." Yes, of course, it all made perfect sense.

In Spanish I asked why when he referred to Antonio Machado he always said *"el buen Machado"* (the good Machado) and not simply Machado? Because, he explained, they had two Machados, both poets, brothers in fact, one Manuel or Manolo as he was often called, and the great Antonio. Did they call Antonio the good Machado because he was the superior poet? Only partly, Sr. Rusiñol assured me. Manolo had been something of a dandy, a fop, a popular figure in the Madrid of his day who lived the high life, wrote some distinguished poems, and devoted most of his energies to enjoying himself. He was what Spaniards referred to as a *"Señorito"*: young men or formerly young men who wallowed in their pleasures and privileges. "Let me show you one of his poems," he said. He rose and peered nearsightedly at his bookshelves until he located a slender paperback that was falling apart. "There's no point in purchasing him in a finer edition," he said, for the frail book he held was exactly what Manolo deserved. The poem, "Felipe IV," focuses mostly on the king's wardrobe, which is dark and tasteful and contrasts with his pale complexion and frail, blue-veined hand. It reads like a portrait of a portrait by Velasquez.

"Very elegant," I said. "It's a sonnet, isn't it."

"Yes, elegant is one word you might use."

"And another?" I said.

"Decadent would do even better. Notice that the king has put aside the scepter in favor of a *'guante de ante,'* a suede glove, which was more likely part of the costume of Sr. Machado. I've seen him painted with a book in hand but never a suede glove."

"Is this typical of his work?" I asked.

Sad to say, it was, and though the subject left Sr. Rusiñol cold, he admired the craft of the poem, which was as studied as Sr. Machado's style of dress. "That was the point: to be preoccupied with style during an era of social upheaval. From this it was only a small step to a portrait of Charles V, and then another smaller step to the Generalisimo." It was clear he was referring to Franco, for Manuel—who outlived Antonio by eight years—had done well under the dictatorship.

"And Antonio," I asked, "what were his affiliations?" I grew bolder, "What were his politics?"

Sr. Rusiñol took a deep breath and measured me carefully. "Antonio Machado, our greatest poet of this century, was naturally a man of the people. He put his whole soul into the struggle for *libertad*." Did he mean that the good Machado took the side of the Republic during the Spanish Civil War? "I mean exactly that," he said, staring me down, "and when our side lost he gave up his life." I had not failed to hear that crucial "our," which Sr. Rusiñol had so fearlessly uttered in the presence of a man he had no good reason to trust, although we were brothers in poetry.

The Rusiñols had crossed the border from Catalunya into France in 1939 just before the fall of the last Republican forces. At that time Juan was only a boy of fourteen, but he remembered the events with remarkable clarity. Once on the French side of the frontier they had been interred with other Republicans in what one could only properly call a concentration camp, where they lived until the onset of World War II, which was only six months in coming. Once the so-called "fake war" was over and the Nazis grew serious about taking France, many of the refugees saw what was coming and escaped. Some returned to Spain, some joined the *maquis*, and others merely survived the best they could. But the most indelible event that etched itself on the tablets of the memory of Juan was the death of the great Spanish poet, Antonio Machado, who had crossed the border in their company. "It was as though Spain itself were dying," he said.

"Did you know who he was?" I said.

"Everyone knew who he was. And, of course, my father told me how great a poet he was and that he had written poems in defense of the Republic."

"Was your father also a poet? Or a literary man?"

No, his father had been and still was an auto mechanic. He seldom worked with his hands anymore, for now he owned the large repair shop on the road to Gavá, but back in '39 he was employed as a mechanic in the Republican army. But he was a Spaniard and a Catalan so he knew the literature. "To this day I think he regrets he was not one of those who offered to fulfill the poet's last wish."

"What was that?" I said.

"He asked to be buried in Spanish earth. He did not ask to be buried in Spain itself, for even at the end he was the same considerate, gentle man. To have taken him back to Spain for burial could have cost the lives of those who returned him and God knows what the fascists might have done with his body. He merely said '*la tierra de España*,' the earth of Spain. Those were his words. My father was there and heard them. Over the years he's repeated those words to me many times."

"How did they do that?"

"They simply crossed the frontier at night and dug sacks of the true soil of Spain and returned. When he was buried they packed around the coffin this earth from Spain." He, Sr. Juan Rusiñol, only a boy of fourteen, was there at the end; he would remember that day for the rest of his life. I asked if it had been a rainy Thursday. No, it had not been a day out of a poem. "Perhaps," he said, "Vallejo did die as he predicted, on a day of downpours in Paris, but Machado was buried on a beautiful day in early spring. That was the irony, the day was very beautiful, a day he would have loved. It might have been a Thursday; I do not recall everything. I was not yet a poet, so I did not truly know how much I was losing."

Once again Sr. Rusiñol rose and went to his bookcase. This time he returned with a book bound in boards, the spine covered with what appeared to be cracking red-dyed leather going white. He held it up for me to read the title, *Nuevas Canciones*, and above the title also in gilt letters and in very small print the author's name, Machado. Along the length of the spine were five star-shaped golden blossoms each framed by a golden vine. He moved his chair around the table and sat next to me and opened the book, leafing patiently past the title page, yellowing with age and stiffening, to the dedication page, which read "*A la memoria de D. Cristobol Torres.*" Underneath the dedication at a 45-degree angle in black ink gone brown was the one name clearly though inelegantly inscribed, "Machado," the poet's own signature.

He stopped leafing through the pages when he reached a poem that began, "*Hacia Madrid, una noche, / va el tren por Guadarrama.*" He read in a slow, somber voice but a voice that was his own, without melodrama or incantation. When he'd finished he asked, without looking directly at me, if I'd understood the poem. I said I'd followed some of it. A train is traveling at night toward Madrid; it travels under something in the sky. "A rainbow," he said, "a rainbow made of water and moonlight." I confessed I'd lost the next few lines. He recited from memory, "*Oh luna de abril, serena, / que empuja las nubes blancas!*" "Oh, moon of April, serene / that pushes the white clouds." He nodded his approval, and began to recite again, looking down at the book or pretending to do so. A mother holds a little boy in her lap, and the child in his sleep sees the green countryside pass by with its sunbrightened little trees and golden butterflies. "Yes, even at night, in his dreams," said Sr. Rusiñol, "the child sees the daylight world bursting with promise, for what he sees is his own world coming into being, and that world has all time to grow in. And the mother?" Once again he recited, "'*Ceño sombrio / entre un ayer y una mañana, / ve unas ascuas mortecinas / y una hornilla con arañas.*' And the mother's face is fixed in time," he went on, "for the life of the child is her burden as well, perhaps, as her joy. She sees the fire dying, she sees in her mind, the fire dying in the oven invaded now by spiders." He recited the last line slowly, ending, "'*y una hornillo con arañas.*'" He smiled, "Before there were in your house ants who did not know you, there were spiders in the oven, but García Lorca would have been the first to admit his debt to Machado."

"The tragic passenger who talks only to himself, is he Machado?"

I asked.

"No," said Sr. Rusiñol, "though others have read the line that way. Antonio Machado would never enter his own poem as the tragic passenger. No, that man is simply the tragic passenger of the poem, he who must travel the way of life alone."

"But wasn't his life spent largely in solitude? Didn't his young wife die very early?"

Yes, that was true, that was no doubt how he learned intimately how tragic life could be, but never would he refer to himself as the "tragic passenger." "You see," he said, "he enters in his own person in the following lines," and he held the book up closer to me so that I might verify his claim. And he read, "'*Yo pienso en campos de nieve / y pinos de otras montañas.*' This is Machado speaking, for he has his dreams of winter landscapes, of fields of snow, and the high pine trees of other mountains."

"And then God enters," I said.

"Yes," he said, "Machado often invites Him into his poems, for there is room for everything in his writing. In this case a God by whose light all of us see and who in turn sees all of us, and he asks this God of his a single question. Do you know what the question is?"

"He asks if he will ever see his face."

"Yes," he said, "he asks if that day will ever come, for He sees all of us, our hearts and souls, at all times, but will we ever see even His face?" Sr. Rusiñol closed the book slowly and pressed his thumbs down on the back cover. He was sorry he could not lend me this book, for it was a gift, but he would gladly loan me a paperback edition, an *antologia*, a selection of the poet's best work. He would be pleased to help me read these poems, for this way I might come to better understand both the Spanish language and the Spanish people.

Quite abruptly Hardie moved to Castelldefels. He gave up his rent-controlled apartment in Barcelona. He claimed he was sick of the noise of the streets and the overpowering stink of diesel exhaust. A lawyer friend—a man he'd met the week before in a bar—had arranged it. He did not trust my "Herr Breen," for, he told me, a Dutchman was not to be trusted. We sat in the living room of his brand-new *torres* enjoying a glass of sherry. Antonio was glued to the television on which *Real Madrid* was as usual trashing the Barcelona soccer team. A small fire of damp oak smouldered on the hearth; this was something Hardie had never before enjoyed, and he took great pride in the elegance of his newfound home. True, so far the plumbing had proved a disaster. When I asked how much rent he was paying, he avoided answering. Instead he assured me that save for the month's rent to his agent, the lawyer friend, there were no hidden costs like those my Herr Breen would spring on me before I departed.

I changed the subject to the anthology. Could I work on some translations of Machado? Why, he asked, did I want Machado? I told him of my conversations with Sr. Rusiñol, the Catalan poet. "Every gentleman in Catalunya is a poet, including your Sr. Rusiñol," of whom he had never heard. "No, I'm sorry," he said, "I've assigned Machado to Bly." Bly had a particular affinity to the difficult Machado. It was not simply that both men led a solitary rural life, it was also their constant striving for simplicity and wisdom.

"But Bly is married and has kids," I said, "He's surrounded with friends and cronies, he is outgoing, boisterous, a shrewd literary entrepreneur, an influential editor. He has a bountiful nature, but he's essentially theatrical, exactly what Machado was not."

Hardie casually waved me away. I was taking the whole thing too personally. His attention had strayed to the contest between *Real Madrid* and Barcelona. "Look, *Los Niños*," his nickname for *Real Madrid*, "are going to score." The Madrid crowd was also standing and shouting as one, the players were dancing about and hugging each other. Each year it was the same. The two cities revealed their natures on the fields of sport.

The speed and élan of Madrid triumphed over the stolid persistence of joyless Barcelona.

"I think you would do well with Unamuno," said Hardie, closing down the literary discussion.

While experimenting with his breathing, my son Mark passed out, hit his chin on the arm of a wooden chair, and received a nasty cut, which in spite of home bandaging was still oozing blood the next morning. I asked Señora Fuertes, who lived across the street, the name of a reliable doctor, and she sent me to a Dr. Esteban Ruiz with offices just off the town's main square. The doctor saw patients at ten a.m., and his office was a daunting sight, not perhaps as daunting as St. Vincent's emergency room at one thirty in the morning, but bad enough to leave a sane person quaking. The huge waiting room was crowded to overflowing with a variety of people, bandaged and otherwise, many of whom appeared to be unconscious in the heavy haze of cigarette smoke. I was struck by the fact that most of the men had been injured in some way about the head: eyes, ears, foreheads, entire skulls were hidden in great swaths of graying cotton. I was immediately seized by several elderly women in black and ushered to the front of the room where a woman in ordinary street clothes sat behind a simple deal table with a large notebook. The women urged me forward and asked me to explain the purpose of my visit. I told the attendant, a rather elegantly turned out woman in her thirties, the nature of my son's injury and indicated with my fingers that stitches might be required. *Sí, sí!*, the doctor would determine the nature of the remedy. She took my name. The elderly women then led me to an empty chair, awakened the man seated in the adjoining chair, and asked him to move so that the *estranjero* and his *joven* could be seated side by side.

Across from us sat another father and son. The father had buried his face in his hands, and the son—a boy of no more than eight years—was whispering into his ear. When the father looked up I recognized him immediately, for he was one of the younger officers from the local *Guardia Civil* barracks a few blocks from my house. He had removed his jacket and wore wide leather crossed belts across his shoulders and a wide black belt at his waist from which his holstered automatic pistol hung. He nodded gravely at me and once again hung his head, breathing deeply like one who has just finished a difficult race, his chest heaving under the gray-green shirt. The boy whispered again in his ear, but the man merely shook his head no, and went on gasping for breath. Expecting a long wait I had brought a copy of Orwell's *Homage to Catalonia*, which I'd wrapped in butcher paper to hide the title. I questioned the wisdom of reading it.

The next time the officer sat up the boy took a pack of cigarettes from his father's pocket, selected one, and pushed it toward his father's mouth; the man accepted it without comment and leaned to the flaring match his son produced. The officer rose and began to pace back and forth the length of the room. At last he stopped and leaned into an illuminated wall of glass bricks; the day was a brilliant one, the sky of Catalunya a deep blue, the light lacking the golden dust for which it is famous. He was a short, sturdily built fellow so wide across the shoulders his shirt seemed about to burst its seams. He leaned his head into the glass bricks and then drew it back; a moment later he let his head fall with a sharp report. Before he could withdraw it and repeat the act, his son was on his feet. The boy was tall for his age, dressed in a white shirt which, though he wore no tie, he had buttoned at the throat. He was very slender and wore gray shorts that seemed too small for him. For a moment the noise in the room, largely made up of coughs and groans, subsided. The boy began to stroke his father's hand until at last he caught his attention, and then he led him slowly back to his seat, where he sat beside him, comforting him with little pats on his back as he whispered in his ear.

Suddenly I was aware that my name had been called; the door which bore the name of Dr. Esteban Ruiz had opened and a nurse—or at least a woman in a nurse's starched white uniform—had called out my name.

Several of the women in black indicated with gestures that I should arise with my son and go forward. Before we could reach the door the young officer was there ahead of us, his son behind him pulling back on one hand. "My wife," he said, "where is my wife?"

"In a moment," the nurse said, "in only a small moment. Please, be patient."

Dr. Esteban Ruiz looked amazingly like my friend the poet Peter Everwine, though he was shorter and his moustache a bit fuller and darker. He was seated behind his desk in a small room lined with glassed-in bookshelves which looked as though they hadn't been invaded in years. He had been reading the sports section of *La Vanguardia*, one of Barcelona's worst and most widely read newspapers, which he shoved to one side as he rose to greet me. Alas, Dr. Ruiz did not speak English. In Spanish he asked what the problem was.

Mark immediately took over the conversation. "Here," he said in Spanish, "I've wounded my chin."

Dr. Ruiz removed the bandaid and stared lovingly at the wound. "It pains you?" he asked. He was assured by father and son that the cut no longer caused pain. "Then what is the problem?" We explained: the wound continued to bleed. Would stitches be required? The good doctor mused. He had no affection for stitches. Not in such a case. First they must be put in, which required great care; then they must be removed, which required a second visit. And there was the likelihood of a scar, not a large scar, but not a welcome sight on the chin of so handsome and blond a young man. No, he had a better solution. He rummaged in his top desk drawer until at last he located a great round piece of adhesive tape. He peeled away the plastic backing, studied my son's chin for some seconds, and then abruptly slapped on the tape. Mark staggered back. The doctor apologized, and then carefully tamped down the edges of the tape. "Perfect," he said. "You will be sure to remove it in a week, and you will still be very handsome."

"And so blond," I added.

I paid the woman at the desk. She also shook my hand and expressed her pleasure in serving the father and his handsome, blond son. She was none other than Señora Ruiz, the wife of the doctor. I could see the Guardia officer and his son nowhere. The old women in black pointed me toward the door, nodding their approval.

When I told Hardie of the extraordinary civility of the women in the doctor's waiting room, he stared at me in disbelief for several seconds and then laughed. He turned to Antonio and related my tale. Antonio shrugged and muttered a few, indecipherable words which Hardie translated. "Those old women have nothing to do but hang around all day waiting for someone to die."

"What did the doctor charge you," Hardie asked. I told him how tiny the fee had been, five hundred *pesetas*.

"Five hundred *pesetas* is not a tiny fee. It's eight dollars. You were paying for half the patients that morning, that's why they ushered you up to the front. Once the doctor got your eight dollars he could treat the others without regret for what they had to give him. We don't have socialized medicine here, this isn't Europe." The injured workers were covered by a form of compensation that paid $1.50 for an office visit. The rest bring eggs or maybe a slab of ham *serrano* or maybe a few sausages. Had I noticed a certain pungency in the air? Now he was howling with laughter at the spectacle of this street-wise American city boy being suckered by a bunch of village widows. I said nothing about the young officer and his son.

At the dining room table he presented me with my first translation assignment: a poem by Unamuno which deals with a blackened sculpture of the dead Christ in the Church of the Cross at Palencia. Although the language is slightly elevated and the poem more rhetorical than most American poetry of the '60s, I found it presented a stunningly intimate portrait of the poet's feelings toward this God-man or man-God whose deity the poem struggles not to accept. I was surprised by how much I liked the poem. "What do you think of the poem?" I asked Hardie.

"It doesn't matter what I think of the poem. It is Unamuno. It is an important poem by one of the key figures of the Generation of '98, one of the keys to an understanding of what took place in this country's poetry. You must hear this calm, clear, unembroidered voice, the voice of a serious man speaking to serious men." I knew I'd triggered a lecture that could go on until the small hours of the morning, but somehow I couldn't let go of the subject.

"To you this is a calm, clear voice?"

He took a deep breath and explained I was not reading American poetry or even English poetry. If I knew what was being written before the Generation of '98 I would come to understand what a revolution these poets had fostered.

"As significant a revolution as the one Wordsworth fostered a century before when he turned English poetry toward the language of ordinary people?"

"Far, far more significant," he said, smiling, for it had produced poetry of much greater importance.

With its serious adult voice addressed to any and all adults, with its hope to create faithfully and in every detail the homely scene, with its naked passion for its subject and its nostalgia for a lost faith, how wonderfully and hopelessly out of fashion this poem seems.

From *The Dead Christ Lying in the Church of Santa Clara*
(Church of the Cross) *in Palencia*

This Spanish Christ that hasn't lived,

black as the dung-ripened fields,
lies like an immense plain,
horizontal, packed down,
without soul, without hope,
with closed eyes, his face to the sky
that hoards its rain and scorches our bread.
And with his black feet, hooked like an eagle's,
he seems to want still to imprison the earth.

Or perhaps God, penitent,
dressed in this miserable rag,
wanted to taste the death of this world,
in order to flush his conscience of guilt
for having made man, and with man
evil and pain.

Popular superstition imagines that his nails
and hair bring in
from this life the callused, the shelled,
dry superstitions,
whatever he scratches up, whatever he binds around
his harvested head.

This motherly piety of the poor daughters
of Santa Clara has skirted
with cloth of white silk and gold
the repulsive privates,
although this pouch of bones and pus
is neither male nor female;
this Spanish Christ without sex
lies far beyond that difference
that is the tragic knot of history,

for this Christ is ground of my ground.

Is there a poetry magazine in America that would accept such a direct poem, with its unapologetic appeal to our deepest beliefs? I can almost write the rejection slip myself from the *American Poetry Review*.

Dear Mr. Michael Unamuno,

I regret to say that only three issues back we published another poem dealing with Jesus Christ. We appreciate the seriousness of your commitment, but we find this poem more than a little out of touch with what's going on in recent poetry. We would be willing to look at newer work, especially anything that dealt with your journey down from the mountains to make the revolution.

Sincerely,
Jack Hatchett
for the editors

I shudder to think of what our current batch of killer-reviewers would do with poetry of such frank concern for the human estate. Imagine Mary Kinzie or Marjorie Perloff unleashed by *APR* on the unsuspecting Mr. Unamuno. Not a pretty thought.

One night, feeling a bit downcast in the terrible weather of the end of autumn in Catalunya, I stopped for a drink at a small bar on the road to Sitges, a lovely little fishing village down the coast from Barcelona. At the rear of the bar was a large square window through which I could see the waves crashing against the rocks below the terrifying coast road. "Bad day," said the bartender, a paunchy middle-aged fellow who wore a white apron tied around his middle like a cummerbund. He poured himself a Tio Pepe and drank to my health and then poured me a second brandy on the house. Over the window hung two crossed pitchforks, a display I often found in bars and inns throughout Spain; the tines were twisted and knotted like arthritic fingers. The rain was whipping in from the low dark clouds scudding over the hills to the west of us. All that afternoon I had been sure it would snow, though my neighbors assured me it was out of the question. It was too early in the year, said one; another claimed it snowed only once every ten years and this decade had already had its snowfall. As I tramped along the highway or padded, head down, along the shore, I was sure I caught glimpses of snowflakes falling through the air. I had been walking for hours every day. I would spend much of the mornings in bed, the warmest place in the house, trying to urge a frozen poem into being, and then after a small lunch of bread and *chorizo* I would go for a long walk to escape the smell of butane or the smoke from the fireplace. Usually in the late afternoon my youngest son, Teddy, would accompany me on the long walks along the shore, but today he was taking part in a game of soccer in the large field behind our house. Although my sons were not proficient at the game, they had to be included because Teddy owned the single ball in our neighborhood that could be substituted for an actual soccer ball, which no one owned. With Teddy by my side the walks were far more rewarding, for we would question each other about the events of our day, how the year was going, and usually wind up casting about in our memories for our fondest images of home. Lacking his company I had sought relief in this tiny roadside bar.

The door swung open and a blast of cold damp air invaded the place. Two Guardias hung their ponchos and leather tricorn hats on hooks by the door. The younger of the two also hung his tommy gun there while the other slung his rifle over his shoulder. "One bad day," he said to me, and drew a stool up next to mine. Before seating himself, he saluted me, and then laughed and extended a wet hand, which I shook. "Tomas

Garcia," he said, "at your service." I presented my name, and he looked at me quizzically. "You are not a Catalan?" he said. I told him he was right. "How odd," he said, "you look exactly like a Catalan." He went on to explain that a week before he had come in out of the cold and introduced himself to a man at the bar, and the man, shorter than I and perhaps a bit older, had presented him with his calling card, which he extracted from his wallet. It read *C. Blanco, Catalan Fisherman.* "What a country, eh, we all have calling cards."

I told him I lacked a calling card and asked if he had one. "No," he said, "no one seems to doubt the nature of my employment." His comrade laughed and added that it was difficult to figure out what they were doing on a miserable night like this. "What do you think we are doing?" he asked me.

I would have preferred not to have been drawn into this conversation, but it was too late for that. "I think you've been getting wet," I said.

"You are very observant," said the first and more cheerful Guardia. "Our mission is to make sure the enemies of Spain do not deliver great bales of hashish to this shore. There are hundreds of vessels out there in the dark just waiting for us to come into this bar and get drunk so they can unload their cargoes of drugs. Were you aware of this?" I told him I was not. "Then you do not read the newspapers; they are full of warnings. Every day they publish a new warning against the fleets of our enemies." He unshouldered his rifle and handed it to me. It was actually a tiny, bolt-action carbine; it weighed no more than a .22 and looked about as effective. He had inserted a cork into the end of the barrel, no doubt to shield it from the salt air. "This is what they have given me to defend the sacred shores of Spain from the Communist fleet. I haven't a chance. The string on the cork is broken; one shot and I'm through."

"I cannot say if it is a good translation," said Sr. Rusiñol. He knew the poem so well he couldn't really imagine it other than it was. It was a poem his father had shown him when he was still in his teens, when he was struggling with his own religious doubts. Indeed his father had given him an *antologia* of the poems of Unamuno.

I asked if Unamuno was one of his father's heroes. He was silent for a while, and then he said, "Unamuno is like a great monument for us all: philosopher, novelist, poet, savant, educator. He was the director of our greatest university as well as our greatest literary figure. As Machado is for us the soul of Spain, he is the conscience."

"Do you like his poetry?" I said.

"Always you ask this question, 'Do I like...?' Who am I, Juan Rusiñol, to like or dislike this giant?" The only significant question would be, he explained, "What Unamuno would think of the writings of Juan Rusiñol."

"Do you read him for pleasure?" I asked.

"Pleasure? Do you read Walt Whitman for pleasure?"

I told him that of course I did, that when I read "Song of Myself" there were times I could barely contain my joy. I had to get up and put the book down and dance about the room or sing, even though I had no singing voice.

"You are lucky, very lucky," he said. "We parade solemnly around our Unamuno with hushed voices, we do not dare dance and sing in his presence. Like this poem, he was august, far larger than life. He lived in the same room with God, all his life he spoke with God as one might speak to a brother whose love you were unsure of. He was like a God himself, and then he died with such courage and grandeur to remind us what a man can be, to remind us that man is created in the image of God or God is created in the image of man." I had never seen Sr. Rusiñol so passionate. He went to the window and pointed down at the dismal yard where the pines and the few shoddy, leafless trees bowed to the sea winds. "You know he was a Basque, Miguel de Unamuno, but at the end he defended us too, the Catalans. Although he was not of the left, he defended those of the left; he defended everything alive in Spain that stood for life. It is impossible to believe today," and he gestured out the window at the yard below, "that this poor earth of Spain could again give us a man like Unamuno."

"How did he die?" I asked.

"You do not know? Then I will tell you." And so the whole sad story unfolded: how as rector of the University of Salamanca, Unamuno was forced to take part in a celebration of Nationalist Spain which turned out to be a celebration of death. He had sat on the podium with Franco's wife and listened to an insane speech by the fascist General Millan Astray, who had spoken of the one half of Spain as a cancer which must be removed by a surgical process. He had whipped up the audience—largely Falangists—to a frenzy, and soon they along with the General began the fascist chant of "*Viva la Muerte!*" (long live death). When the audience finally calmed, Unamuno rose.

Sr. Rusiñol went to his desk and rummaged about in one of the side drawers until he located a small magazine that resembled a comic book in its flimsy structure. "I would like you to hear his words, for they are famous to us." He read them slowly in Spanish. At the end without looking back he began to translate and paraphrase what he had read. At times it was a lie to remain silent, Unamuno had said, and so he would speak. As a philosopher he had dealt in paradoxes all his life, but this meaningless, necrophilous cry "Long live Death!" repelled him. "General Millan Astray is a cripple," he said. This was true, for he'd lost an arm and an eye in combat as head of the Foreign Legion. "And if he has his way, the General will create many more cripples. The General would like to create a new Spain in his own crippled image." At this point the General could not contain himself and screamed, "Death to the intellectuals! Long live death!" A machine gun was pointed at the head of Unamuno, but it did not silence him. Sr. Rusiñol bowed again to the text and translated with precision. Unamuno spoke:

This is the temple of the intellect, and I am its high priest.

It is you who profane its sacred precincts. You will win, because you have more than enough brute force. But you will not convince. For to persuade you would need what you lack: reason and right in your struggle. I consider it futile to exhort you to think of Spain.

Amazingly enough when Sr. Rusiñol finished he was dry-eyed. He looked at me directly and remarked that it was General Franco's wife who probably saved the poet from being murdered on the spot, though it hardly mattered, for six weeks later he died of a broken heart. "I understand your Walt Whitman died an old man, in bed. Whereas our García Lorca died against a wall, still in his youth. We love our poets."

I decided the best thing I could do was select a short poem by Machado and do my best to translate it. If I waited for permission from someone, even from myself, it would never come. I chose one that began, "la casa tan querida" because I could translate the first two lines without consulting a dictionary. Also it did not rhyme, and the lines seemed of no fixed length, so most of the usual formal considerations were irrelevant. The syntax of the first stanza—which was a single, very complex sentence— gave me fits. I wanted not to have to resort to breaking it into two or even three sentences. Hours passed, and I felt I was simply moving words around and not getting any closer to a version of the poem I'd be happy with, but a curious thing was happening during these hours: I was falling in love with the taste of the Spanish on my tongue.

I went for a long walk down by the sea and began quoting passages from the poem. To my great surprise I had memorized all of it, though I no longer recalled how I'd translated most of it. The poem concerns a man who goes back to view a house that was very dear to him because once a certain woman lived there. The place is now an uninhabited wreck, and the wreck reveals its worm-eaten skeleton. The short second stanza goes:

La luna está vertiendo
su clara luz en sueños que platea
en las ventanas. Mal vestido y triste,
voy caminando por la calle vieja.

We discover it's night. The moon "is shedding / its clear light of dreams / that silver the windows." Why would the windows still remain in a junked house? Perhaps the speaker is remembering it as it was even though he places the experience in the present. Perhaps he is demonstrating how the past takes preeminence over everything. I repeated the final sentence over and over, for I was describing myself, alone, bundled in thick, coarse sweaters against the sea winds, feeling each of my thirty-seven years twice over. "Shabby and sad / I made it down the old street." And like Machado or the speaker in the poem, the experience was utterly not mine, for there was no woman of romance anywhere in the world whose loss I still regretted, but there was in me a yearning for a place of the past, a house to which I could return and be taken in, a place that had once mattered and still mattered. No such place existed. I had had the American experience of finding the old house replaced by a parking lot, and this was 1965—two years before what in Detroit would come to be known as the Great Rebellion—and much of the neighborhood of my growing up was still unburned. It would take another twenty-five years to show me how fully Machado's poem dealt with a life I could never live, for by the time I truly became that shabby old man the places of growing up had been obliterated. The American experience is to return and discover one cannot even find the way, for the streets abruptly end replaced by freeways, the houses have been removed for urban renewal that never takes place, and nothing remains, not even a junked skeleton "silvered by moonlight." When I want to find an image of my Detroit I go to the poetry of World War II—for instance, to this passage from Miroslav Holub's "Five Minutes After the Air Raid":

In Pilsen,
Twenty-six Station Road,
she climbed to the Third Floor
up stairs which were all that was left
of the whole house
she opened her door
full on the sky
stood gaping over the edge.

Once again I shared my translation with Sr. Rusiñol. He pored over it for several minutes, and then looked up at me. "You are pleased with this first sentence?" I had to admit I was not. It sounded graceless and awkward. I was certain I was doing a great disservice to the original. No doubt I was right, he murmured, but still it was a noble effort, this effort to create one sentence out of so complex a sentence. He was sure I had understood the original and got the meaning right, but he could not help me, for his English was not up to the task. "May I ask you a somewhat personal question?" he said. "Did you get any pleasure from reading this over and over, as you must have?" and he smiled broadly.

I told him it had given me a profound and curious pleasure I could not explain and one that I was unprepared for, and suddenly I found myself reciting the second stanza as I had done so many times to myself. When I had finished, Sr. Rusiñol nodded his approval and said, "You have crossed the border into Spain."

I struggled another day with my little Machado poem and finally decided to share it with Hardie. He took it immediately to the dining room table, which served as his office, got down his Machado from a shelf, and compared the translation and the original for a full ten minutes. "Bly likes this poem too," he said. "He translated it, but I doubt I'll use it in the anthology. He did a better job than you."

"I don't believe it," I said.

From another shelf he removed a large envelope, went through it swiftly, his reading glasses slipping off his nose, and finally withdrew the Bly translation and handed it to me. After reading it carefully, I said, "You're wrong, Hardie, it stinks." Hardie was clearly taken aback. I was not trying to question his taste where Spanish poetry was concerned; I felt my ear for English was adequate for the judgment. "Look," I said, "how he cheats. He creates a parenthetical sentence where there isn't one, and it sounds awkward as hell. This man deep in a meditation on the past blurts out in Bly's version, 'she lived there.' Doesn't that strike you as a violation of the whole poem? And '*maltrabado*' doesn't mean 'badly lasting.' Look how graceless the second stanza is in his version and how lovely it is in mine. I admit we both louse up the first stanza; it's untranslatable."

"Nothing is untranslatable," he said, "but you're right, neither of you do well with the first stanza."

"And the second?" I said.

He laid the two side by side and studied the original again. I knew this was serious business for him; his commitment to Spanish poetry was his life. Finally he raised his head and put his reading glasses back in his breast pocket. "They're different. Robert's is Robert's, an effort at rendering the original as exactly as possible. Yours takes a few more chances. What I'm curious about is why the two of you were attracted to this poem. There's nothing remarkable about it."

Somehow I didn't dare say that I'd known all the words in the first two lines and so decided impulsively and on such thin evidence that this was the right poem for me, nor did I want to admit how many hours I'd spent poring over the dictionary, and how much I was still in doubt about my rendering of the first stanza. Instead I said something about the universality of the theme, that we all imagined going back to a place of first love, a place of beginnings, and how going back we did not find the place or found it utterly different from the place stored in memory.

"It's a familiar poem about lost love," he said.

"It's far more than that," I said, "far more. Each of us harbors a dream of a place that retains some magic for us. We believe that if we could return to that place and time and begin again our lives would somehow be different, fuller, and so we return. It's almost a quest. Machado's portrait of it is so moving and surprising; the place is at once nothing, a wreck, a pile of junk, and yet at the same time the false vision remains as true as what's before his eyes. We may go away totally denied and defeated, but our capacity for belief remains, even the evidence of our actual sight fails to kill it: '*La luna está vertiendo* . . . The moon is shedding / its clear light of dreams / that silver the windows.' The capacity to dream is limitless."

Hardie shook his head and clasped his small, delicate hands before him on the table. From the other room Antonio could be heard howling with laughter over some incident from "I Love Lucy," a local favorite. "I hate to say this, Phil, but you're beginning to sound like a Spaniard."

I translated one more poem by Machado, "Amencer De Otoño" ("Autumn Begins"), but this time showed it to no one. When our sons' Christmas break came we went south to the great cities of Andalusia. On the way there we passed through the small town of Lorca, the first of the so-called "white towns" we'd seen. At noon we parked in the center of the town and walked around buying bread, cheese, salami, and wine. I knew it was not the home of García Lorca, but nonetheless I felt it was a place of poetry. Going west from Alicante on the way to Granada we passed close to the birthplace of Miguel Hernandez; back then he was only a name to me, though before the next year ended I discovered his amazing poems and failed to translate them with grace or accuracy and so joined all his other translators. We found the Alhambra on a clear, cold afternoon, the courtyard of stone dogs, the great floating vista from the battlements. In Sevilla we stayed at the worst hotel in the world, all five of us for $1.60, and when I awakened in the middle of the night I found peasants sleeping in the hallways, each on his mattress of newspapers. One small fellow, fully dressed, looked up at me, and half his face was smeared with black ink. I would never lose that image of public lies become personal affronts. There was a little balcony outside my room, and from it I looked down into the rail yards. All night the switch engines chuffed in the darkness. This was a comforting image, for I had worked a year in the rail yards behind the Michigan Central Terminal a few blocks from Tiger Stadium.

The next day in Córdoba I was walking in the brightness of noon with Teddy, and we were speaking Spanish for the practice of it. A man, dressed in suit and tie and also with a small boy, approached me and asked if I was Catalan. He was quite sure my accent was Catalan. I said I was, and we shook hands and exchanged a few words, for this was New Year's Day, and the whole city was in a festive mood. To be in Córdoba with the sun shining on New Year's Day, I thought, what else does one need to know one is blessed. Teddy asked me why I had lied to the man and said I was Catalan. I told him that I hadn't wanted to shame the man in front of his son and tell him he was eight thousand miles off target. I reminded him what a man on the Gran Via in Barcelona had said to me, a perfect stranger who had interrupted a similar conversation to tell me not to speak Spanish to my son because I'd only ruin his perfect accent. "Look how considerate this man was even if he didn't know what he was talking about," and we laughed at the recollection of the earlier event.

I thought that perhaps Sr. Rusiñol had not been lying and my accent wasn't bad and that people actually took me for a Catalan. People were always coming up to me on the streets in Barcelona and speaking to me in Catalan, and when I answered them in Spanish as best I could, they would apologize. When I told this to Sr. Rusiñol, he had said again that I looked Catalan, and now that my clothes were from Spain it was natural for people to assume I was one of them. I had asked what he meant when he'd said I look Catalan. "We are all part Jewish," he'd said. "From your family name I assume you are Jewish, of the tribe of Levi." I nodded. "You look like one of us, fairly tall, slender, with the long face, the long slender fingers," and he'd held up his hands. "You could be my brother."

On the way back from Córdoba it began to storm. The narrow, two-lane road toward Madrid was awash and slippery. Again and again I could feel the VW give a moment, begin to slide, and then take hold. To the west the gray disk of the sun kept breaking through the clouds, and I hoped for some relief that never came. It was a Sunday, before noon, with no truck traffic on the road. Here and there we passed a solitary man on a bicycle or walking under a yellow plastic poncho. At a crossroads west of Jaén, two Guardias in leather helmets had parked their motorcycles on the shoulder. One stepped into my lane, held out a palm, and I stopped. He peered in the driver's-side window, which I rolled down. His aviator sunglasses were dotted with raindrops; rain dripped off his helmet and ran down his face.

"You are Hollanders?" he said.

"No," I said, "North Americans."

"Where are you going?"

"Jaén." I said.

He pointed toward the east and stepped back. I could hear the creaking of his heavy, wet jacket. "The road is clear, you may go," and with an impatient wave he commanded me forward.

A few miles later an old black Citröen, what my boys called a gangster car, had stopped in my lane facing me. I slowed almost to a stop. Two men were peering under the hood. One straightened up, placed his hands at the small of his back, and stretched as though in pain. Before diving in again to his labors, he turned and gave us a broad smile from under his black fedora.

"Jaén is where Machado lived much of his adult life," I said to my wife. "I'd like to stop there." From the backseat Teddy asked if we were going to find the hillside where he'd been shot. No, I told him, Machado had not been shot. He had simply lived here and taught high school French, lived alone after his young wife died. "He was a humble man," I said, "He just taught and wrote. I doubt his students or neighbors knew he was a great poet."

"If you don't ask someone where the hillside is, you're never going to find it. You should ask that Guardia; they know everything."

"I can't ask the Guardia. They were probably the ones who shot him. And that was Lorca back in Granada."

"All we do is drive up and down country roads in the rain," Teddy said to no one in particular, "looking for a good hillside to shoot someone. Up and down the roads. And we don't ask anyone."

In Bailén, due north of Jaén, the rain was coming down in such great sheets I could barely see to drive. I pulled over and parked. We sat while the roof drummed on and on. A thick-bodied woman in black wearing a gray apron splashed by as best she could in her felt carpet slippers. We made a clumsy dash for the doorway of a bar. Inside the place seemed to be swimming in its own mild drizzle. At the far end three men sat playing a game with tiles; a naked bulb hung over their heads casting a faint greenish light.

"Can I be of service?" said a bartender who suddenly appeared from nowhere. I shook out my raincoat and hung it from a peg on the wall. I cleaned my glasses, and the place came to order. We asked for ham and cheese sandwiches and orange sodas for John and Teddy. Fran had a coffee, and Mark and I had red wine. "This is Sunday weather," said the bartender. "For several hundred years it has rained every Sunday."

We did not turn south toward Jaén. The bartender assured us the rain was heavier there on Sundays, and the cathedral, though very old and sacred, was shabby. "Part of the roof is missing, and on Sundays everyone gets soaked. It is the capital," he said, "so it has many courthouses and a *plaza de toros*." By now I was not sure if Machado lived in the province of Jaén or the town. I had the impression he'd lived in a small village, one he could walk to the edge of on spring afternoons when his classes were over. It may even have been here in Bailén, which ended so abruptly that we were instantly in the country driving between plowed fields that turned their brilliant red earth toward the grim sky.

La Mancha was more of the same, though the earth turned brown and then farther north a dull gray. The white cities vanished, replaced by unwalled towns the color of mud that seemed to hold their breath against the weather. Just south of Valdepeñas a solitary hunter with an air rifle slung across his shoulder waved at us from a field of stubble. "Wouldn't it be great to see Toledo under this sky?" I said. "It's pure El Greco." From the backseat Teddy said, "Pop, you wouldn't do that to us." Discouraged by the rain, I turned east and headed for the coast.

In a seaside village just north of Valencia, Fran and I took a long walk after dinner in the clear balmy air. It had been a brilliant afternoon when we'd arrived, the promenades thick with families out for their Sunday strolls, and all five of us had joined them, glad to be uncooped from the car. Catalans would tell you that this was part of their world, but the people had a southern gaiety that the Barcelonese usually lacked. Returning to the hotel, we found Teddy asleep in our bed. We unfurled the huge road map of Spain and retraced that day's course east from Córdoba, north to La Mancha, and then east again over the mountains to Valencia. "We can make it home tomorrow easily," I said.

From the bed Teddy mumbled, without opening his eyes, "That's our vacation. We get in the car and drive, drive, drive, and then stop and take pictures of the church, and get back in and drive, drive, drive."

"You left out the part about getting wet," I said.

"I left out the part about getting wet," he said.

Sr. Rusiñol had never seen the great jewels of the south, Granada, Sevilla, and Córdoba. The *estranjeros* saw much more of Spain than most Spaniards, who rarely travelled in their own country. The farthest he had ever been from home had been a few visits back to what he called "French Catalunya" to see relatives and friends of the family who had chosen not to return to Spain or whose political activity before or during the Civil War made it impossible. (The Franco government did not declare a general amnesty until 1969, thirty years after the surrender of the Republic.) I described the magnificence of the Alhambra. I described the ancient quarter that climbed the great hill with its narrow streets with their channels of running water that added a strange and constant music to the place. He had read much about the beauty of the city and of Sevilla, with its stunning antiquities. I neglected to tell him how we had passed the famous Ghiralda without stopping, believing it so ordinary it could not be the place. Nor did I mention our hours in the Jewish quarter, huddled in doorways in a vain attempt to stay dry. I spoke instead of the great sadness of the railroad station, of the solitary soldier who sat there alone in the late afternoon waiting for the train for home, a train I was sure would never come. Outside the light was falling; it would soon be New Year's Eve, and sitting there alone in the great station, he became for me a symbol of my own distance from the life I knew. I spoke of the mean little hotel we'd stayed at, and how standing on the balcony outside my room I'd made the mistake of looking in the window of the room next door and there saw a soldier in bed with a woman. Her garments were scattered across the floor; his rifle leaned against the door. In a moment this had registered on my memory, and I was certain it would remain forever. I had turned away and tried to imagine the care with which he had slowly and precisely dressed the chair and placed his boots at the foot of it.

And Córdoba, what had I thought of her? he wanted to know. I spoke of the great mosque now converted into a Catholic house of worship: how on the outside it had seemed like nothing, a sort of dun-colored warehouse, but when we entered, it had exploded in a maze of brilliant marble arches, and how on that Sunday, the first Sunday of the new year, the chorus of children's voices had floated ethereally from the baroque Catholic corner, and how my wife and I had merely stood for half an hour in awed silence.

Then I spoke of the ride home and how we had stopped so near the former home of Machado. "No," he said, "Machado lived neither in Jaén or Bailén but in Baeza, a village east of the city of Jaén though in the province of Jaén." It was, he had read, a very ancient mountain village, and probably nothing like the hideous mercantile, rain-swept Bailén. "You can feel the beauty and dignity of Baeza in his poems," but it was of course "cold Soria" which had at first been the most inspiring landscape of his life. It was there he had lived with his young bride before she died, and it was from Soria he had fled to save his sanity. I asked if I'd been near Soria. "No, Soria is in the north, in Castile, on the banks of the Duero. That is the landscape of his greatest poems." He began to recite from memory, "*Yo voy soñando caminos / de la tarde*" until he completed this famous poem. "Even after he had left he still dreamed of walking those roads in the afternoon. Always I see him walking 'among the golden hills, the green pine trees, the dusty live-oaks' and asking where the road leads. In my mind I hear the wind stirring in the trees along the river. We know the beauty and sadness of the Duero from his poems." He took my notebook and drew a rough outline of the Iberian peninsula; then he marked a city, and said, "It is in that cold land that Soria sleeps."

"Sleeps?" I said.

Yes, it slept, for that is how Machado presented it. He knew that region only through the poems of Machado. In one poem even the stones seemed to be dreaming. "What happened to you on the balcony of the hotel in Sevilla: that is what took place in the soul of Machado." He had suddenly switched to English. The light was failing outside, though the days were growing longer. Sitting across from me, his back to the window, Sr. Rusiñol was only a dark presence whose features I could no longer make out, but the voice went on. "Anyone who writes poetry knows that experience you spoke of, and no one knew it better than Machado. At the end of his great poem 'Fields of Soria' he writes of that world, 'You have settled in my soul,' and then he asks, 'or were you there from the start?' At such moments it is impossible to believe that who you are and what you behold are not one and the same. Do you know what I mean?"

Yes, of course I knew what he meant, but I had been surprised on that balcony because I did not expect the experience in so foreign a place.

"Nothing is foreign," he said, and offered no explanation.

He flicked on a small light over his desk, which I suddenly noticed was devoid of its usual clutter of books and papers. By my watch I saw it was past five, and so I rose to end our lesson, but Sr. Rusiñol gestured for me to be seated again. He bowed his head and spoke quietly. "I must tell you that I am going away, and so for a while these lessons must come to an end. I have enjoyed them very much. I will miss our discussions of your poets and ours, but in truth I do not think you require any more lessons. You speak Spanish now with great facility." I'm sure even in the dim light he could see my surprise. "It is not critical, this going away, it is merely a duty I must perform. We will meet again." And now he rose, and as I rose he hugged me in the traditional Spanish abrazo. I reminded him that I still had his copy of *Spanish Made Simple*. "Please keep it as a memento of these hours," he said, and he saw me downstairs and out into the soft evening air. I never saw him again.

The Castelldefels I knew is gone. Barcelona came out to meet it, and it's now a suburb of over forty thousand souls, many of them housed in hideous cement high-rises. It has joined the modern world and possesses its own traffic jams, drug merchants, and topless bars. The train still comes in every two hours from Gavá, but even on a Sunday morning in June it's not crowded with picnickers, maybe because the beach is oil-smeared and the truck traffic has fouled the air. The little tobacco store that sold stationery and pens is no longer there, or if it is I couldn't find it, though I did find my *torres* and learned from the new Dutch agent I could rent one like it for $1,500 a month, American. Hans Breen retired, and after all his years of wandering went back to Holland to settle down. The elder Rusiñol's garage has become a new car agency and flogs VWs manufactured in Spain. At the bakery I learned the Rusiñols were long gone, and no one I talked to remembered the poet.

Perhaps that is why when my old friend José Elgorriaga asked me to help him translate Machado, I agreed to do so. I knew it could not be done, I argued against the venture, I insisted my style as a poet was all wrong, but my friend only agreed. Everything I said was true, but he needed the help of a poet, and I was the poet he had. He handed me a sheaf of Xeroxed copies of his favorite poems that almost disappeared in the spiderwebs of his notes and with them yellow-lined sheets with trots in English. And then he sat me down and read me the poems in his beautiful Castillian Spanish, occasionally rising in the dusty center of his tiny campus office to declaim a passage that moved his soul with its beauty. I had not witnessed such love of Spanish poetry since the departure of my Catalan friend.

Have you ever been moved in the soul? I know that is a ridiculous question, but I ask it because much of my life I didn't know such a thing was possible. I grew up with no concept of the soul, and when the conversation turns to the nature of the soul I will remain at sea forever. As a young Jew I prayed, but never for my immortal soul, and as an older Jew I never prayed at all. (In a recent poem entitled "Soul," I recount a true tale in which a Mrs. Morton made my brother Eddie and me go down on our knees and recite for company the prayer that should we die before we wake God would take our souls. We found the spectacle so appalling that no threat of punishment could ever induce us to repeat it. We were saved when my mother caught Mrs. Morton stealing her jewelry, and she was sent "packing—with no references—into the larger Christian world.") As solitary observer and memorializer of the Castillian landscape, Antonio Machado is often moved in the soul. He tells us again and again without the least reserve, he tells us with such simplicity and clarity we come to believe him absolutely, and in doing so we come to understand our own deepest experiences and to believe entirely in their authenticity. It is hard to imagine a more useful poetry.

In Machado's poems nothing hurries, for the world has been as it is for centuries, though of course it constantly changes so that it can return to what it was. "Mounted on small brown donkeys," he writes, "the travelers are lost from sight / where the roads drop below / the rolling hills, though now they rise / in the distance of afternoon, tiny painted figures / that stain the blazing canvas of dusk." We could be in ancient Chinese poetry or traveling with Yeats's figures carved in lapis lazuli. When "the wind stirs in the river poplars" you know that once again this autumn the dry leaves will deliver their ageless "chant to the water's song." Yesterday the branches "bent to the weight of nightingales" and tomorrow "the scented winds of spring will hum through the branches." All time is one time in the soul of Antonio Machado, and there is a time for everything. The world whirling in its endless dance of time does so with a poise and dignity our lives lack—or lack until we read Machado, until we pour ourselves into his poetry and he in turn pours his vision into us. The inner landscape of his heart is a "city in ruins," his Soria, and viewing it each day the "heart deepens with sadness," a sadness—as he says—"like love." He looks out over this world—I suppose his contemporary in English poetry might say he "gazes" out over this world—and he sees it as it is and at the same time as it has been for centuries, for to him nothing has changed except that it all lives in time and so is never the same. The whole history of Castile is the history of Machado, an empire gone to ruins, and the moment which is his life, the lasting moment he lives and relives, becomes the place itself. Think of being the very world you behold, of having been that world since time began, think of the present moment stretching back to no beginning and forward to no ending, and you too might say, "Fields of Soria / where the stones seem to be dreaming, / you go with me."

Think of being a world of country trails, meadows, outcroppings of rock, fields of brambles, thorns, thistles, briars, burdocks, bees and their honeycombs, jackdaws, sheep. Think of the roads closed in snow, the high frigid winter plains of Castile rife with the memories of a Spanish empire long lost, the towns with their collapsing churches, stone fountains, belfries, the houses with their rusty gates and barred windows. From his Andalusian days the water wheel turns like a clock, the nightingale sings in the dark, water runs in troughs to the music of time. Where there is a tool it is an axe, where there is food it is dark bread, where there is perfume it is the lemon tree in blossom, where there is a weapon it is the crossbow, where there is music there is a lyre. Logs smoulder on the hearth, an old man wrapped in wool shudders by the fire, his woman sews, and the lost son never returns.

And they go on waiting, for the lesson of this great maestro—he taught far more than high school French—is patience, the greatest lesson the poet can learn, for without it he or she is subject to every corrupting influence. Impatience is our nightmare. As Kafka wrote, "There are two main human sins from which all the others derive: impatience and indolence. It was because of impatience that they were expelled from Paradise; it is because of indolence they do not return. Yet perhaps there is only one major sin: impatience. Because of impatience they were expelled, because of impatience they do not return." Reading and rereading the poems of Machado it becomes impossible to believe even a single poem was rushed into being or hurried toward some form of completion. Consider this: I am writing about one of my contemporaries.

I delight to imagine Machado at his evening walk. The world comes to him whether he is on the cold roads of Soria or in a mountain town of Andalusia. A river comes into view curved like a crossbow, the boughs of the plane trees bend to the weight of bees, the wind stirs in the long grasses at the edges of sight where a few travellers appear over the green mounds of the distant hills; they speak back and forth in a language as soft as water overflowing cisterns; the rocks empurpled in the dusk dream in eternity. The air deepens and stills in the fields; time stops. Something like a vision rises in the golden dust of sunset, a vision of a world sweet enough to welcome the human heart freed from vanity and greed. I delight to imagine Antonio Machado alive in a world of others as good as he, a world as glorious as the simple language he found to create it.

Flight Home[1]
(1958)
W.S. Merwin

(In August 1956, Merwin flew home after seven years in Europe. The notes that follow are taken from a journal he kept at the time.)

Aug. 27, 1956, a barber shop in St. John's Wood

They say that after seven years every cell in your body has changed. You are a different person.

I wish I could remember what day it was, in July, 1949, that I landed in Genoa. Or the day (one or two days before?) when we first came in sight of the Spanish coast.

Strange, now I am going back, to think that I have been in Europe without a break, ever since I was a minor. Ever since I was twenty-one.

On the chart one does not see the long line of wanting to go back.

---

1. "Flight Home" first appeared in *Paris Review*.

Editor's Note: W.S. Merwin, "Flight Home" from *Regions of Memory: Uncollected Prose 1949–1982* (Urbana: University of Illinois Press, 1987).

Beginning in my case before I set out, and rising through delight and hostility and wonder and everything that has been the experience of Europe. The line rising clear off the chart at last and stabbing into the air above it, without footing, but without coming down, for how many years now?

Part of the confusion, once the desire to go back got off the chart, arose from the suspicion that this was simply, at least in part, the first shock of maturity: a realization that home, where you grew up and belonged— belonged with and without your own volition—no longer exists. The desire to return to it, the moment you know it no longer exists. I had been away long enough, and surrounded by Europeans thoroughly enough, to get these mixed up. European friends wondering, as they say, what I will make of it. Probably nothing at all. Wishing, they say, that they could be here, like a fly on the wall, to watch, when I get back. How can I explain that I do not want to go back in order to form opinions. That, unless I am very wrong, opinions will have nearly nothing to do with the main thing of being back. Home is a place that does not exist, about which your opinions are irrelevant.

Aug. 27, 1956, 11:30 p.m., PAA Clipper Carib

It is nearly impossible, afterwards, to remember at what point I began to believe that I was really going. Believing comes elusively, not when you expect, most often, but both earlier and later, only gradually filling in the place where it will be. Unpredictable, like a season changing.

It would come over me all at once that I was, say, sitting in that barber's chair for the last time before I went. It would take the imagination by shock. The next minute I didn't believe it at all. I was sure I'd go on and have the next haircut in that same chair (with the barber who'd learned what I enjoyed was not having him talk to me, but having him carry on animated conversation with other customers, to which I could listen), and the one after that, and the one after that. When I got around to having haircuts at all. Somewhere else in the mind the imagination suddenly looks down the long vistas of time where one will not walk. The possible lives that one will not lead.

And twenty-four hours before I was due to go, when everything was reminding me that it was happening for the last time—a rhythm that had gathered speed until it was unbroken—I would find myself going through the motions of the place's most familiar habits, and not be able to believe.

I was sure I was going in a thin way like a hum in your ears, yesterday, as the desk gradually grew bare and everything in the study was either packed or put away. Not feeling anything about it but a certain emptiness independent of the emptying room; but sure. Feelings? I suppose they were there, after all, but like beasts patient as immigrants, waiting to move in on the emptiness when their time came.

And sure yesterday as my key case kept getting lighter, and the keys one by one were used for the last time and then packed in intelligent places where I will never be able to find them again.

Then with all but a few things done, except things that could wait till the last minute, or things that would take too long anyway and must be abandoned, suddenly finding that everything was ready. And time all at once was heavy. Between the intense activity of getting ready, and the farewells and rush of getting off, time was heavy. More so not because I was anxious to go. I'd forgotten that, days before. A week ago. But because of all reasons I did *not* want to go. Wanted not to be going, but since I was going wanted to be gone. How different from most times when I've been going somewhere, thinking almost entirely of where I was going, savoring the whole trip, from the moment I was ready to go. Different entirely from when I left America, for I didn't know how long, seven years ago. Even though a great part of me wanted to stay in America then, and even had an array of reasons. (Why go to Europe when I knew so little of America?) I know just how much and in what ways I'm fond of

Europe, but I didn't know what I felt about America. I regretted leaving, before I had even gone, but I didn't know what I'd really miss until I'd been away for some time. Foreign places, however familiar, defining your feeling about home. But stay away too long and you're bound to confuse that with homesickness. (Which I never in my life felt, except in the mildest ways, until these last few years. Unprepared for it.)

The lassitude that descended, in that pause of an hour or so between the end of getting ready, and the time to go. Not calling the taxi, after all, until almost too late. That dazed lassitude that does not believe in time; or, at the moments when it has to countenance the minutes' passing, panics, and protests, protests, flailing in molasses, shouting under water: "Not today, no, not today." But dazed, languorous, just the same. The lassitude hand in hand with the emotions themselves of good-bye. And they, together, swelling the occasion with their heavy, bewildered, helpless dumbness. The daze still there (like the feeling when you have been in a pub for several hours at lunchtime, and suddenly find yourself out in the sunshine, alone) in the taxi, all the way to the air terminal. Feeling bulky and clumsy, as though your ears had just stopped ringing. The traffic so heavy that the taxi barely made it in time; the excitement of almost missing the bus to the airport, rising through the numbness of departure, and I was grateful for it.

Odd that passing sense of panic that wants to put it off till tomorrow, that hangs around and wants to go all right, but not today; trying to jump back into yesterday. A feeling that can, in the end, find nothing to focus on, and no grounds for itself. Maybe just an intensification of the familiar conviction (when going out to the theater, or leaving a hotel room) that you are leaving something vital behind. As, of course, you always are.

In the rush at the air terminal, again almost missing the bus. Never having felt any departure so contradictorily, I was never before so aware of the way the efficient bustle, the professional voices on loudspeakers, the assembly line rounding up and processing of passengers, resembles the ward-walking manner of nurses. Admirably impersonal. Cheery. For the benefit of everybody especially, designed to brisk, shame, and cozy you along. I've always found this amusing, a tiny bit irritating (making me want to ask them stupid questions and delay everything, and see just how long everything could be made to wait, just how elastic it could all be), and rather pleasant. And this time I wished it wouldn't all rush through so fast, so that I could have a chance to watch the effects of the helpful manner on the other passengers, especially those who were parting at the air terminal itself. (My incurable vulgar curiosity.) Partly to get away from too clinging a concern with my own departure and what I was leaving.

But in England, up to the very last, there's always the weather to concern you. The morning had been overcast and rainy, but as the taxi drove away the sun came out. And the airport bus was stuffy and hot, turtling through the Kensington and Hammersmith traffic in the sunny muggy London late afternoon. The sort of weather that would have women swanning up and down Knightsbridge, and the London shopkeepers and charwomen groaning. A nice summer day, or a bit of one. One of the Bright Periods whose Second Coming the London papers will mendaciously prophesy for months to come. The few English people in the bus quietly sweltering in their dark inconspicuous tweeds (one splendid man with a white mustache and a dirty gabardine raincoat on over his) and the many Americans peeling off their conspicuous pressed, newly bought-in-England woolens. Two collegiate characters, each just twelve pounds overweight, in white shirts, talking seriously about expansion of some kind, somewhere in Connecticut. A glum, brown-dressed, green-faced thin, young New Yorker next to me, filling his embarcation card with that particular expression of unimpressionable, slightly sour-natured boredom which is peculiarly New York. Two ugly girls from Baltimore talking to a handsome woman from further south, up ahead of me. Several South Americans, Brazilians. A collection of Turks, and one family with Turkish diplomatic passports. A group of American Greeks going back to Greece, with the accent of the mother country, the intonation of my country, driving through England.

THE STRANGEST OF THEATRES

England, where nearly all intonations of the language except the few variants of what they call "standard English," tend to be considered comic, or ugly and undesirable if you have to take them seriously. A system which, I can see, is good for acting, but strikes me as deadly in most other ways. About as healthy for writing, I should think, as the French deliberate limitation of their literary vocabulary was for French poetry. Socially handy, it seems. This preoccupation with class distinction which no longer means much. A preoccupation which, after five years off and on in England, I still find as foreign as sampans. Continuous effort and argument with myself, not to find this amount of preoccupation with class distinctions more than a little vulgar. In a way which, to me, looks sterile. Probably this is a case, among so many, where the illusion that we speak the same language registers against my ability to understand.

When we got to the airport the day had gone dark with clouds; there was a raw wind, and the rain had started again. There must have been several inches of water in some places on the tarmac. Rain sweeping over the wings of the waiting planes. The big planes taxiing around on the wet runway, and the rain and real wind skating across it in goose-flesh streaks like flaws rushing across mica. The slipstreams of the planes tore up long plumes of spray, the water streaking out flat and whipping away like grass does out on the airfield. The engines, idling or warming up, actually bared and dried the tarmac, for a second, just in back of the wings. And when a plane would take off, as one did right in front of us, the water on the tarmac would lie gashed and open for a moment, bared over a bone, and then flow back hesitantly to fill the place and smooth it over, after the plane was airborne, just as it would have over a ship that had sunk. The genies of controlled violence reminding you that the control is artificial, that they're all one family and never forget each other and that two-thirds of the world is violence.

With everything so organized and sterilized and herded and heated and air-conditioned, it seemed strange that one should be walking in real rain, even for a minute. The taxiing around the airport, that always robs me of the last shred of my sense of direction, wherever I am, as though you had to be robbed of that before you could be hurled straight toward your destination as the crow flies. The houses and allotments around the airport turning and turning. You have to be dizzied, after being robbed of volition; be the Blind Man. The voices in the plane coming from far away, as through the sleep of a child, over the noise of the engines; the pressure of everything seeming to build up in the plane. Wanting to sing, as always, when the engines, one by one, were gunned and roared, at the end of the runway before the takeoff, and the plane shook itself free of the ground. As excited as a child, as always, by the takeoff. And at the same time, this time, suddenly caught in an immense depression, as though all the dead weight of the lassitude of an hour, two hours, before, had fallen on me at once, and was carrying me down. As the plane rushed down the runway and the wedge between us and the ground widened, and the line of houses streaked by, I had a distinct impression of a cloth being violently torn. I would have rushed out of the plane that minute, had it been still; or have been tempted to. And back onto it, the moment my feet touched the ground.

England looked soaked, sodden, from the air. Whole fields lying under water. The standing water in sheets of glassy gray, no color, white, no color; showing the contours of all the hollows and low patches. As though a sheet of some sort of metal had been slid through the land. The ponds looking higher than their banks, and the Thames looking as though it lay on top of the countryside. Landscape and sky all lights and shades of gray, in every direction. Even the sunlight gray and laden with rain: pregnant. The sky dark with tons and tons of water as we flew toward Wales; and the towns beneath looking as if they had never been dry.

A nun looking like an albino buffalo with dyspepsia had got on at London, with another of her cloth, and I with my superstitions had to keep my fingers crossed all the way to Catholic Shannon because where could I find two dogs on an airplane to cancel the nuns? Though we were flying over towns full of Englishmen all loving dogs as Americans are supposed to love their mothers.

We were in and out of long feathers of black cloud, over Wales; after dusk with the lights on in the towns, but the dark not final yet, and the coast of Wales clear and sharp as we flew over.

Next to me a young thin Jewish doctor, my age, from Philadelphia, who has been all over Europe as surgeon to a traveling Black basketball team.

He has been to see his grandfather's four ancient sisters in Liverpool but I have been able to extract few details from him other than their ages (69, 72, 78, 82), the fact that two of them are almost blind, and that they are too old to cry. This last seems to be quite a drawback, since although they had never seen him before they apparently all wanted to cry as soon as they knew he was there, their brother's son whom they thought they'd never live to see; and it seems they were all of them pretty choked up as long as he was there. But enjoyed it, if he is any indication. Probably quite genuinely glad to see each other...

Cloud over Ireland until we got to the west. And then the low-running hills looking green as in the storybooks, in the almost dark dusk. Long pennons of water winding in from the coast, with lights along them, and everything low. We came in over water.

And Shannon was better than I could have hoped. The low, dark green buildings, temporary and whorish. The feeling that they'd sell you their genuine Machree grandmother if you expressed an interest in such baggages and had the green money. People lined up ten deep at the liquor counter, buying the limit. Watches, perfumes, Irish linens and tweeds, pipes, souvenirs of olde Erin impossibly clean and already looking like the belongings of tourists. A long waiting room with asbestos walls, where fifty travelers sprawled and smoked and drank and sat guard over packages and looked as dejected as though they had just learned they were going to live there. None of them seemed to be speaking to each other. Loudspeakers in the walls asking for Father O'Brien every two minutes, or if not Father O'Brien, Father Malloy. We were led into a dull supper of thumb soup with pretensions to mushrooms and flannel beef.

Taking off from Shannon, we had a searchlight beam on us, and the light in the propellers made big, slow-widening spirals of light, with spirals of shadow inside them that spread outward from the propeller shafts. Like those tops I had as a child, where the colors melted outward as the top spun.

12:35 a.m. London time

I wonder whether it is raining in London. Probably. I wonder whether the rags that I left in the attic joists won't get too heavy in the ceiling and bring it down with a sodden crash all over the floor.

The Dipper is as bright as I remember it in Spain, just outside the window. A regatta of little triangular clouds, far below, as we fly west. And one great mountainous cloud which we have just flown through had a long promontory which ran out into nothing, and made me feel vertigo for the cloud. I remember seeing a promontory in Majorca, on a day so still that its reflection in the sea was as sharp and clear as its own shape; they made a single shape running out into the colorless sea that looked like a sky, and it seemed they must certainly fall. And that first summer in France, the day when I swam out into the Mediterranean trying out a pair of underwater goggles, which I'd never worn before. Warm with pleasure at the first long view of the jagged seafloor shifting with light and blue shadows. Fish, fronds, sea anemones, swimmers, and sliders and weeds washing. The pocked snags and sloping ridges maybe thirty or forty feet below me as I rocked and swayed and swam out. They deepened a little and then rose toward the surface again, a hundred feet out. And then suddenly ended. The sharp edge dropped off into dark blue nothing, in which occasionally a tiny fin would flash light for a second. I was out over nothing at all, and it felt cold, and nowhere but in my dreams had I ever known such vertigo.

Every time you leave it is the last time.

Even if passionately addicted to talking about myself, how difficult it would have been to explain to friends in England (and to some Americans) this thing of *not expecting anything* from going back. I know things have changed. I know too that, as I've felt it all receding from me, I've made it up, invented it. I knew at the time that I was doing it.

I don't expect to be disappointed at finding that my invention was false, that the place isn't like that at all, that even the things I never liked, and remember disliking, have changed. I expect to be immensely relieved to be able to abandon the fiction entirely, and let the real thing take over. Because the real fiction was a fence to keep people away from what of America I felt I had managed to hang on to. And I was aware that it would end by keeping me away from it too. I look forward to being able to admit to an honest dislike of something right there and my own. A thing that I've hardly allowed myself to do for months, not because I was concerned with anyone's opinions, but because of a fear that such admission might push the smallest detail of home, even an unpleasant one (especially an unpleasant one) further away from me. But remembering, in private as deliberately as anything else, sordor, squalor, waste, ugliness, injustice. One thing I do not expect is to respond to the place simply, with delight, or admiration, or repulsion, as I do in Europe. Not one feeling at a time. But several of them or all of them, all me, at once.

I have loathed that fiction, and myself for fostering it. Like finding oneself insisting that the person one loved was pretty. Finding myself betraying everything, out of my desire not to betray it. Only let me waste no time now even for penance. It redresses nothing, least of all balance. Let me find instead a hard eye.

I don't think that Europeans get the same sort of passion for home. Generations and generations having worked out a way of regarding the place, taught them where to fix the feeling, what to see and how to communicate with it. And just the confidence which must come from the awareness that it all has been there so long already. And allow themselves even nostalgia without so much danger of sentimentality running riot. They can do it all more gently, more gracefully. Two qualities that we, quite often, must manage without.

I suppose it would be simpler to say that they have loved their place for generations, centuries; and know it, without having to make a fuss about it. Whereas, by comparison, we begin as a loveless people. Generation after generation having cared little for the place. Our fathers began by caring little enough about Europe so that they could leave it. We've used the place, wasted it. It has made us prodigal, restless. And we are attached to it in still-raw ways that we aren't aware of, most often. We ought to know that we couldn't hate it as fiercely as we do sometimes without there being something honest in our attachment to it. But there is always the sense of surprise, of inarticulate awkwardness, at discovering that the name for what you feel is love.

The black sea down there doesn't even need sleep, all the way to Labrador; and the night is splendid, and above it all.

The Antilles: Fragments of Epic Memory[1]

Nobel Lecture, December 7, 1992

Derek Walcott

Felicity is a village in Trinidad on the edge of the Caroni plain, the wide central plain that still grows sugar and to which indentured cane cutters were brought after emancipation, so the small population of Felicity is East Indian, and on the afternoon that I visited it with friends from America, all the faces along its road were Indian, which, as I hope to show, was a moving, beautiful thing, because this Saturday afternoon *Ramleela*, the epic dramatization of the Hindu epic the *Ramayana*, was going to be performed, and the costumed actors from the village were assembling on a field strung with different-coloured flags, like a new gas station, and beautiful Indian boys in red and black were aiming arrows haphazardly into the afternoon light. Low blue mountains on the horizon, bright grass, clouds that would gather colour before the light went. Felicity! What a gentle Anglo-Saxon name for an epical memory.

Under an open shed on the edge of the field, there were two huge

---

1. Derek Walcott, "The Antilles: Fragments of Epic Memory" (Nobel Lecture, 1992). Later collected in *What the Twilight Says* (New York: Farrar, Straus and Giroux, 1998).

armatures of bamboo that looked like immense cages. They were parts of the body of a god, his calves or thighs, which, fitted and reared, would make a gigantic effigy. This effigy would be burnt as a conclusion to the epic. The cane structures flashed a predictable parallel: Shelley's sonnet on the fallen statue of Ozymandias and his empire, that "colossal wreck" in its empty desert.

Drummers had lit a fire in the shed and they eased the skins of their tablas nearer the flames to tighten them. The saffron flames, the bright grass, and the hand-woven armatures of the fragmented god who would be burnt were not in any desert where imperial power had finally toppled but were part of a ritual, evergreen season that, like the cane-burning harvest, is annually repeated, the point of such sacrifice being its repetition, the point of the destruction being renewal through fire.

Deities were entering the field. What we generally call "Indian music" was blaring from the open platformed shed from which the epic would be narrated. Costumed actors were arriving. Princes and gods, I supposed. What an unfortunate confession! "Gods, I suppose" is the shrug that embodies our African and Asian diasporas. I had often thought of but never seen *Ramleela*, and had never seen this theatre, an open field, with village children as warriors, princes, and gods. I had no idea what the epic story was, who its hero was, what enemies he fought, yet I had recently adapted the *Odyssey* for a theatre in England, presuming that the audience knew the trials of Odysseus, hero of another Asia Minor epic, while nobody in Trinidad knew any more than I did about Rama, Kali, Shiva, Vishnu, apart from the Indians, a phrase I use pervertedly because that is the kind of remark you can still hear in Trinidad: "apart from the Indians."

It was as if, on the edge of the Central Plain, there was another plateau, a raft on which the *Ramayana* would be poorly performed in this ocean of cane, but that was my writer's view of things, and it is wrong. I was seeing the *Ramleela* at Felicity as theatre when it was faith.

Multiply that moment of self-conviction when an actor, made-up and costumed, nods to his mirror before stopping on stage in the belief that he is a reality entering an illusion and you would have what I presumed was happening to the actors of this epic. But they were not actors. They had been chosen; or they themselves had chosen their roles in this sacred story that would go on for nine afternoons over a two-hour period till the sun set. They were not amateurs but believers. There was no theatrical term to define them. They did not have to psych themselves up to play their roles. Their acting would probably be as buoyant and as natural as those bamboo arrows crisscrossing the afternoon pasture. They believed in what they were playing, in the sacredness of the text, the validity of India, while I, out of the writer's habit, searched for some sense of elegy, of loss, even of degenerative mimicry in the happy faces of the boy-warriors or the heraldic profiles of the village princes. I was polluting the afternoon with doubt and with the patronage of admiration. I misread the event through a visual echo of History—the cane fields, indenture, the evocation of vanished armies, temples, and trumpeting elephants—when all around me there was quite the opposite: elation, delight in the boys' screams, in the sweets-stalls, in more and more costumed characters appearing; a delight of conviction, not loss. The name Felicity made sense.

Consider the scale of Asia reduced to these fragments: the small white exclamations of minarets or the stone balls of temples in the cane fields, and one can understand the self-mockery and embarrassment of those who see these rites as parodic, even degenerate. These purists look on such ceremonies as grammarians look at a dialect, as cities look on provinces and empires on their colonies. Memory that yearns to join the centre, a limb remembering the body from which it has been severed, like those bamboo thighs of the god. In other words, the way that the Caribbean is still looked at, illegitimate, rootless, mongrelized. "No people there," to quote Froude, "in the true sense of the word." No people. Fragments and echoes of real people, unoriginal and broken.

The performance was like a dialect, a branch of its original language, an abridgement of it, but not a distortion or even a reduction of its epic scale. Here in Trinidad I had discovered that one of the greatest epics of the world was seasonally performed, not with that desperate resignation of preserving a culture, but with an openness of belief that was as steady as the wind bending the cane lances of the Caroni plain. We had to leave before the play began to go through the creeks of the Caroni Swamp, to catch the scarlet ibises coming home at dusk. In a performance as natural as those of the actors of the *Ramleela*, we watched the flocks come in as bright as the scarlet of the boy archers, as the red flags, and cover an islet until it turned into a flowering tree, an anchored immortelle. The sigh of History meant nothing here. These two visions, the *Ramleela* and the arrowing flocks of scarlet ibises, blent into a single gasp of gratitude. Visual surprise is natural in the Caribbean; it comes with the landscape, and faced with its beauty, the sigh of History dissolves.

We make too much of that long groan which underlines the past. I felt privileged to discover the ibises as well as the scarlet archers of Felicity.

The sigh of History rises over ruins, not over landscapes, and in the Antilles there are few ruins to sigh over, apart from the ruins of sugar estates and abandoned forts. Looking around slowly, as a camera would, taking in the low blue hills over Port of Spain, the village road and houses, the warrior-archers, the god-actors and their handlers, and music already on the sound track, I wanted to make a film that would be a long-drawn sigh over Felicity. I was filtering the afternoon with evocations of a lost India, but why "evocations?" Why not "celebrations of a real presence?" Why should India be "lost" when none of these villagers ever really knew it, and why not "continuing," why not the perpetuation of joy in Felicity and in all the other nouns of the Central Plain: Couva, Chaguanas, Charley Village? Why was I not letting my pleasure open its windows wide? I was enticed like any Trinidadian to the ecstasies of their claim, because ecstasy was the pitch of the sinuous drumming in the loudspeakers. I was entitled to the feast of Husein, to the mirrors and crepe-paper temples of the Muslim epic, to the Chinese Dragon Dance, to the rites of that Sephardic Jewish synagogue that was once on Something Street. I am only one-eighth the writer I might have been had I contained all the fragmented languages of Trinidad.

Break a vase, and the love that reassembles the fragments is stronger than that love which took its symmetry for granted when it was whole. The glue that fits the pieces is the sealing of its original shape. It is such a love that reassembles our African and Asiatic fragments, the cracked heirlooms whose restoration shows its white scars. This gathering of broken pieces is the care and pain of the Antilles, and if the pieces are disparate, ill-fitting, they contain more pain than their original sculpture, those icons and sacred vessels taken for granted in their ancestral places. Antillean art is this restoration of our shattered histories, our shards of vocabulary, our archipelago becoming a synonym for pieces broken off from the original continent.

And this is the exact process of the making of poetry, or what should be called not its "making" but its remaking, the fragmented memory, the armature that frames the god, even the rite that surrenders it to a final pyre; the god assembled cane by cane, reed by weaving reed, line by plaited line, as the artisans of Felicity would erect his holy echo.

Poetry, which is perfection's sweat but which must seem as fresh as the raindrops on a statue's brow, combines the natural and the marmoreal; it conjugates both tenses simultaneously: the past and the present, if the past is the sculpture and the present the beads of dew or rain on the forehead of the past. There is the buried language and there is the individual vocabulary, and the process of poetry is one of excavation and of self-discovery. Tonally the individual voice is a dialect; it shapes its own accent, its own vocabulary and melody in defiance of an imperial concept of language, the language of Ozymandias, libraries and dictionaries, law courts and critics, and churches, universities, political dogma, the diction of institutions. Poetry is an island that breaks away from the main. The dialects of my archipelago seem as fresh to me as those raindrops on the statue's forehead, not the sweat made from the classic exertion of frowning marble, but the condensations of a refreshing element, rain and salt.

Deprived of their original language, the captured and indentured tribes create their own, accreting and secreting fragments of an old, an epic vocabulary, from Asia and from Africa, but to an ancestral, an ecstatic rhythm in the blood that cannot be subdued by slavery or indenture, while nouns are renamed and the given names of places accepted like Felicity village or Choiseul. The original language dissolves from the exhaustion of distance like fog trying to cross an ocean, but this process of renaming, of finding new metaphors, is the same process that the poet faces every morning of his working day, making his own tools like Crusoe, assembling nouns from necessity, from Felicity, even renaming himself. The stripped man is driven back to that self-astonishing, elemental force, his mind. That is the basis of the Antillean experience, this shipwreck of fragments, these echoes, these shards of a huge tribal vocabulary, these partially remembered customs, and they are not decayed but strong. They survived the Middle Passage and the *Fatel Rozack*, the ship that carried the first indentured Indians from the port of Madras to the cane fields of Felicity, that carried the chained Cromwellian convict and the Sephardic Jew, the Chinese grocer and the Lebanese merchant selling cloth samples on his bicycle.

And here they are, all in a single Caribbean city, Port of Spain, the sum of history, Trollope's "non-people." A downtown babel of shop signs and streets, mongrelized, polyglot, a ferment without a history, like heaven. Because that is what such a city is, in the New World, a writer's heaven.

A culture, we all know, is made by its cities.

Another first morning home, impatient for the sunrise—a broken sleep. Darkness at five, and the drapes not worth opening; then, in the sudden light, a cream-walled, brown-roofed police station bordered with short royal palms, in the colonial style, back of it frothing trees and taller palms, a pigeon fluttering into the cover of a cave, a rain-stained block of once-modern apartments, the morning side road into the station without traffic. All part of a surprising peace. This quiet happens with every visit to a city that has deepened itself in me. The flowers and the hills are easy, affection for them predictable; it is the architecture that, for the first morning, disorients. A return from American seductions used to make the traveller feel that something was missing, something was trying to complete itself, like the stained concrete apartments. Pan left along the window and the excrescences rear—a city trying to soar, trying to be brutal, like an American city in silhouette, stamped from the same mould as Columbus or Des Moines. An assertion of power, its decor bland, its air-conditioning pitched to the point where its secretarial and executive staff sport competing cardigans; the colder the offices the more important, an imitation of another climate. A longing, even an envy of feeling cold.

In serious cities, in grey, militant winter with its short afternoons, the days seem to pass by in buttoned overcoats, every building appears as a barracks with lights on in its windows, and when snow comes, one has the illusion of living in a Russian novel, in the nineteenth century, because of the literature of winter. So visitors to the Caribbean must feel that they are inhabiting a succession of postcards. Both climates are shaped by what we have read of them. For tourists, the sunshine cannot be serious. Winter adds depth and darkness to life as well as to literature, and in the unending summer of the tropics not even poverty or poetry (in the Antilles poverty is poetry with a V, *une vie*, a condition of life as well as of imagination) seems capable of being profound because the nature around it is so exultant, so resolutely ecstatic, like its music. A culture based on joy is bound to be shallow. Sadly, to sell itself, the Caribbean encourages the delights of mindlessness, of brilliant vacuity, as a place to flee not only winter but that seriousness that comes only out of culture with four seasons. So how can there be a people there, in the true sense of the word?

They know nothing about seasons in which leaves let go of the year, in which spires fade in blizzards and streets whiten, of the erasures of whole cities by fog, of reflection in fireplaces; instead, they inhabit a geography whose rhythm, like their music, is limited to two stresses: hot and wet, sun and rain, light and shadow, day and night, the limitations of an incomplete metre, and are therefore a people incapable of the subtleties of contradiction, of imaginative complexity. So be it. We cannot change contempt.

Ours are not cities in the accepted sense, but no one wants them to be. They dictate their own proportions, their own definitions in particular places and in a prose equal to that of their detractors, so that now it is not just St. James but the streets and yards that Naipaul commemorates, its lanes as short and brilliant as his sentences; not just the noise and jostle of Tunapuna but the origins of C.L.R. James's *Beyond a Boundary*, not just Felicity village on the Caroni plain, but Selvon Country, and that is the way it goes up the islands now: the old Dominica of Jean Rhys still very much the way she wrote of it; and the Martinique of the early Césaire; Perse's Guadeloupe, even without the pith helmets and the mules; and what delight and privilege there was in watching a literature—one literature in several imperial languages, French, English, Spanish—bud and open island after island in the early morning of a culture, not timid, not derivative, any more than the hard white petals of the frangipani are derivative and timid. This is not a belligerent boast but a simple celebration of inevitability: that this flowering had to come.

On a heat-stoned afternoon in Port of Spain, some alley white with glare, with love vine spilling over a fence, palms and a hazed mountain appear around a corner to the evocation of Vaughn or Herbert's "that shady city of palm-trees," or to the memory of a Hammond organ from a wooden chapel in Castries, where the congregation sang "Jerusalem, the Golden." It is hard for me to see such emptiness as desolation. It is that patience that is the width of Antillean life, and the secret is not to ask the wrong thing of it, not to demand of it an ambition it has no interest in. The traveller reads this as lethargy, as torpor.

Here there are not enough books, one says, no theatres, no museums, simply not enough to do. Yet, deprived of books, a man must fall back on thought, and out of thought, if he can learn to order it, will come the urge to record, and in extremity, if he has no means of recording, recitation, the ordering of memory which leads to metre, to commemoration. There can be virtues in deprivation, and certainly one virtue is salvation from a cascade of high mediocrity, since books are now not so much created as remade. Cities create a culture, and all we have are these magnified market towns, so what are the proportions of the ideal Caribbean city? A surrounding, accessible countryside with leafy suburbs, and if the city is lucky, behind it, spacious plains. Behind it, fine mountains; before it, an indigo sea. Spires would pin its centre and around them would be leafy, shadowy parks. Pigeons would cross its sky in alphabetic patterns, carrying with them memories of a belief in augury, and at the heart of the city there would be horses, yes, horses, those animals last seen at the end of the nineteenth century drawing broughams and carriages with top-hatted citizens, horses that live in the present tense without elegiac echoes from their hooves, emerging from paddocks at the Queen's Park Savannah at sunrise, when mist is unthreading from the cool mountains above the roofs, and at the centre of the city seasonally there would be races, so that citizens could roar at the speed and grace of these nineteenth-century animals. Its docks, not obscured by smoke or deafened by too much machinery, and above all, it would be so racially various that the cultures of the world—the Asiatic, the Mediterranean, the European, the African—would be represented in it, its humane variety more exciting than Joyce's Dublin. Its citizens would intermarry as they chose, from instinct, not tradition, until their children find it increasingly futile to trace their genealogy. It would not have too many avenues difficult or dangerous for pedestrians, its mercantile area would be a cacophony of accents, fragments of the old language that would be silenced immediately at five o'clock, its docks resolutely vacant on Sundays.

This is Port of Spain to me, a city ideal in its commercial and human proportions, where a citizen is a walker and not a pedestrian, and this is how Athens may have been before it became a cultural echo.

The finest silhouettes of Port of Spain are idealizations of the crafts-man's handiwork, not of concrete and glass, but of baroque woodwork, each fantasy looking more like an involved drawing of itself than the actual building. Behind the city is the Caroni plain, with its villages, Indian prayer flags, and fruit vendors' stalls along the highway over which ibises come like floating flags. Photogenic poverty! Postcard sad-nesses! I am not re-creating Eden; I mean, by "the Antilles," the reality of light, of work, of survival. I mean a house on the side of a country road, I mean the Caribbean Sea, whose smell is the smell of refreshing pos-sibility as well as survival. Survival is the triumph of stubborness, and spiritual stubborness, a sublime stupidity, is what makes the occupa-tion of poetry endure, when there are so many things that should make it futile. Those things added together can go under one collective noun: "the world."

This is the visible poetry of the Antilles, then. Survival.

If you wish to understand that consoling pity with which the islands were regarded, look at the tinted engravings of Antillean forests, with their proper palm trees, ferns, and waterfalls. They have a civilizing decency, like Botanical Gardens, as if the sky were a glass ceiling under which a colonized vegetation is arranged for quiet walks and carriage rides. Those views are incised with a pathos that guides the engraver's tool and the topographer's pencil, and it is this pathos which, tenderly ironic, gave villages names like Felicity. A century looked at a landscape furious with vegetation in the wrong light and with the wrong eye. It is such pictures that are saddening rather than the tropics itself. These delicate engravings of sugar mills and harbours, of native women in cos-tume, are seen as a part of History, that History which looked over the shoulder of the engraver and, later, the photographer. History can alter the eye and the moving hand to conform a view of itself; it can rename places for the nostalgia in an echo; it can temper the glare of tropical light to elegiac monotony in prose, the tone of judgement in Conrad, in the travel journals of Trollope.

These travellers carried with them the infection of their own malaise, and their prose reduced even the landscape to melancholia and self-contempt. Every endeavor is belittled as imitation, from architecture to music. There was this conviction in Froude that since History is based on achievement, and since the history of the Antilles was so genetically corrupt, so depressing in its cycles of massacres, slavery, and indenture, a culture was inconceivable and nothing could ever be created in those ramshackle ports, those monotonously feudal sugar estates. Not only the light and salt of Antillean mountains defied this, but the demotic vigour and variety of their inhabitants. Stand close to a waterfall and you will stop hearing its roar. To be still in the nineteenth century, like horses, as Brodsky has written, may not be such a bad deal, and much of our life in the Antilles still seems to be in the rhythm of the last century, like the West Indian novel.

By writers even as refreshing as Graham Greene, the Caribbean is looked at with elegiac pathos, a prolonged sadness to which Lévi-Strauss has supplied an epigraph: *Tristes Tropiques*. Their *tristesse* derives from an attitude to the Caribbean dusk, to rain, to uncontrollable vegetation, to the provincial ambition of Caribbean cities where brutal replicas of modern architecture dwarf the small houses and streets. The mood is understandable, the melancholy as contagious as the fever of a sunset, like the gold fronds of diseased coconut palms, but there is something alien and ultimately wrong in the way such a sadness, even a morbidity, is described by English, French, or some of our exiled writers. It relates to a misunderstanding of the light and the people on whom the light falls.

These writers describe the ambitions of our unfinished cities, their unrealized, homiletic conclusion, but the Caribbean city may conclude just at that point where it is satisfied with its own scale, just as Caribbean culture is not evolving but already shaped. Its proportions are not to be measured by the traveller or the exile, but by its own citizenry and architecture. To be told you are not yet a city or a culture requires this response. I am not your city or your culture. There might be less of *Tristes Tropiques* after that.

Here, on the raft of this dais, there is the sound of the applauding surf: our landscape, our history recognized, "at last." *At Last* is one of the first Caribbean books. It was written by the Victorian traveller Charles Kingsley. It is one of the early books to admit the Antillean landscape and its figures into English literature. I have never read it but gather that its tone is benign. The Antillean archipelago was there to be written about, not to write itself, by Trollope, by Patrick Leigh-Fermor, in the very tone in which I almost wrote about the village spectacle at Felicity, as a compassionate and beguiled outsider, distancing myself from Felicity village even while I was enjoying it. What is hidden cannot be loved. The traveller cannot love, since love is stasis and travel is motion. If he returns to what he loved in a landscape and stays there, he is no longer a traveller but in stasis and concentration, the lover of that particular part of earth, a native. So many people say they "love the Caribbean," meaning that someday they plan to return for a visit but could never live there, the usual benign insult of the traveller, the tourist. These travellers, at their kindest, were devoted to the same patronage, the islands passing in profile, their vegetal luxury, their backwardness and poverty. Victorian prose dignified them. They passed by in beautiful profiles and were forgotten, like a vacation.

Aléxis Saint-Léger Léger, whose writer's name is Saint-John Perse, was the first Antillean to win this prize for poetry. He was born in Guadeloupe and wrote in French, but before him, there was nothing as fresh and clear in feeling as those poems of his childhood, that of a privileged white child on an Antillean plantation, *"Pour fêter une enfance,"* *"Éloges,"* and later *"Images à Crusoé."* At last, the first breeze on the page, salt-edged and self-renewing as the trade winds, the sound of pages and palm trees turning as "the odour of coffee ascents the stairs."

Caribbean genius is condemned to contradict itself. To celebrate Perse, we might be told, is to celebrate the old plantation system, to celebrate the bequé or plantation rider, verandahs and mulatto servants, a white French language in a white pith helmet, to celebrate a rhetoric of patronage and hauteur; and even if Perse denied his origins, great writers often have this folly of trying to smother their source, we cannot deny him any more than we can the African Aimé Césaire. This is not accommodation, this is the ironic republic that is poetry, since, when I see cabbage palms moving their fronds at sunrise, I think they are reciting Perse.

The fragrant and privileged poetry that Perse composed to celebrate his white childhood and the recorded Indian music behind the brown young archers of Felicity, with the same cabbage palms against the same Antillean sky, pierce me equally. I feel the same poignancy of pride in the poems as in the faces. Why, given the history of the Antilles, should this be remarkable? The history of the world, by which of course we mean Europe, is a record of intertribal lacerations, of ethnic cleansings. At last, islands not written about but writing themselves! The palms and the Muslim minarets are Antillean exclamations. At last! the royal palms of Guadeloupe recite *"Éloges"* by heart.

Later, in *"Anabase,"* Perse assembled fragments of an imaginary epic, with the clicking teeth of frontier gates, barren wadis with the froth of poisonous lakes, horsemen burnoosed in sandstorms, the opposite of cool Caribbean mornings, yet not necessarily a contrast any more than some young brown archer at Felicity, hearing the sacred text blared across the flagged field, with its battles and elephants and monkey-gods, in a contrast to the white child in Guadeloupe assembling fragments of his own epic from the lances of the cane fields, the estate carts and oxens, and the calligraphy of bamboo leaves from the ancient languages, Hindi, Chinese, and Arabic, on the Antillean sky. From the *Ramayana* to *Anabasis*, from Guadeloupe to Trinidad, all that archaeology of fragments lying around, from the broken African kingdoms, from the crevasses of Canton, from Syria and Lebanon, vibrating not under the earth but in our raucous, demotic streets.

A boy with weak eyes skims a flat stone across the flat water of an Aegean inlet, and that ordinary action with the scything elbow contains the skipping lines of the *Iliad* and the *Odyssey*, and another child aims a bamboo arrow at a village festival, another hears the rustling march of cabbage palms in a Caribbean sunrise, and from that sound, with its fragments of tribal myth, the compact expedition of Perse's epic is launched, centuries and archipelagoes apart. For every poet it is always morning in the world. History a forgotten, insomniac night; History and elemental awe are always our early beginning, because the fate of poetry is to fall in love with the world, in spite of History.

There is a force of exultation, a celebration of luck, when a writer finds himself a witness to the early morning of a culture that is defining itself, branch by branch, leaf by leaf, in that self-defining dawn, which is why, especially at the edge of the sea, it is good to make a ritual of the sunrise. Then the noun, the "Antilles" ripples like brightening water, and the sounds of leaves, palm fronds, and birds are the sounds of a fresh dialect, the native tongue. The personal vocabulary, the individual melody whose metre is one's biography, joins in that sound, with any luck, and the body moves like a walking, a waking island.

This is the benediction that is celebrated, a fresh language and a fresh people, and this is the frightening duty owed.

I stand here in their name, if not their image—but also in the name of the dialect they exchange like the leaves of the trees whose names are suppler, greener, more morning-stirred than English—*laurier canelles, bois-flot, bois-canot*—or the valleys the trees mention—*Fond St. Jacques, Matoonya, Forestier, Roseau, Mahaut*—or the empty beaches—*L'Anse Ivrogne, Case en Bas, Paradis*—all songs and histories in themselves, pronounced not in French—but in patois.

One rose hearing two languages, one of the trees, one of school children reciting in English:

I am monarch of all I survey,
My right there is none to dispute;
From the centre all round to the sea
I am lord of the fowl and the brute.
Oh, solitude! where are the charms
That sages have seen in thy face?
Better dwell in the midst of alarms,
Than reign in this horrible place ...

While in the country to the same metre, but to organic instruments, handmade violin, chac-chac, and goatskin drum, a girl named Sensenne singing:

Si mwen di 'ous ça fait mwen la peine
'Ous kai dire ça vrai.
(If I told you that caused me pain
You'll say, "It's true.")
Si mwen di 'ous ça pentetrait mwen
'Ous peut dire ça vrai
(If I told you you pierced my heart
You'd say, "It's true.")
Ces mamailles actuellement
Pas ka faire l'amour z'autres pour un rien.
(Children nowadays
Don't make love for nothing.)

It is not that History is obliterated by this sunrise. It is there in Antillean geography, in the vegetation itself. The sea sighs with the drowned from the Middle Passage, the butchery of its aborigines, Carib and Aruac and Taíno, bleeds in the scarlet of the immortelle, and even the actions of surf on sand cannot erase the African memory, or the lances of cane as a green prison where indentured Asians, the ancestors of Felicity, are still serving time.

That is what I have read around me from boyhood, from the beginnings of poetry, the grace of effort. In the hard mahogany of woodcutters: faces, resinous men, charcoal burners; in a man with a cutlass cradled across his forearm, who stands on the verge with the usual anonymous khaki dog; in the extra clothes he put on this morning, when it was cold when he rose in the thinning dark to go and make his garden in the heights—the heights, the garden, being miles away from his house, but that is where he has his land—not to mention the fishermen, the footmen on trucks, groaning up mornes, all fragments of Africa originally but shaped and hardened and rooted now in the island's life, illiterate in the way leaves are illiterate; they do not read, they are there to be read, and if they are properly read, they create their own literature.

But in our tourist brochures the Caribbean is a blue pool into which the republic dangles the extended foot of Florida as inflated rubber islands bob and drinks with umbrellas float towards her on a raft. This is how the islands from the shame of necessity sell themselves; this is the seasonal erosion of their identity, that high-pitched repetition of the same images of service that cannot distinguish one island from the other, with a future of polluted marinas, land deals negotiated by ministers, and all of this conducted to the music of Happy Hour and the rictus of a smile. What is the earthly paradise for our visitors? Two weeks without rain and a mahogany tan, and, at sunset, local troubadours in straw hats and floral shirts beating "Yellow Bird" and "Banana Boat Song" to death. There is a territory wider than this—wider than the limits made by the map of an island—which is the illimitable sea and what it remembers.

All of the Antilles, every island, is an effort of memory; every mind, every racial biography culminating in amnesia and fog. Pieces of sunlight through the fog and sudden rainbows, *arcs-en-ciel.* That is the effort, the labour of the Antillean imagination, rebuilding its gods from bamboo frames, phrase by phrase.

Decimation from the Aruac downwards is the blasted root of Antillean history, and the benign blight that is tourism can infect all of those island nations, not gradually, but with imperceptible speed, until each rock is whitened by the guano of white-winged hotels, the arc and descent of progress.

Before it is all gone, before only a few valleys are left, pockets of an older life, before development turns every artist into an anthropologist or folklorist, there are still cherishable places, little valleys that do not echo with ideas, a simplicity of rebeginnings, not yet corrupted by the dangers of change. Not nostalgic sites but occluded sancties as common and simple as their sunlight. Places as threatened by this prose as a headland is by the bulldozer or a sea almond grove by the surveyor's string, or from blight, the mountain laurel.

One last epiphany: a basic stone church in a thick valley outside Soufrière, the hills almost shoving the houses around into a brown river, a sunlight that looks oily on the leaves, a backward place, unimportant, and one now being corrupted into significance by this prose. The idea is not to hallow or invest the place with anything, not even memory. African children in Sunday frocks come down the ordinary concrete steps into the church, banana leaves hang and glisten, a truck is parked in a yard, and old women totter towards the entrance. Here is where a real fresco should be painted, one without importance, but one with real faith, mapless, Historyless.

How quickly it could all disappear! And how it is beginning to drive us further into where we hope are impenetrable places, green secrets at the end of bad roads, headlands where the next view is not of a hotel but of some long beach without a figure and the hanging question of some fisherman's smoke at its far end. The Caribbean is not an idyll, not to its natives. They draw their working strength from it organically, like trees, like the sea almond or the spice laurel of the heights. Its peasantry and its fishermen are not there to be loved or even photographed; they are trees who sweat, and whose bark is filmed with salt, but every day on some island, rootless trees in suits are signing favourable tax breaks with entrepreneurs, poisoning the sea almond and the spice laurel of the mountains to their roots. A morning could come in which governments might ask what happened not merely to the forests and the bays but to a whole people.

They are here again, they recur, the faces, corruptible angels, smooth black skins and white eyes huge with an alarming joy, like those of the Asian children of Felicity at *Ramleela*; two different religions, two different continents, both filling the heart with the pain that is joy.

But what is joy without fear? The fear of selfishness that, here on this podium with the world paying attention not to them but to me, I should like to keep these simple joys inviolate, not because they are innocent, but because they are true. They are as true as when, in the grace of this gift, Perse heard the fragments of his own epic of Asia Minor in the rustling of cabbage palms, that inner Asia of the soul through which imagination wanders, if there is such a thing as imagination as opposed to the collective memory of our entire race, as true as the delight of that warrior-child who flew a bamboo arrow over the flags in the field at Felicity; and now as grateful a joy and a blessed fear as when a boy opened an exercise book and, within the discipline of its margins, framed stanzas that might contain the light of the hills on an island blest by obscurity, cherishing our insignificance.

Improvisations: The Poem as Journey[1]

Charles Wright

"I am writing to you from a far-off country," "I am writing to you from the end of the world," Henri Michaux, the French Surrealist poet, says. Precisely. Most, if not all, good poems come from that place, or those two places if they have become separated by intent or degree. Like the continents and like imagination, they started as one mass, but both have devolved to a movable attitude. Dante wrote from the Empyrean, a far-off country, indeed. Others write from next door, which often can be the end of the world.

So many journeys. So many destinations. Orpheus descending through the byways and back canals of the human body, Ulysses and Aeneas blown to and from all those lands and islands of the natural world, Dante and Leopardi arrowing in and out of the various heavens and the stars.

---

1. Delivered as the second Claudia Ortese Lecture in American Literature, May 14, 1992, L'Universitá Degli Studi di Firenze, Florence, Italy.

    Editor's Note: Charles Wright, "Improvisations: The Poem as Journey" from *Quarter Notes: Improvisations and Interviews* (Ann Arbor: The University of Michigan Press, 1995).

And what is the ultimate resting place of all these peregrinations, the landscapes we travel through, the roads we go back and forth on, or the time it takes us to get there or fail to arrive?

"A journey is a fragment of hell," Bruce Chatwin says in *Songlines*. An inch or a thousand miles, I say, in whatever direction, up or down. But that's the road the good poem takes. Most everyone thinks it's the road that counts, that the traveling is the point of the journey, both in life and in art. I disagree. I think it's what's at road's end that is important, that where the road leads is where the meaning is: it's not the telling of the story that's important, it's what the story has to tell. The telling is interesting, but the point is what's transcendent. As a younger man, I thought that process was meaning. I now know that meaning is meaning, and that journey's end is the end of the journey, not some intermediate point—the road to Campostela leads to Campostela, the road to Assisi ends in Assisi, not at Gròpina.

Poems are not just *about* journeys, of course, they *are* journeys—surreptitiously, silently, staying in one place the way plants do. Like any organism, the good poem is a self-contained adventure, both physically and metaphysically. What Eihei Dogen, the Japanese Zen master, said about the plantain in the century Dante was born can as well be said about the good poem: "A plantain has earth, water, fire, wind, emptiness, also mind, consciousness and wisdom as its roots, stems, branches, and leaves, or as its flowers, fruits, colors and forms. Accordingly, the plantain wears the autumn wind, and is torn in the autumn wind. We know that it is pure and clear and that not a single particle is excluded." If it lacks these essential components, the plantain does not grow to its fullest expectations. If the poem lacks them, it goes nowhere. Moribund and ill-equipped, it becomes a shell—without the interior journey, the exterior one is impossible. The true journey is a healthy plant; the true poem is the same thing.

At the heart of every poem is a journey of discovery. Something is being found out. Often the discovery is merely technical—architectural, metrical, or spatial—though, when lucky, the technical revelation is not just "merely" but is an uncovered new thing. Poetic structures sometimes end up in that fortunate "field." New concepts of lineation often do as well. From time to time the discovery is spiritual, a way of looking at the world that affects the way we lead our lives, or how we think of them. Poems that cause us to say, after having read them, "Oh, that's nice," or "Ummm, not bad," do not participate in this voyage of discovery. No matter how new their paint job is, no matter how smart and crisp their sails, they never get out of the harbor. The journey belongs to others.

Two twentieth-century Italian poets—Dino Campana and Eugenio Montale—make an interesting comparison. Campana, who restlessly writes of almost nothing but journeys on foot, by sea, or all manner of transportation, to both spiritual and quotidian places, has a turbulent and frenzied surface to his poems, but underneath a Romantic standstill and stasis. Montale, on the other hand, whose poems have, for the most part, placid and one-place-at-a-time surfaces, underneath have a miraculous sense of voyage to previously undiscovered or forgotten states of being. Another famous twentieth-century poet, Giuseppe Ungaretti, in his minimalistic sensibility, also constantly carries us elsewhere. His two-word, two-line poem "Mattina"—"M'illumino / d'immenso"—says about all there is to say on the subject of epiphanic discovery (and is my favorite example of why translation is ultimately impossible). To finish off the parallelism, Pier Paolo Pasolini, whose movies were a constant exploration of both physical and psychic revelation—as were his novels—had to my way of thinking a very ordinary and unadventurous venture in his poems. His life, as we know, followed his novels and films, even to its abrupt, and sad, ending.

The imagination is, of course, the starter's pistol of all journeys. As

Federico García Lorca, the great Spanish poet of the 1930s, has said, "it travels and transforms things, endowing them with their purest sense, and it identifies relations which had never been suspected.... Imagination is the first step, the foundation of all poetry." Inspiration, the dark twin and demiurge of imagination, can, he later counsels, send the traveler farther and deeper than imagination alone, creating a poetry where "a man more rapidly approaches the cutting edge that the philosopher and the mathematician turn away from in silence." That "cutting edge," where all true poems climb from and return to, is the edge where the void begins. And it is inspiration, pure instinct, to which Lorca eventually pays the greater homage. Imagination is closely allied to intelligence and logic/reasoning. And intelligence, he said, "is often the enemy of poetry, because it limits too much, and it elevates the poet to a sharp-edged throne where he forgets that ants could eat him or that a great arsenic lobster could fall suddenly on his head." The journey is always into the unknown, into the mystery and darkness where great lobsters fall on our heads and great unseen wings graze our faces and vanish.

Back to Montale for a moment. Just about thirty years ago, I translated into English (American, really) a section of his poems "Lampi e Dediche" ("Flashes and Dedications") from his book *La bufera*. These little poems had such a profound effect on me that I then went on to translate the entire book—the first time, I might add, that the complete *La bufera* had been done in English. It has since, of course, become a mountain that many have climbed. However, my point here is with the short, diary-like section, "Lampi e Dediche." What first drew me to these poems was their strong, and strange, religious overtones. This is rare in Montale's work and, even here, it is not "religion" per se, but rather a peculiar sort of mysticism, little apocalypses, immense journeys in tight and loaded little packets.

The opening poem in the series, "Verso Siena," serves to show that God is a possibility, though how He is to be taken, and how Montale takes

Him, we are never sure. This uncertainty gives the power of the unknown, the mystery, and the journey's end as an addition to the imagistic pyrotechnics in the poems themselves. The reader—after going through such other poems as "Sulla colonna più alta," "Incantesimo," and "Vento sulla mezzaluna"—knows he has traveled to a different universe indeed in things Montaliane, a universe almost completely comprised of nothingness (a familiar place at first). But this time nothingness is not all; there sometimes appear certain perceptions (*lampi*) that carry almost metaphysical overtones of faith.

Montale's world, as we know now, is a fascinating one, with a sense of time as a steady destroyer, of existence as entropy, an inevitable process of decay. But it is the added dimension found in "Lampi e Dediche" that gently alters that world, which hints of the changes that came later in *La bufera*, when the journey went down and down, deeper into the darker waters of personal history, and the century's history. "*O voi chi siete in piccioletta barca*," as Ezra Pound had it from Dante. Out of my way. *Pista!*

And speaking of Uncle Ez, as Montale called him, and as he called himself on Italian radio, we have a fine example of someone who tried the ultimate journey in his work, a Dantean-Joycean voyage that ended up, by his own admission, shipwrecked on the rocks of history, prejudice, and Western culture in general, the very land's end he was headed for all along. Having had his epic—his non-narrative epic (which Montale said was a contradiction in terms)—progress *in periplum*, where the winds took it, and not on any preset, direct-narrative course, this is not surprising. But it remains one of the most spectacular and gorgeous literary wrecks, in English, of the century, and the lyrical songs that continue to rise from the wreckage, and the incredible music and visions of many of its parts continue to seduce us toward that same shore and those same shoals, a broken bundle of mirrors though they may be.

Having said that about Pound, let me say something else, something more personal about his work and its early effects on me. I have said this before in another place, but it bears repeating when we are speaking of journey and poetry, as it concerns the beginning of my own journey, without Ariadne's thread, into the maze. All first loves are ultimately sad. They begin in such light and splendor and end in darkness and disillusion. Later they are brought back up to shine again like discovered lost treasure from the old waters of indifference. My poetic first love was no different from this. And it was Ezra Pound.

I have written at some length, and almost continuously, for over thirty years about my first stay in Italy, which began in January, 1959. Such obsessive attempts at re-creation are some slight indications of the abiding effect of the country and its culture, and my initial baptism by total immersion in it, had—and continues to have—on me.

My most momentous occasion, at least in what was to preoccupy me from then on, and what I still, as I once said, "waste my heart on," was a trip I took to Lake Garda from Verona, where I lived, and particularly to Sirmione, the peninsula at whose tip Catullus, the legend goes, had a villa, the ruins of which to this day stun the unwary foreign traveler when he comes upon them. I was such a traveler, clutching in one hand the *Selected Poems of Ezra Pound*, bought two years previously in New York City and still unread. My friend Harold Schimmel, with me in the army in Verona, had borrowed it in the first weeks of our friendship and had returned it with the admonition to read the poem "Blandula, Tenulla, Vagula," which was about the very spot I would be visiting. And so I did, the late March sun pouring through the olive trees, reflecting off their silver and quicksilver turns in the lake wind, the lake itself stretched out below me and into the distance, the pre-Alps above Riva cloud-shouldered and cloud-shadowed, the whole weight of history and literature suddenly dropping through the roof of my little world in one of those epiphanic flashes that one is fortunate enough to have in one's lifetime now and then if one is ready. I was ready. The continuous "desire to write" that I had had since high school had finally found its form—the lyric poem. The irresistible force had met a movable object. A week later Schimmel and I took off for a week's leave—down to Bologna, over *La Futa* and the Apennines, through Florence, Rome, Naples, and finally to Paestum in southern Italy—and my focus was set for the rest of my life, as hyperbolic as that might sound. I still have that little paperback book, and it still has the heavy, army-issue-paper slipcover on it that Harold made back in 1959. The number 1302 is written in ink on the cover, a number that means nothing to me.

But the book means something to me, and the poems meant something to me in my green time. One's personal poetic journey has to begin before the journey inside the poem can get under way.

And speaking of Verona, it was there, I think, that a girl I knew back in 1959 or 1960 said to me one afternoon, during the course of a courtship that went back and forth between Milano, where she lived, and Verona, where, as I say, I lived, "*Guarda*, Charles, *quando io faccio una cosa, io vado fino in fondo, sai*." *Ostrighetta!* I was a young guy then, and young guys just want to have fun. Fun for her meant something else, however. It meant, finally, "*andare fino in fondo*." She did, I didn't.

Such a course, "*Andare fino in fondo*," was no fun for John Berryman, an American poet of a recent generation who did just that in both his life and his poems. The voyage to the bottom of the soul. He took it and his poems took it. It was tragic in his life and brilliantly redemptive in his art. It was just such a journey that a group of poets, called the Confessionals, all but one of them of the same generation, took: they were Berryman, Robert Lowell, Anne Sexton, W.D. Snodgrass, and Sylvia Plath. Delmore Schwartz and Randall Jarrell were peripheral members. Four of them committed suicide, two died young, and one, probably the originator of the kind of writing the group was known for, though not its most illustrious member, is still alive. Some journeys from the void know secret shortcuts, some have no return ticket.

Berryman and his alter egos, Henry and Mister Bones, dance the

Dance of Death, that dark and monotonous soft-shoe, across the stage of *The Dream Songs*, a huge book of almost exclusively eighteen-line poems about the foibles, momentary triumphs, and endless vicissitudes of Henry as he shuffles inexorably off stage left to his predestined and preternatural doom. The entire enterprise is a kind of *commedia dell'arte* stage setting, the characters, especially Henry, rather like marionettes or puppets just waiting to collapse or to be pulled under at any moment. We are not disappointed. In brilliant set piece after brilliant set piece, the excruciating ritual is played out to its appointed end, Henry and Berryman himself, puppet and puppeteer, finally subsumed by the journey itself. Ars brevis, vita brevis est.

Franz Kafka, in one of his entries in *The Blue Octavo Notebooks*, writes: "Before setting foot in the Holy of Holies you must take off your shoes, yet not only your shoes, but everything; you must take off your travelling garments and lay down your luggage; and under that you must shed your nakedness and everything that hides beneath that, and then the core and the core of the core, then the remainder and then the residue and then even the glimmer of the undying fire. Only the fire itself is absorbed by the Holy of Holies and lets itself be absorbed by it; neither can resist the other." This is the kind of journey we are talking about....

For many of us in our youth, Hart Crane was the ultimate American poetic icon. His poem "The Bridge" is second only to Pound's *Cantos* as the most spectacular and seductive failure of the twentieth century in American poetry. There is something irresistibly sexy and alluring about ambition and the failure of that ambition, especially if its scattered or gathered parts have a kind of glittering perfection, as those of both the *Cantos* and "The Bridge" do.

The wake of the SS *Orizaba* had hardly closed over Crane's body before his personal legend began to take shape. His literary one was not far behind. He had tried for the impossible in his poem—his great, shattered poem—a journey across time, history, and personal recognition that refused to redeem either him or literature and refused to come together—two lacks that mirrored the disconnections in his own life. The way out seemed the way in, and he took it. The verb "to voyage" is just as inaccessible and untranslatable in the heart as it is in the poem.

Hart Crane was unafraid in his literary ambitions. Many, of course, profess to be unafraid and are willing "to try anything." The vast majority of such people say and do such out of ignorance and foolhardiness. Crane did it out of talent, genius, and a vision, a vision that was not to be thwarted. True vision *is* journey. True vision is a bridge from here to there. Crane saw his road and set out on it. At its end was the end. Had he known that before he set out, I'm convinced he would have acted no differently. Genius must keep its appointments. We are still picking up and examining the dazzling flotsam and jetsam, just as we are from the *Cantos*. Hart Crane and Ezra Pound, the two fallen angels in the American twentieth-century poetic firmament. How they shine and flare in their fiery arcs.

Does the journey currently seem shorter and less ambitious? Have the truly incredible occurrences of this century shrunk and shortened the reach of poets and poems? E.M. Cioran accuses Paul Valéry of corrupting generations of French poets, he and Stéphane Mallarmé, by their insistence that every poem be an exercise in the impossible, that every poem be a leap from a high wall by the poetic body. Rather like the famous photograph staged by the French artist Yves Klein, where he is shown in midair, stretched out, having just jumped from a high stone wall down to a Parisian stone street. We now know that the photograph is a collage and that, in actuality, there was a net beneath the original leap to catch him, now excised, with a cleverly added picture of the street creating the physical disaster he seems headed toward.

Indeed, most journeys are, perforce, of this kind in poems. And that's all right, I think. Otherwise the landscape and the history of literature would be strewn with bodies and maimed poems. Short journeys are not only acceptable, they are necessary to make the longer ones possible and legendary. Dante needed Lapo Gianni and Guido Cavalcanti. Montale needed Cesare Pavese and Salvatore Quasimodo. An inch or infinity, to the stars or to the *norceria*, through the thickets of the soul or the thickets of language, down the boulevards of the heart or the thoroughfares of technique. The journey remains the same in the good poem—it goes from point A to point B. Distance does make a difference and depth does make a difference, but vision is still vision, whatever its scope or manifestations.

Emily Dickinson was stationary. By that I mean her life was stationary. Her mind was a long-distance runner, unstill, never ceasing. Her imagination and inspiration were lightning-strikes and full of a great illumination. She sat in her room and the galaxy unrolled beneath her feet. She sat in her room and the garden and orchard outside her windows took on the ghostly garments of infinity. In her finest poems, and everywhere throughout her letters and the rest of her poetry, there has seldom before been such expansiveness in such small containers. Her poetry was an electron microscope trained on the infinite and the idea of God. Such distances under her fingertips! Inside the tube of the climbing rose, the River of Heaven flowed. Under the oak's throat, the broken ladder to Paradise waited for reassembly.

During the last ten years of her life she apparently seldom left her room, or at least the second story of her house. For most of her life she had been reclusive. Yet her poems are immense voyages into the unknowable. To leave she had to stay still, something Dino Campana was unable to accept, for instance, or was incapable of doing.

There was the famous white dress. There was the famous white flower. There was the famous "white election." And there was the famous last letter she wrote, the day before her death, to her two cousins, Louise and Fannie Norcross—"Little Cousins—Called back. Emily"—sounding almost as though she were an alien, some extraterrestrial who was here on a visit. She does seem "inhabited" in a way. Or perhaps she was Manichaean, a kind of Cathar whose chip of light was to begin its last, and longest, journey back to the original and unthinkable source of all light, leaving this darkness for good. Whatever, she remains one of the great lyric poets of all time. Sappho casts no shadow on her, her sherry-eyed opposite....

Every journey is the same journey, and every journey is different. The journey in life, as the song says, is a lonesome valley. The journey in the poem runs toward higher ground, the ridgebacks and upper slopes, hilltop to mountaintop. The movement, in other words, tends to be upward. At least it has been that way for me.

The iconic book in my life, the work toward which all my work has aspired, is the *Confessions* by Saint Augustine. It is that kind of autobiography, in a more temporal—though no less spiritual—sense, I suppose, that my poems want to describe. Or to show their inability to describe. In either case, the journey is the same journey, even if the station reached is dramatically different. One goes where one is called.

The journey in the Chinese poem, which has also been of interest to my work, is otherwise. Where our Western movement, as I say, tends to be upward, the Chinese aim deliberately downward, at the earth, at the landscape and the tactile world and their tenuous place within it. It is a poetry of seeing, and their spiritual strength is in that seeing and in the things of this world they look at. And since they have no belief in a future world—as, say, Christians do—they love what they look at with a passion the Western tradition does not contain. Their sense of the permanence of the world is as strong as our sense of its transience.

It has been said that Buddhism has provided a spiritual basis for Chinese landscape poetry. One does sense the great interior Zen journey, that long and arduous trek to the still, quiet center of things, reflected in the description of landscape and in the patience and absolute faith of certain onlookers such as Cold Mountain (Han Shan) or Wang Wei. The poets and poems from the T'ang Dynasty (618-907) are generally accepted as being the finest examples of this, though the T'ang poets were using forms and song patterns, we now know, which were themselves up to four hundred years old, brought down from the time of the Han. If, as Gustave Flaubert said, the Good Lord does live in the detail, then these short poems which often centered upon the enduring problems of man's life can be said to be large spiritual voyages as the Chinese looked around themselves and told how it was to be here at this time, in this place, letting the waters of the River of Heaven slide over their heads and the waters of the Yangtze slide under their feet. The enormousness of the material world and all the roads that wind through the ten thousand things!

While it is not poetry but fiction, the writing of Ernest Hemingway has been very influential in my life. The book that I read as a young man and never quite got out of my system is *The Short Stories of Ernest Hemingway*. There is a purity of description, a purity of language at its most effective, that has always been seductive to me in his writing, and I find it—or found it so when I was younger—most prevalent in his stories. It is a purity of language in action that I have often aspired to in my poems.

Such stories, for example, as "A Clean, Well-Lighted Place," "Hills Like White Elephants," and "The Short Happy Life of Francis Macomber" seemed to me perfectly articulated and took the reader to a faraway place, an effortless journey of narrative and style. It is such a place I wanted my poems to have access to, and the roads that led there I wanted my poems to be able to travel. Especially the early, crystalline vignettes of *In Our Time*. Like Chinese poems, they gave a sense of the long journey through the possibilities of language, its exclusions as well as its inclusions. I thought they were "true" in the way Hemingway liked to use the word, and I loved them.

It's always been my contention that the shorter the distance, the harder the journey. By that I mean there is less time and less space to get said what has to be said. For that is the real journey after all—what you've got to say. We can metaphor and simile and weave intricate euphemisms till our pencils stub out of lead, but the fact remains that what you have to say is where you have to go. How you say it, of course, can grease the wheels and fuel the engine (here we go metaphoring again) and can sometimes actually be what you are talking about, but for the most part, you've got to say your way to seize the day. And the more condensed the poem is, the less maneuvering room there is, the stronger the message and the greater the journey is after the fact, which is where all real journeys start out. Dante is an example of this.

But there are contemporary poets who illustrate my point as well as Dante, including Jorie Graham, an American with significant connection to Italy. Jorie grew up in Rome and, in 1966, was a member of the army of students who came to help salvage books from the Arno's mud after the floods here. When I asked her to respond to my view of the journey in our poems, Jorie Graham replied in a letter, and gave the following explication. Her explanation helps make the case for that "journey of technique" I mentioned earlier. I want to present first her poem "San Sepolcro" and then what she says about the poem:

San Sepolcro

In this blue light
    I can take you there,
snow having made me
    a world of bone
seen through to. This
    is my house,

my section of Etruscan
    wall, my neighbor's
lemontrees, and, just below
    the lower church,
the airplane factory.
    A rooster

crows all day from mist
    outside the walls.
There's milk on the air,
    ice on the oily
lemonskins. How clean
    the mind is,

holy grave. It is this girl
    by Piero
della Francesca, unbuttoning
    her blue dress,
her mantle of weather,
    to go into

labor. Come, we can go in.
    It is before
the birth of god. No-one
    has risen yet
to the museums, to the assembly
    line—bodies

and wings—to the open air
    market. This is
what the living do: go in.
    It's a long way.

And the dress keeps opening
    from eternity

to privacy, quickening.
    Inside, at the heart,
is tragedy, the present moment
    forever stillborn,
but going in, each breath
    is a button

coming undone, something terribly
    nimble-fingered
finding all of the stops.

If I consider "San Sepolcro," the journey seems especially a *formal* journey—an experiment with elements of style which led to the discovery of a layer of "voice" I could call mine, or inhabit, for a period of my life.

First of all I should say that many of these devices might seem on the one hand too obvious to be of use— except to one who doesn't avail herself of them habitually. And, too, that, the taking on, only apparently arbitrary, of stylistic devices—the inhabiting of them until they become the garment of one's spirit life, the method by which one touches the world, the means by which one can be touched oneself, and changed—all of these mysteries are the reason the act of writing holds such powerful and enduring sway over my life. The changes I made in my "technique" are changes that occurred to my life: I became the person I couldn't have otherwise been by these small devices, habits. In other words, the journey is made up of, and created by, technique. The soul-making Keats refers to as the goal of poetry is a web composed of small techni-cal attempts which lead to a new voice—a deeper voice, one at a more morally and historically and spiritually engaged level than the personal voice. A voice one can only build by the *act* of writing, an act which grows dead and automatic if not constantly reinvigorated by strange-ness of strategy.

In "San Sepolcro" I tried to slow down the act of *speak-ing*. I tried all sorts of devices to this end and finally settled on the shortened line, the antiphonal indentation, the sin-gling out of individual words by frequent use of mid-line sentence breaks.

I was delighted in my soul by the slowness of pace I dis-covered. I started thinking of it (*feeling* it, really) as a kind of solemnity—as when one walks in a cathedral and every sound one makes—footfalls!—seems heightened, signifi-cant, held open for inspection, *accountable*. I liked what for me felt like a new nakedness—as if the underpinnings were visible on the surface and no lies could be masked. I have always troubled the area surrounding the "veracity" of an assertion or an image—and so the slowness the inden-tation thrust upon my habitual way of proceeding thrilled me by its sense of *enforced*, solemn, accountability. Every word seemed suddenly to matter *on its own*—it seemed to resist the kind of easier truthfulness, easier beauty, the sentence could effortlessly (deceitfully?) effect. So: word vs. sentence—fragment brought to the surface. And yet a surface that still had an insistent patterning, order, of its own.

Connected to all this was my (at the time rather terrify-ing) use of direct address: "In this blue light / I can take you there." Its use flew in the face of all other imagined listeners

I had imagined or posited unconsciously up to that point. It forced me down into a far more intimate *voice*—at least tonally intimate—not *personally* intimate.

And this led, I believe, to the use of far more contemporary (vernacular) details (the airplane factory, the assembly line, etc.)—it is the specific admixture—the intermingling without dilution of the dramatic difference—of the spiritual and the physical worlds in this poem that led to the impetus for the writing of the whole book, *Erosion*. The two levels of "going-in" were actually sprung into *life* for me by the sudden appearance of the airplane factory (more than the open-air market which seemed, still, to partake of the aesthetic and historical Italian landscape). The factory—actually glimpsed rounding the hill off Montefalco (so *ugly*, I thought at the time, marring the "view")—the new Italy, if you will—helped me *turn*, in my spirit life, back to Italy and my whole past (family, inheritance, the problematics of memory—historical and personal—the *history*, the wars Europe endured, etc.).

I don't think I could have gotten to the place in my "role of soul-making" where I turned back to Italy and that constellation of aesthetic/historical and personal problems without that airplane factory. I had despaired of ever being able to make the landscape of my *actual* childhood and its art (so utterly literal to me as I played hide-and-seek in the churches of Trastevere as a child) anything other than symbolic or otherwise "unreal" in the context of the America I was living and writing in. The sudden, thrilling, jarring appearance of that airplane factory changed the whole situation. In that sense it actually created a juncture out of which a stage in the journey would unfold.

Our subject matter, the Poem as Journey, or the Journey at the Heart of Poetry, is surely the largest, most extensive that exists in the art. From Homer through Dante and Chaucer, through Shakespeare and Milton, through Leopardi and Goethe, through Zanzotto and Luzi, there is everything to be said and nothing more to say. It is one of those subjects you shadowbox with, since everyone who has ever written who was any good at all is an example to hold up to the light. For every good poem, as we've said, contains a serious journey. Dante, Homer, Chaucer, Shakespeare—what's to say? Eliot, Pound, Akhmatova, Mandelstam, Yeats and Lorca, Miłosz and Hikmet: the list might run as long as memory and appreciations permit.

Still, a few more words, perhaps. About Theodore Roethke, an American poet of the generation of Lowell, Berryman, Elizabeth Bishop, and Randall Jarrell. He subsumed the exterior landscape into his interior journey as well, if not better, than anyone in the United States in the second half of this century. His major work is a group of longish long-line meditations on the self, existence, and the landscape entitled "North American Sequence." Six poems that delve into the heart of the American landscape and into the heart of the spiritual self, the long voyage inward through the rocky creekbeds and river gulches, the windy cliffs that contain the dark wave-edge of the soul.

At least I thought that when I first read these remarkable, underappreciated, very American masterpieces. Like Dante's journey, his ends in an image of the rose—in Roethke's case an actual one, though its literary and religious reverberations are unmistakable—a rose in the soul's wind, which tears at reality and the difficult beliefs we sometimes choose to live our lives by.

Roethke, like Hart Crane, has the courage and vision in these poems to go the length of the dead-end road, the road that disappears into the vast expanse of unknowing and incredulity inside us, to come to the end of that road and keep on going; the courage to take the landscape and its significance on its own terms, to take the soul and the soul's self on their own terms and try to come to a workable spiritual balance with them. This is, of course, hard to do, and most writers, like most people, usually avoid it at any cost. Roethke's triumph is that he was fearless in his pursuit of himself and his place in the American literary and spiritual landscape.

As I noted a moment ago, there is just so much one can say in general about a topic as large as ours, and I think I have had my say for the time being. One final comment, though, and a slightly more personal one.

W.B. Yeats, the great Irish poet, wrote once in a verse that when he had said what he had to say, and had begun to enumerate old themes, he had to go back to the starting point: "I must lie down where all the ladders start, / In the foul rag-and-bone shop of the heart." Presumably to start contemplating the real ladder again. This is, of course, the void I was talking about earlier, out of which all journeys begin and to which they all return.

The journey my own poems took, and continue along, may have physically begun at Lake Garda in March, 1959, where I finally found a ladder I had to climb, but the first rung of that journey, out of the heart's void, was surely taken the afternoon a week later when my Volkswagen made a sharp turn on *La Futa* around a cypress tree and I was confronted with the enormity of Brunelleschi's dome on Santa Maria del Fiore rising, it seemed, almost out of the road itself in front of me, so near, so huge, the sunlight flashing off its curves and angles. And once we descended, the dome coming into and out of view, ever closer and larger, there was never a turning back.

A Bookshop, a Fishing Boat, a Trek Through the Andes:

A Roundtable of Poets Who've Lived Abroad

The draw to leave home can be strong and the promise of adventure so alluring that it can be tempting to just pick up and go. Alas, traveling abroad is not so simple. There are countless considerations; the trip will likely defy expectation; and when a situation does go awry, knowing how to respond can be difficult.

To prevent prospective travelers from making mistakes already made, forestall unnecessary work, and redirect anxious casting about, the editors and I asked fourteen traveled poets questions often posed when planning international travel. Their reflections constitute a conversation, which is printed here. The conversation can be read straight through, or, if one or two poets catch the eye, his or her responses can be tracked from question to question.

The result, I hope, is an illumination of the broad spectrum of reasons, excuses, and impulses that lead poets abroad. While advice may not supplant the value of lived experience, the contributors' collected wisdom offers guidance and encouragement, making it easier to know what to expect and how to prepare as we color the world with our presences.

—*Jared Hawkley*

Meet the Roundtable

Elizabeth Austen is a Seattle-based poet who has traveled extensively in Bolivia, Ecuador, and Peru.

Derick Burleson has worked as a Peace Corps volunteer in Rwanda. He lives in Two Rivers, Alaska.

Gregory Dunne has traveled to and now permanently resides in Japan, where he teaches at Miyazaki International College.

Karen Finneyfrock has traveled in Nepal as a Cultural Envoy through the US Department of State, performing and teaching poetry. She lives in Seattle.

Kathleen Graber has traveled as an Amy Lowell Poetry Travelling Scholar, traversing Germany, Hungary, Malta, and the United Kingdom. She lives in Virginia.

Garth Greenwell has traveled to and now resides in Sofia, Bulgaria, where he teaches secondary school.

Adrie Kusserow has traveled to Bhutan, India, Nepal, South Sudan, and Uganda as a cultural anthropologist. She lives in Vermont.

Sandra Meek has worked as a Peace Corps volunteer in Botswana. She lives in Georgia.

Aimee Nezhukumatathil has traveled in India and the Philippines. She lives in New York State.

Jacquelyn Pope lived for seven years in the Netherlands, working as a bookseller and translator in Amsterdam.

Srikanth Reddy lived a year in Oaxaca, Mexico, on research leave from the University of Chicago. He lives in Chicago.

Emily Ruch has served in South Korea and Iraq as a soldier in the United States Army. She lives in Santa Fe, New Mexico.

Donna Stonecipher has traveled to and now resides in Berlin, Germany.

Katharine Whitcomb led a summer study abroad for her Central Washington University students in France. She lives in Washington State.

What particular circumstances allowed you to live abroad?

MEEK: I was a Peace Corps volunteer. I think I had always been aware of the Peace Corps, and for my BA and MFA degrees, I went to Colorado State University, a school that's had a connection with the Peace Corps from the start. I joined the Peace Corps immediately after completing my MFA degree program, twenty years ago.

GRABER: I received the Amy Lowell Poetry Travelling Scholarship [amylowell.org] for 2008 to 2009. I knew many other poets who had applied for it. Elizabeth Bishop was a Lowell Travelling Scholar.

AUSTEN: In the fall of 1996, I quit my day job managing Freehold Theatre Lab Studio, a Seattle not-for-profit company. I sold my Honda Civic and bought a one-way ticket to Quito, Ecuador. I told friends and family that I wanted to learn to speak Spanish, do some volunteer work, and hike in tropical rain forests. But the true intent of my open-ended trip was to change my life. Because of some recent work I had done with poetry and dance theater, I had a strong hunch this meant becoming a writer, and I didn't know how to make sense of that or where to begin. Being a poet is, after all, perhaps the only vocation less practical than being a stage actor.

RUCH: I spent the majority of my time abroad as a soldier in the United States Army. I was stationed for a year in South Korea and deployed twice to Iraq.

KUSSEROW: I am an applied cultural anthropologist, so I am somewhat required to travel to "earn my keep." I teach cultural anthropology at a college in Vermont, so I usually bank on travel during winter vacation, summer break, and sabbatical leave from the college. I also travel with students to do international service-related projects in Bhutan, South

Sudan, and Uganda, so my travel funds come from the college when I take students. Initially, my travel was partially funded through Harvard, where I got my PhD. My travel since then has been funded through a combination of anthropology grants, college faculty fellowships (from the college where I teach), college funding for a study-abroad service learning course I am leading, my own personal funds and fundraising, and in the case of Bhutan, the government of Bhutan. It is never enough money, and I barely scrape by on my trips.

WHITCOMB: I applied for and received a one-month residency at La Muse from September to October 2010 while I was on sabbatical from my job teaching creative writing at Central Washington University. I had first read about La Muse [lamuseinn.com], a writers' and artists' retreat in southern France, in a posting on Facebook by a friend, the poet Sheryl St. Germain. After returning to the United States, I codesigned a class to be housed at La Muse and proposed it for a summer study abroad through Central Washington University. I completed this study abroad with one other faculty member and eight students during July 2011.

NEZHUKUMATATHIL: I lived for a month in Kerala, India, in 1999 and for three weeks in 2006 and then in Pangasinan, Philippines, in 2002 and 2007.

BURLESON: I applied to the Peace Corps because my wife at that time had always dreamed of being a Peace Corps volunteer, so joining the Peace Corps was a condition of marriage. We had both heard about the Peace Corps all our lives. During the application process, it seemed we would most likely be assigned to Eastern Europe, and we started taking classes in European history. When the assignment came and we were going to Rwanda instead, we were surprised and delighted and had no idea what would be in store for us there. We were both writers finishing MA degrees at Kansas State University and hoped going to Rwanda would give us something to write about.

GREENWELL: I've been working full-time as a high school teacher for the two years I've lived in Bulgaria. Several agencies specialize in international placements in secondary schools: Search Associates and International Schools Services are two of the biggest. I've worked with Carney, Sandoe & Associates, a company mostly focused on US placements that has been expanding its international portfolio.

FINNEYFROCK: I traveled to Nepal in December 2010 through the US Department of State and the US embassy in Nepal as part of a Cultural Envoy Program called Slam Poetry Fortnight. There was no application process, although I was asked to send work samples and an artist résumé. The embassy arranged all travel and lodging.

REDDY: The last time I lived abroad, during the academic year 2008–2009, I stayed in Oaxaca, Mexico. I was on research leave from the university where I teach. I didn't have to apply for this leave—it was part of my contract as junior faculty at the University of Chicago.

DUNNE: I applied to work aboard Japanese fishing vessels operating in the Bering Sea as a biologist and observer through the US Fisheries Observer Program. I was interested in Japan and its culture and felt that such work would introduce me to the culture. I worked aboard the ships for two to three months at a time without returning to port at Dutch Harbor in the Aleutian Islands. Insofar as I was living aboard a Japanese fishing vessel and surrounded by Japanese men and their culture and language, I felt I was living in a foreign country—a floating country. I was the only English speaker aboard the vessels. I continued with this work for three years. The experience increased my interest in Japan: its culture, language, and literature.

If you applied to a program, what did the application process entail?

BURLESON: Applying to the Peace Corps in the late 1980s was a fairly daunting experience, with interviews, background checks, and health checkups all required. Some of my students and friends have applied in recent years, and it seems the process hasn't changed much. The Peace Corps wants to find volunteers who will stay at their posts for two years, so the application process is quite detailed.

MEEK: The Peace Corps application involved a written application, including short essay questions, and an interview at the regional recruitment office, which in my case was in Denver. Also required were fingerprints for a criminal record search and a medical exam.

FINNEYFROCK: Although there was no application process for my particular Cultural Envoy Program, it is helpful to know that many embassies are interested in featuring writers as part of cultural programming.

DUNNE: I filled out an application and mailed it to the National Oceanic and Atmospheric Administration (NOAA) in Seattle. I was interviewed in Seattle for the position and attended a two-week mandatory training program.

GRABER: The application process for the Lowell Scholarship could not be simpler. There is a one-page form in addition to a writing sample. There is no fee. I put a copy of my first book, some new poems, and this little application in a priority envelope, and off it went. Months later, I got a very unexpected phone call from the executors of Amy Lowell's estate informing me that I had been selected.

WHITCOMB: La Muse had a standard e-mail application. I did have to submit a writing sample and describe a project that I would work on during the residency.

GREENWELL: International independent schools require at least a BA degree in a candidate's subject area; most prefer advanced degrees. Some experience teaching is usually required, and some schools require US state certification. I don't have this. Increasingly, international baccalaureate certification, which can be easily earned through online programs, is desired.

At Carney, Sandoe & Associates, the agency I used, I was required to submit a CV, a philosophy of teaching, and letters of reference. They passed along my dossier to schools with openings, letting me know when they did so. It was up to me to contact schools that I was interested in.

There are several fairs in Asia, Europe, and the United States where candidates interview with schools. Most schools do require in-person as well as phone interviews, though there are sometimes exceptions.

What would be useful for others to know before applying?

DUNNE: Applicants to the US Fisheries Observer Program need to have at least an undergraduate degree in the sciences. NOAA prefers applicants with degrees in biology, fisheries, and other sciences. The process is moderately competitive.

GREENWELL: I think the level of competition for international teaching placements varies widely. Positions in what are seen as the most desirable cities can be hugely competitive, especially at high-prestige schools. In places such as Eastern Europe, where recruitment is more difficult, new college graduates with no teaching experience may sometimes fill positions. Most require an initial two-year commitment, and penalties for breaking a contract can be fairly heavy.

KUSSEROW: For anthropology grants, the process is quite competitive. These cannot be grants in which I state that I will also be writing poetry—I wouldn't be taken seriously. These grants require elaborate bibliographies, explicit statements about contribution to the discipline and anthropological theory, a CV, a doctorate, letters of reference, and an explanation of why the proposed research is important.

College-funded trips that I lead are less competitive; I usually have to give a long written rationale for why the college should offer the course. Being a professor at a college has been an immense resource in terms of travel funding related to curriculum development or research.

BURLESON: The most important thing for Peace Corps applicants is to be flexible about where and when they hope to go. The process also requires persistence. It is competitive, and experience in teaching definitely gave me an edge over much of the competition.

MEEK: Try to plan ahead. The application process can take many months, and it is competitive. You should always check with the Peace Corps website and/or the regional recruitment offices for the most up-to-date advice, but applying eight to twelve months ahead of the time you'd ideally like to go is not unreasonable. Certainly, if you are available more quickly than that, you should apply anyway and let the recruiters know when you are able and willing to go. The more flexible you are, the better your chances of placement. Although I graduated in May, my program didn't begin until November. I ended up getting a temporary job at a local factory until departure, which was totally outside my experience up to that point—and was itself great preparation for the Peace Corps!

If you are a college student, or if you've already graduated and think you may want to join the Peace Corps sometime further down the road—and Peace Corps volunteers are all ages, though having a college degree is a requirement—consider getting some kind of volunteer and cross-cultural experience. This will help on the application, but more important, it will help you learn whether volunteering is the right direction for you. For instance, many communities have programs for teaching English to recent immigrants; this type of volunteer work is not only valuable in itself but will also provide you with both cross-cultural and teaching experience. Most Peace Corps positions involve some type of teaching, even if you aren't placed in a classroom situation.

GRABER: You have nothing to lose by applying, even though the Lowell Scholarship is very competitive. Once the judges narrow the field, I am sure that there are many equally deserving applicants in any given year. When I was a recipient, there was only one scholar per year. Now there are two.

WHITCOMB: La Muse is not very competitive. It does offer some full fellowships, which might be harder to get. It also sometimes offers barter stays in exchange for manual work. These barter exchanges are not always available. I paid for my stay, but the fee is very reasonable when compared to staying in a hotel in that region for a month. La Muse is equipped with a large communal kitchen with a professional range and plenty of cooking equipment. One can eat wonderfully and cheaply by shopping for local food, cooking in the kitchen, and eating in the dining room or on the terrace. The Aude department—and in particular the village of Labastide-Esparbairenque, where La Muse is located—is an exceptionally beautiful, lightly traveled area of France. The experience is very rural. A national forest of fir and chestnut trees; narrow, winding roads; and mountains and rivers surround the village.

**If a scholarship or another program did not finance
your travels, how did you find places to live?**

REDDY: My wife had been to Oaxaca many years earlier, and she'd always wanted to return. This, in combination with other poets' rave reviews of the place, sparked our initial interest in spending the year in this part of Mexico. Eliot Weinberger's essay on Oaxaca also made it seem like the perfect place to live for a year and write poetry. Last but not least, my university has a study-abroad program in Oaxaca, which gave us various contacts on the ground there when we arrived.

KUSSEROW: When I travel, I go to places that I can afford and that aren't too removed from the indigenous culture. I try not to live in expat enclaves. I often stay near the organization or nonprofit I am working with, such as the Education and Leadership Initiative offices in Yei, South Sudan, or a guesthouse near the Bhutan Centre for Media and Democracy.

GREENWELL: Most international schools provide assistance with accommodations. Many schools maintain their own apartments, and others help teachers find their own.

AUSTEN: Before I left the United States, I joined SERVAS, an international grassroots organization founded in Denmark after World War II to foster peace through one-on-one contacts between people of different nations. As a member, I received a list of hosts in the countries where I would be traveling and with whom I could stay for a couple of nights. This connection to local people was tremendously important, especially in large urban centers such as Lima, where it's easy to feel isolated. SERVAS families also provided a conduit to cultural events such as poetry readings.

As soon as I arrived in Quito, I enrolled in language school, which included placement with a local family. Over the course of about six weeks, I stayed with three different Ecuadorian families.

Did you take any jobs while you were abroad?
What were they?

POPE: I bought a bookshop in Amsterdam, so that narrowed everything down. That isn't a path open to most people, of course. To back up, I married a Briton who had grown up in Amsterdam. We met in Chicago, where we were both in the book business; each of us had the ambition to own a bookshop one day. The opportunity arose to buy a store where he'd worked for several years prior to coming to the United States. Because I'd always had a desire to live abroad and he wanted to move back to Europe, we borrowed money and bought it.

When we moved to Amsterdam, we were able to rent an apartment in the house his mother owns, so we never had to look for a place to live. That was extremely fortunate because housing in the city center was and is pretty scarce. It was a five-hundred-year-old house on a canal, and I was extremely lucky to live in those surroundings.

Once I had some rudimentary Dutch-language skills, I began working in our bookshop. However, I hadn't anticipated the many differences between the way bookstores are run in the United States and in the Netherlands, not to mention differences in customer behavior and the existence of some outright hostility toward an American's part ownership of the shop. This was balanced by most people's insistence on treating my husband as sole proprietor.

Over time, and I mean after several years, this eased. By then I'd begun doing some freelance translation for a few people, which led to work for the Anne Frank Foundation and then later to a job as the in-house Dutch-English translator for the language center at the University of Amsterdam. I liked being able to switch between environments, and at the university I was constantly meeting other translators, all of us with an accent and a story and usually something else going on. Many were artists.

STONECIPHER: I've always worked while living in Berlin, first for American publishers and now for a German publisher, editing art books. I also work as a translator and occasionally earn money from writing.

AUSTEN: Toward the end of my time in South America, I accepted a monthlong volunteer position at the Lima office of the South American Explorers Club. In return for a private room in the SAEC "clubhouse," three meals a day, and a small stipend, I helped run the office and researched in-country volunteer opportunities for members.

I volunteered with the Fundación Jatun Sacha in Ecuador, an environmental organization focused on preserving Ecuador's biological diversity. Initially, while studying in Quito, I assisted in the plant library, basically filing dried specimens. Very exciting work. Later, I spent ten days at Bilsa, the foundation's remote ecological station of tropical premontane wet forest. I worked in the *vivero*, planting seeds and transplanting seedlings, and helped the station botanist collect seeds and plant specimens on daylong hikes through the 5,500-acre reserve.

KUSSEROW: I do volunteer when I travel—for example, at orphanages in Kathmandu, Nepal, or Kampala, Uganda; at a girls' high school in Yei, South Sudan; at the Tibetan Children's Village in Dharamsala, India; or at the Bhutan Centre for Media and Democracy in Thimphu, Bhutan.

DUNNE: The Japanese fishermen had mentioned that I could teach English in Japan if I had a degree in English—I already had a degree in biology. I decided to study English at the University of Washington, in Seattle. There I met a Japanese woman, Kae, who was studying in the United States. We dated for about a year, and then she returned to Japan. I finished my English degree six months later and decided to travel to Kyoto, where Kae was living, and teach English there. I was fortunate to find work at the Berlitz School of Languages in Kyoto.

After four years in Kyoto, I returned to the United States to pursue studies in creative writing (MFA in poetry) with a secondary emphasis in TESOL (teaching English to speakers of other languages). After I completed my studies, Kae came to the United States, and we married. Immediately after our marriage, we returned to Japan where I was able to resume work at Berlitz while looking for part-time university work. Once I began working part-time at one university, finding jobs at other universities was reasonably easy. The most effective way to find a university teaching job was to have someone recommend me for the position. In this sense, networking and word of mouth were indispensable. After a few years of part-time teaching, I was able to begin applying for full-time positions.

Did you discover any resources that were helpful in your stay?

AUSTEN: The South American Explorers Club was especially useful because it helped me meet other hikers and offered timely, accurate, and localized information about current conditions on the ground. During the time that I was in Peru, the Sendero Luminoso (Shining Path) was still an active threat in specific parts of the country. Having access to nearly real-time information about this was essential because much of my travel involved tiny villages and the nearby hiking areas.

KUSSEROW: Universities are tremendously helpful—but there aren't many in Bhutan or South Sudan—as are places that support college semester-abroad learning experiences for students. The School for International Training [sit.edu] is excellent, as is the Alliance for Global Education.

FINNEYFROCK: Suvani Singh and Pranab Singh, the owners of the bookstore Quixote's Cove [www.qcbookshop.com] in Kathmandu, are working hard to build a vibrant literary arts scene in the city. They work with schools and colleges to provide library development services and helped establish the Word Warriors, Nepal's first slam poetry group. The Singhs are working toward publishing an anthology of Nepali poetry.

Quixote's Cove is also a literary events management company. It conducts a variety of literary events, including creative-writing groups; a monthly literary discussion series, Tavern Tales; and an annual international literature festival, Kathmandu Literary Jatra [www.litjatra.com].

GREENWELL: In Bulgaria, the Elizabeth Kostova Foundation is a wonderful organization that organizes workshops, readings, and other activities to make connections between Anglophone and Bulgarian writers.

REDDY: A local language school called the Instituto Cultural Oaxaca manages my university's study-abroad program. The institute's director, Lucero Topete, was a wonderful resource for everything from living arrangements to local attractions. Oaxaca is also full of bookstores, libraries, and museums that welcome foreign travelers. The English-language bookstore, in the middle of town, is very useful in particular, as is the English-language Oaxaca Lending Library. Information on all these resources is readily available in any good travel guide to the area.

POPE: One resource in Amsterdam that provided a connection to the writing world was the John Adams Institute, which promotes cultural exchange between the United States and the Netherlands. The institute sponsored readings and lecture series that were great—the writers were mostly novelists, not poets, but the evenings there were always thought provoking.

What do you wish you had known before living abroad?

DUNNE: With regard to the US Fisheries Observer Program, I suppose it would have been good to know how difficult and isolating an experience it can be, especially when one cannot fully communicate with the men aboard the vessel. This is not to say that I would not do it again but simply to make a note that to be culturally isolated in that way can be trying.

This said, such isolation can also be stimulating and rewarding. It forces a person to consciously consider identity and cultural values, among other things.

With regard to teaching at the university in Japan, it would have been good to know how very different the Japanese university system is from the US system. The differences are directly related to culture. Although it would have been good to know more about the university system before I came, I also believe explanations can go only so far in helping prepare for the experience. To a large degree, I think the differences between the university systems simply have to be experienced—lived.

MEEK: Actually, I felt pretty informed by the time I went. I talked to as many people as I could about the program, and about the country, before leaving the United States. I definitely recommend that. Everyone's experience is going to be different, so no one should be too alarmed— or enchanted—by the narrative experience of the first person he or she talks to. People should read about programs they are interested in and get names of people who have done similar programs and try to contact them. Former volunteers for groups like the Peace Corps tend to be very generous about talking to potential volunteers; regional recruiters will likely be willing to provide names of returned volunteers.

WHITCOMB: It would have been very helpful to have rented a car for my stay at La Muse for my initial residency. I was pretty place-bound except for a weekly shopping excursion to Carcassonne. I made sure to rent a car when we returned the next year with the study-abroad students.

GRABER: I wish I had known immediately upon learning that I had been selected that I would need a long-stay visa, and I wish that I had understood how best to get one. The Lowell Scholarship is not affiliated with any foreign academic institution, and it is time consuming—one needs about four to six months of lead time—to procure a long-stay visa for an

EU country in which one has no official contacts or business.

There is also now an accord—the Schengen Agreement—between most European nations to facilitate travel for EU citizens between the member nations, but one of the consequences is that it severely limits the amount of time a foreigner can stay cumulatively in all of them. You can stay in all of the EU nations collectively for only 90 days out of any 180 days. Your passport is checked only when you enter the EU and when you leave, but you don't want to risk being suddenly kicked out or, worse, being denied reentry to the country in which you've left everything you own in a rented apartment!

Because I could not secure a long-stay visa before I left, I spent a lot of time moving between Britain, where I could stay longer—up to six months at a time—and the continent itself. I finally threw myself on the mercy of the government of Malta, which graciously expedited a long-stay visa application for me. Generally, you *must* have your visa in hand upon arriving in your initial port of entry. The Maltese authorities were, however, very understanding and helpful. Of course, the fact that nearly everyone speaks English there was a tremendous help. I would recommend that all Lowell Scholars traveling to Europe enter through Malta!

I wish I had managed to find a way to stay in one place for the whole year and to simply travel out from there as I wished. Once you are in Europe, it is easy and very inexpensive—if you have only a carry-on bag; bag fees on discount airlines can actually run hundreds of dollars!—to fly from place to place, especially if you are not locked into a schedule. But you really need a solid, inexpensive hub, a place to set up some sort of "home" and to leave most of your belongings.

I also wish I had known how weak the dollar actually was. The exchange rates were unfavorable, and goods were simply much more expensive in many places. Malta, for instance, is in the middle of the Mediterranean. People have to import nearly everything. Hence, most things cost a good bit more there, and no one seems to get rid of anything. There are no charity shops or thrift shops. If you need a spatula, you must apparently purchase it with the thought that you will pass it on one day to your children! There are, moreover, only one or two self-serve laundries. If you do not rent an apartment with a washing machine, you discover that you must send your laundry out to be washed, which is shockingly expensive! In these sorts of economies and radically different consumer cultures, I discovered that I was suddenly quite poor. It is easy to think when you first arrive that you are on a terrifically extended vacation. You cannot, however, afford to live that way! You have to be very, very diligent about your budget.

I also wish I had known that I would not have access to some fairly essential websites (iTunes, for instance, and Netflix). This has to do with how various companies negotiated their worldwide distribution rights. Having a computer abroad was and is a complex scenario. You cannot purchase anything from a US site when your computer is detected as being out of the country. But you also cannot purchase anything from a foreign site with a US computer and only a US credit card! I hear that it is now possible to install a program that masks the location of your computer. That would be one way to avoid this problem. I also think that it could help to open a bank account in your nation of temporary residence in order to get a debit card with a chip—a feature all European cards have—and a European account number. That might allow you to purchase some of the downloads from the European branch of iTunes or at least order books from AmazonUK. Anyone would think that an iPad or iPod or a Kindle would provide access to all the reading and viewing materials necessary or desired, but if you don't download those files before you leave, you cannot buy them abroad!

FINNEYFROCK: I found the pace of the program exhausting. Cultural Envoy Programs last a minimum of ten days, and several days included long stretches of both teaching and performance. In many cases, the workshops were longer than ones I would teach in the United States and were held in the afternoons, before performances. There wasn't much time to rest between day and evening programs.

GREENWELL: As anyone with experience in secondary education knows, teaching high school students is extremely demanding. To continue being productive as a writer requires discipline and efficiency. I didn't write at all for the first year I worked as a teacher.

AUSTEN: There's an adage in the backpacking community that your confidence is inversely proportional to the amount of gear you carry. That was certainly true for me. I took my body weight in stuff. I wish I was being hyperbolic. Hauling all that around created its own set of problems and, ironically, made me feel more vulnerable as my attention was diverted to dealing with the unnecessarily difficult logistics of getting all that stuff—what, they don't have shampoo in Ecuador?—from one place to another. The metaphorical aspect is obvious, I'm sure.

KUSSEROW: Each country totally differs, as does each program. Mostly it is best to let go when you are in another country, to try not to hold on too tight to preconceived ideas of experiences you should have or what people should be like.

Did you encounter unexpected difficulties as a poet living in an unfamiliar land?

BURLESON: Rwanda was undergoing a civil war when we arrived in 1991, and that continued until we were evacuated in 1993. Even though life went on as usual, there were military checkpoints to navigate and Peace Corps meetings on how to avoid stepping on land mines. We became used to hearing gunfire at night, especially in the northern part of Rwanda. When the Rwandan Patriotic Front took and held the northern third of the country in early 1993, the decision was made to evacuate all the volunteers and close the program. The genocide that began in April 1994 changed everything. Peace Corps Rwanda finally reopened a couple of years ago.

AUSTEN: It turns out that if I have a gift for language, it's only for English. My brain proved strangely resistant to Spanish. Despite previous exposure growing up in San Diego, intense study, living with Spanish speakers, and the daily practice that traveling alone afforded, I never managed more than about a second-grade proficiency, even at the end of my trip. Most of the time, I spoke Spanish with the nuance and complexity of a three-year-old. As someone whose primary sense of identity had always been located in verbal skill and ease, this was intensely alienating and disorienting.

FINNEYFROCK: Food and water in Nepal is often unsafe for Westerners, and despite the incredible generosity and care of my hosts, I got sick. I was forced to cancel two days of my program and was lucky that the other poets traveling with me were able to cover the workshops and performances. I also learned that the US Department of State insurance would cover my medical expenses while I was in the country. Also, the air quality is very poor in Kathmandu. I'm a performer, and I struggled to keep my voice in working order.

STONECIPHER: The only real difficulty I experience is a significant one— I do not live in the country in whose poetic community I participate. I write in English primarily for English speakers, yet I don't live in an English-speaking country.

WHITCOMB: It is hard to call this a difficulty, but I loved being in France again so much that it was hard to sit in my room and write all day. I wanted to explore and experience where I was and sometimes found it impossible to concentrate on recording my impressions.

GRABER: I was very lonely and homesick, and I am among the least patriotic, least social individuals I know. I think, however, that this deep sense of dislocation and this confrontation with my own American-ness were very good for me in the long run.

My sense of displacement was probably somewhat exacerbated by the simple fact that I am a real homebody. I'm very domestic. I missed having my own essential objects around me. I missed having good pots for cooking! By the last few months, I was traveling with one good kitchen knife, a knife sharpener, a wooden spoon, a cutting board, a French press, and a skillet. I was down to two pairs of jeans and six T-shirts. And a few wool sweaters and boots. I kept replacing the clothing in my suitcase with housewares! I came to see what really mattered to me. You don't really need a fancy dress or a tie and nice shoes when you wake up in a strange place after traveling for twenty-four hours straight! You need some good coffee and a pair of quick-drying socks.

In many places, you are going to have limited access to English-language texts. Unless you ship your library with you, you are going to feel some frustration. I did not have a Kindle or an iPad with me, but I'm not sure that that would have given me what I was seeking. And, of course, one part of being a real "thing" person is the desire to hold the book as an object in your hands. You have to be prepared for the fact that there might only be six books in English in a used bookstore. I think I paid $35 for a used hardback edition of Oliver Sacks's *Musicophilia* in Budapest. And it was worth it! The library on Gozo had no poetry after modernism. These limitations forced me to value deeply whatever was at hand. I read all of H. D., and I reread Pound's prose on poetry. And Eliot's essays. This was terrific. I was thrilled when the librarian there agreed finally to give me my own library card and let me take the books home!

MEEK: In my case, it was difficult to get books. I knew it would be an issue, but I didn't fully anticipate how expensive books would be and how little access I would have to them. At times, I was really starved for poetry. A gift package of books from my mother could seem as revitalizing as a blood transfusion. My advice here is to find out about where you are going—will you have access to a library? If so, will there be books in English? Will there be poetry? You will likely have very little or no access to books of contemporary American poetry. I found it was really important to have that infusion of the living voice of my own culture, even as I was living in a different culture and trying to absorb all I could there. Try to be proactive with this—if you have supportive family members and friends, consider asking as many of them as you can if they could send you a new book of poems occasionally. Postage can often be very expensive, so diffusing these costs among multiple friends and family members will be appreciated.

DUNNE: I think the difficulties were pretty much anticipated: few bookstores with English books, few opportunities to hear poetry being read in public (in English), a fractured poetry community—poet friends living far and wide within the country—difficulty in finding like-minded souls to talk with about poetry. Though these difficulties were anticipated, I was surprised by how desperately I actually missed them in my daily life—the luxury of walking into a good bookstore with stacks of poetry books to peruse.

REDDY: One thing I found difficult was accessing English-language books. The local English-language bookstore was helpful in special-ordering texts, but it took some time for volumes to arrive. The local English-language library was a wonderful place, but holdings in my particular (i.e., eccentric and eclectic) areas of interest were spotty. I couldn't access my university's online collection while living in Mexico, so I relied on sources such as the Questia online library to patch in holes wherever I could. But still, there were times when I would have loved having access to the stacks of a major research university's collections.

POPE: I had deeply underestimated the effects of living in a foreign language and culture, the simple and pervasive level of disorientation involved. Many of the writers I admired had been expatriates at some point, and I think I naïvely felt it was a pretty common rite of passage, something that enhanced rather than hindered the work.

I also underestimated how it would feel to be away from my friends, and it was hard to keep in touch—this was before e-mail. Phone calls cost a fortune, and the six-hour time difference was tricky. Letters took a week to get from one continent to the other. I really lived for them, though.

It seemed sort of ridiculous to miss US culture when Hollywood movies and certain TV shows were readily available, not to mention mass-market books, but after the first couple of years, I did miss it. Not the mass-market stuff—small things, regional things, particularities, the stuff Europeans can't believe exists in the United States. I especially missed the invention and playfulness of English. I know that this was intensified by the effort to live in another language, which entails strait-ened expressive circumstances for quite some time, but I think it also had to do with some of the essential differences between the two languages. I also missed the small-press culture—there was nothing comparable to it in the Netherlands.

Were there unexpected joys?

REDDY: The unexpected joys were everywhere. But this is part of living abroad—you never know what you'll miss the most upon departure. Even the things I found irritating when I first went to Oaxaca—the dogs barking from the rooftops at every passerby, the fireworks going off in the middle of the night—became part of the wonder and joy of the place in good time. And I'm not even mentioning the pleasures we discovered in the food, the culture, and the friends we made during our time in Mexico.

GRABER: Every difficulty was also a strange joy, though you might be dis-traught in the moment. Loneliness is a joy because it asserts that you at least like *some* other people! It felt very good to discover that I had some actual affection for the United States. I stayed up all night in London streaming the 2008 election results on my laptop, and I wept. I was as proud as I have ever been of my country, especially as I had encountered so many Europeans who were convinced that Obama would never be elected, even though the polls had him ahead. The election radically changed what it meant to be an American in Europe. That is not an overstatement. It was a real blessing to be able to see firsthand the world's perception of the nation change quite radically and suddenly.

AUSTEN: One of the most surprising and humbling experiences was how often very poor people showed spontaneous generosity toward me. It's hard to say how much of this was because I was a woman traveling alone, but many bus and train rides included someone offering to accompany me to my destination or to feed me. Even Quechua speakers, whose Spanish was often only marginally better than mine, would make the effort to use the small shreds of language we shared in common to connect in an act of generosity. A family of six would open their cloth manta with a simple lunch—perhaps their only meal of the day—and invite me to share it.

These experiences and the fact that I was living on about fifteen dollars a day for months at a time, including transportation, shifted my relationship to money in a significant, long-lasting way. Not that I live now with anything remotely like that kind of austerity, but my attitude toward what I consider a necessity versus a luxury was permanently altered.

The depth of solitude I encountered, especially when backpacking alone for several days in a remote national park in central Ecuador, did not feel joyful at the time. However, during that experience I was more intensely in contact with my own vulnerability and resourcefulness than ever, and there was a certain—perhaps not joy exactly—but satisfaction in recognizing that after the fact.

WHITCOMB: I loved how easy it was to explain having a profession as a professor and a poet.

BURLESON: Rwanda was and is an incredibly beautiful place, and the people there were very welcoming and friendly. I grew close with a number of people and am still in touch with those who survived the genocide. My best friend, Roger Remera, came and lived with me for several years in the United States after he managed, though shot and left for dead in the forest, to survive the genocide. He just returned to Arusha, Tanzania, this past year to testify at the International Criminal Tribunal for Rwanda against the man who shot him and killed his brother. Seventeen years have elapsed in the meantime. His finally getting to tell what happened from his own perspective was an important moment for us both. Living with Roger, hearing night after night his story and the stories of our friends who were killed or who managed to escape, made me see the world in a new way.

FINNEYFROCK: The US embassy staff could not have been more accommodating. As a spoken-word artist who sometimes writes pieces that are critical of US policy, I was concerned about being censored abroad. Instead, I found the embassy staff encouraging my right to perform any poem and state any views I held. Likewise, my Nepali hosts were among the warmest people I've met. We spent many nights with Nepali poets, drinking and laughing and talking about poetry in the warm evenings after dinner.

GREENWELL: I encounter unexpected joys every day in Sofia, where after two years I'm still discovering new things almost every day. It helps that new things are being uncovered nearly every day as well; new ruins are being found as the city continues developing its metro. The language is also a continuing, unexpected joy; I had never studied a Slavic language before and am constantly delighted by the quirks and challenges of Bulgarian.

STONECIPHER: Living in a city that constantly offers me ideas and stimulation and interesting people and endless reflection is a joy. Learning German was (and is—it's a lifelong process) a joy.

POPE: Most of my joys were connected to the point when I achieved a level of fluency in Dutch that allowed me to express myself beyond perfunctory exchanges, to read more than newspapers, and most of all to enjoy Dutch humor.

NEZHUKUMATATHIL: A small thing, but I was able to watch and help my four-foot ten-inch grandmother prepare several meals in her modest kitchen, was able to see and touch and smell all the glass spice jars delicately arranged on the windowsill. I hadn't planned that quiet intimacy, could not even afford to dream it up, me, a girl who grew up feeling a palpable sadness at not being able to spend time with my grandmothers (my grandmother in the Philippines died a few weeks after I was born in Chicago). Had I elected to stay at a hotel or resort, I never would have experienced those rich moments. The best decision I ever made about my time abroad was that, with the exception of a handful of days over the course of more than two months abroad, I always stayed in the homes of my cousins or uncles. I feel hugely blessed to have been embedded in those cultures, if only for a few months.

DUNNE: Because poetry friends were hard to find, when I did find them, I tended to value them greatly. Those relationships seemed to take on greater significance and meaning than they might have otherwise. They became a sort of lifeline. Years ago in Kyoto, for example, some interested folks began meeting in coffee shops to talk about poetry and to exchange books. Eventually, the group grew. In time, we began to meet at the home of the expatriate American poet Cid Corman. He graciously held weekly poetry meetings and took on the role of mentor for many of us. At these gatherings, poetry was read and talked about for hours and hours. It filled a vital need, and we recognized that need as something elemental in our lives.

Another joy came in time through learning the Japanese language. This deepened my appreciation of the culture and its literature. I began to realize how much of what we experience and understand is mediated through language. A further joy came from simply having the opportunity to experience a different culture and all that entails. This experience helped me understand my own culture more—its values, assumptions, and aesthetics.

MEEK: Of course, there were many highs—and lows—during those two years. A significant unexpected joy was how fascinating the smallest day-to-day workings of the natural world and the village community could be: the flight of termites after rain, dung beetles doing their exhaustive work. And certainly, the amazing personalities of free-range goats!

KUSSEROW: Countless joys, infinite, mind-boggling—every day is like being in an altered state of consciousness. This is why I travel. Everything about it makes you grow; you realize your own smallness, your insignificance. You realize you are not the norm, your ethnocentricity suddenly becomes crystal clear, you hopefully become more humble because of this, you fall in love with other truths, other faiths, other norms, so that you become a more agile and tolerant human being, one who is less judgmental, more expansive, more compassionate.

Did you need language skills for your travels?

WHITCOMB: No, but they would have been an asset. I occasionally had some difficulty because of my limited French, but that is to be expected.

I had one incident with language at a wonderful restaurant in Roquefère, a town neighboring Labastide-Esparbairenque. The coteacher and I had arranged to take our study-abroad class down to have a big Sunday lunch. In my efforts to help the students navigate the menu, I mistakenly translated *écrevisse* on the menu as shrimp (crevette)—only to have big bowls of crawfish arrive, looking very much like large pink bugs in butter-herb sauce. Fortunately, the students rolled with it and gamely attacked the écrevisse.

BURLESON: I studied French and Kinyarwanda.

FINNEYFROCK: Most Nepali people I encountered spoke English and translated their poems into English.

MEEK: I was a volunteer in Botswana, which has two national languages, English and Setswana. The Peace Corps provided us with two months of language training in Setswana, in-country, before sending us to our job posts. I used English as a teacher; the basic knowledge of Setswana I received in training helped with communication around the village, with polite conversation, and with understanding the specific challenges my Setswana-speaking students had in learning English.

This will vary; for some countries, knowledge of Spanish or French, for instance, will give you a competitive advantage in applying, but for other countries or programs, no prior language skills will be expected. Your recruiter will take into consideration any language abilities you have when matching you with a program, but language ability (or lack thereof) is just one factor for placement. Don't assume, for instance, that if you are fluent in Spanish, you will necessarily be sent to a Spanish-speaking country; at least one volunteer in our group was fluent in Spanish, and there was absolutely no use for her Spanish in Botswana.

GREENWELL: British and US international schools use English as the common language, and in Sofia, at least, it is possible to get around without the language. That said, I think any international experience is extremely limited without some access to the language of the place.

KUSSEROW: I have been able to get by on English in Bhutan, India, Nepal, South Sudan, and Uganda. But knowing the language at least a bit opens many doors and is vital insofar as it is symbolic of attempts to appreciate and respect the other culture.

POPE: I wasn't in a program, but I certainly needed language skills, and I would emphatically recommend that any American traveling anywhere learn at least a handful of words in the local language, even if the trip is only for a short time. A willingness to try using the local language counts for a great deal, wherever you go. Because we have lousy foreign-language education in the United States, we don't usually get the chance to practice, experiment, and become more comfortable with trying basic exchanges, but trying is essential. The unwillingness to do so is perceived as rudeness or another demonstration of Americans' sense of superiority, which ironically is the opposite of what many of us feel, especially when attempting to communicate.

DUNNE: Language skills were not required—but language skills were always an asset. I did a lot of independent study. While in Kyoto, I studied Japanese at a language school.

GRABER: Language skills would have been awesome, but I don't speak any language other than English. I can read or semiread a few, but I am too shy to try to make the right sounds! I got around fine in Budapest, and I don't know any Magyar at all. Hence, I'd say you don't *need* another language. On the other hand, I was on the subway one day when the train stopped in the tunnel and an announcement came on. Oddly, there was no one else in the car I was riding. It was in the middle of the afternoon on an extraordinarily hot day. That was a frightening moment. I had no idea what I was being instructed to do. Eventually the train started up again, and we went on our way. Similarly, in the middle of the night, a car drove up and down the streets playing a recorded message through a loudspeaker. I have no idea even now what that might have been. I looked out the window, and no one seemed to be evacuating her home or otherwise bracing for a disaster, so I just went back to bed.

What advice can you offer about staying in touch with loved ones, managing money issues, arranging storage, and taking care of domestic matters?

AUSTEN: The Internet has changed this aspect of travel so profoundly since my trip. I'm sure many things that were difficult in 1996 to 1997 would be much easier now. At that point, when Internet cafés were still a rarity and before texting became the cheap international mode of communication, keeping track of what was happening with my bank account or contacting family and friends was difficult. These matters depended on involvement with something like a language school or the South American Explorers Club in order to access a general e-mail account or fax.

I had two periods of thirty-plus days when no one at home knew exactly where I was, and there was no way to contact me. Internet cafés didn't exist in the remote areas where I was traveling, and at any rate, I didn't have a personal e-mail account. Phone calls were prohibitively expensive, and I was often in places with few phones and an intermittent power supply.

Now it would be much rarer to be out of communication range. But the fact is that I engaged most deeply with my surroundings, and with the intensity of the experience, during those unconnected weeks. The depth of my aloneness—though often overwhelming and unwelcome—was essential to the kind of transformation I was seeking. If I'd been able to check in via e-mail or text every few days, I would have missed the most significant and transformative confrontations with my own fears and limitations. Instead I turned to my journal, where I talked to myself in order to understand, remember, and process what I was seeing and experiencing.

So my advice would be to manage the expectations of people at home so that you can fully immerse yourself in the experience at hand. Having to check in all the time can mean never quite fully giving over to being where you are and might deprive you of the unexpected gifts of solitude.

WHITCOMB: A lot of places I visited recently have wi-fi, which makes things easy. I also got international calling and data plans for my BlackBerry, which worked perfectly in France and Spain. Flash drives are essential. Make sure the data roaming on your phone is not turned on, especially if you receive e-mails on your smartphone. This can really rack up the bills.

BURLESON: I knew I'd be gone for two years, so I put everything in order—and sold a lot of stuff—before I left. Staying in touch was tricky with a postal system that usually worked but took a long time. Letters from folks back home were especially welcome when they did arrive!

GRABER: I am still recovering from the financial cost of having been fortunate enough to receive back-to-back fellowships (the Hodder Fellowship at Princeton and then the Amy Lowell Poetry Travelling Scholarship). These both required me to live somewhere other than in the home I own. I don't think these opportunities were necessarily designed for individuals with mortgages and pets. I could have self-selected out, but I didn't, and I'm obviously glad that I had these two years, which were so essential to my work and which profoundly changed my understanding of who I am. At the same time, I could barely live on the Lowell Scholarship stipend, given the very unfavorable exchange rates at that particular moment, and then I still had to pay my own mortgage, my home insurance, my property taxes, et cetera.

The Lowell Scholarship does not come with a health care package, and after a certain point in your life, you really need good health insurance. The sort of health insurance that travelers purchase did not seem to me to be enough. I was not worried about breaking my arm; I was worried about being diagnosed while I was abroad with a very serious condition that might require long-term treatment. I felt I needed health care such that I would be able, if necessary, to return home to get whatever care I needed. I wanted coverage that would be good worldwide. Fortunately, I was able to negotiate with my home university to provide that for me, but not all Lowell Scholars will have "home institutions."

FINNEYFROCK: My program was short, lasting only two weeks, but it still placed demands on my teaching schedule in the United States. The planning period for the trip was only a few months, and I was lucky that my job with Writers in the Schools was accommodating. The US Department of State was prompt with payments, so money issues were not a problem for this trip. Our hotel provided Internet access, so video chats were the best way to talk to people back home.

GREENWELL: For money issues, be sure to acquire credit cards with addresses in the United States, and keep an open bank account in the United States as well. Banks have widely differing policies affecting ATM fees and customer support internationally.

For staying in touch with family in the United States, Skype has been indispensable. Video chat is great, and it's very cheap to maintain a US phone number through Skype that friends and families can call from their regular phones. This number needs to be arranged while you're still in the United States.

POPE: Staying in touch is so much easier now that it can be done electronically for minimal expense and in a way that isn't time dependent. Money issues are tricky because US systems are so different than they are in much of the world, but at least it's easier to use ATMs in most places. I had a postal giro account—a fantastic system that doesn't exist anymore because of privatization. People I know who have traveled abroad for extended periods have lived on credit cards and shared a checking account with someone in the United States who received and paid their bills.

DUNNE: During my time in Japan—about twenty-five years, on and off—technology has advanced to such a degree that staying in touch with family and friends is no longer much of a problem. In addition to frequent Skype calls and e-mail, I like to return to the United States about once a year to stay in touch with friends and family.

Storage is a problem, however, and I have not found any successful way around it, other than the obvious: try to minimize the amount of my possessions.

REDDY: The one thing that made our year abroad possible was finding a good subletter for our apartment. Our tenant was pretty much ideal. She forwarded our important mail to us in Mexico, kept the apartment clean as a whistle, and paid her rent on time every month. Without her, I don't think we could have managed to transport our lives south of the border for that precious year abroad. The other things, such as staying in touch with family and accessing bank accounts in the United States, were a piece of cake. With things such as ATMs and Skype, the details generally worked themselves out.

RUCH: While I was stationed in South Korea, it was very easy to find inexpensive, used cell phones set up to work with calling cards, and I primarily stayed in touch with my family in this way. Friends who were stationed in Germany found similar resources available there. There were also numerous Internet cafés throughout the metropolitan areas I visited in South Korea, and I've found that to be true of many other countries as well.

Automatic bill pay probably saved my credit score while I was stationed overseas. Everything that can be paid by automatic bank draft every month should be set up that way for peace of mind while you're abroad. Put things such as your cell phone service and auto insurance on hold until you get back home.

Paying for a monitored security service was well worth the expense for the peace of mind it gave me while I was deployed. At a minimum, arrange to have someone keep an eye on your house and check on it from time to time in case of unexpected issues, such as frozen pipes or leaky roofs. This person should also regularly collect any newspapers, phone books, or flyers that are left in the driveway, on the front door, or on your car windshield. Obviously, this person should know how to get in touch with you.

If you will be away only for a month or two, have the post office hold your mail until you return. If you will be away longer, consider having your mail forwarded to a family member or friend. The person can send along the important correspondence once a month or so.

If you plan to be out of the country for an extended period, you should consider leaving a very trustworthy individual with a limited power of attorney. If your roof blows off in a tornado or your basement floods or your front door is kicked in (you get the idea), this person will be able to access the necessary funds and sign off on any repairs quickly to resolve these issues before they lead to more costly problems.

It's also not a bad idea to prepare a will before you leave the country, especially if you will be traveling to any politically unstable destinations. Leave a copy in a safe-deposit box and a copy with a close friend or family member, along with photocopies of your passport, driver's license, major credit cards, health insurance card, and itinerary. In the event that these items are lost or stolen, you will be able to expedite their replacement by having this information on hand in a safe location.

I cannot stress enough how important it is to find a willing and responsible caretaker for your pets, a person who understands how much they mean to you. While I was deployed, one of my dogs was put down without my consent for a treatable condition that I had successfully managed for some time. My dog's caretaker had been fully briefed about his condition and how to treat it before I left the country, but she failed to administer the appropriate medication and as a result chose to have my dog put down without even consulting me. I am telling this story only to illustrate the potential repercussions of this decision. Take it very seriously.

MEEK: I was in the Peace Corps twenty years ago, and it was a whole different world, communication-wise, back then. Now cell phones are widely used even in what might be considered quite "remote" areas. I have traveled for extended periods in southern Africa in recent years as well, though, and I would suggest that you have a cell phone but that you don't use it constantly to call "home." As much as you can stay in the place, do so. My suggestion: if you are dying of loneliness, call someone. If your family is afraid for you, set up a plan for regular contact. But focus on where you are now—the place you went to a lot of trouble to experience fully. Writing letters can be a good way to process your experience through language and to keep in touch with loved ones without being pulled abruptly out of your new place.

Do you have any technical equipment suggestions?

RUCH: A digital voice recorder is small, easy to pack, relatively inexpensive, and extremely handy for collecting stories that can later be transcribed and written directly or indirectly into your work. Make sure you have a large enough memory card or possibly more than one if you won't be able to download your recorded files onto a computer until you get home. Also make sure you will be able to find the batteries your device requires, or take a supply with you.

AUSTEN: This may be obvious, but be clear about what you need the equipment to do—is broadcast quality essential?—and get the smallest, lightest equipment you can afford that will provide that functionality.

POPE: I had pens and notebooks and, later, a manual typewriter.

MEEK: Definitely I'd recommend a small digital camera and audio recorder—and video, if that's something you'd like to do. Go for compact sizes first! If you are going to stay in one country for an extended time, take a phone and buy a SIM card in that country. If you are going to be traveling in multiple countries, consider buying an international cell phone, which will allow you to travel across international borders without losing service. You can get an international cell phone and pay by the minutes you use, with no monthly fees. This can be good because it will help you limit your conversations!

GREENWELL: I'm a big fan of Dropbox, especially given the unreliability of computers in many international schools.

STONECIPHER: Skype—for something like thirteen dollars a month, you can make all the phone calls you want to American landlines and cell phones.

NEZHUKUMATATHIL: I didn't have access to these at the time of my trips to India and the Philippines, but I would say Skype and a small, light-weight video camera would now be indispensible for communicating with people at home and recording sights and sounds.

DUNNE: I don't really have any suggestions here—other than Skype. I do all my international calling on Skype and find it to be of great value and highly dependable.

REDDY: We just took our laptops with us. Setting up a phone and an Internet connection was time consuming, but our landlords in Oaxaca were helpful on that front. Once we were hooked up with wireless in the apartment, everything else came along pretty easily.

KUSSEROW: I have a whole host of things I take as an anthropologist that probably wouldn't be relevant to poets. But definitely take a laptop. Internet cafés are everywhere now, even at Everest base camp. I also like giving the locals my camera—it's fascinating to see what they find worthy of a picture. In the places I travel, there are often norms around picture taking, so you need to clue into those before you start snapping. You can be thrown in jail in South Sudan for taking a picture, whereas in Bhutan it can bring on a flood of eager and giggly kids dying to see their images.

FINNEYFROCK: I wish I had taken a video recorder. That footage would be worth so much to me now.

Being There

Did you read the poets of the countries you traveled to either before or during your time there?

GREENWELL: There's not much in the way of translation from Bulgarian into English, but a couple of anthologies have been published since 1989. The most beautiful translations I've found are three poems of the great poet Valeri Petrov translated by Richard Wilbur. A number of exciting young writers work in Bulgarian; thanks to the efforts of the Elizabeth Kostova Foundation and others, it is becoming easier to find them in English.

GRABER: I tried to make a point of reading the poets of each region I visited. I read the Hungarian poets when I was in Hungary (in translation, of course). I read Walter Benjamin every day I was in Berlin. I read W.S. Graham in Cornwall, John Burnside in Scotland.

MEEK: I read what I could of regional poets before I left but could not find at that time the work of any Batswana poets available in the United States. Once in Botswana, I found a bookstore in Gaborone that carried local writers, including a few poets whose work I then was able to read. However, the work of a number of South African poets and many southern African novelists, including Bessie Head (who emigrated from South Africa to Botswana), was available in both the United States and Botswana. I read as much as I could find, both before, during, and after my two years in Botswana.

WHITCOMB: In France, I did not. The region around La Muse is the legendary land of the troubadours, and I read a lot of history of the area. In preparation for the study-abroad class, the coteacher and I assembled a course pack with readings for the students to look at on the plane. It contained excerpts from books on medieval architecture, the history of the Cathars, maps, and a key essay on creativity and the unknown by Peter Turchi.

BURLESON: I taught English at the university in Rwanda and had the chance to read Rwandan poets in translations to French and English. My colleagues at the university were very helpful in explaining the history of Rwandan poetry, an art form very much respected and central to the culture.

FINNEYFROCK: I did read short stories by a Nepali writer who is well known in the United States, but I didn't find books by any Nepali poets before leaving.

KUSSEROW: The countries that I work in don't seem to have many modern poets who have written bodies of work that were available to me before leaving. But I always try to find any anthropologists who write poetry about the country to which I am going. I subscribe to and am a member of *Anthropology and Humanism*, which publishes anthropolog-ical poetry. I often get great recommendations of travel poets from other anthropologists at the American Anthropological Association meetings. These happen each year in the United States, and I often lead poetry workshops for anthropologists and give readings with other anthropolo-gists at these. The meetings are a great place to make connections, hear about books, and be encouraged to write poetically as an anthropologist.

STONECIPHER: The best thing about learning German was then being able to read Celan, Rilke, Goethe, et cetera, and contemporary poets in the original. Rilke, for example, was a complete revelation. The English-language Rilke is a fabrication.

POPE: I didn't read any Dutch poets before I left, though I did read some fiction in translation. There was and is not a great deal of Dutch literature in English translation. While I was living in Amsterdam, I began reading Dutch poets. Spending my days in a bookshop made the value attached to poetry clear—it was read by a real cross-section of book buyers, very unlike in the United States. Dutch people would often tell me that their poets were far more accomplished than their novelists, that what they did with the language was far more ambitious and significant. Once I found a few writers whose work attracted me, I began trying to translate poems as a change from all the commercial translation I was doing, in which the language was far from interesting.

NEZHUKUMATATHIL: Yes, especially Kamala Das, Rabindranath Tagore, Eric Gamalinda, Alfred A. Yuson, and Marjorie Evasco.

DUNNE: I read the work of Japanese poets prior to coming to Japan. Their poetry prompted me to come to Japan. I was captivated by the aesthet-ics that I found there. While in Japan, I have continued to read Japanese work, although I tend to read primarily in English translation.

REDDY: I'm embarrassed to say no, I didn't really read the poets of Mexico before or during my time in Oaxaca. Just before leaving the country, I did stop by the local university bookstore to pick up some Latin American poetry—people such as Dario, Huidobro, Hernández, and others—but I didn't really focus on Mexican poetry in particular.

AUSTEN: While living in Quito and then in Lima, I went to several poetry readings and dance-theater performances that involved poetry. My reading was largely focused on understanding tropical rain forest and altiplano ecology and the history and present-day effects of Spanish colonialism and the indigenous human-rights movement.

Did you interact with other poets while living abroad?

FINNEYFROCK: I was introduced to several poets by our hosts, Suvani Singh and Pranab Singh, from Quixote's Cove bookstore in Kathmandu. They had been running open-mic poetry nights already and were thrilled to introduce us to the small band of poets in Nepal who had already heard of poetry slams. We had several informal, social nights together and two performances with the local poets.

GREENWELL: The Elizabeth Kostova Foundation, which I've already mentioned, is a great resource for making connections with writers here. For teachers working in secondary schools, the alumni network is also a terrific resource. The majority of the writers I've met here have been friends of an alumnus I met more or less by chance.

STONECIPHER: I interact with lots of poets in Berlin. I meet them in the usual ways, through friends, by going to readings, et cetera.

AUSTEN: I had brief conversations with a couple of poets in Lima. They were friendly and receptive, but my Spanish was so limited that it was extremely frustrating to try to talk about poetry with them—I just didn't have the vocabulary. My pleasure in hearing their poems read in Spanish wasn't dependent on understanding them, but conversation, of course, requires comprehension.

WHITCOMB: I met a group of experimental visual artists who were introduced through the owners of La Muse. During my initial residency, we made a "land art" project in the woods above Saint-Julien by shaping shards of the native slate into a giant egg-shaped sculpture. When I returned to La Muse with the study-abroad group, I met many of these artists again at a party in the village.

BURLESON: Though I didn't have the chance to interact with other poets, I did work with a Rwandan novelist, Daniel Kanyandekwe, who was my colleague at the university. He later won a scholarship to study in the United States and finished a PhD in New York. He unfortunately died young while still in the United States, and his remarkable fiction remains mostly unpublished.

POPE: I didn't know other poets in Amsterdam. I knew some prose writers and a number of painters who were serious readers of poetry and sometimes incorporated it in their work.

NEZHUKUMATATHIL: Through the helpful coordination of Filipino literati star Mr. Krip A. Yuson, I was to read at the MagNet performance space at Ateneo de Manila University, but alas, I was pregnant and nauseated during that time and could not make the six-hour drive over winding roads to Manila.

DUNNE: I have interacted with a number of poets while living in Japan. I have interacted with poets whom I have translated and with Japanese editors of literary magazines. I have also interacted with many expatriate,

English-speaking poets from around the world: Australia, Canada, India, Ireland, Nigeria, and New Zealand.

I met most of my contacts through word-of-mouth connections. Cid Corman enjoyed connecting people he thought would enjoy meeting one another. I am indebted to him for having introduced me to a number of contacts who became friends. In this sense, Corman was something of a central connection for me, a hub.

KUSSEROW: I have never met another poet (at least not someone who described himself or herself as such) in the countries I have visited. But in some countries, the word *poet* has a very different meaning that cannot be separated from other religious roles.

REDDY: My wife and I didn't make friends with any Mexican poets while living in Oaxaca, but, oddly enough, we became close friends with two American poets during that time. Joshua Edwards, who was in Oaxaca on a Fulbright grant, and Lynn Xu, his partner, were living in the city that year and became our constant companions. It would have been a lonelier and less artistically productive experience without them.

Were you aware of opportunities for publishing your poetry in the magazines and periodicals of other countries? How did you learn of these opportunities?

FINNEYFROCK: Yes. In fact, I have kept in touch with many of the poets I met in Nepal through social media sites. Quixote's Cove is currently finishing a compilation of spoken-word poetry from Nepal and asked me to contribute poems to the anthology.

STONECIPHER: Journals and magazines are as monolingual in Germany as they are in the United States. If one's poetry is to be published in them, it has to be in the form of translation.

DUNNE: I was aware of several magazines in Japan that published work in both Japanese and English. These magazines were mentioned in Dustbooks' *Directory of Poetry Publishers*. Some of them are associated with major universities in Japan.

POPE: Those opportunities were few and far between. I learned about them from magazines. My impression is that there is a lot more opportunity now—because of the Internet, of course, but also because the greater degree of mobility of citizens within the EU has resulted in the creation of more English-language venues.

Have you written about the countries where you lived?

NEZHUKUMATATHIL: I've written and continue to write poems and essays about both India and the Philippines. In fact, a good portion of my new manuscript deals with my travels and observations while living in southern India, particularly in the state of Kerala, where my father was born.

Kerala has one of the forty-two tiger reserves set up to protect some of the estimated 1,706 tigers left in India. I'm currently writing about the ecotourist trade there, in particular with the tiger preserves. Tourists who come along on various tours and preserve maintenance operations become involved in the conservation of the forests of Periyar and help generate some valuable revenue for the community too. People who once made a living by illegal operations in the forests have since become forest protectors and earn their livelihood through these programs. My husband and I participated in one of these tours for our first anniversary, and I've been studying the physiology and conservation efforts of the majestic tiger ever since.

POPE: My first book of poems, *Watermark*, was in large part about Amsterdam and my experiences living there. I've also written a lot of prose about that period.

DUNNE: I have written broadcast essays for NHK radio. I have also written at some length about my mentoring under Cid Corman. Presently, I am writing a mixed-form (prose and poetry) memoir that explores my life in Japan and my journey into the vocation in poetry.

AUSTEN: In one sense, no, I haven't written about Ecuador, Peru, or Bolivia in a way that would be clear to the reader. But in another sense, my experiences there informed everything I've written since. For example, "The Girl Who Goes Alone" is the title poem of my first chapbook. In its final form, the poem is situated in the landscape of the Pacific Northwest, but the original draft was actually about a three-day solo backpacking trip I did in Sangay National Park, a particularly remote area of central Ecuador. I discarded the literal details of that trip in subsequent revisions, but my experience of being completely out of my depth in terms of the extremity of the physical challenge I'd set for myself, and the way my own fears kept me from enjoying what was, in retrospect, an amazingly beautiful trip, gave me the subject matter in the deepest sense of that phrase.

GRABER: Almost all the poems in the last section of *The Eternal City* are set in foreign landscapes. There are poems set in Berlin and Budapest, Cornwall and Gozo.

FINNEYFROCK: I have tried several times to write about Nepal. For me, this trip marked my first visit to Asia and my first trip to a developing country, one of the world's poorest. As a privileged person from the first world, I struggle to find ways to write about my experience there that honor the country and the people of Nepal while acknowledging my perceptions as a Westerner. In trying to avoid the exploitative or voyeuristic elements of writing about a culture that is not my own, I find a challenge in creating work that is engaging and honest.

MEEK: My first book of poems, *Nomadic Foundations*, centers on my experience living in Botswana and traveling in southern Africa. I have returned to the region four times in the last three years, and the poems generated from this experience, in the context of having also lived there twenty years ago, when southern Africa was a vastly different world, are really the centerpiece of the book of poems I am currently working on, *An Ecology of Elsewhere*.

GREENWELL: My first book, *Mitko*, is set in Bulgaria and draws a great deal from my experiences in my first year here. My new project is also about Bulgaria, and I have written a number of essays about teaching and living here as well. I suspect that I will continue to find inspiration in this place for a long time.

BURLESON: My first book of poems, *Ejo: Poems, Rwanda 1991–94*, centers on my experience in Rwanda and what happened to my Rwandan friends, colleagues, and students during the genocide. I wrote the book as a memorial for those who had been murdered, and it wasn't a project I had any choice about. The poems demanded to be written. As William Carlos Williams wrote:

> It is difficult
> to get the news from poems
>   yet men die miserably every day
>   for lack
> of what is found there.

I had a story that I had to tell over and over, and poetry seemed to me to be the best vehicle to get at that story, to transform my experience and the experiences of my friends into a solid object that would last—a memorial for those whose voices were silenced.

How did living abroad affect your work?

RUCH: My time overseas affected my work profoundly. Those experiences gave my writing purpose and direction and a much larger scope, and they play a central role in most of what I write today. Everything—from the ethical dilemmas I struggle with when deciding which stories to tell to the language I use to tell them—has been influenced by many long months lived in these two war-torn countries. Sometimes I can't write the things I want to write. I've been told it takes seven years before a person can effectively write about traumatic experiences. War changed me, irreversibly; war changes everyone. How could it not change the very soul of my work?

POPE: I am still discovering ways in which it affected my work. Foremost was the experience of living in another language and now living with the ghost of that language. It also led to my involvement in literary translation, and that's been valuable in itself. I know that I was exposed to the work of a lot of writers I wouldn't have encountered otherwise—Dutch, British, French, and others. There were even American writers whose work I might not have read at all if I hadn't encountered them there, in a different context, where I could pay a different kind of attention.

I learned something about what it's like to be from a minority culture, what it means when a person's native tongue is a minor language. Beyond that, I became aware of what linguistic minorities are—people in the United States don't encounter these distinctions and issues of identity.

Underneath the effects that had to do directly with writing, the experience of such a profound degree of strangeness, the work of figuring out so much from the ground up, is something that fundamentally changed my life and how I think.

BURLESON: Living in Rwanda for nearly two years and the reverse culture shock I experienced after returning to the United States utterly changed the way I experienced the world. I had a breakdown in the cereal aisle at Safeway shortly after I got home. There were just too many choices, and the neon colors were overwhelming. I haven't really eaten cereal since. Living in Rwanda made me reconsider my life and how and what I ate, what I really needed to survive, as opposed to what my own culture suggested I might want. I began to grow and gather my own food and to avoid the supermarket as much as possible.

NEZHUKUMATATHIL: I'm keenly aware of and sensitive about not exoticizing the landscapes of my parents, because I feel at once very much at home and very much a visitor. I try to take care not to present "tourist poetry" but instead to sing the songs of all the beauty of the people and the topography of those two lands in a very accessible and dynamic way. In a way, I feel like I'm always essentially writing unrequited love songs for India and the Philippines.

KUSSEROW: Going abroad is everything. It "makes/creates" my work, my poetry. Ethically, I'm not sure I could write about a country without living there; this is sort of the anthropologists' code of honor. In anthropology, no one takes you seriously if you write about a culture you haven't lived in for a while. You are considered a fraud. I also tend to distrust poets who write about cultures they have never been to or lived in.

AUSTEN: Before responding to these questions, I reread the journals from my time in South America, and I see, fifteen years later, how certain things I was trying to work out on that trip—about my relationship to making art, to being female, to learning to love generously—unfolded in the years after I came home. Reading the journals now, in my mid-forties, I find myself thinking, Be patient—the time horizon for some kinds of growth is very, very long. I mean this in a positive sense, that some things can't be approached directly; they are influenced by factors people can't control.

It occurs to me now that this understanding is foundational to my writing practice. The role of the will is to get me to the page, but after that, the will has little—nothing?—to do with the finished poem.

Once I had been in Ecuador for a month or so, I realized that my true agenda was to have no agenda—to simply pay attention to the world directly around me and to practice putting it into words. At this point, I was journaling and writing letters and not yet writing poems.

The way I learned to inhabit my body while traveling alone has translated now into the ability to relinquish the idea of "productivity" in order to become deeply receptive, to enter fully into that "apparently unproductive" state that leads to poems.

Another important way my travels have affected my work: I now have a day job at Seattle Children's Hospital, and one of the things I do there is offer poetry and journaling workshops for the staff. The main skill I teach through journaling is how to direct compassionate attention inward, to befriend the self on the page. This is a direct result of my own relationship with journaling on my trip.

GRABER: I have had readers say that the book that I wrote on the Lowell Scholarship has an air of isolation to it, and I believe that. Of course, some of the images are lifted from those landscapes and some micronarrative moments. I could feel history around me in Europe, especially in Budapest and Berlin, in a way that I think I am immune to at home. Its weight is rather terrifying, which may be why we humans turn away from our own history so often. Malta is perhaps the most colonized parcel of land on Earth. I was thinking a good bit about empire before I left, and European history only drives those ruminations deeper. Now, of course, I can feel the weight of US history much more than I felt it before. I've also changed cities since coming back. It is hard not to feel history in Richmond! But I feel that my work will have an outward-facing aspect in the future that it did not have in the same way before.

FINNEYFROCK: I did several performances while in Nepal. It struck me during these shows how cultural specificity lives in the references and images in my poems. Particularly in the case of humor, I found the translation of my work culturally, rather than literally, problematic. Since returning from Nepal, I'm more interested in work on universal themes. Themes such as love, raising children, modern dependence on oil all seemed relevant to the world audience; US politics, humor, and religion didn't relate as well.

My work was affected, but in a larger way, I was affected. I have more awareness of how wealth and lifestyle in the United States compare with those in the developing world. I witnessed the environmental toll that poverty and civil war take. An embassy guide who grew up in Nepal told me, "Fifteen years ago, Kathmandu was Shangri-la. Now, I don't want to stay." He told me this after we crossed over the sacred Bagmati River, now barely moving because of the piles of trash that clog it.

MEEK: Arriving in a radically new landscape and culture and having to learn how to live and hopefully do some useful work there gave the opportunity for much practice in the arts of looking and listening, in developing a habit of receptivity and expectation. Any moment could bring something completely unfamiliar or a new angle of perception, as when I was told that the plovers I heard shrieking in the early mornings were called the birds-who-never-sleep and were in league with witches, or when, during evening studies at the school, the first night we had electricity a curious cobra came into the classroom, swelling its hood between two student desks. I think my work became much more grounded in place. That heightened sense of discovery that this deep travel provided changed the focus of my work and life completely, as I sought new experiences and deeper connections to other landscapes and cultures from this point forward.

GREENWELL: This is a hard thing to talk about. I'm certain that my work has been affected profoundly. I have been writing a lot more prose since coming here, perhaps simply because I still feel so overwhelmed by new information and impressions. I also think the sounds and rhythms of a new language will have an unavoidable effect on one's work. I've been moved and inspired by the availability and visibility of history and its traces in Bulgaria, whose history includes so many years under the occupation of various empires.

STONECIPHER: My poetry thrives on newness, difference, tension, difficulty, and friction. Placing oneself in a foreign context supplies plenty of those things.

DUNNE: This is a hard question for me to answer. I think that is because I have lived in Japan for so long that in some sense Japan has become home—too familiar. It is hard for me to analyze how it has affected my work. Still, I think I can say that in many ways living in Japan has made me more patient in my approach to poetry. I have come to see poetry as an intrinsic part of my life and have come to feel less anxious about success, whatever *success* means. I have come to this understanding partly though the example of Corman but also because of the Japanese culture, which seems to emphasize a lifelong commitment to process in art while downplaying immediate accomplishment and gain.

REDDY: Though I didn't write about Oaxaca or Mexico while living there, the simple fact of dwelling in such a simultaneously lively and tranquil environment had a major impact on my work. I was able to abstract myself, as it were, from my everyday existence in Chicago and enter more fully into the imaginative world of the poem—now out under the title "Voyager"—that I was writing at the time. I didn't have the conventional sort of relation to writing about place while I lived abroad. I wrote neither about the place I was in—Mexico—nor about the place

I'd left—Chicago—but about an imaginary place inside my head that I couldn't have accessed without the experience of travel.

Did you pitch any stories to magazines either before or during your stay? How did it work out?

STONECIPHER: Many years ago, I wrote one travel article about Berlin for *Alaska Airlines Magazine* and won't write any more. I don't want to write about Berlin for commercial purposes; I want to hoard it all for my own work.

POPE: I did, once—I'd written an essay about coming from a big country and living in a small country and about perceptions/misperceptions of the United States and Americans. I knew a Czech writer who had a connection to the *San Francisco Chronicle*, so I pitched it there, but it didn't go anywhere, and, unfortunately, I didn't try anywhere else.

KUSSEROW: I don't pitch anything, but I usually imagine the poems from my experience will end up in both anthropology literary magazines and formal poetry journals. I also use my poetry to teach anthropology courses. I assign my books to teach students about other cultures and certain concepts they need to learn. I also am sometimes asked to put my poems on websites that are working for a cause, such as STAND (Students Taking Action Now Darfur).

DUNNE: I submitted work to Japanese journals both while living in Japan and while living back in the United States. I was most successful in placing work when I was living in Japan.

Coming Home

What did you hope to glean from your time abroad? What was your purpose in traveling as a poet?

MEEK: I wanted to do something that I could feel good about and at the same time widen my experience; other than a couple of very brief trips to Mexico, I had never been out of the country before I joined the Peace Corps. Certainly as a young poet, I was looking for what might "matter," for new encounters with "subjects." Part of me winces when someone says that I—or any another poet—travel in order to "look for poems," though there is a level of truth to this. I like to see it a little more holistically, though, a little less coldly utilitarian; as human beings, we all need to find out what most engages us, what we are passionate about, what makes us alive. We will write out of these relationships that matter to us, whether these involve the towns we grew up in or places we fell in love with half a world away. All are valid for poetic exploration, and of course, they aren't mutually exclusive. Traveling abroad can also deepen people's perspective on "home," including their private histories. I certainly feel this is the case in my own experience.

GRABER: I don't think I had an agenda before I left. I wanted to go to Berlin. I had loved Walter Benjamin for so long. I wanted to stand in his city, which no longer exists. At least I was able to stand where it was.

I was already middle-aged when I was selected for the Lowell Scholarship. I thought it was too rare an opportunity to pass up, even though the logistics seemed overwhelming. It came to me as an adventure when all the adventuring already seemed done.

WHITCOMB: When I was in my early twenties and learning and reading about art history, culture, and world politics, I wanted to go to France— Paris in particular—so strongly that it was almost like a physical pain.

Luckily, I was able to travel to France twice during my twenties and thirties and became a complete Francophile. In the following years, my life became very busy and at the time of my residency at La Muse, I had not been abroad in a decade. I was starving again for the experience of being away, especially in France. Writers thrive on experience; we spend our lives re-creating those experiences on the page, in many iterations. I was hoping the residency at La Muse would help me immerse myself in my writing and provide the opportunity to get to know a new part of France. Part of my purpose in going to a residency abroad was to meet other writers and artists from around the world and to make some connections and friendships.

BURLESON: I hoped to gain a new subject for my work, new experiences, new languages, a new way of seeing. I gained all those things. But the genocide also taught me to be careful about what I wish for. I happened to be in Rwanda at a key historical moment, both for the people of that country and for the planet. But I also wish it had never happened.

FINNEYFROCK: I was hoping for the opportunity to visit the Himalayas, to meet Nepali people, and to hear poetry from a culture outside my own.

POPE: I wanted to throw myself into something altogether different, and that I certainly did. Sometimes I thought of it as having thrown myself off the edge of my known world. I wanted to learn another language—to do more than read in another language—and I did. I wanted experience, pure and simple, that would expand the ground for poems, and I found that. I wanted to get away from the huge, hollering buzz of US mass media, and I enjoyed my years of respite. But what I'd really meant to do was to make a life there, and in that respect, it didn't work out. I had seven years, not the decades I had planned.

NEZHUKUMATATHIL: It was like looking into a slightly foggy mirror. So much of what I thought was bizarre and strange, such as dogs given full rein to leftovers from each meal or sleeping in little *bahay kubos* in the Philippines or thatched houseboats in India, was just considered a way of life there. For a gal who had grown up in usually the only Asian American family in predominantly white towns, this was especially necessary and satisfying, as one could imagine.

DUNNE: When I came to Japan in 1986, I was trying to become a poet. I was interested in Japanese poetry and aesthetics. I was also attracted to Zen Buddhism. I felt that I might be able to work and write here. Because I could teach English, I could afford to stay in Japan for a significant period. Furthermore, my teaching duties took place primarily in the evening, so I had the daytime to study and write. I felt that the experience in Japan would broaden me, allow me to see the way other human beings ordered and expressed the experience of living. Japan did help me with vocation because it provided models that I could have faith and confidence in. I could see a way to approach a life in poetry here that I could not as readily see in the United States.

KUSSEROW: I travel for many reasons: to be humbled, to be widened, to be awestruck, to gain perspective, to foster a big mind, to attempt to help in a situation where there is suffering or inequality in my role as an applied anthropologist. The countries I go to have high degrees of disease, maternal mortality, blindness, extreme poverty, modern-day slavery, pretty blatant forms of social inequality, and lack of education, especially for girls. If I am in a country, I want to try to help or respond. I could never just go and hang out and write poems about a place unless I could use those poems to teach back at my college or unless they were published in a mainstream journal where enough people would read the poem and become aware of an issue and hence might give to a nonprofit. For example, I try to list africaeli.org in my bio of a South Sudan poem. I also use poems to reveal subtleties about a culture that students don't get from boring academic texts: the hips, heart, soul, and saliva of a people.

AUSTEN: For some months before the trip, the superstructure of my life had been disintegrating—I finally admitted to myself that I was disillusioned with acting and theater, a major relationship ended, and I began having nightmares about Freehold's artistic director's demanding I help her perform autopsies in her office. I also began having a recurring daydream in which I saw myself somewhere at extremely high altitude, with a very clear blue sky overhead. As everything I assumed I knew about the shape of my life lost its meaning, I became convinced the transformation I was seeking involved finding that specific sky.

I traveled abroad, in a very real sense, in order to *become* a poet. This had less to do with what I actually wrote while I was there and more with temporarily giving up all the ways I had previously defined myself. For all the miles I hiked, the real terrain explored was internal.

The job I held for several years before going to South America involved working to support other artists' visions. Though that's a worthwhile thing to do, for me it had become a way of avoiding the risk of developing my own voice. This became clear to me when, about eight months before going to South America, I created a short dance-theater piece based on three poems I'd written. The experience of generating the poems and choreographing and directing three dancers made painfully clear how little genuinely creative work I'd done since becoming Freehold's managing director and how disenchanted I really was with the kinds of theater I'd been doing for the past couple of years. Making that piece showed me how off track my life was, how disconnected I was from my own voice.

So one purpose of the trip was to radically alter my context and remove the familiar reference points—friends, family, language, occupation—and see what remained, with the hope and expectation that I would know and hear myself more accurately, more deeply, as a result. One surprise was how much this did in fact happen and how it was followed almost immediately—meaning, as the next thought—with the desire to write and publish.

REDDY: I wanted to write during my year abroad. I didn't want to write about the place I was going to visit, and I didn't want to write about home—I just wanted to write.

Did you fulfill your purpose? Did travel have any unforeseen effects on your work?

DUNNE: I was able to fulfill my purposes in Japan. I read a lot about Japan while in Japan. I studied its history, literature, and language. I was also able to find a temple where I could practice zazen on a regular basis and receive instruction. During my initial four years in Japan, I was able to produce a portfolio of poetry that I submitted for my application to graduate school.

One of the most fortuitous and unforeseen effects of my travels was my coming to meet the poet Cid Corman in Kyoto. Corman was an American expatriate poet and a long-term resident of Kyoto. In many respects, he took me under his wing and gave me valuable instruction in poetry.

WHITCOMB: After my return from residency, I resumed a conversation I had tentatively begun with a photography professor at the university where I work about coteaching a study abroad in France, maybe Paris. It was very clear to me after my experience at La Muse that it would be fantastic to take a group of students *there* and to design an interdisciplinary writing and photography class around the story of the Cathars.

Seven months after my first visit to La Muse, I was back again with eight students and the aforementioned photography professor in tow. The class was called Constructing the Creative Castle: Creative Writing and Photography in Medieval France. The students received credit in both art and English. We had designed the assignments to be as collaborative and interdisciplinary as possible: one project involved each student choosing a spot around the village and visiting that exact spot five times in five days, spending time there shooting photos and writing. The accumulated impressions were then edited and assembled into a digital collage, a small book, a short film, or whatever vehicle the student chose. One student chose the village spring, another a perch on the wall overlooking the village.

La Muse has a gallery space on street level with the village, and the students put on an exposition of their projects, complete with a reading and refreshments, the last night we were there. They named their exposition *The New Cathar Resistance!* and made flyers and signs to advertise around the village. Our bus driver for the excursions liked the class group so much that she rode her motorbike up from Carcassonne to attend the exposition, much to the delight of everyone. John and Kerry, the owners of La Muse, helped the students make pizzas and apple tarts for the event. And the evening ended with a hugely violent thunderstorm and the students outside watching the lightning streak across the mountains and the valley.

BURLESON: I came to doubt everything I had believed before I went, and that doubt continues to drive my poetry even though I haven't written much about Rwanda since that first book. Travel, in the way that I traveled, gave me a certain degree of Keats's "Negative Capability," I think, and that has turned my work in directions I couldn't have expected at the time.

REDDY: I got a lot of writing done. There's something about the pace of life in a provincial Mexican town that lends itself to daydreaming and getting those inner wanderings down on paper. The most unforeseen effect of travel on my work was the lack of travel's effects on the page. The book I finished while abroad could have been written in Pittsburgh,

Bombay, Rome, or Oaxaca. As it happened, it was in the latter location. And I'm grateful for it.

I was also quite happy to be away from the United States during that election year. The race simply would have been too distracting for me to get any writing done if I'd been home during that time. So that's another curious advantage to leaving the country for a time.

GRABER: It was much more illuminating than I could articulate in a brief space. I learned a good bit about what really matters. I learned what I could take, as in tolerate, and take quite well, in fact. I learned the difference between necessity and everything else! And I think that that attitude will inform my thinking and writing for the rest of my life.

I lived a very spare, hard life for a year, moving around from place to place with one suitcase. The world changed radically while I was away. I was in Europe when the global markets first began their declines, which have continued. I came home to a terrible personal financial disaster. I could not have passed through that as resolutely as I have if I had not already gotten quite used to doing without many, many things. I still live in an apartment that has only a two-burner hotplate and a countertop oven (the last bit of austerity, I hope), and that would have been inconceivable to me if I had not lived in very similar circumstances for extended periods while I was abroad. I learned how little of my self-image is actually linked in any meaningful way to conventional economic success. That being said, I like to be able to buy food, to take a bath, and to turn the heat on when I'm cold! Lots of times, I had very little heat in Europe! For four months, I lived in a stone cottage with only a wood stove, a big forest, and a little saw.

FINNEYFROCK: I did fulfill my purpose, although the travel was more challenging than I had expected. I was very tired and felt constantly affected by the air pollution and the noise pollution.

MEEK: I knew I would write about my experience, but I didn't know how much the experience would change my life, how deeply southern Africa would enter my work, so that twenty years later, I'm back there again—physically, mentally, emotionally—for the book I'm now writing. This experience also changed me as a reader and teacher; I had no experience with African or even postcolonial literature before I lived in Botswana, and now I teach this literature, as well as creative writing, in my capacity as an English professor.

Twenty years later, those two years still resonate through my life. What they taught me as a poet was to work to be more open to the world in all its particularities and contradictions, to be more mindful that every view is partial, every subject, multiple. What being a Peace Corps volunteer gave me is a place across the world to return to but also the desire to go elsewhere and to go deeper, into the here, into the now.

GREENWELL: It is difficult to have a genuinely immersive experience when teaching in an international school because I have to teach in English, and some of my colleagues are Americans. But yes, I do think that I am having a meaningful engagement with another language and another culture.

STONECIPHER: I wasn't expecting to become a translator, so I consider that an unforeseen and very happy effect of traveling.

POPE: Although I did mostly fulfill my purpose, the effects on my work are pretty different from what I had imagined, perhaps chiefly because I returned to the United States. I worked for a long time to fit in—I know I wanted to claim something permanent after I'd spent my whole life moving from place to place—but that was never going to work out. I did get good enough to pass—not to be called out as an American. But passing is a strange experience in itself. People began asking me when I was going to start writing in Dutch, and I always knew the answer was "never." The question then became this: was the writing going to stay hidden, or was I going to leave? The longer I stayed, the sharper that dilemma became for me.

There were many unforeseen effects on my writing: I developed a much more elastic ear, an appreciation for literary styles and eras I had previously dismissed, an attraction to the work of exiles and expatriates in general, and a highly reinforced sense of marginality. I have a sense of estrangement from my own culture now, which was there before but to a different degree. I like playing with notions of "foreignness." It is a gift to see how so much of what we know or think we know is culture-bound.

NEZHUKUMATATHIL: I write with the intersection of three cultures always looming over my shoulder—Indian, Filipino, and American. That provides my writing with a layering and fusion of pop culture and customs. As a poet, I find a perfect solution to capturing these blended traditions. I serve as interpreter, investigator, and historian. Worlds rife with fauna and flora—king cobras, cuckoo wasps, violet guavas, sea dragons, and whale sharks—come alive for me in this way. I hope to demonstrate how one can be situated without being rooted—can travel without getting lost.

RUCH: I didn't write anything during the entire five years I served on active duty. While I was deployed, I rarely took notes or photos of my everyday experiences because I didn't want to remember them. When I finally began to write again and realized how powerfully therapeutic it could be, I regretted my failure to document the things I'd seen and done, not because I have forgotten but because I might have written about them with greater accuracy. Now, telling my own stories and those of my fellow soldiers feels necessary, vital, even if it takes a lifetime to do so.

AUSTEN: Two quotes from my journal illustrate how much I did fulfill my purpose in knowing myself more deeply. I wrote this during a particularly low period while traveling briefly in Bolivia: "I can't pretend anymore that I could live my life without making art. Looking at those three Bolivian indigenous women made me realize that."

It's typical of my immature writing skills of the time that I left out the necessary details of this event: who were those women? What were they doing? What was my relationship to them? What was I noticing that led to the realization? This is probably the main reason I don't have poems "about" Peru, Bolivia, or Ecuador—it wasn't until I came home and began to study writing as a craft that I understood the need to set the scene, to include sensory details rather than simply report the epiphany.

But it's also typical of my experiences traveling that the transformative moments were absolutely not linear; they did not conform in any way to my expectations of cause and effect. In this way, I came to understand and value unstructured time as an essential ingredient—time and leeway to follow my instincts about what to give my attention to, what to read, what to write, whether to follow an obsession or a hunch or what seems at first like a whim.

And, finally, this, written in the final week or two before I returned to the United States: "... the next big adventure is taking myself seriously as an artist."

How did your experiences and the poets, writers, and artists you discovered influence your poetics?

FINNEYFROCK: I was excited to find a deep, cultural love for poetry in Nepal. I teach poetry in high schools in the United States and too often hear groans when students find out they will be writing poetry. There is a palpable reluctance around poetry in the United States. In Nepal, however, students were on the verge of cheering when they heard they would be writing poetry. Many students could already recite poems by other poets and were naturally expressive onstage reading their work. It was helpful for my work as a writer and as a teacher to be reminded that young people are not naturally turned away from poetry.

POPE: I have access to this other language now, one that so few people outside the Netherlands speak that it's like having a secret code at my disposal—my greatest ambition as a kid. Translating poetry sort of extends that idea.

Something entirely unanticipated was an appreciation that life could be slower, that stillness is a good thing. Not every American needs to leave home to learn that, but I know I would never have learned it without that time abroad.

I was already deeply interested in painting, but in Europe I discovered the work of many artists, living and dead, who were new to me—their work has also influenced my ideas about poetry.

WHITCOMB: Another interesting effect of the travel on my work as a poet came in the recurrence of imagery, namely that of wild boar. I was running on the mountain trails late one afternoon during my residency and was surprised by a very large, black, hairy pig running across the trail in front of me, scooting from undergrowth to undergrowth. I had been told boar were everywhere in the woods of the area. Every Wednesday and weekend in the fall, the village shuts down for the *grand chasse* (the "big hunt"). The men drive their tiny trucks up to the old forest roads and let their little dogs out of their kennels; you can hear them blow the hunting horns all over the valley. I wrote what became a group of poems about the forest, the boar, the dogs, and the old roads. The image of the boar was very metaphoric and became emblematic in the poems of that region of France, of its remoteness and profundity. *Boar* is also kind of funny, from an American perspective, and I found using that word to be a light way to play with language and tone.

GRABER: I think that I was politicized in some way by the aesthetics of the European poets. There is not as sharp a divide between the personal and private narratives and the public discourse of the speakers in many of those poems. I also admire the lingering influence of the surreal, but

I cannot emulate it at all! Perhaps one day.

MEEK: In "The Road To," a prose poem from my first book, *Nomadic Foundations*, I wrote about being on the back of a truck in rural Botswana when the driver ran down a flock of beautiful blue-helmeted guinea fowl, and the Batswana women on the back of the truck with me nodded and said, "Nice meat." Yes, it was a surprise when that driver turned into, not away from, that flock of guinea fowl, but it made me much more aware of what a luxury it is to be able to look at a bird solely in aesthetic appreciation instead of also seeing it as something that could fill a family's stomachs. Those two years offered many such moments of experiencing viscerally a new way of seeing, how perspectives can be multiple and conflicting.

Those years also gave me a new and uncomfortable sense of being seen, of being implicated by history, a white, middle-class person living in a then-undeveloped country where many of the people worked in apartheid South Africa. So many times, particularly when I had to leave my own village, I wished that I were invisible or at least not white. But I could no more escape my own cultural identity than I could my confrontation with self, as, for instance, in the issue fundamental to teaching in Botswana: to beat or not to beat. I remember naïvely, though at the time I thought high-mindedly, saying in my Peace Corps interview that I wouldn't beat my students but also wouldn't condemn those Batswana teachers who did. I didn't anticipate that parents would come to the school to complain to the headmaster about American teachers who won't beat their kids; I didn't expect, after being ordered to use the *thupa*, the stick, how used to it I would become.

That's one thing I was hoping the book title *Nomadic Foundations* would evoke—that even what you think is the most fundamental base of the self can shift. This led to my idea of deep travel, which I first wrote about in my dissertation in graduate school following my Peace Corps service, how in what I called deep travel, the self is not simply a static observer, not an objective or transparent or omniscient presence but rather is radically implicated in scene, in image, in word.

When I returned to the United States, how I looked at everything had shifted—and not just in how overwhelming it was to go into a grocery store or mall or library. I didn't want to lose the highs of discovery resulting from an increased receptivity to the world. Okay, so I couldn't hike to a water hole to watch baboons come to drink, but I could drive into the mountains near my home in Colorado to see marmots. I'd grown up in Colorado, and I had never thought to look for them. I was no longer living on the edge of the Kalahari Desert, but the Great Sand Dunes were just a few hours away. I'd been there before, but had I really looked at them? It seemed I was seeing everything for the first time, and that's a feeling I still work to cultivate, whether abroad or at home. Maybe I was just addicted to the high of discovery—and really, what poet isn't?—but travel and place became and remain central to my work, along with a newfound interest in the environment, in the relationship between people and place.

STONECIPHER: Living in Berlin has influenced my poetry and my thinking about poetry in innumerable ways. I only worry from time to time that my poems don't engage enough with problematics of my home soil. But I can't choose what I write, and I can't force subject matter on my poetry.

REDDY: The Americans abroad, Joshua Edwards and Lynn Xu, were a real lifeline to me while living in Mexico. They gave me a sounding board for what I was doing, and I hope I provided the same service to them. Unfortunately, I didn't make any friendships with Mexican writers while living in Oaxaca. But if my Spanish had been good enough to do so, I'm sure I would have benefited greatly from the experience.

DUNNE: Cid Corman had a great influence on me—not so much in how I write but more in how I went about approaching the life of poetry. He gave me a deep and abiding appreciation for the vocation of poetry. Perhaps this faith came in part from the *way* in which he saw the Japanese poets of the past embrace the way of poetry, or perhaps it came from the contemporary Japanese poets whom he knew and was working with in his translations. In any event, he helped point me toward the poem itself—and the life of poetry—as opposed to the marketplace, as opposed to fame and name. He helped me—at a time when I really needed it—to believe in the value of poetry, and he did this not by words but through his example of a life lived in poetry, a life that was austere in material terms, strict in discipline and practice, and yet generous and open—gracious.

He always made time to talk with younger people who were interested in poetry. One afternoon, while I was visiting him at his home, he said the following to me: "Poetry is the most important thing that human beings can be aware of. Poetry is life itself, a central thing. It is the most important element in the world, the human world and even beyond the human world because it gives us respect for everything else. It is taking everything into account and bringing it to point."

In Japan, poems are published every day in newspapers. In this respect, poetry is more visible and more a part of people's lives than it is in the United States. It was good for me to live in a country in which poetry was understood to be a part of the everyday life of the community. It helped me to believe in its centrality in life.

AUSTEN: I don't think it's an overstatement to say that I found my primary mode of working—receptive, intuitive—and much of my subject matter during those six months in South America. The experience of confronting my fear and taking physical risks changed my sense of myself and my place in the world as a woman. Part of that was the particular cultural mirroring associated with living in Latin countries—in Ecuador and especially Peru, ideas about the roles and limitations of women are very macho. Local people in villages or the paths nearby often stopped me to ask if I was really alone, exclaiming in disbelief, "*¿¿Solita!?*"—"You're here by yourself?!"

Once I went home and began writing poetry, my voice first began to coalesce around a sense of spirituality rooted in the natural world, in the specific gravity of particular places—the forests of the Cascades, the Olympic coast, my own garden—and then around pivotal questions of female identity—whether or not to mother, sexual power, patriarchal religion.

My willingness to go in search of that particular blue sky is a direct antecedent to my willingness now to follow the call of an image without first needing to attach any meaning or purpose to it.

As it turns out, just a week before I flew home, I did find the sky that had prompted my journey. I was hiking with a Peruvian man I had met through my work for the South American Explorers Club. Our destination was a glacier on Huaytapallana, an eighteen-thousand-foot peak in the central Andes. A few hours after dawn, as we crested the lip of the *páramo*, a small lake came into view, the glacier rising above it. I immediately recognized the place—not just the color and clarity of the sky but also the lake, the scrubby plants, the mountain. I felt as though the bones at the roof of my skull—the ones that fuse together shortly after birth—had dilated open. A sensation I can describe only as electrical shook me—my body rang the way it had when, at five years old, I had put a metal house key into an electrical socket. I wept but not with pain or fear. I felt rinsed with elation, every cell alert, alive, at home in my skin.

Are you still in touch with the poets you met while living abroad? If so, how have you kept in communication? Any collaborations?

DUNNE: I remain in touch with many poets from around the world. I met those poets here in Japan and in the United States. For the past five years, the Japan Writers Conference has been a location at which writers from inside and outside Japan have gathered. It has furthered the connections between writers. Communication is kept up through blogs, e-mail, Skype, and literary magazines.

KUSSEROW: Through e-mail, I doggedly stay in touch with writers, both anthropologists and poets, who write poetically about cross-cultural experiences.

FINNEYFROCK: We have a Nepali spoken-word poetry group on Facebook called Word Warriors.

GREENWELL: As my language skills improve, I would like to work on translations with young Bulgarian writers; that's a kind of collaboration I would like to pursue actively.

POPE: I am translating the work of a Dutch poet, Hester Knibbe, whose work I encountered while I lived in Amsterdam, though I did not meet her until after I'd left. We communicate via e-mail, and I was able to spend time with her when I visited the Netherlands two years ago.

REDDY: I'm still in touch with Joshua Edwards and Lynn Xu back here in the United States. We e-mail regularly, and we try to see each other every few months, though they live out West in California these days, and we're settled back in Chicago. We haven't collaborated formally yet, but the conversation itself feels like a collaboration, one that will yield much over the years to come.

What do you think other poets learned from their experiences abroad, and how, in your opinion, did it change their poetics?

POPE: Well, Sylvia Plath found it was fatal. Before her death, though, she became sharper both intellectually and poetically than she would have been had she remained in the United States—she could be serious in England in a way she probably wouldn't have allowed herself to be in the United States. Elizabeth Bishop created a whole new life in Brazil, but it seems to me many of her letters ache with homesickness. When she returned to the United States, something was askew in her life and remained that way; she was never able to feel at home here. It certainly seems that her poems were never again as strong as they had been. Charles Wright, on the other hand, encountered Italy and seems to have had the experience of walking out into the product of his own poetic imagination—his connection to that country is so deep that it always strikes me as having a spiritual cast. Rita Dove has written very interesting poems and prose about her years abroad, and her translations are just fantastic. The sheer range of her work seems to me to be related at least in part to her experience of different countries and languages.

I translate the work of a South African poet, Elisabeth Eybers, who exiled herself to the Netherlands and lived there for more than forty years. She published in both countries and developed quite a literary reputation, all the while stubbornly writing in Afrikaans, her father's native language. She wrote highly crafted poems that were often very sly about her longtime position as an outsider, which is clearly what she felt she was, despite being embraced by the Dutch literary world. There is something so particular to poets about that—that insistence on one's own language, even in situations like hers where compromise wouldn't necessarily cost so very much.

BURLESON: The poets I know who have traveled deeply all say that their experiences have profoundly affected their work and the way they see the world. Even when they're not writing directly about their travel experience, the new way of seeing they gained abroad influences everything they write.

DUNNE: I think many poets learn to broaden their aesthetic sensibilities. When an American person lives in a country like Japan, she has to confront, at some level, the realization that her ideas of what constitutes the beautiful are shaped or determined to a significant degree by forces at work within her own culture. A Japanese rock garden will challenge many Americans at first glance—so too may a Japanese essay, which tends to develop in a much less logically determined fashion than a US essay. Encountering differences such as these is an exciting experience and one that bears directly on the vocation of the poet. The poet learns from these different aesthetic sensibilities—from various ideas of what constitutes the beautiful—and goes on to test their applicability. In this way, the experience of living abroad might be said to bring a healthy richness to the poet, a wider appreciation of beauty in various forms, and an inquisitive mindset that can lead forward into experimentation, innovation, and refinement of poetics.

REDDY: Off the top of my head, I'd mention that Elizabeth Bishop seemed to learn a great deal about surrealism and perception from her time in Brazil, that Dante learned his rage and melancholy from the experience of exile, that Pound learned his unfortunate politics in Europe. The list goes on and on.

MEEK: When I was editing *Deep Travel: Contemporary American Poets Abroad*, a collection of poems by thirty-four poets who have lived or spent significant time abroad, what drew me to these poets' international work was what I saw as a heightened attentiveness, an openness, a willingness to discover that deepens and layers the work. I don't want to suggest that any writer who travels will do better work or that travel is the only path to good poetry; again, as I tried to get at with the term "deep travel," it's about a generative interaction between a particular poet and a particular place, not simply the injection of "exotic" subject matter. But for those poets who are attentive travelers—attentive to self as well as other—and who write out of this same openness to discovery, the fusion in their work of experience and language, the engagement of word and world, can be truly extraordinary.

Anything to add?

RUCH: As a woman soldier living in Iraq, I discovered that carrying a book with me and being seen reading it made local males more likely to talk to me. Because of my book, they concluded that I was literate and therefore educated—at least that's what one of them told me—and so they broke with customs based on social and religious taboos and stereotypes, and held conversations with me on a few occasions. I heard a number of interesting stories that would have been entirely inaccessible to me without that book in my back pocket.

FINNEYFROCK: I'm impressed by the ways our work in Nepal kept making an impact after we returned home. My group of three poets went to Nepal to teach about the history and traditions of poetry slams and the spoken-word poetic form. We worked with both youth and adults and produced Nepal's first poetry slam. After we left, I found out that a group of the young poets we had worked with took a trip outside Kathmandu to visit an orphanage. They did a poetry workshop with the younger kids and then had a poetry reading with the older kids after the little ones went to bed. When I read about their trip and thought about the ways the work continued after we left, I was surprised and moved.

I had specific concerns about introducing poetry slam to Nepal. It is a populist art form that seeks to engage the idea that "anyone can decide if a poem is good." We take the competitive elements found in publishing poetry, generally arbitrated by editors, selected juries, and professors, and put the decision-making power in the hands of people who attend poetry readings. We do this by handing scorecards to five audience members and asking them to rate the poets.

Poetry slams were intended to spoof literary contests, to make a spectacle out of the concept of judging art. However, the movement has changed over the twenty-five years of its existence and has become, for many poets, a sincere competition with career benefits based on winning. Poetry slam grew out of particular conditions in the US literary community involving access to audiences and success for poets outside of higher education.

I'm not sure that the idea of the poetry slam as a gimmick, or tongue-in-cheek show, translates well to other cultures. As poetry slams crop up around the globe, each country has adapted the slam to fit the needs of the people and the poetic climate. I struggled to find ways to teach about poetry slam without imposing US ideas of poetry slam on Nepal; I wanted to present the ideas driving the form without rigidly presenting the form.

REDDY: I guess the most important thing to me about the experience of travel is that there is no one way to experience it. Some poets travel abroad and come home laden with poems about what they've seen. Some poets leave home and return empty-handed. (Often the ones who didn't write anything while they were away turn out to have learned the most from their travels). Some travel to escape their lives, some to find them. You don't have to write about where you are or where you've left. You just have to write. And somehow, for some inscrutable reasons, travel can make that happen in the most circuitous of ways.

How to Write Your Way Out of the Country

Our battered suitcases were piled on the sidewalk again;
we had longer ways to go. But no matter, the road is life.

—Jack Kerouac

Opportunities for Traveling, Living, and Working Abroad

Catherine Barnett, Rachel Galvin, and Brandon Lussier

Introduction

Opportunities are abundant for poets who want to travel: you can teach English abroad, attend an international writing residency, attend a literary festival, pursue translation opportunities, volunteer, or win a fellowship, grant, or scholarship, among other possibilities. In this section, you'll find lists of places and programs that provide these opportunities. The lists are punctuated by "voices from the field"—suggestions, insight, and encouragement from poets who have spent significant time abroad and who speak of—and from—the hold that traveling has had on them. "I've returned to Bosnia twice since that first experience ... and now, sixteen years after my first experience, I am still writing poems about my time there. It haunts me," says Susan Rich, one of the editors of this anthology and a Seattle-based poet. Jess Row, a fiction writer and Buddhist chaplain, says his work in Hong Kong completely transformed his career: "My first book is about Hong Kong, and everything I've written thereafter has been shaped by my experiences there in one way or another."

The word *transformative* crops up frequently when writers describe their experiences. Garth Greenwell, who has taught English at the American College of Sofia in Bulgaria for three years, says his experiences in Sofia have changed his writing profoundly. "Since moving here I've written about little else," he says. "I'm fascinated by what I see, by the people I interact with, by the experience of living in another language and another culture. The most dramatic effect has been a shift in genre: in my first months here I began writing prose." Reflecting on the decision to move to Europe, Greenwell says, "I do think my writing is better, more open to the world and to other people, for the choice."

"Whenever I work surrounded by a different language, my sense of English becomes heightened," says Susan Briante, who has been a resident at Fundación Valparaiso, in Almeria, Spain. "I am fluent in Spanish, having lived in Mexico for six years during the 1990s. It was actually that first experience of learning Spanish that made me both a translator and a poet. I learned English while living in Spanish."

Patricia Chao, a poet and fiction writer, has had extensive experience in countries where many people do not speak English. "If you spend enough time in your daily life in another language," she says, "you come back to English and it feels like a new language, which is wonderful. You become much more sensitive to it—sound, rhythm, syntax. It's a very good perspective, particularly for poetry."

Jennifer Scappettone spent a year in Rome as a recipient of the Rome Prize and acknowledges that her own writing was "profoundly influenced by the Italian language, in both lexical and syntactical senses, in both conscious and unconscious ways." Her time in Rome helped her finish a manuscript of translations with "the Italian language as the soundtrack of my dreaming."

Certainly less rhapsodic but equally essential for anyone planning to travel are the cautionary tales and advice shared by those who have first-hand experience. Some of the poets queried for this section, particularly those who accepted foreign teaching positions—either volunteer or paid—met with the uncertainties of bureaucracy, political instability, and violent insurgency. Many writers mention the destabilizing power of culture, which, says Jess Row, "works in both directions. It has to be taken seriously. Hong Kong was where I first had the experience of being a member of a racial minority—a tiny minority—and I was astonished at how difficult, and how interesting, that was. My thinking about race, culture, and justice was all changed as a result." Tiffany Tuttle Collins, who volunteered for the Peace Corps in Kyrgyzstan, says she hit a low point around six months into her service, when "I had a sense of my own cultural incompetence and isolation but had not quite made the strong relationships that later integrated me into the local community." She says not to be surprised if 25 to 30 percent of your group—"and that may include you"—goes through early termination, for personal or medical reasons. To reduce the chances of this happening, be sure to research not only the obvious details of visas, inoculations, and health care before you go (see "Additional Resources" at the end of this section for more information) but also the place itself, its history, politics, and art.

Fellowships, Grants, and Scholarships

Traveling on a fellowship or grant provides both financial and creative support, but applications for such opportunities often require specific projects. Recipients of this form of support often end up becoming both insiders and outsiders, a simultaneity that can be fruitful for poets who seek to navigate between the known and the unknown. "It was the most extraordinary and rare gift of freedom I've ever had," says Jill Jarvis of the Fulbright fellowship she held in Sri Lanka. "It transformed my thinking."

Before applying, consider what your long-term goals are and how the specific scholarship that you are interested in will help you meet them. Can you demonstrate that you have already taken concrete steps to meet your goals? Are those goals in line with the mission of the organization or institution that administers the scholarship?

If you are going to apply for a fellowship, scholarship, or grant, avoid the most common applicant mistake: do not form future goals based on what you think a committee wants to hear. This almost never works because scholarship committees tend to value not just the long-term goals of candidates but also what candidates have already done to work toward those goals.

The following funding opportunities have an international focus and are best for self-motivated individuals who feel comfortable moving to another country, finding their own housing, and immediately getting to work on their projects. Although they are not specifically for poets, they all support activities (language study, travel, et cetera) that can enrich a poet's experience, perspective, and language. Be aware that culture shock, exploring a new place, and being away from friends and family can all make it more difficult to accomplish work at the pace you are used to. Go abroad with a plan that details major goals as well as smaller milestones.

Fellowships, grants, and scholarships are awarded on a competitive basis. Here is a partial list of funding opportunities:

-» **Akademie Schloss Solitude**, located in Stuttgart, is funded by the German government and offers three–to–twelve–month residencies to artists and scholars under the age of thirty-five (or to those who have finished a college or graduate degree within the last five years; several additional fellowships are offered regardless of age). Fellowships include lodging and a stipend. *www.akademie-solitude.de*

-» **The American Academy in Rome** offers the Rome Prize to thirty emerging writers and scholars, providing housing, meals, a studio, and a generous stipend for either six or eleven months. Fellowships usually begin in September. Literature fellows are nominated by the American Academy of Arts & Letters. *www.aarome.org*

-» **The American Council of Learned Societies** offers summer grants (among others) for intensive summer study of Eastern European languages, including Albanian, Bosnian-Croatian-Serbian, Bulgarian, Czech, Estonian, Hungarian, Latvian, Lithuanian, Macedonian, Polish, Romanian, Slovak, and Slovene. Grants can be used in the United States or abroad but must be used for an intensive, university-run program and not for tutoring or less intensive opportunities. Awards are intended primarily for graduate students in Eastern

---

VOICES FROM THE FIELD

According to poet Roy Scranton, who spent time at Akademie Schloss Solitude, this residency provides "fruitful digressions" in an urban setting. "It is competitive-entry, interdisciplinary, energetically international, and very well organized," he says. "Schloss Solitude had a collegiate and institutional feel, but at the same time, there was much more ambient intellectual and artistic energy.... The people at Schloss Solitude were all very hip and engaged."

European studies who will use these languages in academic research or teaching or in work for US government agencies or nongovernmental organizations. Grants have been given to poets seeking further knowledge of a language for the purpose of translation. Recipients must find appropriate study opportunities, enroll on their own, and plan their own travel and living arrangements for their period of study. For those who need to study abroad to take courses in languages that are infrequently taught in the United States, it is important to plan ahead and make contact with universities that teach intensive summer courses to avoid missing application/enrollment deadlines. *www.acls.org*

-» **The American-Scandinavian Foundation** (ASF) offers fellowships (up to $23,000) and grants (up to $5,000) that enable individuals to study or conduct research in one or more Scandinavian countries for up to one year. The foundation's materials note that "all fields are eligible, but applicants must have a well-defined research or study project that makes a stay in Scandinavia essential." Candidates should have some ability in the language of the host country, even

---

VOICES FROM THE FIELD

For Jennifer Scappettone, a recipient of the Rome Prize whose creative and scholarly projects center on Italy, the residency in Rome "represented a culmination of passions surrounding Italian culture and translation as well as a unique opportunity to pursue my individual research and writing agendas in an interdisciplinary setting in the heart of Rome, a city I love. I was surprised by how busy the Academy kept us with conferences, lectures, readings, walking tours, book launches, concerts and other performances, and exhibition openings." Scappettone was completing two decade-long book projects during her residency and says she imagines "It would have been even more amazing to be at the Academy at the beginning rather than the end of a project—at a point of one's career during which one can be truly open to every influence."

if it is not essential for the proposed research or study. The foundation recommends that candidates who plan to do translation work wait to apply until they have the necessary proficiency to do the work without assistance. The $23,000 fellowships typically, although not always, go to candidates at the graduate level for dissertation-related study and/or research, so most applicants should apply to the grant program for a shorter stay. At the time of application, candidates must provide confirmation of an invitation and/or affiliation from an institution and/or individuals in the host country. *www.amscan.org*

-» **The Amy Lowell Poetry Travelling Scholarship**, which provides financial underwriting for poets to travel abroad, allows the recipient to make his or her own logistical arrangements. If you plan a trip on your own through this or another similar scholarship, consider setting up a home base from which you can easily travel to other places. *www.amylowell.org*

-» **The Bellagio Center** offers residencies at its site on Lake Como, Italy, for literary as well as academic writers; the goal is to support interdisciplinary exchange among residents. Most residencies last

---

VOICES FROM THE FIELD

Poet and journalist Eliza Griswold won a Rome Prize for her poetry: "The beauty is overwhelming, but the wrecked-ness of some of the Roman landscape provided a lot of deep solace for me because that combination of beauty and wreckage is something that I really identify with in my work." She reflects that the time "was extraordinarily healing—just the sheer beauty of the city and its history helped me to process many of the things I'd seen and experienced. It's historically at the center of so much geopolitical strife that it also helped me to put some of what I know of contemporary conflicts into a longer historical trajectory."

one month; all provide a room, a private bath, a studio, and meals. Transportation fees are generally not included. The Bellagio Center prefers to support writers who have a record of outstanding achievement and are interested in global issues, and whose work "contributes to the well-being of humankind."
www.rockefellerfoundation.org/bellagio-center

-» **The Brown Foundation Fellows Program** at the Dora Maar House in Ménerbes, France, is geared toward midcareer artists. Travel expenses, lodging, and a per diem are provided for fellows.
www.mfah.org/doramaar

-» **CEC ArtsLink Project Support Grants** provide up to $10,000 in funding to US artists, curators, presenters, and arts organizations undertaking projects in any of thirty-two eligible countries (see the website for a list). Applicants must be working with an artist or organization in that region, and projects should be designed to benefit participants and audiences in both the United States and the host country.
http://www.cecartslink.org

VOICES FROM THE FIELD

While holding an Amy Lowell Poetry Travelling Scholarship, poet Kathleen Graber's sense of time was deeply altered, a transformation that helped shape her second book of poems. "Even the distant past is very palpable in parts of Europe, certainly in the Mediterranean," Graber says, "and the recent past can be felt quite powerfully and disturbingly in places like Budapest and Berlin. The landscapes of many of these spots and the rumination those landscapes precipitated appear in my second book."

-» **The US Department of State Critical Language Scholarship** (CLS) Program offers funding to enable study at intensive summer language institutes overseas. Only study of foreign languages considered of "critical need" will be funded. At the time this guide was printed, the eligible languages were Arabic, Azerbaijani, Bangla/Bengali, Chinese, Hindi, Indonesian, Japanese, Korean, Persian, Punjabi, Russian, Turkish, and Urdu. Students enrolled in undergraduate, master's, or doctoral programs are eligible to apply. People who have international fellowships or plan to study abroad and want to improve their language skills often receive Critical-Language Scholarships. *http://clscholarship.org/index.html*

-» **DAAD Scholarships** are granted for an academic year of study in Germany, with the possibility of a one-year extension to allow completion of a degree. Those enrolled in US master's degree programs or who have graduated from an undergraduate institution in the past six years are eligible to apply. Candidates in the arts and humanities are expected to have a good command of the German language. Recipients receive a monthly stipend of approximately 750 euros

---

VOICES FROM THE FIELD

"It's helpful to be attached to an institution when applying for the Fulbright," says Jill Jarvis. "For research Fulbrights, it's crucial to have a strong case for why you want to go to a particular country and also helpful (though certainly not necessary) to have already been there or have already studied the relevant languages." Less popular sites may have less competition in the application process. For her Fulbright, Jarvis researched a recent movement to reinstate higher ordination for Theravada Buddhist nuns in Sri Lanka. "I also became involved at the university in the town where I lived," she says. "There I helped with editing a philosophy journal and acted in a friend's Sinhala translation of Ionesco's *Bald Soprano*, which was staged at the university in an unforgettably hilarious production."

plus health insurance coverage, a rent subsidy, and a family allowance, if applicable.
www.daad.org

-» **Fulbright Fellowships**, sponsored by the US Department of State's Bureau of Educational and Cultural Affairs government, are designed to increase mutual understanding between the people of the United States and the people of other countries. Fellowships are for US citizens to study, teach, and conduct research abroad and for citizens of other countries to do the same in the United States. The application is notoriously challenging, so applicants should plan on starting work on their projects three to six months before the application is due to allow time to contact people, organizations, and institutions in the country of interest. This demonstrates a seriousness of purpose and makes it possible to obtain letters of support. Fulbright also offers teaching fellowships (see "Teaching English" in this section). It is important to remember that the Fulbright mission is not to train writers, artists, or scientists; its mission is to facilitate opportunities for Americans to form lasting ties to other countries. Projects that will involve collaboration with citizens of the host country are more likely to be funded, and long-term goals should

VOICES FROM THE FIELD

The program, Japan-US Friendship Commission is connected to the International House in Tokyo, where an initial orientation takes place, explains poet Brian Turner, one of the editors of this anthology. "The I-House, as it's called, has an incredible library which is available to those who become members," he says. "I became a member and immediately began working with the librarian to track down obscure information and source material connected to my fellowship study. In essence, I had a great research librarian working on my behalf. Invaluable."

include plans to stay engaged with the host country and its people. Conditions and support levels will vary by location. See Susan Rich's essay, "Solitary: Spending a Fulbright Year in South Africa," for more information.
www.iie.org/fulbright

-» **The Japan-United States Friendship Commission** offers $20,000 grants plus up to $2,000 travel expenses for US artists and creative writers to spend three months working in Japan. Writers must be published and have a compelling reason to live and work in Japan; collaboration with Japanese artists and writers is encouraged. The program is competitive; five artists and writers are chosen annually. Once in Japan, writers work independently, although logistical support is available.
www.jusfc.gov/creative-artists-programs/

-» **Marshall Scholarships** are given to "young Americans of high ability" to study for degrees in any field in the United Kingdom for two to three years. The goal of the program is to fund future leaders in order to strengthen the relationships between British and US citizens and their governments and institutions. A candidate must have a four-year undergraduate degree and a minimum GPA of 3.7. The program is one of the most competitive scholarship programs in the world but provides full study and living costs as well as international travel funds.
www.marshallscholarship.org

-» **Mitchell Scholarships** fund one year of study in Ireland or Northern Ireland. Any field of study is acceptable. Eligible candidates are US citizens with four-year undergraduate degrees who are between the ages of eighteen and thirty. A demonstrated commitment to community and public service is essential, as well as a strong academic record and the proven ability to serve as a leader. Successful candidates have demonstrated a "significant, tangible impact" on their communities or schools. Five strong letters of recommendation are required. *www.us-irelandalliance.org*

-» **Princeton in Asia Fellowships** are yearlong, service-oriented fellowships. Each year, more than 150 fellows are placed in one of eighteen Asian countries to work in the fields of education, international development, environmental advocacy, journalism, and law or business. Although many fellows work as English teachers at universities and high schools, specific positions in nongovernmental organizations (for example, working on the protection of old city buildings and culture or for foreign affairs publications) are also listed on the organization's site each year. Graduates of accredited four-year colleges and universities are eligible. Applicants should be prepared to pay for the following: round-trip travel to Princeton twice (once for interviews and once for orientation), necessary vaccinations and a health screening, round-trip travel to Asia, and a TESL certificate. Living expenses in Asia are covered. (See "Teaching English" in this section for more information.)
piaweb.princeton.edu/

International Writing Residencies

International residencies provide writers with opportunities to focus on their work and to experience new environments and cultures that may provide inspiration for current or future projects. They range in length from a few months to a few weeks. A residency may be an excellent way to see if you'd like to pursue sustained time overseas.

"Your richest experiences will not be sitting in your studio doing your art," says Patricia Chao, who was a resident at the Sacatar Foundation in Brazil, "but being out in the streets, hanging out with new people, attending festivals. Most of the residents end up doing a project involving the community in some way." Many writers report taking up new activities or hobbies that change their work significantly. Relationships built during a shared residency often blossom into long-term friendships and professional exchanges, though some residencies function as a retreat where you can focus quietly on your own work. In these cases, the residency may offer little by way of outside stimulation, so it's up to you to structure your time.

Keep in mind that some residencies require community engagement (readings, teaching workshops, et cetera). The organizations that run residential centers usually cannot afford to cover all costs for those accepted but often provide help with travel costs, housing, and/or food.

Choosing a Residency

-» Residencies look for writers at different points in their careers.

-» Some residencies welcome writers without significant publications, some require a history of published work, and others ask that candidates be alumni of their American residencies before applying to an international residency.

-» Residencies that require a fee may be less competitive.

-» Some residencies are geared toward fostering interdisciplinary collaboration.

-» Some residencies pay airfare.

-» When planning a residency, it is usually up to the candidate to take care of paperwork. If you are aiming for a relatively short residency (one month in a European country, for example), you won't need a special visa. Different countries have different requirements.

Some central resources for locating and choosing an international writing residency include the following:

-» Alliance of Artists Communities
www.artistcommunities.org

-» Beltway: A Poetry Quarterly
http://washingtonart.com/beltway/resid.intl.html

-» Mira's List
www.miraslist.com

-» Poets & Writers posts the online Conferences & Residencies database.
www.pw.org
www.pw.org/conferences_and_residencies

-» Res Artis
www.resartis.org (click "Residencies"; from there, you have the option of viewing a complete list of residencies or searching for a residency matching your particular interests and needs)

-» Trans Artists
www.transartists.org

-» Some American residency programs, such as the Virginia Center for the Creative Arts, also coordinate a robust offering of foreign programs for their former residents.
www.vcca.com/main/international

A sampling of international foundations, residencies, and retreats follows. Although this list is not comprehensive (opportunities number in the hundreds), it will help get you started in your research. Please be aware that fees change regularly; the estimates included here simply provide general guidelines. Dollar signs indicate relative prices according to the following:

-» $ ($500 and under/week)
-» $$ ($500–$1,000/week)
-» $$$ (more than $1,000/week)

-» **Anam Cara Writer's and Artist's Retreat** in West Cork, Ireland, houses five residents at a time and its fee includes meals and amenities. In addition to retreats, six weeklong workshops are offered each year in poetry, fiction, nonfiction, and publishing. *www.anamcararetreat.com* • *$$*

-» **Art Workshop International** in Umbria, Italy, offers summer workshops with Anglophone writers. *www.artworkshopintl.com* • *$$$*

-» **Arvon Foundation** is a charitable foundation that offers weeklong writing programs around the UK. These workshops are held in historic houses in secluded rural areas. Participants attend for a fee, although grants are available that cover the full cost of the course. *www.arvonfoundation.org* • *$$*

-» **The Baltic Writing Residency** in Latvia is available on a competitive basis to one poet, fiction writer, or playwright each year. The one-month residency takes place in July in Riga and provides the winning resident with housing in a boutique hotel and $1,000 to offset travel costs and costs of living. *www.balticresidency.com* • *$*

VOICES FROM THE FIELD

"At Anam Cara you become part of village life in a faraway corner of West Cork," says Susan Rich, poet and an editor of this anthology. "A fisherman may bring a salmon just caught that morning for evening dinner, or you may arrange for a visit with Mary, the village oracle. I met writers from Denmark, England, Ireland, and the United States—in half the cases, the writers were returning for a third or fourth stay. Writers have moved to the tiny village of Eyeries after first discovering it through a residency at Anam Cara. The rooms look out over Coulagh Bay and over mountains and cow fields. There are two bars in town, one teashop (which is also a family's front room), and one main shop. Cheese comes from the local cheese maker, and walking is the preferred means of transportation."

-» **The Banff Centre** in Canada offers, with its Leighton Artists' Colony for Independent Residencies, nine studios to artists (not just writers) who are recognized in their fields and to emerging artists. This is a solitary retreat environment placed within a larger artistic community.
www.banffcentre.ca/leightoncolony • *$*

-» **Camac's Arts Center**, in the village of Marnay-sur-Seine in the Champagne-Ardenne region of France, offers retreats of one to two months to artists, composers, and writers from around the world. Each resident has a private room with a private bathroom and can prepare meals for breakfast and lunch (kitchen and food are provided). Dinner is provided Monday through Friday. Although the center does not cover the cost of the residency, it offers help in applying for scholarships, in particular the UNESCO-Aschberg grant. In addition, a fully funded Ténot Bursary is given annually to one writer, one visual artist, and one musician. These residencies, which provide travel, room and board, and a separate studio, are available on a competitive basis.
www.camac.org/english/intro.htm • *$*

-» **The Fundación Valparaiso**, located in the village of Mojácar, near Almeria, Spain, offers retreats for writers and artists who are professionally recognized as well as the occasional emerging artist of exceptional creative talent. Eight residents stay for a month at a time;

VOICES FROM THE FIELD

"The Fundación [Valparaiso] is housed in a beautiful home surrounded by olive and lemon groves as well as a striking semiarid landscape," says poet Susan Briante. "From the Fundación, you can walk about twenty to thirty minutes into the center of Mojácar, a gorgeous whitewashed mountain village with views to the Mediterranean."

---

applicants submit proposals for the work they intend to do while at the foundation. Grants cover meals and housing; residents pay for their own travel, medical insurance, and materials. *www.fundacionvalparaiso.es* • *$*

-» **Hawthornden Castle** in Scotland is open to international writers, whether they have published a book yet or not. The residency does not maintain a website, but interested writers may request applications by phone (+44-0131-440-2180) or by writing to Hawthornden Castle, The International Retreat for Writers, Lasswade, Midlothian EH18 1EG. Fellowships cover all expenses except travel to and from the castle. • *$*

-» **La Muse** is a retreat for writers and artists in the small mountain village of Labastide-Esparbairenque in the Languedoc-Roussillon region of southern France. Run by two former New Yorkers who wanted to find an easier environment to write in, it offers rooms for one-week and three-week retreats. Regular and barter fellowships are also available. *http://lamuseinn.com* • *$*

-» **The M Literary Residency** awards three-month residencies in Shanghai and Bangalore. Transportation, accommodation, and meals are provided gratis to recipients along with $1,000 for expenses. The

---

VOICES FROM THE FIELD

According to poet G.C. Waldrep, "Hawthornden Castle was very accommodating to a nervous American who had not really been abroad before." He adds, "There is no Internet at all at Hawthornden, and cell phones don't work in the castle either. To use a cell phone, you have to walk up the drive to the road; for the Internet, we all walked into Bonnyrigg (about two miles) and used the public library."

program provides space and time for writing and research on site and aims to foster deeper knowledge of contemporary life and writing in China and India. One writer is selected for each location yearly. *www.m-restaurantgroup.com/mbund/Ms_residency.html* • *$*

-» **Red Gate Residency** in China offers residencies ranging from one to six months. The program helps writers connect with local arts and culture but does not cover any costs. Accommodation consists of apartments and lofts in Beijing. Applications are accepted on a rolling basis, but residencies are generally filled six months in advance. *www.redgategallery.com/residency* • *$*

-» **Sacatar Foundation**, on Itaparica Island off Bahia, Brazil, seeks applicants who wish to work on a specific project; the foundation covers travel costs, accommodation in private rooms, a separate studio, and most meals. Sacatar encourages residents to share their work with the local community and warns that the setting is fairly undeveloped. *www.sacatar.org* • *$*

VOICES FROM THE FIELD

According to writer Roy Scranton, La Muse welcomes "writers in the early stages of their writing careers. It's not a competitive residency, in part because you pay for it—it really is buying time in a great place to get some work done." Scranton recommends La Muse for independent people who like to get outside. The owners of La Muse offer a ride plan, with weekly grocery trips and even a visit to the medieval city of Carcassonne. They strongly suggest that you sign up for their plan or rent a car. "The nearest *épicerie,* which has a very limited selection, is a forty-five minute walk into the next valley," Scranton says. "Bread and grocery trucks visit the village, and you can buy eggs, rabbits, and vegetables from the neighbors."

-» **Sage Hill Writing Experience**, in Saskatoon, Saskatchewan, Canada, features a poetry colloquium in May and workshops in July and August. All ages and levels are welcome to apply. Scholarships are available on a competitive basis.
www.sagehillwriting.ca • *$*

-» **Sanskriti Foundation**, near New Delhi, India, offers writing residencies and opportunities to work with local traditional craftspeople. Residents can stay from two to twelve weeks. The foundation houses three craft museums.
http://sanskritifoundation.org • *$*

-» **Tyrone Guthrie Centre** in Annaghmakerrig, Ireland, hosts residencies and retreats up to six months in length in a rural setting in County Monaghan. Accommodation, which can include board, is in farm cottages and a large manor house. Candidates may apply directly and must pay their own way. The cost varies according to facility. You may also participate with a VCCA exchange or a Djerassi exchange if you've already been to their American residencies.
http://www.tyroneguthrie.ie/homepage • *$–$$$*

VOICES FROM THE FIELD

According to Patricia Chao, the best candidates for a residency at Sacatar would be accomplished artists with considerable world travel under their belts and, optimally, a working knowledge of Portuguese, or at least Spanish or Italian. "If you have traveling chops and an open mind," she says, "you'll do fine at Sacatar. Itaparica often feels more third world than first, so that kind of travel experience would be invaluable. English is not spoken in the general population, so you'll have to learn at least a smattering of Portuguese if you want to leave the compound and have adventures. I'd say a sense of adventure is paramount! You are pretty much on your own, so focus and a detailed project are important."

Literary Translation Opportunities

For poets who have some experience with or interest in translating, there are opportunities abroad. Here is a list of some resources and opportunities for literary translators who want to work and travel.

-» The American Literary Translators Association, based at the University of Texas at Dallas, offers a wealth of resources for translators, including a list of grants, awards, and residencies available for literary translators.
www.utdallas.edu/alta/resources/grants-and-awards

-» The European Council of Literary Translators' Associations is an umbrella organization that features news about European residencies and prizes for international translators.
www.ceatl.org

-» Additional information for literary translators can be found at the websites of the Canadian Association for Translation Studies and UNESCO's section on Literature & Translation.
www.uottawa.ca/associations/act-cats/English/Home.htm
http://portal.unesco.org/culture

Here is a small selection of translation opportunities:

-» The Banff International Literary Translation Centre (BILTC) offers a residency program with the primary aim of offering literary translators a working retreat within a community of international colleagues.
www.banffcentre.ca

-» **ATLAS** (Assises de la Traduction Littéraire), in Arles, France, is a cultural association that offers residencies and workshops for translators working with all languages, not just to or from French. *www.atlas-citl.org*

-» **The French-American Foundation** offers a translation award and holds annual conferences that bring together Francophone and Anglophone writers. *http://www.frenchamerican.org/publishing-and-translation*

-» **Ekemel**, the European Translation Centre, features workshops and paid residencies for translators. *www.ekemel.gr/Home.aspx?C=3*

Literary Festivals

Literary festivals offer opportunities to attend workshops, give and attend talks, and hear memorable readings by poets from around the world. The festival environment, in which hundreds or even even thousands of writers gather—sometimes in spectacular settings—can provide heady experiences for practitioners of the trade. The following databases are useful resources for learning about international festivals.

-» The American Literary Translators Association website
www.utdallas.edu/alta

-» The Book and Periodical Council in Canada
www.thebpc.ca/the-resource-file/literary-festivals

-» The University of Pennsylvania, which curates an up-to-date list of calls for papers for conferences and festivals
http://call-for-papers.sas.upenn.edu

-» PEN International, which sponsors festivals across the globe
www.pen-international.org/events-festivals

-» Poets & Writers Conferences & Residencies database
http://www.pw.org/conferences_and_residencies

The following list is a sampling of international festivals; it is by no means comprehensive. Before finalizing plans to attend any festival, consult the US Department of State's warnings and information site.

CANADA

-» The International Festival of Authors in Canada is held in October in Toronto.
www.readings.org

-» The Ontario Writers' Conference is held in May.
www.thewritersconference.com

-» Summer Literary Seminars are held in Montreal in June. (See Kenya and Lithuania for two other sessions of Summer Literary Seminars.)
www.sumlitsem.org

COLOMBIA

-» The annual International Poetry Festival of Medellín is held in June.
www.festivaldepoesiademedellin.org

CZECH REPUBLIC

-» The Prague Summer Program is held in June and July.
www.praguesummer.com

-» The Prague Writers' Festival is held in April.
www.pwf.cz

GERMANY

-» The International Literature Festival is held in Berlin in September.
www.literaturfestival.com/aktuelles-en

-» The Literaturwerkstatt Berlin poetry festival is held in June.
www.literaturwerkstatt.org/index.php?id=1016&L=0

IRELAND

-» The Cúirt International Festival of Literature takes place in Galway
during the last week in April.
http://www.cuirt.ie/

ITALY

-» Sirenland in Positano is held in March.
www.sirenland.net

-» The Umbria Writing & Publishing Workshop is held in June and July.
www.noahcharney.com/writing/index.htm

-» A Writers' Workshop is held at the Amalfi Coast Music Festival in July.
www.amalfi-festival.org

JAMAICA

-» The Calabash International Literary Festival is held in Jamaica each
May.
www.calabashfestival.org

KENYA

-» Summer Literary Seminars are held in December in Nairobi and Lamu. (See Canada and Lithuania for two other sessions of Summer Literary Seminars.)
www.sumlitsem.org

LITHUANIA

-» Summer Literary Seminars are held in Vilnius in July and August. (See Canada and Kenya for two other sessions of Summer Literary Seminars.)
www.sumlitsem.org

MEXICO

-» San Miguel Poetry Week is held in January.
www.sanmiguelpoetry.com

-» San Miguel Writers' Conference is in February.
www.sanmiguelwritersconference.org

NETHERLANDS

-» The Maastricht Poetry Festival is held in October every other year.
www.maastrichtpoetry.com

-» Poetry International Rotterdam, one of the oldest poetry festivals in Europe, takes place in June. The website contains one of the most comprehensive literary anthologies of poetry from around the world currently available on the web.
www.poetryinternationalweb.net

NICARAGUA

-» Granada International Festival of Poetry is one of Latin America's most popular poetry festivals.
www.festivalpoesianicaragua.com/

PORTUGAL

-» Dzanc Books, in collaboration with Portuguese cultural organizations and Summer Literary Seminars, Inc., has recently established DISQUIET International, which takes place in July in Lisbon and for which grants are available on a competitive basis.
http://disquietinternational.org

REPUBLIC OF MACEDONIA

-» Struga Poetry Evenings, one of the oldest poetry festivals in Eastern Europe, is held each August in Struga.
www.svp.org.mk/

SLOVENIA

-» Days of Poetry and Wine, one of the most popular festivals for younger Eastern European poets, is held at the end of August.
www.poezijainvino.org/2011/en/home

SOUTH AFRICA

-» The Poetry Africa international poetry festival in Durban is held every October.
http://www.cca.ukzn.ac.za/index.php?option=com_content&view=article&id=93&Itemid=75

SWITZERLAND

-» The Geneva Writers' Conference is held in February.
www.genevawritersgroup.org

UNITED KINGDOM

-» The National Association of Writers in Education conference takes place in November.
www.nawe.co.uk

-» The Great Writing International Creative Writing conference is held in June or July.
www.greatwriting.org.uk

-» The Winchester Writers' Conference is held in June.
www.writersconference.co.uk

-» WordTheatre Writers' Workshop and Retreat takes place in Edale, England, in July.
www.wordtheatre.com/writersretreat

Teaching English

Teaching abroad can provide not only valuable professional experience, but also the chance to become involved in a local community. There are many international teaching opportunities; the list that follows includes placement agencies as well as specific programs. When selecting a program, school, or agency, consider not only the location but also the level of preparation the organization will expect and the training it provides.

Poets hoping to teach in a foreign country should conduct research well in advance of hiring cycles (at least a year before the desired departure date). For teaching secondary school internationally through private organizations, an MFA can be a meaningful credential.

Here are some agencies and specific programs that may help you get started with your research; the list is not comprehensive. Organizations marked with an asterisk will give you the instruction you need to teach English.

-» Berlitz is one of the world's largest ESL schools and places those interested in teaching English at a Berlitz center for one year or more. Candidates must be interested in teaching both adults and children, and although it is possible to apply to teach in a specific country, flexibility will make acceptance more likely. Those with previous teaching experience who are willing to be abroad for more than one year are most likely to be hired. Be aware that Berlitz is a corporation, so work is usually at a language center in a corporate environment. Pay varies by country and teaching assignment but is better than for many other international teaching opportunities.
www.berlitz.com

-» Carney, Sandoe & Associates is a recruiting agency that represents both US and international schools.
www.carneysandoe.com

-» Those selected for the program, Connecting Schools to the World, live with families in rural pueblos throughout Argentina. The program provides teaching English as a second language (TESL) training in Buenos Aires, after which teachers spend four to nine months living with families in regions rarely visited by tourists. Housing costs are covered, and a monthly stipend is provided in exchange for up to twenty-five hours per week of teaching. The program is most suitable for those with at least Spanish proficiency, although Spanish language skills are not required.
http://www.connectingschools.com.ar

-» Dave's ESL Cafe is an online resource for those interested in teaching English abroad. The site includes job listings and a portal where résumés can be uploaded so that those seeking English instructors can contact candidates qualified for their positions.
www.eslcafe.com

-» The French embassy coordinates the Teaching Assistant Program in France, which hires English teachers for French schools. This government program guarantees a French visa, full access to French health care, subsidies to defray half the monthly transport costs, and some rent. According to Michelle Coghlan, who taught in the program, "The program offered minimal training but did supply us with basic lesson plan ideas and a set of targets students should reach by the end of the year."
www.frenchculture.org/assistantshipprogram

-» Fulbright English Teaching Assistantships allow US citizens to live in another country for an academic year and teach English in a local school. These opportunities are less competitive than the Fulbright fellowships (see "Fellowships, Grants, and Scholarships" in this section) but still provide the chance to have an immersive cultural

experience and to get to know local literary culture. Teaching assistants are encouraged to pursue individual study and research plans in addition to their teaching responsibilities, and they receive stipends that allow for comfortable living in their host countries. (For more information about the Fulbright Program, see Susan Rich's essay, "Solitary: Spending a Fulbright Year in South Africa.")
http://us.fulbrightonline.org/english-teaching-assistantships

-» Japan Exchange and Teaching (JET) Programme, sponsored by the Japanese government, arranges for teachers from the United States and more than thirty-five other countries to teach English in Japan. This is one of the world's largest exchange programs. JET participants function as cultural ambassadors for their countries of origin. JET acts as the intermediary among Japanese educational authorities, some private schools in Japan, and Americans wishing to spend a year in Japan teaching. JET provides a very useful list of teaching opportunities on the website Alternatives to the JET Programme: English.
www.jetprogramme.org
http://jet-programme.com/jet_alternatives.htm

-» The Peace Corps has provided opportunities to live, work, and serve in developing countries since President John F. Kennedy started the program in 1960. Volunteers serve more than seventy countries in Africa, Asia, the Caribbean, Central and South America, Europe, the Middle East, and the Pacific Islands. The volunteer term is twenty-seven months, and volunteers provide support in six program areas: education, youth and community development, health, business and information/communication technology, agriculture, and environment. The Peace Corps application process can be lengthy and does not allow the applicant much input regarding where he or she will be stationed. Most positions require a bachelor's degree. The Peace Corps takes care of visas, inoculations, and health care. It also provides follow-up care for ongoing health issues that need to be addressed once you return to the United States. Service to the Peace Corps will allow you to defer your student loans while you are abroad. Travel expenses to and from the country of service are provided, as well as a monthly stipend for living expenses and medical and dental insurance. Volunteers who complete their terms receive a stipend of approximately $7,500. Federal Perkins student loans are eligible for cancellation of up to 70 percent of the loan (15 percent canceled for completion of each of the first two years and 20 percent cancelation for the third and fourth years). The Peace Corps experience is known to be extremely challenging because of both the length of stay and the difficult conditions in most placement communities. (See "Volunteerism" in this section for additional information.) *www.peacecorps.gov*

VOICES FROM THE FIELD

"Approximately ten hours each week were spent on technical training—in the case of TEFL (Teaching English as a Foreign Language) trainees, that meant teaching techniques and lesson planning," says Tiffany Tuttle Collins of her work for the Peace Corps. "We received a number of teaching materials to work with as well, from beginner to advanced level instruction, and we spent two weeks at 'model school.' There, pairs of trainees planned and taught classes to local children and were observed and given feedback by American staffers, other active volunteers, and host country teachers." The training proved useful, she says. "We learned to create effective lessons from scratch." She also notes that the process of acquiring a foreign language gave volunteers some insight into their students' learning. "The application process takes several months, including a written application, an interview with a Peace Corps recruiter, and extensive medical and dental screening," she explains. "You can indicate what continent you would like to work on, and you can refuse an invitation to serve, but the application states that the pickier you are, the longer it will take to find another assignment."

-» Princeton in Asia Fellowships provide the opportunity to work in one of eighteen Asian countries. Placements are in education, international development, environmental advocacy, journalism, and law or business. (See listing in this section under "Job Opportunities Abroad" for more information.)
http://piaweb.princeton.edu/

-» Search Associates is an international agency that provides a database of positions available for applicants looking to teach abroad. An application is required.
www.searchassociates.com

-» Teach Abroad provides an online database of English-teaching opportunities. Do some research before pursuing an opportunity. Ask an organization if it can put you in touch with someone who has taught abroad through one of its programs. If it is unable to connect you with someone, it may be a sign that the organization is poorly run and/or that participants have negative feelings about their experiences.
http://www.goabroad.com/teach-abroad

-» Teach Away places teachers in Africa, Asia, Europe, the Middle East, and South America. Successful candidates typically have one or two years of teaching experience. Monthly salaries are based on local economies and are competitive ($6,000–$6,500 per month in Hong Kong, for example). Airfare is also included for most placements, and some provide a monthly travel stipend as well. Teach Away positions have the potential to become long-term jobs, with room for promotion and increased pay.
www.teachaway.com

-» Teach English in Mexico finds jobs for those interested in teaching English in Mexico and also finds housing placements. In exchange for a fee paid to the organization, Teach English in Mexico guarantees a paid placement and gives teachers access to a representative in Mexico who can provide advice and support before and after arrival. *www.teach-english-mexico.com*

-» The US Department of State provides many resources for locating international schools that are looking for teachers. *www.state.gov/m/a/os/c16899.htm*

Job Opportunities Abroad

Job opportunities abroad can be anything from short-term legal work as an electoral monitor to securing a position as a journalist or joining an emergency medical team for short-term disaster relief projects. As in the United States, jobs abroad depend on employment history and level of education. However, there are positions that welcome a generalist background in farmwork, for example, or environmentally focused projects.

-» The American Bar Association (ABA) facilitates legal internship opportunities for US law students interested in international law. *www.abanet.org/intlaw/intlinternship.html*

-» The American Medical Student Association (AMSA) maintains a directory of opportunities for those with medical experience who wish to gain experience abroad. *www.amsa.org/global/ih/ihopps.cfm*

-» BackDoorJobs.com is an online database, including opportunities to teach, work on sustainable farms, lead youth trips, and intern abroad. *www.backdoorjobs.com/*

-» The Riley Guide is one of the most thorough online listings of job search resources and search engines by region and country and is recommended if you wish to search for a job without using a placement agency. *http://www.rileyguide.com/internat.html*

Volunteerism

These volunteer opportunities, ranging from just a couple of weeks to more than two years, are excellent for getting to know other cultures, improving language skills, and meeting other people who want to work for a better world. Long-term volunteer appointments, in particular, provide chances to meet local writers and become involved in the literary culture, which is possible with many short-term appointments as well.

Volunteer travel is one of the most intimate and unpredictable ways to experience a foreign country. Take stock of your skills and research the possibilities for contributing your strengths to a place or a community in need. If you have special skills—medical training, for example, or agroforestry experience—you may be eligible for some remarkable volunteer opportunities.

Be aware that volunteer work in developing countries can be psychologically and emotionally challenging. If you have not traveled to a developing country before, it is recommended that you try one of the two-to four-week opportunities before considering a long-term appointment. Each organization provides experiences that will alter your perspective on the world. If you are self-motivated, you can seek out opportunities and get to know local writers.

The following books by former international volunteers provide useful insight into what to expect: *Only Bees Die: Peace Corps Eastern Europe*, by Robert Keller (CreateSpace, 2010); *The Village of Waiting*, by George Packer (Farrar, Straus and Giroux, 2001); *Whispering Campaign: Stories from Mesoamerica*, by Lawrence F. Lihosit (iUniverse.com, 2009).

Volunteer Resources

-» Doctors Without Borders seeks medical and nonmedical aid workers to provide vital medical help for people threatened by war, epidemics, natural disasters, and other catastrophes. The Nobel Prize–winning organization operates in more than fifty countries. *www.doctorswithoutborders.org*

-» Habitat for Humanity International Volunteer Program allows participants to help build and rehabilitate affordable housing around the world. Typical assignments for long-term volunteers include work in administration, communications, finance, programs, resource development, and volunteer coordination. In addition to the long-term, international program, Habitat for Humanity also runs two-week trips for volunteer teams under the Global Village Program (www. habitat.org/gv). In some cases, the host country provides assistance with local transportation or housing; in all cases, volunteers are responsible for international medical insurance, most housing costs, food, and travel to and from the United States. *www.habitat.org/ivp*

-» The International Volunteer Programs Association is an association of nongovernmental organizations that run volunteer and internship programs. Whether or not you have professional skills (medical, technical, or business), the IVPA can help you choose an international volunteer program. *www.volunteerinternational.org*

-» Peace Corps volunteer positions most often require a bachelor's degree. Volunteers receive thorough training in language and cross-cultural instruction. The Peace Corps features some programs for which specialists are keenly desired, such as agroforesters,

engineers, urban planners, deaf-education teachers, and university-level teachers. (See "Teaching English" in this section for additional information.)
www.peacecorps.gov

-» Service Civil International (SCI) offers work camps in numerous fields and locations worldwide. Most volunteers work for two to four weeks, but it is possible to commit for up to one year. SCI provides participants the chance to learn about other cultures and contribute to local communities in concrete ways. Examples of volunteer activities include planting trees in Iceland, building classrooms in Mexico, and running activities for refugees in Kenya. There is also a long-term program for those who want to volunteer for three to twelve months. Volunteers cover most of their own expenses and pay a participation fee that helps support the volunteer centers.
www.sciint.org

-» Volunteers for Peace offers placement in international volunteer projects in more than one hundred countries. Volunteers work for approximately five hours per day and have built community centers, created hiking trails, provided activities for orphans or refugees, worked in community gardens, et cetera.
www.vfp.org

-» World Wide Opportunities on Organic Farms (WWOOF) is a membership organization that provides the opportunity to receive free room and board at any of the thousands of WWOOF farms throughout the world. The program is recommended for those with a genuine interest in learning about organic growing, country living, or ecologically sound lifestyles. No previous farming experience is necessary, and volunteers do not pay for housing while abroad. It should be noted that working on a rural farm will provide less opportunity to get to

know the nation's literary culture than community-based volunteer opportunities; however, it may still be excellent for language acquisition and provide a great deal of inspiration.
www.wwoof.org

Additional Resources

This section provides information on how to prepare for travel abroad. Along with an extensive and straightforward checklist every traveler should consult before leaving home, you'll find discussions of issues of special interest to gay, lesbian, bisexual, and transgender travelers; to minority travelers (both ethnic and religious minorities); and to travelers with disabilities. Suggestions for preparing for medical issues while abroad are provided along with other basic information useful to the traveler.

Traveling Abroad: A Checklist

To prepare yourself for your time abroad and to help avoid or mitigate negative experiences:

❏ Research **visa** requirements for the country you are going to, and comply with all requirements. Begin the process of applying for a visa as soon as you know you will be going abroad. For some countries, the processing time can be more than three months. Most countries require that applicants appear at the consulate that serves your host country in person (some require that applicants appear in person twice), so plan ahead. You can find all the necessary visa information on consulate websites; pay careful attention to the instructions, as consulates are notorious for refusing to process incorrectly prepared visa applications. Most countries require a visa for stays longer than three months, and many countries require them for visits of any length, even a weekend. **Do not** assume that because you have received a grant or been accepted into a program, you will receive a visa. It is up to you to complete the necessary requirements. For a list of foreign countries that have embassies/consulates in the United States, visit www.state.gov/s/cpr/rls/dpl/32122.htm. You should also familiarize yourself with the US embassy or consulate in the country you are visiting. Visit www.usembassy.gov.

❏ Make sure your **passport**, which is the only universally accepted form of identification, is valid. You cannot travel internationally without one. Passport applications can be obtained at many local US post offices. For more information and for the latest passport fees, visit travel.state.gov/passport/passport_1738.html.

If your trip will be longer than one month, make sure your passport is valid for at least six months after the date that you plan to return to the United States. Many countries will not admit travelers with a passport that is about to expire.

❒ Make **two copies** of your travel itinerary, program contact information (if going through an organization or institution), airline tickets, passport photo page (and visa, if you have one), and medical insurance cards. Keep one copy separate from the originals at all times while traveling and abroad; give the other copy to a friend or family member in the United States.

❒ Arrange for a **physical checkup, an eye examination, and dental work** before you leave the United States. Immunizations are required to enter many countries and recommended for travel to many more (see below).

❒ Get your required **immunizations.** In the developing world, special immunizations are often required, even for short stays and often in advance of your arrival into the country. You should check to make certain all your shots are up-to-date, including vaccinations for measles, meningitis, mumps, rubella, polio, diphtheria, and tetanus. If you expect to travel outside Western Europe, you should contact the Centers for Disease Control and Prevention at 1-800-CDC-INFO (1-800-232-4636) for information about health precautions and immunization requirements for travel to other countries. You can also visit the website at www.cdc.gov/travel.

❒ Pack a **first-aid kit.** When traveling, carry your own basic drugstore supplies, such as ibuprofen or acetaminophen, motion-sickness medication, laxatives, antacids, antihistamines, decongestants, antiseptics, and bandages. Depending on where you are going and how long you are staying, your doctor may recommend that you take antibiotics with you in the event that you become ill overseas. Make sure all medications are in their labeled containers, and carry a copy of the written prescription with generic names. Do the same with glasses and contact lenses. Take an extra pair of glasses and/or contact lenses. Be sure to pack contact lens solution; you may not find the kind you use abroad. If you have a health condition that could be serious (such as diabetes, an allergy to penicillin, et cetera), wear a medical alert bracelet.

❐ Make additional preparations for **medical care** while abroad (see below).

❐ Check out **travel warnings**, conditions, and general information about the country or countries you will be traveling in at http://travel .state.gov.

❐ Register at https://step.state.gov/step/ so the **US Department of State can better assist you in an emergency** and will be aware of your location. By registering, you help the embassy or consulate locate you when you might need it most. Registration is voluntary and costs nothing but should be part of your travel planning and security. The US embassy or consulate in your host country will issue a new passport or replace one that is lost or stolen while you are abroad; contact the US Department of State at embassy expense for further instructions if you cannot verify your citizenship; and help you find medical or legal services in case of an emergency and help notify friends or family members. The US embassy or consulate **will not** give or lend money, serve as a travel agent, provide interpreters or courier services, or arrange for free medical or legal services (they will assist you only in finding a doctor or lawyer appropriate to your needs).

❐ If you plan an extended stay in one place, it is a good idea to **know where the US embassy is** located. In many countries the embassy or consul will have an English-language library and other resources you can access.

☐ In many countries, it's useful and necessary to **register with the local ward office, immigration department, or local police station** shortly after arrival at your destination. This is especially true if you are living in the country using a work visa or a cultural activities visa (as in the case of the Japan–United States Friendship Commission Fellowship). It's often easiest to inquire about this prior to arrival— you can check with embassy or consulate officers about this process.

☐ Do some **research on the cost of living** in your host country, and draft a budget so that you have a good idea of how much you can spend each week from the first week of arrival.

☐ Take several forms of **money.** You should be able to get local currency from an ATM machine after you arrive, but in case of immediate problems with ATMs, carry approximately $200, changed into local currency.

☐ If you plan to use **credit cards** abroad, Visa and MasterCard are the most widely accepted. Discover and American Express are not as widely used in many countries.

☐ **Call your credit card companies and banks** to notify them of your travel plans and inquire about applicable fees. Notifying them that you will be abroad is essential. Without notification, they may freeze your accounts because of "suspicious activity" when you begin making purchases and withdrawing cash abroad. You may also want to open a bank account with a bank that does not charge ATM fees abroad.

❐ If you plan to use **debit cards**, Cirrus or Plus ATM machines are easy to find all over westernized countries. Be sure to check with your bank about transaction fees, and open an account with a bank that charges no, or very low, fees abroad if you will be staying for a long time. Make sure your PIN is only four digits and not six (many ATMs abroad do not accept six-digit PINs).

❐ **Write down phone numbers for each credit card** and for your debit card in the event you lose your cards or they are stolen. Keep these numbers in a safe place separate from the cards. E-mail a copy to yourself as well as to a trusted friend.

❐ If you will be studying while you are abroad, purchase an **International Student ID Card** (visit www.isic.org). The card provides health insurance as well as hundreds of discounts on electronics, travel, clothing, and other essentials. You can also purchase additional insurance coverage for personal belongings such as laptops and cell phones, in case they are lost, stolen, or damaged during your travels.

❐ Be sure all your **gadgets**, from cell phones to laptops to electric shavers, can work while abroad. There are two standard voltages in the world: 110 (used in the United States) and 220. An appliance designed for 110 volts cannot run on 220 without a converter. In addition, outlet types vary and require adapters. If you will be abroad for an extended stay, consider buying necessary appliances abroad. If you are going to pack an appliance from the United States, purchase a converter that can convert 110 to 220 volts. You will also need a socket adapter to use the appliance. An international socket adapter set is recommended in any case because you may need it if you travel outside your host country during your time abroad.

❐ Almost all laptops have converters built into their power cables so they can be used internationally, but you will still need a **socket adapter** in most countries. To be certain that your laptop will work abroad, check the power pack. It should read "INPUT 100-240V–50/60HZ." If it does not, you may need to purchase a different power pack for your computer.

Gay, Lesbian, Bisexual, and Transgender Issues Abroad

Customs, attitudes, laws, and social practices relating to gay, lesbian, bisexual, and transgender people vary throughout the world. Some countries are more progressive than the United States in their perspectives on GLBT issues. Many other countries are far more conservative and restrictive in their policies and practices. GLBT travelers will want to inform themselves about relevant issues in their host countries and in all their travel destinations.

Most country-specific travel guides will have a section on GLBT issues. Use these and other books to become informed. The following websites provide additional information and resources:

-» Information for GLBT travelers worldwide
http://gayguide.net/index.html

-» The International Lesbian, Gay, Bisexual, Trans and
Intersex Association
www.ilga.org

-» The International Gay & Lesbian Human Rights Commission
www.iglhrc.org.

Political Awareness for Travelers

Just as in the United States, political issues or lack of tolerance can make some groups of people targets for mistreatment. Political rallies and certain dates, such as anniversaries of historical events, can spur ethnic and religious conflicts in many countries. Take the time to research minority issues in your destination country and talk with scholarship or placement organization staff if you are concerned.

Travelers Who Have Disabilities

Resources and facilities for individuals who have disabilities may not be the same abroad as they are in the United States. Disabled people traveling abroad may also be the victims of prejudice and stereotyping. In many countries, there are no standards or requirements for providing access for disabled people. Wheelchair ramps, handicap-accessible parking spaces, Braille signs, and other aids may be nonexistent in parts of the host country, especially in rural areas.

In addition to a lack of services provided for the physically disabled, there may also be a lack of services provided for those who have learning disabilities or psychological or emotional disorders.

If you know that you will likely need special arrangements abroad, you should be in touch with your scholarship or volunteer/job placement program before you apply; ask what may be possible in the country you are considering for your time abroad.

For physical disabilities, you can also consult with Mobility International USA (MIUSA). Call 541-343-1284, or visit the website at www.miusa.org. MIUSA also offers several trips abroad each year for persons with physical disabilities. Travelers can choose from "inbound" and "outbound" programs to countries such as China, Spain, and Jordan.

Medical Care While Abroad

Be aware that the manner in which people obtain medical help, the ways patients are treated, the conditions of overseas medical facilities, and the ways health care is afforded abroad often differ markedly from US practices. US health care values, assumptions, and methods are not universally practiced. Even ideas regarding the onset of illness or points at which expert attention is required are to some degree cultural phenomena.

If you have a **physical or psychological problem** that requires ongoing treatment by a doctor, you should consult with your physician or mental health professional about the prospect of spending an extended period abroad. Most programs and opportunities listed in this guide do not employ mental health professionals, nor is mental health treatment widely accessible or comparable to mental health treatment in the United States in many locations abroad. For your own welfare, you should consult with a US mental health professional or physician to discuss the potential stress and physical challenge of living abroad and ways to cope with issues if you cannot access the same medical care you depend on in the United States.

If you take **medication**, discuss with your physician the type of care you may need while abroad and the best way to continue your regimen. Not all drugs are available in all countries, and when they are available, they may have been given a different commercial name. You will most likely need to take enough medication to cover the duration of your time abroad; consult your health insurance provider about obtaining enough medication for your entire stay. Be aware that not all medications can be given in the amounts you may need, and some may not be allowed into the country at all. These include many types of narcotics (including some painkillers) and certain medications prescribed for mental health conditions. Do not try to secure the medication abroad unless you have done research and are certain that the exact dosages and medicines you need are available and that you can obtain them. You may also need a written note from your doctor to take a medication into another country. Please note: it is difficult, if not impossible, to ship medications internationally. Even if legal, the shipment must clear customs, which may take weeks.

It's also a good idea to see if your prescriptions are available in your host country. The same medication may be under a different brand name.

"Questions of Travel"[1]
Elizabeth Bishop

There are too many waterfalls here; the crowded streams
hurry too rapidly down to the sea,
and the pressure of so many clouds on the mountaintops
makes them spill over the sides in soft slow-motion,
turning to waterfalls under our very eyes.
—For if those streaks, those mile-long, shiny, tearstains,
aren't waterfalls yet,
in a quick age or so, as ages go here,
they probably will be.
But if the streams and clouds keep travelling, travelling,
the mountains look like the hulls of capsized ships,
slime-hung and barnacled.

Think of the long trip home.
Should we have stayed at home and thought of here?
Where should we be today?
Is it right to be watching strangers in a play
in this strangest of theatres?
What childishness is it that while there's a breath of life
in our bodies, we are determined to rush
to see the sun the other way around?
The tiniest green hummingbird in the world?
To stare at some inexplicable old stonework,
inexplicable and impenetrable,
at any view,
instantly seen and always, always delightful?

1. Elizabeth Bishop, "Questions of Travel" from *The Complete Poems, 1927–1979*. (New York: Farrar, Straus and Giroux, 1984).

Oh, we must dream our dreams
and have them, too?
And have we room
for one more folded sunset, still quite warm?

But surely it would have been a pity
not to have seen the trees along this road,
really exaggerated in their beauty,
not to have seem them gesturing
like noble pantomimists, robed in pink.
—Not to have had to stop for gas and heard
the sad, two-noted, wooden tune
of disparate wooden clogs
carelessly clacking over
a grease-stained filling-station floor.
(In another country the clogs would all be tested.
Each pair there would have identical pitch.)
—A pity not to have heard
the other, less primitive music of the fat brown bird
who sings above the broken gasoline pump
in a bamboo church of Jesuit baroque:
three towers, five silver crosses.
—Yes, a pity not to have pondered,
blurr'dly and inconclusively,
on what connection can exist for centuries
between the crudest wooden footwear
and, careful and finicky,
the whittled fantasies of wooden cages.
—Never to have studied history in
the weak calligraphy of songbirds' cages.
—And never to have had to listen to rain
so much like politicians' speeches:

two hours of unrelenting oratory
and then a sudden golden silence
in which the traveller takes a notebook, writes:

"Is it lack of imagination that makes us come
to imagined places, not just stay at home?
Or could Pascal have been not entirely right
about just sitting quietly in one's room?

Continent, city, country, society:
the choice is never wide and never free.
And here, or there...No. Should we have stayed at home,
wherever that may be?"

Contributors

Kazim Ali, associate professor of creative writing and comparative literature at Oberlin College, is the author of numerous books of poetry, fiction, and essays, including most recently *Orange Alert: Essays on Poetry, Art, and the Architecture of Silence* (University of Michigan Press) and the cross-genre poetic memoir *Bright Felon: Autobiography and Cities* (Wesleyan University Press). He has translated volumes of poetry by Ananda Devi and Sohrab Sepehri and is founding editor of the small press Nightboat Books.

Elizabeth Austen is the author of *Every Dress a Decision* (Blue Begonia Press), *The Girl Who Goes Alone* (Floating Bridge Press), and *Where Currents Meet* (one of four winners of the 2010 Toadlily Press chapbook award and part of the quartet *Sightline*). Her poems have been featured on *Verse Daily* and Garrison Keillor's *The Writer's Almanac*. She was the Washington State Roadshow poet and is the literary producer for KUOW 94.9 public radio in Seattle.

Catherine Barnett is the author of two collections of poems, *Into Perfect Spheres Such Holes Are Pierced* (Alice James Books) and *The Game of Boxes* (Graywolf Press). She has received the 2012 James Laughlin Award, a Guggenheim Fellowship, a Whiting Writers' Award, a Glasgow Prize for Emerging Writers, and a Pushcart Prize. Her poems have appeared in the *American Poetry Review*, the *Kenyon Review*, *Pleiades*, *TriQuarterly*, *Virginia Quarterly Review*, the *Washington Post*, and other publications. She works as an independent editor and teaches at Barnard College, The New School, and New York University.

Ashley Brown (1923–2011) was professor emeritus in English and comparative literature at the University of South Carolina. He was founder of the literary magazine *Shenandoah* and a

confidant of novelist Flannery O'Connor and poet Elizabeth Bishop.

Derick Burleson's most recent book of poems is *Melt* (Marick Press). His first two collections of poems are *Never Night* (Marick Press) and *Ejo: Poems, Rwanda, 1991–1994* (University of Wisconsin Press). His poems have appeared in the *Georgia Review*, the *Kenyon Review*, the *Paris Review*, the *Southern Review*, and *Poetry*, among other journals. Burleson directs the MFA program in creative writing at the University of Alaska Fairbanks and lives in Two Rivers, Alaska.

Katharine Coles's fifth poetry collection, *Reckless*, is forthcoming from Red Hen Press; she has also published novels and essays. She is a professor at the University of Utah, where she codirects the Utah Symposium in Science and Literature. In 2010, she traveled to Antarctica on a grant from the National Science Foundation's Antarctic Artists and Writers Program. In 2009 and 2010, she served as the inaugural director of the Poetry Foundation's Harriet Monroe Poetry Institute.

Gregory Dunne is the author of two collections of poetry: *Home Test* (Adastra Press) and *Fistful of Lotus*. His nonfiction book, *Quiet Accomplishment, A Remembrance of Cid Corman*, is forthcoming from Ekstasis Editions. His poetry and prose have appeared in numerous magazines, including the *American Poetry Review*, *Manoa*, *Poetry East*, and *Kyoto Journal*. He lives in Japan and teaches in the Faculty of Comparative Culture at Miyazaki International College.

Karen Finneyfrock's second book of poems, *Ceremony for the Choking Ghost*, was released by Write Bloody Publishing. Her young-adult novel, *Celia, the Dark and Weird*, is due from

Viking Children's Books, a division of Penguin. A member of four National Poetry Slam teams, she has toured nationally and internationally as a spoken-word artist.

Nick Flynn has worked as a ship's captain, an electrician, and a caseworker with homeless adults. His most recent book is *The Captain Asks for a Show of Hands* (Graywolf Press). His poems, essays, and nonfiction have appeared in various venues, including the *New Yorker*, the *Paris Review*, National Public Radio's *This American Life*, and the *New York Times Book Review*. A professor in the creative writing program at the University of Houston, he teaches each spring then spends the rest of the year in (or near) Brooklyn, New York.

Carolyn Forché directs the Lannan Center for Poetics and Social Practice and is the Lannan Visiting Professor of Poetry at Georgetown University. Her fifth collection of poems, *In the Lateness of the World*, is forthcoming from HarperCollins. Her book *The Country Between Us* (Harper Perennial) received the Poetry Society of America's Alice Fay Di Castagnola Award and was a Lamont Poetry Selection of the Academy of American Poets. Her honors include a Lannan Literary Award in Poetry and fellowships from the Guggenheim Foundation and the National Endowment for the Arts.

Rachel Galvin earned a PhD in comparative literature at Princeton University and has recently joined the Humanities Center at The Johns Hopkins University as a Mellon Fellow. Her essays appear in *The Blackwell Companion to Translation Studies*, the *Los Angeles Review of Books*, and the *Wallace Stevens Journal*, and poems and translations appear in the *New Yorker*, *McSweeney's*, and *PN Review*. A book of poems, *Pulleys & Locomotion*, was published by Black Lawrence Press, and her translation

of *Hitting the Streets* by Raymond Queneau is forthcoming (Carcanet Press).

Kathleen Graber is the author of two collections of poems: *Correspondence* (Saturnalia) and *The Eternal City* (Princeton University Press), which was a finalist for the National Book Award and the National Book Critics Circle Award. She has received fellowships from the National Endowment for the Arts and the Rona Jaffe Foundation. An assistant professor of English at Virginia Commonwealth University, Graber also teaches in the low-residency MFA program at Fairleigh Dickinson University.

Garth Greenwell's first book, *Mitko*, won the 2010 Miami University Press Novella Prize. His poetry has appeared in the *Yale Review*, *Boston Review*, *Poetry International*, and *Gulf Coast*, among other journals, and has received the Grolier Prize, the Rella Lossy Poetry Award, and the Dorothy Sargent Rosenberg Poetry Prize. Greenwell lives in Sofia, Bulgaria, where he teaches at the American College of Sofia, an independent secondary school.

Eliza Griswold received a 2011 J. Anthony Lukas Book Prize for her *New York Times* best seller *The Tenth Parallel* and a 2010 Rome Prize from the American Academy in Rome for her poetry. Having won awards for both her nonfiction and her poems, she is currently a senior fellow at the New America Foundation. A former Nieman Fellow at Harvard University, she reports on religion, conflict, and human rights. Her first book of poems, *Wideawake Field*, and *The Tenth Parallel*, an examination of Christianity and Islam in Africa and Asia, were published by Farrar, Straus and Giroux. Her reportage and poetry have appeared in the *New Yorker*, the *Atlantic*, the *New York Times Magazine*, *Harpers*, the *New Republic*, and many other publications.

Jared Hawkley is a poet and freelance editor from Vancouver, British Columbia. He's been a contributing editor to *The Best American Nonrequired Reading* (Mariner Books); *Blue Collar, White Collar, No Collar* (Harper Perennial); and books of student writing for the educational nonprofit 826michigan, including *Don't Stay Up So Late: A Treasury of Bedtime Stories*. He has written for newspapers and blogs, designed record jackets, led hikes up fourteeners in Rocky Mountain National Park, and given dogsled tours in the northern woods of Minnesota. He lives in Oakland, California.

Jane Hirshfield is the author of seven poetry collections, most recently *Come, Thief* (Knopf). *Given Sugar, Given Salt* (Harper Perennial) was a finalist for the National Book Critics Circle Award. Lay ordained in Soto Zen in 1979, she is a current chancellor of the Academy of American Poets. *The Ink Dark Moon* (Vintage) is her cotranslation of the work of Ono no Komachi and Izumi Shikibu, two classical-era Japanese women poets.

Ilya Kaminsky is the director of the Harriet Monroe Poetry Institute at the Poetry Foundation. He is the author of *Dancing in Odessa* (Tupelo Press) and coeditor of *The Ecco Anthology of International Poetry*.

Yusef Komunyakaa is the author of numerous books of poetry, most recently *The Chameleon Couch* (Farrar, Straus and Giroux), which was a finalist for the 2011 National Book Award. He has received multiple fellowships, and his awards include the Kingsley Tufts Poetry Award and the Pulitzer Prize. In addition to poetry, Komunyakaa is the author of several plays, performance literature, and libretti, which have been performed in venues that include the 92nd Street Y, Opera Omaha, and Sydney Opera House. He currently teaches in New York University's graduate creative writing program.

Adrie Kusserow is a professor of cultural anthropology at Saint Michael's College in Vermont. She works with the Bhutan Centre for Media and Democracy and Africa ELI: Education and Leadership Initiative (Bridging Gender Gaps Through Education) in South Sudan. She has written two books of poetry: *Hunting Down the Monk* (BOA Editions, A. Poulin, Jr. New Poets of America Series) and *Refuge* (American Poets Continuum), also from BOA Editions.

Denise Levertov (1923–1997) was a British-born American poet who published more than twenty books of poetry, criticism, and translations. Among her many awards and honors are a Shelley Memorial Award, a Robert Frost Medal, a Lenore Marshall Poetry Prize, a Lannan Literary Award in Poetry, a Catherine Luck Memorial Grant, a grant from the National Institute of Arts and Letters, and a Guggenheim Fellowship. From 1982 to 1993 she taught at Stanford University. She spent the last decade of her life in Seattle.

Philip Levine was named the eighteenth US poet laureate by the Library of Congress in 2011. His most recent book of poetry is *News of the World* (Knopf). His awards include the Pulitzer Prize for *The Simple Truth* (Knopf), two National Book Awards, the National Book Critics Circle Award, the Ruth Lilly Poetry Prize, two Guggenheim Fellowships, and the Harriet Monroe Memorial Prize. He was born and raised in Detroit and currently lives in Brooklyn, New York, and Fresno, California.

Brandon Lussier's poems and translations have been published in the *Harvard Review*, the *Virginia Quarterly Review*, the *Columbia Review*, and elsewhere. His translation work has been anthologized in *New European Poets* (Graywolf Press) and *A Sharp Cut: Contemporary Estonian Literature* and was reviewed in *Boston Review*. He has spoken about literary translation at Princeton University and the American Literary Translators Association and is a former creative writing Fulbright Scholar and the recipient of a Javits Fellowship in poetry. Lussier is a National Endowment for the Arts Fellow in literary translation and assistant director of International Programs at Trinity College in Hartford, Connecticut.

Sandra Meek is the author of four books of poems: *Road Scatter* (Persea Books); *Biogeography*, winner of the Dorset Prize (Tupelo Press); *Burn* (Elixir Press); and *Nomadic Foundations* (Elixir Press). She also edited *Deep Travel: Contemporary American Poets Abroad* (Ninebark Press). Meek served as a Peace Corps volunteer in Manyana, Botswana, from 1989 to 1991. Recipient of a 2011 National Endowment for the Arts Fellowship in Poetry, she is director of the Georgia Poetry Circuit, poetry editor of the *Phi Kappa Phi Forum*, a cofounding editor of Ninebark Press, and a professor of English, rhetoric, and writing at Berry College.

W.S. Merwin was the seventeenth poet laureate of the United States. He is the author of more than fifty books of poetry, prose, and transla-tions. His most recent awards include the National Book Award for *Migration: New and Selected Poems* (Copper Canyon Press) and the Pulitzer Prize for *The Shadow of Sirius* (Copper Canyon). Past honors include the Ruth Lilly Poetry Prize, the Shelley Memorial Award, and fellowships from the Guggenheim Foundation, the National Endowment for the Arts, and the Rockefeller Foundation. He lives in Hawaii and is dedicated to restoring the islands' rain forests.

Aimee Nezhukumatathil is the author of three poetry books, most recently *Lucky Fish* (Tupelo Press), winner of the Hofer Grand Prize and the gold medal in poetry from the Independent Publisher Book Awards. Other awards for her writing include a poetry fellowship from the National Endowment for the Arts and a Pushcart Prize. She is an associate professor of English at SUNY Fredonia.

Naomi Shihab Nye has received a Lannan Literary Fellowship in Poetry, a Guggenheim Fellowship, a Witter Bynner Fellowship from the Library of Congress, and four Pushcart Prizes. Her collection *19 Varieties of Gazelle: Poems of the Middle East* (Greenwillow Books) was a finalist for the National Book Award, and her collection *Honeybee* (Greenwillow Books) was awarded the Arab-American Book Award. She is currently serving as a chancellor of the Academy of American Poets. She has edited several poetry anthologies, including *Time You Let Me In* (Greenwillow Books), *What Have You Lost?* (Greenwillow Books), *Salting the Ocean* (Greenwillow Books), and *This Same Sky* (Simon & Schuster Books for Young Readers), and she is the author of the novels *Habibi* (Simon & Schuster Books for Young Readers) and *Going, Going* (Greenwillow Books). She lives with her family in San Antonio, Texas.

Jacquelyn Pope's first collection of poems, *Watermark*, was published by Marsh Hawk Press. Her poems have appeared in various journals, including *Poetry*, the *New Republic*, *Gulf Coast*, *FIELD*, and the *Southern Review*. Her translations from Dutch and Afrikaans have been published in journals in the United States and abroad and have been featured on the *Poetry Daily* website. Pope has received the José Marti Prize and awards from the Academy of American Poets and the Massachusetts Cultural Council for her work.

Claudia Rankine is the author of four collec-tions of poetry, including *Don't Let Me Be Lonely* (Graywolf Press), and the plays *Provenance of Beauty: A South Bronx Travelogue* (commis-sioned by the Foundry Theatre) and *Existing Conditions* (coauthored with Casey Llewellyn). Rankine is also coeditor of *American Women Poets in the 21st Century: Where Lyric Meets Language* (Wesleyan University Press). She writes and directs the Situation videos in collaboration with John Lucas and organizes the Open Letter Project at www.newmediapo-ets.com/claudia_rankine/open/open.html.

A recipient of fellowships from the Academy of American Poets and the National Endowment for the Arts, she is the Henry G. Lee Professor of English at Pomona College.

Srikanth Reddy is the author of two books of poetry—*Facts for Visitors* and *Voyager* (both from University of California Press)—and a critical study, *Changing Subjects: Digressions in Modern American Poetry* (Oxford University Press). A graduate of the Iowa Writers' Workshop and the doctoral program in English at Harvard University, Reddy is currently an assistant professor of English and creative writing at the University of Chicago.

Susan Rich has traveled to Bosnia and Herzegovina, South Africa, and the West Bank as a human rights activist and an electoral supervisor. She has worked as a Peace Corps volunteer and a program coordinator for Amnesty International and now teaches English and film studies at Highline Community College outside Seattle. She is the author of three collections of poetry: *The Alchemist's Kitchen*, named a finalist for the ForeWord's Book of the Year Award and the Washington State Book Award; *Cures Include Travel*; and *The Cartographer's Tongue: Poems of the World*, winner of the PEN USA Award for Poetry, all published by White Pine Press. Rich has received awards from the *Times Literary Supplement* of London and Peace Corps Writers and a Fulbright Fellowship.

Emily Ruch was raised in the mountains of southern New Mexico. Her formal education has been diverse and includes fine arts, interior design, and ranch management. She graduated from the Evergreen State College with a focus in writing. Her work has been published in *Crab Creek Review*, and she was a finalist in the annual Winning Writers War Poetry Contest in 2010. As an Army mechanic, she served in South Korea and deployed twice to Iraq. She currently lives in Santa Fe, New Mexico.

Donna Stonecipher is the author of three volumes of poetry: *The Reservoir* (University of Georgia Press), *Souvenir de Constantinople* (Instance Press), and *The Cosmopolitan* (Coffee House Press), which won the 2007 National Poetry Series. She also translates from French and German; her translation of Ludwig Hohl's novella *Ascent* will appear from Black Square Editions. She currently lives in Berlin, Germany.

Brian Turner is the author of *Here, Bullet* and *Phantom Noise* (both from Alice James Books). He received a USA Hillcrest Fellowship in Literature, a National Endowment for the Arts Literature Fellowship in Poetry, an Amy Lowell Travelling Scholarship, a Japan–United States Friendship Commission grant, a Poets' Prize, and a Lannan Literary Fellowship in Poetry. His work has appeared on National Public Radio, the BBC, the PBS *NewsHour*, and *Weekend America*, among other networks and programs. He is the director of the low-residency MFA program at Sierra Nevada College.

Alissa Valles is the author of the poetry collections *Orphan Fire* (Four Way Books) and *Doctor Salvage* (forthcoming). She studied at the University College London School of Slavonic and East European Studies and at universities in Russia, Poland, and the United States. She has worked for the BBC Russian Service, the Dutch Institute for War Documentation in Amsterdam, and the Jewish Historical Institute and La Strada International, an anti-human-trafficking group, in Warsaw. She now lives and works in the Bay Area as an independent writer, editor, and translator, most recently of the work of Polish poet Zbigniew Herbert.

Derek Walcott is a Saint Lucian poet and playwright. He received the Nobel Prize in Literature in 1992. His latest book of poetry, *White Egrets* (Farrar, Straus and Giroux), was awarded the T.S. Eliot Prize, though he is best known for the Homeric epic poem *Omeros* (Farrar, Straus and Giroux). His honors include a MacArthur Foundation "genius" Fellowship, a Royal Society of Literature Award, a Eugenio Montale Prize, and a Queen's Gold Medal for Poetry. He resides in Saint Lucia.

Katharine Whitcomb is the author of three collections of poems: *Saints of South Dakota and Other Poems*, chosen by Lucia Perillo as the winner of the 2000 Bluestem Award; *Hosannas* (Parallel Press); and *Lamp of Letters* (Floating Bridge Press). Her awards include a Stegner Fellowship at Stanford University and fellowships to the Fine Arts Work Center in Provincetown, the Wisconsin Institute for Creative Writing, and the Prague Summer Seminars.

Charles Wright's most recent collection of poetry is *Bye-and-Bye: Selected Late Poems* (Farrar, Straus and Giroux). His book *Country Music: Selected Early Poems* (Wesleyan University Press) won the National Book Award, and *Black Zodiac* (Farrar, Straus and Giroux) won the Pulitzer Prize. Other honors include the PEN Translation Prize, the American Academy of Arts and Letters Award of Merit medal, and the Ruth Lilly Poetry Prize. He is recently retired from the University of Virginia in Charlottesville.

The Harriet Monroe Poetry Institute is an independent forum created by the Poetry Foundation to provide a space in which fresh thinking about poetry, in both its intellectual and its practical needs, can flourish free of any allegiance other than to the best ideas. The Institute convenes leading poets, scholars, publishers, educators, and other thinkers from inside and outside the poetry world to address issues of importance to the art form of poetry and to identify and champion solutions for the benefit of the art.

The Poetry Foundation, publisher of *Poetry* magazine, is an independent literary organization committed to a vigorous presence for poetry in our culture. It exists to discover and celebrate the best poetry and to place it before the largest possible audience. The Poetry Foundation seeks to be a leader in shaping a receptive climate for poetry by developing new audiences, creating new avenues for delivery, and encouraging new kinds of poetry through innovative partnerships, prizes, and programs.

The Poets in the World Series is an HMPI project that supports the research and publication of poetry and poetics from around the world and highlights the importance of creating a space for poetry in local communities in the United States.

Current Publications

Katharine Coles, HMPI inaugural director

Poetry and New Media: A Users' Guide, report of the Poetry and New Media Working Group, Harriet Monroe Poetry Institute, 2009

Blueprints: Bringing Poetry into Communities, edited by Katharine Coles (University of Utah Press, 2011)

Code of Best Practices in Fair Use for Poetry, created with American University's Center for Social Media and Washington College of Law, 2011

Forthcoming Projects

Ilya Kaminsky, 2011–2013, HMPI director

Open the Door: How to Excite Young People About Poetry, edited by Jesse Nathan, Dominic Luxford, and Dorothea Lasky (McSweeney's, 2013)

15 Essential Poems from Latin America, edited by Raúl Zurita and Forrest Gander (Copper Canyon Press, 2013)

On the Road, edited by Eliot Weinberger (Open Letter Books, 2013)

New Cathay: Contemporary Chinese Poetry, edited by Ming Di (Tupelo Press, 2013)

An Anthology of European Poetry, edited by Valzhyna Mort (Red Hen Press, 2013)

An Anthology of Anglophone Poetry, edited by Catherine Barnett (Tupelo Press, 2013)

Fifteen Iraqi Poets, edited by Dunya Mikhail (New Directions Publishing, 2013)

An Anthology of Swedish Poetry, coedited/translated by Malena Mörling and Jonas Ellerström (Milkweed Editions, 2013)

Credits